iMuslims

No Children

GODS

ACA Cin

AC SKehD

Islamic Civilization and Muslim Networks
Carl W. Ernst and Bruce B. Lawrence, editors

iMuslims

Rewiring the House of Islam

Gary R. Bunt

The University of North Carolina Press
Chapel Hill

© 2009 The University of North Carolina Press
All rights reserved

Designed by Rebecca Evans
Set in Warnock Pro
by Keystone Typesetting, Inc.
Manufactured in the United States of America

The paper in this book meets the guidelines for
permanence and durability of the Committee
on Production Guidelines for Book Longevity
of the Council on Library Resources.

The University of North Carolina Press has been
a member of the Green Press Initiative since 2003.

Library of Congress Cataloging-in-Publication Data
Bunt, Gary R.
iMuslims : rewiring the house of Islam / Gary R. Bunt.
p. cm. — (Islamic civilization and Muslim networks)
Includes bibliographical references and index.
ISBN 978-0-8078-3258-5 (cloth : alk. paper)
ISBN 978-0-8078-5966-7 (pbk. : alk. paper)
1. Islam—Electronic discussion groups.
2. Islam—Computer network resources.
3. Muslims—Blogs. 4. Jihad—Electronic discussion groups.
I. Title. II. Title: Rewiring the house of Islam.
BP40.5.B857 2009
297.0285'4678—dc22   2008038370

cloth   13 12 11 10 09   5 4 3 2 1
paper   13 12 11 10 09   5 4 3 2 1

For Yvonne, Kane, and Tony,
and for my parents

Contents

Screengrabs, Diagrams, and Tables

Diagrams

Table

Acknowledgments

The research and writing of this book would not have been possible without the help of many people, both in cyberspace and closer to home. Colleagues at the Department of Theology, Religious Studies, and Islamic Studies, University of Wales, Lampeter, provided encouragement for this work during its development. I have enjoyed fruitful discussions with my students on aspects of this research. Colleagues at the Subject Centre for Philosophical and Religious Studies have also given their support. I am grateful to the organizers of a variety of workshops and conferences for allowing me to present aspects of this work. Many people have also discussed aspects of this research and my earlier work with me on a regular basis (on- and offline), and I have welcomed their comments. Thanks are due to series editors Carl W. Ernst and Bruce B. Lawrence for allowing me to contribute to the Islamic Civilization and Muslim Networks series. I have enjoyed dialoguing with Bruce on issues surrounding Islam and cyberspace for several years and have welcomed his insightful comments at every stage of this book's development. I am very appreciative of the thoughtful feedback given by the readers and editors during the shaping of the manuscript. I am particularly grateful for the constructive support and advice of Elaine Maisner and the team at the University of North Carolina Press.

As always, I am grateful to my wife Yvonne for her invaluable encouragement and enlightening sense of perspective during the writing of this book, especially when I was seemingly stuck on my computer for days on end. Kane provided welcome editorial support and musical accompaniment. I had conversations on several aspects of this research with Tony. Other members of my family, especially my parents Betty and Derek, as always provided their enthusiastic support.

Despite the support and input of all the above, the contents and shortcomings of the book remain wholly my responsibility.

Note on Transliteration

Within the main text of this book, I decided not to burden readers with a complex system of transliteration of "Islamic" and other terminology from Arabic and other languages into English. Such a system would be unnecessary and damaging to the flow of the text, especially for nonspecialist readers outside the fields relating to Islamic Studies. However, key transliterated terms with diacritics are provided in the glossary in order to assist readers seeking further information and definitions in specialist sources. The general principles contained in the *Encyclopaedia of Islam: New Edition* (Leiden: E. J. Brill, 1960) and associated systems have been adhered to, with the popular model featured in Ian Richard Netton's *A Popular Dictionary of Islam* (London: Curzon Press, 1991) also applied. Quotations from Internet and textual sources retain their original transliterations; proper names maintain locally applied personal spellings and transliterations; common anglicized spellings of Islamic terms are applied where possible in the text (for example, "mosque" for *mas*djid, and *hajj* rather than *ḥa*djdj). Variants may be found in quotes and in the glossary. When a less-common Islamic term is contained in a quotation, I have given a general definition in parentheses.

iMuslims

Introduction

iMuslims and Cyber-Islamic Environments

The Internet has a profound contemporary impact on how Muslims perceive Islam and how Islamic societies and networks are evolving and shifting in the twenty-first century. While these electronic interfaces appear new and innovative in terms of how the media is applied, much of their content has a basis in classical Islamic concepts. These link into traditional Muslim networks with a historical resonance that can be traced back to the time of the Prophet Muhammad. *iMuslims* explores how these transformations and influences play out in diverse cyber-Islamic environments and how they are responding to shifts in technology and society.

My use of the umbrella term "cyber-Islamic environment" (CIE) acknowledges diversity among and within different zones in cyberspace that represent varied Muslim worldviews within the House of Islam, all of which present a reference point of identity with a conceptualization of Islam. The source encoding of such environments follows specific protocols of identity with particular Islamic reference points, including essential beliefs shared by the majority of Muslims. The encoding is refined and in some cases hacked to engineer manifestations of Muslim understandings that adapt to networks, contexts, histories, and contemporary issues. Islamic diversity encompasses many areas, ranging from elements in the headlines to those outside the realm of the media. Not all aspects of Islam are fully represented online, especially those from Muslim cultural-religious contexts with low levels of Internet connectivity, as well as traditionally quietist elements.

Specific forms of online or digital Islam, distinct from offline or analogue Islam, have developed. A place of religious instruction may only exist in a virtual context. A network or community may only gather online. Their name may not have a real-world equivalent. This is not just a phenomenon linked to so-called jihadi militaristic factions. It is one that is located in other areas of belief, such as elements of Shi'ism where, for personal safety, followers must practice secrecy or dissimilitude—a circumstance that has a long-term historical resonance.

The utilization of the Internet, and in particular the World Wide Web, in the name of Islam has necessitated a reconsideration and reconfiguration of Muslim networks. While elements of historical networking patterns and concepts apply, there are also new issues to address. An innovative knowledge and proselytizing economy has emerged, causing a challenge to traditional "top-down" authority models. A collaborative, horizontal knowledge economy, reliant on peer-to-peer networking, has enveloped areas of Islamic cyberspace. Much of the content is also given away for free, and users are invited to make comments, amend information, and provide contributions in some areas. User input may come as a response to a question, a suggestion for a reference, or a commentary on a particular topic.

This might be described as "wiki-oriented" Islam in relation to the forms of interaction, knowledge sharing, and development that occur. Wikipedia describes the noun "wiki" as "a collaborative website which can be directly edited by anyone with access to it."[1] This collaborative element can be extended into other areas. Don Tapscott and Anthony D. Williams describe such an approach in relation to economics as "wikinomics," based in part on the precedents associated with the evolution of the Linux operating system. The deviser of Linux, Linus Torvalds, shared his version of the Unix operating system with other programmers in 1991 under a license that ensured that all changes would be made available to others for free.[2] The Linux product is now well established as an open-source alternative to Microsoft Windows and other computer operating systems and retains its roots as a collaborative product. The concept of peer-to-peer sharing (or "peering"), for which Linux is such a valuable model, offers a system that lends itself to many other areas of human life and interaction, including Muslim networks and societies.

While there is still a hierarchy in Islamic cyberspace, conventional models have in some cases been shaken to the core or forced to adapt to an open-source model of Islamic understanding and interpretation. Based on a core code of values associated with the Qur'an, new conceptual frameworks have emerged rapidly, accelerated by the collaborative processes of cyberspace. CIES have always had a collaborative element, but this has been redefined through the application of social networking and other online innovations categorized as belonging to so-called Web 2.0.

The notion of Islamic knowledge development through history also had an open-source element. The development of scholarship centered on the collection of the sayings and traditions associated with the Prophet Muhammad, known as hadith, required scholars to network between centers of knowledge production in order to collect and transmit the versions of hadith that they acquired. This activity took place in the centuries following Muhammad's death in 632 C.E. and required extensive travel between Muslim communities in different parts of the nascent Islamic world.[3] These were subject to critical evaluation, sifting, and enhancement by bodies of scholars across the networks of place and time in order that definitive collections of hadith could be compiled. In many ways, this represents one form of open-source Islamic scholarship and collaboration, although it could be argued that the openness was subject to limitations and restrictions over time.

Another precedent would be the refinement over time of Islamic legal knowledge, necessitating a similar process of networking and connectivity. Without contemporary communications media, these processes took centuries. Now, information can be circulated and worked on in a rapid manner by iMuslims. Some of this process reinforces previous forms of knowledge exchange in Islamic contexts, but there are also elements that necessitate what can be described as a "rewiring" of the House of Islam. "Wiring" is something of a metaphor. It has metaphysical and technical connotations. In a literal sense, the individual interface does not have to be hardwired into a network, given the options of wireless networks and Internet-enabled cell phones. Wiring is also suggested in the sense of a connection, both of the individual and the computer, into Islam. Speaking from personal experience, anyone who has been through a rewiring process in their home or workplace will know that it can be a disruptive, chaotic, and at times dangerous process.

In some contexts, the application of the Internet is having an overarching transformational effect on how Muslims practice Islam, how forms of Islam are represented to the wider world, and how Muslim societies perceive themselves and their peers. On one level, this may be in terms of practical performance of Islamic duties and rituals, or on the interpretation and understanding of the Qur'an. On another level, CIEs have exposed Muslims to radical and new influences outside of traditional spheres of knowledge and authority, causing paradigmatic shifts at a grassroots level within societies.

These points will be emphasized in every chapter of this book, with specific examples drawn from diverse contexts. The elements relating to this transformational process are drawn together in the conclusion, which will point a way forward for how Islam and Muslims will continue to apply the Internet as a means of understanding, interpreting, and transmitting forms of religious knowledge to a variety of audiences. The book takes account of how these processes are not static but evolving and how their utilization has become a natural adjunct to traditional forms of Islamic discourse.

iMuslims shows that computer-mediated communication can have a transformative impact on Islam and Muslims in a number of Islamic contexts, while recognizing that there are distinct variables and that some contexts are manifestly unaffected by information technology. What impact there is may be scientifically measurable, while our proximity in terms of time means that it may not be possible to determine other patterns until a greater time has elapsed between the period of observation and the writing of any analysis. Impact may be subtle rather than overt, and it may combine with numerous other factors.

This book emerges from a religious studies context, in which charting specific phenomena and mapping the field are the primary elements. This provides indicators of particular trends and changes associated with the rewiring of Islam, based on sustained monitoring of a range of online materials. Despite its disciplinary origins, it is hoped that *iMuslims* will be relevant to those in other academic areas who may approach this subject area with different foci.

I am aware, through discussing and presenting this research in a variety of academic settings in the United Kingdom and elsewhere, that there are different expectations and approaches to Islam, Muslims, and the Internet. At this stage, it is not my intention to provide a quantifiable, scientific calibration of the transformative capacity or impact of computer-mediated communication on Islam, Muslims, or cyber-Islamic environments. Determining the measures would necessitate extensive, international surveys and resources.

Any study of user communities would require a multivolume international study in order to examine the relationship between online output and offline behaviour within diverse Islamic contexts. Such a study would require several years of sustained effort from teams of academics across numerous disciplines. As with any fieldwork, it would require a great deal of personal access to individuals—in a subject area where respondents and participants would not necessarily be willing to reveal, or feel comfortable offering, sensitive personal information on Web-surfing habits and Islamic lifestyle choices. There may be discrepancies between "expected answers" and data presented. It is hoped that *iMuslims* will help steer future re-search in this area and act as a reflective guide within the processes associated with formulating methodologies and multidisciplinary approaches in the field.

iMuslims shows how the digitization and "wiring" of the House of Islam takes on many thematic and methodological approaches. This process represents one of the most significant historical changes in approach toward how information about Islam and Muslims is processed, networked, and disseminated. As access to the Internet increases exponentially—through a diversity of interfaces and sociocultural contexts—the demand for an academic discourse about these developments intensifies.

A critical consideration is whether the Internet has become the ideal networking tool among dispersed Muslim communities and individuals. This book acknowledges that many Muslims remain unaffected by the Internet, at least directly, while recognizing that for others it has become a crucial adjunct to self-expression and religiosity. In discussing how Islamic ideas of the sacred and of religious identities manifest themselves in complex ways in cyberspace, *iMuslims* considers whether this in some ways reflects the continuum of Muslim understandings located in the nondigital world. This book investigates which elements of Muslim societies might have been transformed through this cyber interaction. It highlights how certain perspectives have raised their profiles via the Web or had their views altered and/or reinforced through values transmitted through the Internet.

iMuslims explains how these changes are taking place in a number of different ways, including through social networking websites and the blogosphere. In this book, I discuss how these resources can be approached and interpreted, incorporating a comparison between and within diverse political-religious frameworks. Blogging has been chosen because it has given access to immediate online publishing and social networking for a vast number of readers and writers. For users with access, the tools are usually open source and free to use, linking into a range of other social networking options. It is an area that rapidly refined itself in terms of subject specialization and achieved opportunities for the articulation of worldviews that have transcended, in many cases, traditional forms of regulation and censorship. Blogging has challenged conventional media, and as language tools have opened up discourse in Farsi, Arabic, and other "Islamic" languages, blogs have become a major conduit of opinion within cyber-Islamic environments.

Jihadi cyberspace, in its multifaceted forms (including blogs), has been chosen for discussion in *iMuslims* because it represents transformation of a different kind. The Internet has dramatically influenced jihad-oriented campaigns by networks such as al-Qaeda and made a significant difference as to how forms of Islamic activism and radicalization have been engendered. *iMuslims* provides a framework through which the Internet output of jihadi organizations can be analyzed. This book draws on practical examples taken from a variety of sites, especially those associated with digital jihadi battlefields in Iraq and Palestine. Jihadi networks and organizations have been using the Internet as a logistical and publicity tool for many years, but after 9/11, attention and speculation surrounding these platforms focused on their Internet presence.[4] Adept application of the net, especially in terms of use of free web space, encryption, and anonymizing tools, allowed al-Qaeda and others to skilfully manipulate press agendas and public opinion across the world in order to promote their worldviews. For some, this represented Islam in its entirety on the Internet. This book seeks to demonstrate that while jihadi output is an important aspect of Muslim expression, and that it requires as much attention and understanding as possible, it is by no means the full picture relating to Islam and cyberspace.

I conclude the book by determining the way forward for the articulation and transformation of diverse understandings of Islam online and describing how Muslim networks will be further shaped through their relationships with the Internet.

The term "iMuslims," which I introduce here, is a synonym for cyber Muslims but focuses on the mercurial *i*. The *i* primarily represents the Internet in its many forms. The *i* may refer in a wider sense to information technology and interactivity. It can also refer to the term "interoperability," evoking the sense of a variety of programs functioning together in a compatible way. There is also a link with a number of popular computer products, such as Apple's iPod, iMac, iPhoto, iTunes, iLife, and iMovie.

The term "Muslim" is applied in this book to describe any person who identifies himself or herself as a believer in Islam. iMuslims are those followers of Islam who function in some capacity in CIEs, that is, within the complex variety of digital contexts that Muslims use to articulate Islam. The central question of this book is: how do iMuslims utilize CIEs in contemporary contexts? To answer this question, one must also understand how the environments themselves shift and evolve in response to changes in technology and the development of new forms of Muslim networks.

Locating Islam in Cyberspace

There is a sense of specific Islamic identity associated with aspects of cyberspace. These may be intentionally designed Muslim-only zones or generic areas of the Web with an Islamic footprint. One might compare the difference between Muslim content on the social networking site MySpace and the general content on the Islamic equivalent MuslimSpace. Islamic-Tube and IslamicTorrents offer video sharing and distribution modeled on non-Islamic equivalents.[1] Does this sense of separateness influence how people who are not Muslim approach CIES? As with other zones of special interest on the Web, some areas of CIES are clearly more open than others. It may, however, be a cliché to suggest that, for some aspects of Islam, openness online may lead to greater understanding and empathy from outsiders. Some sites have endeavored to do this by placing explanations of religious practices on their websites. In reality, explanations of ritual practice may be less valuable to outsiders than seeing the banality and normality of other areas of online Muslim discourse, such as within social-networking sites.

On a number of levels, such developments have facilitated a rewiring of the House of Islam, allowing the Internet a central role in structures of Muslim networks and Islamic expression. Rewiring a structure is not without its disruptive aspects, but it can allow for greater efficiency through the nodes of a network. The "wiring" itself may take many technologies and forms on individual, group, and organizational levels. Some of it is collaborative and undertaken through peer-to-peer networks. Effectively, the connection may also be wireless, allowing for greater mobility and a choice of interfaces.

Through this transformational process, individuals may develop new details of religious knowledge, facilitating a form of Islamic literacy requiring familiarity with a broad range of databases and information sources. These are innovative times, not just for scholars but also for travelers on

Index, MuslimSpace.com, December 2006

the path for religious knowledge in its many forms. One might question whether it represents new forms of religious experience that are more solitary and complex than entry into a religious school or *madrassa*, which may be off-limits to many surfers.

Online, new virtual groupings and affinities develop beyond traditional boundaries, drawing upon multiple identities. These challenge and mutate previously conventional understandings of Muslim identity, transposing familiar elements within a digital interface. CIES provide opportunities for those from nonconventional Muslim backgrounds to promote their own worldviews. These challenges to the status quo have drawn attention from traditional institutions, some of which have sought to proscribe such sites with varying degrees of success. The same mechanics of online debate and identity creation have been targeted as potentially subversive by governmental organizations unable to censor or regulate Internet pronouncements and activities that conflict with their policies.

The ways in which the Internet has been applied in Muslim contexts often reflects the ways that the medium is applied in general. Gossip, rumor, innuendo, and conspiracy theories have their place in CIES, too. Inevitably, conspiracy theories have emerged in chat rooms and elsewhere. For example, in the aftermath of the 2004 tsunami disaster and Hurricane Katrina in 2005, one Internet user exclaimed, "God struck the beaches of debauchery, nudism, and prostitution." Another wrote that "God warns humanity against perpetuating injustice," while a third applauded "the harbinger of the Islamic caliphate."[2]

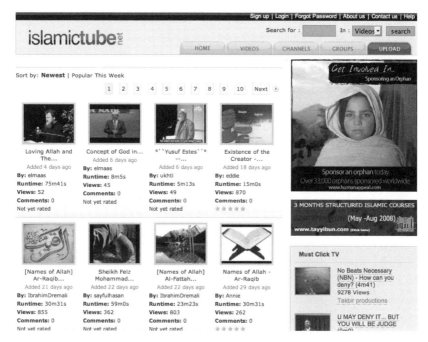

Index, IslamicTube.com, May 2008

The Web is also a space where Muslim groups and individuals convene at a time of crisis. The 7/7 bombings in London saw Muslim organizations in the United Kingdom (UK) quickly issue online statements condemning the attacks.[3] The immediacy of such responses was significant because other media players, such as the mainstream newspapers and broadcasters, placed hyperlinks to them in their reportage. This suggests that some site content is aimed at diffuse audiences, Muslim and other, and that it is accepted practice for references to certain Muslim sites be placed within mainstream media.

Surfers may only visit those sites that reflect their own religious-cultural-political sense(s) of identity; they may keep their visits secret from friends and family out of concern that such visits would challenge conventional ideas about identity and religious values. The anonymity allowed by the Internet can allow for lurking on sites without exposure of a real identity. Avatars allow for exploration of new ideas of religious expression and affinity, which may or may not have a relationship with the surfer's nondigital world.

This introduces issues of physical locations, both of the surfer and the site creators, and what can be described as Islamic Web literacy. Multimedia presents religious encounters in different forms, some relating to interactivity, such as engaging with a scholar from a different context, culture, or language group. The Web offers new influences and experiences, although critics might suggest that not all of these are beneficial to their readers, consumers, and communities. These influences can include exposure to alternate religious sources of authority. These might be web sites containing textual interpretative materials, video clips about religious experiences, online fatwas giving innovative approaches to rites of passage, and statements giving justification for alternate allegiances toward religious authority. One portal may provide sufficient motivation with a complete package of religious activities, guidance, exhortation, sermons, resources, and dialogue.

I am aware of Muslims who will now explain their worldview in terms of identifying with a specific Islamic website, rather than a particular local mosque or religious network. This in itself represents a radical shift of emphasis, while not negating traditional concepts of sacred space and religious authority. In some cases, such approaches suggest an augmentation and fusion of traditional and contemporary outlooks.

In other cases, a website removes the prospect of a compartmentalization of religion, with the potential for some surfers to choose to be always linked to their mosque or worldview by keeping their browser fixed to a particular site. Linking up to e-mail lists and RSS feeds (various formats of feeds derived from the Web that may be located in blogs, podcasts, and regularly updated Web content such as news sites) means that Islam can be "always on," not just in terms of everyday words and actions but through being advised of new alerts to content and networking. Personal Digital Assistants (PDAS), BlackBerrys, and cell phones extend the opportunities to receive alerts of updates and religious information. There is potential for this to become overintrusive. While, for believers, Islam itself should be "always on" and integrated to daily life, Islamic sources also suggest that some compartmentalization of ritual practice is necessary to achieve functionality in society—Islam being, according to the Qur'an, an "easy religion."

The Islamic biographical sources of the Prophet Muhammad note how, during the Night Journey, the Prophet and Moses negotiated the number of daily prayers from fifty per day to a more practical five so that people would be able to fit their normal lives around religious activities. The extent to which iMuslims are always online and tuned into religious content has to be determined. One critical question is: to what extent has using the Internet for Islamic purposes become a religious obligation for some? This book demonstrates that there are many people for whom being online in the name of Allah represents an obligation. How this might be interpreted and monitored is open to question.

Islamic religious authorities have found ways in which the Internet can be applied as a form of regulation within communities. In one extreme example, Saudi Arabian religious police in Medina applied the Internet to allow surfers to anonymously report perceived religious transgressions within their community via a website.[4] There can be a complex relationship between paradigmatic religious practices and technical innovation in which one can often balance out the other. Issues of physical locations, both of the end user and the site creators, become significant. There are fluid ways in which they can find themselves located on a server, divorced from the restrictions of their physical space and potentially away from censorship and monitoring.

Every surfer–content provider relationship is likely to be different. Content has the potential to be an introduction to specific issues of religious authority, and/or it may act as a reinforcement tool for existing patterns and understandings. Innovation is not necessarily encouraged in some Islamic contexts. It is this very resistance to change that has also encouraged other religious authorities to come online to counter influences deemed negative in nature. In some ways, these challenge the wiki-focused collaborative approaches of Net-literate groupings seeking to articulate "new" interpretative approaches to Islam that challenge traditional hierarchies. Surfers may develop new understandings and consequent affiliations through a Web literacy combined with the breadth of Islamic databases and information sources available.

The language in which this is expressed is open to hybridization, reflecting street jargon alongside religious expression. This is true particularly in chat rooms, where participants are in conversational mode utilizing Internet conventions and cell phone slang. The smiley may be wearing hijab. In an analysis of the impact of the Internet on language and vice versa, David Crystal notes that "the prophets of doom emerge every time a new technology influences language, of course—they gathered when printing was introduced in the 15th century." But linguists should be "exulting," he says, in the ability the Internet gives us to "explore the power of the written language in a creative way."[5]

On a related theme, Gilles Kepel, who has integrated reference to online discourse in his analyses of jihadi movements, observes: "On websites in every European language, whether jihadist or pietist, 'trendy' jargon blends in with an intense polemic founded on obscure religious reference to medieval scholars whose work was written in abstruse Arabic."[6] Many examples of slang, polemic, jargon, and creative expression can be found in CIES as part of the undercurrents of contemporary Muslim networks. Content is derived primarily from English and Arabic sources. It is not feasible to monitor Islamic content in all languages, but in the zones that I focus upon, it will be seen that some common issues and themes can emerge from a "snapshot" of Islamic cyberspace.

The Shaping of the Global Islamic Knowledge Economy

The flow of data about Islam that is circulating via the Internet—whether it is the language of slang or the Qur'anic Arabic contained in a sermon—may be appropriate to discuss in terms of a global Islamic knowledge economy. This concept has a link to what Manuel Castells refers to as an "informational economy" in his discussion of twentieth-century global business economics:

> It is *informational* because the productivity and competitiveness of
> units or agents in this economy (be it firms, regions, or nations) funda-
> mentally depend upon their capacity to generate, process, and apply
> efficiently knowledge-based information. It is *global* because the core
> activities of production, consumption, and circulation, as well as their
> components (capital, labor, raw materials, management, information,
> technology, markets) are organized on a global scale, either directly
> or through a network of linkages between economic agents. It is *net-*
> *worked* because, under the new historical conditions, productivity is
> generated through and competition is played out in a global network
> of interaction between business networks.[7]

There is a strong focus on information and knowledge in CIES, although there can be distinguishing features, too. Ideas of religious knowledge can be quite distinct and authoritative and are utilized by many Muslims— hence the focus on the global Islamic knowledge economy here. While not a business in the sense discussed by Castells, this concept possesses these components and networks of interaction. The linkages are not always transparent, and elements of production, consumption, and circulation take on a religious edge within CIES.

The past few years have been a critical phase in Islamic modern history, a period in which this knowledge economy has continued to evolve. However, twenty-first-century developments are also part of a long-term process of development associated with Muslim networks. To quote from miriam cooke and Bruce Lawrence's *Muslim Networks from Hajj to Hip Hop* (2005), one key question is: "How has technology raised expectations about new transnational pathways that will reshape the perception of faith, politics, and gender in Islamic civilization?"[8]

Islam is being reshaped, and the Internet, in particular the World Wide Web, has had an increasing impact on Muslims in diverse contemporary contexts. It is possible to map and analyze the essential elements associated with the development of Islamic cyber pathways and networks. A broad spectrum of Islamic hypertextual approaches and understandings can be located in cyberspace, created by Muslims seeking to present dimensions of their religious, spiritual, and/or political lives online.

Varied applications of the Internet utilized in the name of Islam may combine websites, multimedia, chat rooms, e-mail listings, and/or various degrees of interactivity. While recognizing that these diverse tools interact, the focus of this book is the World Wide Web. The Web can create online notions of Muslim identity and authority that echo and intersect with similar notions in the nondigital real world, but it also nurtures new networks of understandings in cyberspace.

Muslims have creatively applied the Internet in the interest of furthering understanding of the religion for other believers, especially those affiliated to a specific worldview and, in some cases, a wider non-Muslim readership. It may be a natural phenomenon for a Net-literate generation to seek out specific truths and affiliations online, especially when they cannot be accessed in a local mosque or community context. This reflects Dawson's point in a discussion on religion and the Internet: "The Internet is used most often to expand people's social horizons and involvement. People use the Internet to augment and extend their preexisting social lives, not as a substitute or alternative."[9]

Empirical evidence also suggests that generalizations cannot be made in relation to Internet use, with so many iMuslims spending a substantial amount of their lives online, inside and outside of CIES. This has transformed notions of Muslim networking, especially among those who are integrating aspects of Web 2.0 into their consumption and creation of online content.

This book represents a form of research into the "informational society." Castells states that "we need to locate the process of revolutionary technological change in the social context in which it takes place and by which it is being shaped; and we should keep in mind that the search for identity is as powerful as techno-economic change in charting the new history."[10]

This search for identity is a driving factor of CIES. It highlights points made by Castells elsewhere, where he suggests that within the complexities of contemporary circumstances, individuals seek out primary identities. While I would not place Castells's emphasis on "fundamentalism" as a driving force (as there are inherent difficulties with the term), it is interesting to observe how his points on identities play out in CIES—in particular, his belief in the "fundamental split between abstract, universal instrumentalism, and historically rooted, particularistic identities. *Our societies are increasingly structured around a bipolar opposition between the Net and the self.*"[11]

Castells discusses this in the context of a breakdown and realignment of patterns of social communication. While he was originally writing about this in 1996, it would appear to have become a more pertinent issue a decade or so later, certainly in relation to CIES. Particularistic identities have a dominant role in aspects of Islamic expression online, while the selectivity of information exchanges in terms of fulfilling specific goals are represented within a number of online Islamic agendas. However, Dale Eickelman notes that networking is one component of a bigger picture: "More important that just the idea of network are the styles and modes of communication that facilitate the formation of new and overlapping forms of community, trust, and association."[12]

Both Eickelman's and Castells's points are valid: observing iMuslims makes one a witness to the changes in communication styles. The physical and virtual environments in which this is played out are also significant, especially in terms of whether they represent "public" or "private" space. David Holmes takes this point one stage further: "The question of whether interaction, once it is *reduced* to the electronically mediated and technologically extended kinds of access to communication which are enabled from the home, constitutes participation in a public sphere is a pivotal one to ask in relation to CMC [Computer-Mediated Communication]. Certainly the private/public question becomes extremely vexed on the Internet."[13]

This particular question has an added dimension in relation to concepts of Muslim space—for example, in terms of sacred and liminal areas or places where there is gender separation based on religious principles. These factors play out online and offline, where areas of the Net are designated as being private and public areas. In the former category, membership may be limited to vetted individuals who possess passwords. However, possession of a Muslim identity is not a prerequisite for entering CIES. Some might suggest that there is an ease of movement in some contexts for individuals wishing to visit particular zones of the Net that is denied in a real-world context. In my travels, there have been many occasions where entry to a mosque or shrine has been prevented by a gatekeeper because I lacked a Muslim identity or what was perceived as a "Muslim appearance." This is not such an issue online.

This issue can be seen in the context of access to CIES, where the Internet has supplemented, and in some cases supplanted, traditional approaches to Islamic knowledge management and dissemination. The access to Islamic texts and religious opinions, for example, crosses boundaries that earlier generations faced. The traditional concept of "sitting at a scholar's feet" to acquire knowledge about Islam still exists, but it now has a digital equivalent. Levels of participation and membership are also significant indicators within CIES: "Each medium, conceived either as a technical environment or as a form of social connection, is able to facilitate a sense of directly interacting in them. When we leave a television on in the background even when we are not watching it, or download our electronic mail when at work before engaging in face-to-face contact, we are immersing ourselves in forms of media integration."[14]

This sense of interaction and integration takes on multiple forms in CIES, especially when one is a participant in several different websites. The immersion is equally apparent when receiving RSS feeds from a particular site or viewing MySpace and YouTube. It has perhaps intensified, in the sense of those whose daily existence incorporates an "always on" Internet feed or a Blackberry constantly providing e-mail updates from subscription services.

It could be suggested, however, that the "always on" element might reflect those individuals for whom religious reflection and prayer permeates every action and speech throughout the day. It is common in Arabic, for example, to hear religious Muslims punctuate their sentences with phrases invoking Allah and Muhammad. These invocations offer a sense of protection in the everyday world. Perhaps this is analogous to the "always on" Internet feed of Islamic resources dripping from the Internet on a minute-by-minute basis.

CIES also offer a challenge to what has been described as the Electronic Colonialism Theory (ECT): "ECT posits that when exported the mass media carry with them a broad range of values. These values are economic, social, cultural, and sometimes political or religious in nature."[15] This has been interpreted as a Western-oriented, American-centered process by some and relates to the World-System Theory (WST). This "elaborates and extends ECT by dividing the nations of the globe into three categories; it then expands on how the core category works to influence the two subordinate categories."[16]

Many Muslim populations inhabit the subordinate categories within this model. The presence of a vibrant Islamic knowledge economy online goes a small way to counter the impact of a Western-dominated media. It has to be noted that a significant proportion of cyber-Islamic discourse, especially in the early days of the Web, emanated from Western Muslim contexts. The impact of online content authored from within Muslim minorities and presented in a global context has provided status and awareness for those authors within the Islamic knowledge economy. Many CIES incorporate content produced collaboratively from across Muslim networks in diverse contexts.

Consideration might also be given to the "Al-Jazeera effect." The satellite channel's focus in its 1996 launch was initially on pan-Arabic audiences, obviously incorporating many Muslims within its demographic profile. Based in Qatar, the channel offered one outlet for the discussion of Islamic issues, especially on programs such as Yusuf al-Qaradawi's *al-Shariah wal al-Hayat* (*Shari'a* and Life). On this popular phone-in program, the scholar answers viewers' questions on a number of topics. The format has spawned imitators on other channels.

Al-Jazeera has had a profound effect on how news is reported, especially about the Middle East, and its success as a global brand led to the creation of an English-language channel. There is some crossover in content, although one correspondent I spoke to suggested that this was regarded as "Al-Jazeera lite" because it lacked the intensity of its Arabic equivalent. Al-Jazeera's impact extends into cyberspace; it is regularly cited online by broadcasters and bloggers, it draws content from videos and other information posted online, and it has its own websites. Its emergence forced other broadcasters to develop their own Arabic-language content, both in domestic and international markets.

In Al-Jazeera's endeavors to retain the image of impartiality within the pan-Arabic milieu, the channel has established itself as a significant challenge to domestic broadcasters in Middle Eastern contexts and to other channels whose output may be controlled or restricted. Al-Jazeera has, however, been accused of being a mouthpiece for al-Qaeda, in particular in terms of its presentation of jihadi online output—a charge the network strongly rejected.[17] One impact of the Al-Jazeera effect was that it made Islamic online content providers aware of the potential of global media channels in multiple formats. The notion of a global broadcaster also extended into the output of jihadi websites, some of which developed their own programming based on news formats.[18]

Al-Jazeera is one element of a bigger picture. Clearly, it is possible to link varied theories of global communication into exploration of CIES. Discussing these issues has become part of the Islamic discourse online and is a significant object of exchange and analysis by iMuslims, as well as for academics who may or may not operate within a Muslim frame of reference.

Interpreting CIES

There are a complex series of questions at the center of this framing of globalization in an Islamic milieu, associated with notions of so-called orientalism and the media presciently raised by Edward Said.[19] There are also related issues connected with ideas of information flow within local, national and global contexts. The impact of shifts in the ways in which data about Islam is distributed via the Internet, especially through peering, has led to a complex reconfiguration of religious authority models.[20]

Surfers may develop new understandings and consequent affiliations through a Web literacy, combined with breadth of Islamic databases and information sources available. Peter Mandaville notes in this context: "Popular imaginations travel well today. Media technologies are largely responsible for this development. They permit us to reproduce and sustain forms of communal identity across great distance. While the distinction between 'here' and 'there' may still endure, 'there' is no longer very far away."[21] Mandaville tackles this issue through analysis of translocality, where information and opinions flow between and across diverse spaces.[22] The concept of nuanced Muslim communities emerging in cyberspace takes many forms, including individual strands bringing together disconnected individuals.

Determining *who* the audience for this Islamic material is on the Internet can be a critical issue. Specific religious affiliations are likely to be drawn to areas of the Web that represent their own worldview within a digital community. Some sites focus on bringing other Muslims toward their own perspective, while others seek to propagate Islam to people who are not Muslims. Locating a starting point for exploring Islam on the Internet can be problematic. New sites continue to emerge, and simply typing "Islam" into a search engine, a long-standing and time-consuming source of fascination for me, leaves the reader with hundreds of thousands of possible options.

iMuslims have developed expectations about the forms of Islamic discourse available online and the ways that they can contribute to it through distribution, comment, and interaction. Previously reluctant, hesitant, or, in some cases, technologically unaware sectors representing aspects of Muslim beliefs recognized the need to go online to meet the needs of their communities or networks. Through creating attractive portals and online services, shades of the Islamic spectrum have sought to channel readers and manage knowledge associated with their belief perspectives. These are often networked to a wider affiliated global constituency. Jon Anderson suggests that a form of intermediate "creolized discourse" has been produced between different spheres of Muslim interests:

> Islam on the Internet is performative, not merely paradigmatic but a pragmatic engagement of witness and of connection, and . . . these connections grow uniquely in this medium. They include ways that Muslims connect their lives with Islam and extend those connections beyond the parameters of previous networks for a wider range of persons, including women. . . . [T]hese voices, connections, identities and performances represent a "missing middle" between the Islam of intellectuals subject to textual analysis (of thought) and Islam of the folk or masses more likely to be examined in terms of social forces.[23]

This creolizing had an effect, even at bastions of Islamic learning such as Al-Azhar University in Cairo. Whether this missing middle represents an understanding of a top-down authority model—or rather one that offers multiple discourses where top-down authority is subverted—is an intriguing question. The effects of dialogues from the middle may be having an impact in all directions, in particular in the way Muslim cultures and networks are hybridizing to take on elements of other popular cultural values.

This is indicative of the "fusions" of Islamic religious and cultural values as interpreted by Yvonne Seng, in which for some Internet technology there is an integrated element of modern Muslim lifestyles: "The university [al-Azhar] has changed over the millennium. It now stretches far out into the suburbs of Cairo. Students no longer sleep on reed mats in the open air but in air-conditioned, modern dorms. They access the Koran on CD-ROM, communicate via satellite, Internet and e-mail. They study computer technology and tourism (the current careers of choice). Their tastes intermingle East with West: blue jeans with headscarves, Coca-Cola with falafel, Umm Kulthoum with Smashing Pumpkins."[24]

Seng was writing about Al-Azhar, a traditional base for Sunni orthodox education for centuries. The juxtaposition of Umm Kulthoum, an Egyptian singer famous for epic performances evoking traditional Arab and Muslim values, and the long-standing American alternative-rock band Smashing Pumpkins is a telling one. It suggests that there is no contradiction between diverse and apparently conflicting frames of cultural reference. This has a bearing in relation to approaches toward CIES, where there can be an intermingling between traditional values and a contemporary outlook. Such a contemporary, technologically focused outlook is still at odds with some misconceptions about Muslim societies, particularly those functioning in urbanized contexts. For many iMuslims, there is no conflict between technology and living life Islamically. Islam is seen as adaptable to any age and context, while retaining its core values. Incidentally, tracks by both Umm Kulthoum and the Smashing Pumpkins can be downloaded on iTunes.

Researching Cyber-Islamic Environments

Within the digital-Islamic milieu, new developments occur regularly, and it is not possible to record every element of cyber-Islamic expression. Sites, locations, and content change frequently. Formats have makeovers, content evolves over time as technology changes, and content providers enhance their skills. While acknowledging the transformative potential of the Internet on Muslim networks, Anderson highlights the difficulties in analyzing the processes of change:

> Teasing apart this process—actually, multiple intersecting processes—can be devilishly hard. The story is still unfolding, experiments are proceeding, and the evolving interactivity of the Internet as new technologies come online provides an unusual level of responsiveness to the religious "market" for Islamic messages, discourse, and networking, which coevolve with the wider world that they address and in which they are cast. Some of the story has already disappeared, quite literally

gone off-line, as both the Internet and the world have moved on from an initial phase of bringing religion online in pious acts of witness to a more complex one of enacting officializing strategies in a world of multiple, contested, and contesting authorities.[25]

Anderson is correct: substantial material online is lost to study, as it is not formally archived or preserved. I have sought to archive those elements of specific relevance to my research, notwithstanding hard-drive meltdowns, including two during the writing of this book. At times, the acquisition of data has an unstructured, unscientific, and random nature. The publication schedules of online content are not precise and require specific approaches toward data mining.

My own methods for the collection of information pertaining to this research area continue to evolve. An average research day requires daily visits to chat forums, websites, and blogs to read and view a complex array of material. Some of this has to be downloaded and archived, while other elements require entry to secured, password-protected areas of the Internet. The time-consuming element is the sifting of RSS feeds, increasingly fine-tuned with other tools, even as sources grow in number. Research necessitates observation and discussion with Web coordinators and users. The substantive growth in Arabic and other-language materials adds further complex levels to data-mining processes.

In relation to the blogging chapter in this book, a core group of pages was inspected, in part through the use of RSS feeds and aggregators of content. For example, an RSS feed of a portal would link to hundreds of other sites. The selection of such empirical evidence was at times random; one information-rich site would frequently link to several others. A small group of about thirty sites had been observed closely since 2003, but these sites were also portals into hundreds of other blogs in various languages. My focus was on English and Arabic pages, although inevitably I scanned other content as well. Significant pages were observed, themes were tracked, and content was recorded in my personal archive.

A proportion of materials derived from my daily sweeps of the Web are posted on my Virtually Islamic blog, with a brief commentary.[26] This book fills in some of the gaps of my blog, sequencing the information in a coherent framework. A significant percentage of all this data has been recorded and backed up. A lead to a specific new site can require several hours of intensive analysis and recording. Determining site ownership,

checking archive materials (if any), and establishing related links and references are also appropriate activities undertaken to varying degrees.

Some agencies and organizations have teams of staff dedicated to this
task full-time in terms of translation, recording, observation, and analysis.
This is often for specific agendas focused on security concerns. The entirety of this present book is derived from my own output and observation. Mining the Internet for its full extent of Islamic seams of discourse
and knowledge would require enormous information, person, and computer resources, way beyond the scope of one academic. The point was
well made by Daniel Varisco in 2004, when there were substantially fewer
Islamic sites available than at present (mid-2008):

> The ephemeral nature of websites is compounded by the seeming ease
> with which so many different kinds of sites can be found. If there are
> indeed over 8 million webpages that mention Islam, it would theo-
> retically take me over four and a half years of non-stop analysis, eight-
> hours per day, if I only spent one minute on each webpage. Of course
> not all the potential websites would be of value, but how could such a
> massive sample be meaningfully analyzed by hand? Consider also that
> Google does not access every webpage and many of the pages listed no
> longer exist. The data set in itself is seductive, but how could it be use-
> fully related to the people putting up the sites and surfing through the
> pages? A media revolution of enormous proportions is taking place in
> cyberspace. With apologies to Marshall McLuhan, I am not sure that
> the medium is the message for the Internet, but the medium is defi-
> nitely a new kind of methodological challenge.[27]

This book embraces the challenge without apology. The viability of a
snapshot offers contrasts and indications of complexity, providing insight
into how CIES continue to develop and online Muslim networks evolve. I
am increasingly aware that the lines between online and offline have become increasingly blurred within and between CIES and parallel physical
societies.

Distinguishing between online religion and religion online has been a
critical element of pioneering studies of religion and/of the Internet. These
explore the motivation behind placing religious material onto the Web,
which can vary considerably. For some, it is an attempt to digitally distill a
religious experience and place it online. Degrees of "ritual" may appear
or be represented online for many purposes: to explain to outsiders a be-

lief practice, to encourage new adherents, to engender a sense of identity among existing practitioners, and/or to reflect and relate to offline social processes and interactions.

A number of scholars have discussed aspects of the concept associated with specific online religions or belief with no offline equivalent, at least within their developmental stages.[28] Online religion can take many forms, several of which are highlighted in this book.[29] Specific rituals and allegiances have evolved through which networks of Muslims can participate in religious activities that have been specifically shaped for online access, such as prayer or listening to sermons. These may involve degrees of interaction. Questions emerge as to whether the intent and participation associated with an online prayer is the equivalent of one undertaken in the mosque.

International academic conferences have also refined approaches to the field.[30] A number of the developments and innovations of Islamic practices and concepts online discussed in this book have no real offline equivalent, and as such they represent an aspect of "religion online" that should be viewed in conjunction with this scholarly discourse.

The study of Islam in cyberspace remains a developing field of academic endeavor. Jocelyn Cesari suggests, in relation to studies of Islam and the Internet (including those generated by myself), that there is scope for greater investigation into specific forms of online Islam that may be independent of their offline equivalents: "Since September 11, 2001, the study of Internet Islam has primarily concerned itself with the study of Islam-oriented activism."[31]

I have endeavored to balance different elements of interest relating to Islam and the Internet. In 2004 I produced a study of how the Qur'an has been presented online, and within other work I also focused on aspects of networking and electronic *ijtihad*. My books *Virtually Islamic* (2000) and *Islam in the Digital Age* (2003) emphasized how websites could form an extension of other forms of religious knowledge, networking, and authority. It was highlighted that in some cases, distinct new formulations of Islam transcending traditional boundaries of knowledge would emerge. This book seeks to demonstrate unique online Muslim identities and conceptions of Islam as well as the blurring between these and their offline equivalents.

Determining the extent of the cyber-Islamic landscape is a critical element. It is my view that there is scope for a variety of studies into these phenomena, including specific online forms of Islam and what might be described as digital fusions between online and offline Islam. It is certainly pertinent to consider the specific online manifestations of Islam as they present themselves through a variety of contexts, formats, and media. It is also appropriate to undertake grassroots research on the impact of the Internet in diverse contexts, something beyond the scope of this present work.[32]

The Internet has become a critical adjunct for researchers seeking to analyze aspects of Muslim beliefs, especially those focused on content analysis—for whom the Internet is a primary source of information about movements, entities, and networks such as al-Qaeda.[33] Some analysts of Islam have ventured into cyberspace to interpret documents and movements.[34] There is substantial crossover between disciplines in relation to interpretations of Islam and the Internet, especially in regional contexts. The distinct questions that have emerged in relation to the identification and rationalization of Islamic Studies as a discipline—or as a series of disciplines—need to be seen in relation to the study of CIES.

Islamic Studies itself can function through a number of disciplinary foci (not all of which are complementary) and with some diverse agendas. For example, in the UK in 2007, there was a sustained discussion on whether the study of Islam should focus on the Muslim communities present in the UK or on the traditional spheres associated with area studies and linguistics—particularly those associated with the Middle East. I was an executive member of the British Society for Middle Eastern Studies. I am also an academic for whom the study of Islam within Western European contexts has been a primary focus of scholarly endeavor. Therefore, I am positioned midway between these two interest areas, which I have seen as mutually complementary rather than competitive. There is, after all, connectivity between these areas for those with an interest in CIES.

The political ramifications of the study of Islam, even at an introductory level, resonated when Carl Ernst (a coeditor of this book's series) led classes at the University of North Carolina in which a book introducing the Qur'an was the designated subject of study. The ensuing dialogue about academic freedom and impartiality resounded on- and offline. For some who associate themselves with the field within "Western" contexts, there are clear political agendas, associated with the endorsement and support of particular regimes and ideologies.

In some Muslim contexts, the notion of an objective study of Islam is subsumed by political and religious agendas: the motives for Islamic Studies may lie instead in training for religious duties as an imam, or for furthering individual belief frameworks, rather than furthering critical academic enquiry. There can be confusion, and a multitude of explanations, associated with the definition of the study of Islam.

There are also specific issues associated with "insider" and "outsider" identities. On one level, I am operating in the latter category, while also recognizing that one can have a multitude of identities. The insider-outsider debate is a long-standing issue, particularly for one operating both within a Department of Theology and Religious Studies and a Center of Islamic Studies. However, Muslim acquaintances have noted that in certain areas of Islamic discourse, this can facilitate aspects of critical analysis that would be more problematic for those with a Muslim identity. So-called secular Muslims, for example, may present their own interpretation of ritual and receive a dynamic rebuttal from "orthodox" Muslims. Those operating from a particular Sufi outlook would receive short shrift from some legal affiliations within interpretative "schools" of Islamic jurisprudence. Aspects of Shi'a belief do not necessarily recognize one another. Despite these and other factors, I do not wish to convey an air of apology. I recognize that there is scope for numerous perspectives on this subject, particularly from those operating within Islamic Studies. During presentations of related subject matter at conferences and in other discussions throughout the preparation of this volume, I have benefited from discussing these themes with a number of people operating from diverse Muslim worldviews.

In the context of this book, while recognizing that the concept of impartiality may be redundant, effort has been made to produce an academically balanced approach toward understanding CIEs. Responses to my earlier works demonstrated that they have been used equally in Islamic seminary contexts as much as within "secular" university departments (and points in between).

Contemporary Islamic Studies, in particular, have to develop an awareness of this milieu, to which Varisco's earlier comment has further relevance. Bruce Lawrence and miriam cooke developed a conscious approach toward acknowledgment of the potential impact of the Internet amidst forms of Muslim discourse in work leading up to their edited volume, *Muslim Networks*. This incorporated several chapters that refer to the impact of the Internet in Islamic contexts.[35] Dale Eickelman, James Piscatori, and Jon Anderson contributed several important studies referring to the interactions between the media, Muslims, and society. These works recognized the Internet as a significant channel for diverse forms of Muslim communication, integrated into other forms of dialogue and interaction.[36]

This academic recognition has taken numerous forms: Jon B. Alterman pioneered studies associated with aspects of the media, including the Internet, and their impact on the Middle East.[37] Albrecht Hofheinz focused specifically on Arabic-speaking contexts and notions of political liberalization, conducting fieldwork on Internet use in Morocco, Egypt, and the Sudan.[38] Sustained fieldwork was also applied by Deborah Wheeler, who utilized an ethnographic approach in her study of the Internet in the Middle East, which focused on its impact in Kuwait.[39] The impact of the Internet and Islam as a subject of academic discourse meant that it became a significant area for postgraduate studies.[40] There are other examples of developing scholarship focusing on specific issues associated with Islam, Muslims, and the Internet.[41]

Work on Islam and the Internet has become more nuanced in relation to specific aspects of the media and has emerged from departments of theology and religious studies. This has been evident in the work of Göran Larsson, who has surveyed chat rooms and Wikipedia in the context of Islam.[42] Larsson's earlier edited book contained a chapter by Philip Halldén on Salafi jihadi Internet activities, a contribution by Ermete Mariani on forms of Islamic knowledge on the Internet, and a chapter that I wrote about Muslim cyberspace in the UK.[43] Other output and approaches are referred to throughout this book. It is hoped that this present work will also contribute to an understanding of the evolving and shifting Internet landscape in the context of Islam and Muslims. Momentum within this study area continues to intensify as a response to changing global concerns and the development of new technological interfaces mediating between religion(s), their adherents, communities, and observers.

What Makes the Internet Islamic?

According to contemporary Muslim scholars, especially those who are proactive on the Internet, there is no incompatibility between Islam as a religion and its representation on the Internet. That vision is dependent on the purpose and intent for which the media is applied. The determination of what is Islamically appropriate or correct online is best left to the judgment of the individual Muslim. This book demonstrates that a broad spectrum of Islamic hypertextual approaches and understandings are located in cyberspace, which reflect evolving political transmutations of Islamic paradigms and influences and shifting belief patterns responding to interaction with a range of conceptual and interpretative matrices. These are themselves associated with the historical prototypes of knowledge development and communication, which have held a high place in Muslim cultures and societies.

The Prophet Muhammad stated: "Seek knowledge even as far as China."[44] The Internet could be seen as an extension of that quest. It has to be noted that access to the Internet, while improving in many Muslim-majority contexts, is still relatively low. There has been resistance to aspects of the Internet from some Muslim quarters. This has been tempered by pragmatism, given that there is an educated generation that has grown up fully conversant with the application of computer interfaces as part of leisure, education, business, and now religious expression and understanding.

Is all online activity undertaken by Muslims implicitly Islamic? There are clear boundaries where Muslim ethics would suggest otherwise, such as accessing online pornography or participation in online gambling. There are also more subtle zones, especially for those actors who believe that the Qur'an implicitly guides their every action. This raises difficulties for academics, whose representation of these boundaries will not necessarily encompass such considerations. With these points in mind, the focus of this book is primarily on activities online that are overtly religious in their orientation, as defined by the approaches of their Muslim adherents, practitioners, and observers. Some critics have suggested that I should be more overtly critical of some online activities in the name of Islam, but this, in my opinion, would remove attempts at independent observation and objectivity, which are themselves problematic terms, especially in relation to the study of religions.

I have continually emphasized the diversity of conceptualizations of Islam within cyberspace, which really reflects many facets of this fluidity; and indeed how many shades of meaning within the spectrum can be located through searching for "Islam" in cyberspace. I consider that any individual Muslim's perspective on or definition of Islam is legitimate, whether or not it is accepted by a majority or reflects an individual view. This has caused some readers of my work to posit their own opinions about what is legitimate Islam and what goes beyond these boundaries. For example, at various times, descriptions of "gay Muslims" or the Taliban, not usually in the same context, have generated concern that these identities are not Muslim and cannot be incorporated within analyses. However, they have reflected multiple discourses about Islam by Muslims and should, in my opinion, form part of any analysis that speaks in general terms about the religion, its interpretations, its believers, and its diversity as represented in multiple areas of the World Wide Web. This may be indicative of the phenomenological approach to my writing to date, influenced by Ninian Smart and other academic observers of religion. Determination of a single paradigm of Islam and Islamic betrays the reality, on- and offline, with its resonance in the orientalist historical discourse of Edward Said.[45]

Defining what is Islam, Islamic, and/or Muslim is a critical issue. Peter Mandaville discusses a "fluid" conceptualization of Islam, where the single banner of Islam as "master signifier" encompasses "a totalising abstraction through which meaning and discourse can be organised."[46] He speaks of how boundaries set up around different types of "Islams" belie the perspectives of "the vast majority of Muslims" of a single Islam.[47]

How this is determined is really beyond the scope of this book. It has to be said that a number of forms of interpretation, which fall under the banner of either a single Islam or multiple Islams, suggest that their approach is essentially the only legitimate path that can be followed. This is frequently represented in cyberspace. It might be subtle or overt, aggressive or pacific; implicit exclusivity of belief can seek to delegitimize other worldviews within the Islamic spectrums. It can attempt this while paradoxically referring to a single *ummah*, or "community of believers."

When considering elements of knowledge diffusion, censorship, and Internet access within CIES, one significant question is the nature of Internet readership within Muslim contexts. Who are the readers that might utilize the Web to acquire religious knowledge about Islam? Various models can be considered, including those based around consumer marketing and product development, in an effort to determine what makes the product of an Islamic website attractive to different sorts of readers. The product in this context may refer to engendered interactivity and networking as much as to static and/or flowing and regularly updated textual and multimedia content.

Muslims present dimensions of their religious, spiritual, and/or political lives online through spaces that integrate websites, multimedia, chat rooms, e-mail listings, and interactivity through social-networking forums and user-generated content. While recognizing that these diverse tools interact, the primary focus for this book is the World Wide Web. This is the most publicly accessible form of digital content online, requiring no specific memberships (except in closed or membership-only sites) or particular technical skills to access, beyond basic knowledge of how a browser works. A telephone line and basic computer are sufficient to open up a world of content previously off the Islamic knowledge circuits, including areas of the Web requiring membership.

One significant question, which drove my early research in this field, is: how "Islamic" can Internet technology be? This subject has been debated at length online. While not necessarily representative of any mainstream opinion, there were some interpretations and references to technology in an article that appeared on the Hizb ut-Tahrir website khilafah.com.

> Allah (Subhanahu Wa TaÂ'aala) allowed for us to use various types of technology as long as it is in a Halal way. "He it is Who created for you all that is on earth" (Al-Baqarah 2:29). This includes cars, mobile phones, the Internet, satellites, missiles, and DVDs. The Prophet (Sal-Allahu Alaihi Wasallam) utilized the various technologies at his time, he even used the style of digging a trench which [was] taken from Persians, in the Battle of the Ditch, otherwise known as Ahzab. Technology can be used for Halal or Haram, it is not the thing which is Haram it is what you do with it. As an example, the Internet and DVDs can be used for Haram such as promoting indecency or can be used in a Halal way to promote Islam.[48]

This is interesting in its use of the Qur'an and precedents from Muhammad's life to justify certain applications of the Internet within specific boundaries. One must distinguish here between religious and other actions. Some Muslim activities online are not specifically religious or Islamic in their orientation, although their protagonists may exhibit paradigmatic Muslim behavior in their participation and enacting of Islamic principles. The indicator may be subtle, and determining the boundaries between what represents an Islamic activity or Muslim behavior is problematic. An online "al-Salamu 'alaykum" greeting may be enough to present an e-mail as Islamic, even if its content is strictly business. An eBay transaction, which uses a debit card rather than a credit card that accrues interest and which some interpreters would deem un-Islamic, may been seen as a halal activity. There is certainly scope for defining an Islamic Internet etiquette, adapting traditional principles for the information age.

Diversification of Internet content takes many forms, with Islamic platforms establishing new networks of communication in different facets of human life. For example, in Saudi Arabia, an electronic university was planned to project specific Islamic values to domestic and international audiences.[49] This awareness of international audiences was refined by the Iranian Islamic Republic News Agency, which launched a Chinese-language Internet site not only as an effort to reach China's 20 million Muslims but also to project its perspective to other sectors in China's burgeoning Internet audience.[50]

Such activities led to some serious contemplation about the nature of online existence for Muslims in cyberspace: "The increasing 'cyberization' of our lives makes real-life interaction ever more crucial to keep ourselves human. We can allow our shadow selves to be in cyberspace, but we must not lose our souls in cyberspace. In the process of cyberizing Islam, we must see what happens to Islam."[51] This is indicative of wider discussions on the "appropriate" application of the medium in Islamic contexts.[52] Some sought to present specific methodological approaches and controls for the Internet, based on perceived Muslim values. In the UK, a guide was published for Muslim parents seeking to control their children's use of the Internet.[53]

The attendant technological literacy of new generations of readers and site creators introduces new issues into our understanding of CIES. For Muslims seeking religious opinions and advice on such developments, this has also necessitated the scholarly input of 'ulama', self-proclaimed and/or classically trained, who seek to refine elements of Islamic netiquette or manners to match technological shifts and changes in cultural practices. This can include the "suitable" usage of online messengers such as MSN, AIM, and IM and the "appropriateness" of online chatting. In a response to a question on the use of online messenger (and similar chat programs), one scholar noted:

> The Internet is a blessing that Allah Almighty has bestowed on us, and we should thank Him for it. We should express our gratitude to Him by making good use of it. It is an act of ingratitude to misuse the Internet in the ways we know to be indecent.
>
> Online messengers are among the Internet services, but some people neglect the proper Islamic manners while using them. One such neglect is unnecessary chatting between members of the opposite sex, which may involve unwanted risks. We should ward off the evils that Satan whispers in that respect, as he tempts people in many deceiving ways.[54]

The discussion that followed applied Qur'anic references to justify specific behavior patterns in the use of online messengers. This included ensuring that surfers "at the other end" had the time to chat and that the content of a discussion is "decent." An associated response on chatting made the point that "chatting with members of opposite sex, whether they are Muslims or non-Muslims, personally face to face, or on phone or chat lines all fall in the same category. The haram of it is haram, and the halal of it is halal."[55]

This suggests particular patterns of the permitted (halal) and the forbidden (haram), which reflect concepts and principles analogous to other Islamic contexts, as expounded in a further article on Islam Online: "Internet chat is very similar to writing letters or talking to someone on phone. Actually it is a combination of both. Muslims have to observe the same rules as they observe in writing letters or making telephone calls. Islam does not permit love letters or intimate conversations between males and females who are not married to each other."[56]

The development of an Islamic netiquette is part of an ongoing process that includes the application of principles drawn from primary Islamic sources and their interpretation to meet contemporary needs and contexts. In some ways, this approach suggests a form of *ijtihad*, a term that links to the historical and contemporary practices of scholars in deriving interpretative and analogous meaning from Islamic sources to suit the exigency of a situation.

The highlighting of the perceived dangers of the Internet and computer technology has a currency way beyond CIES. Combined with the discussion of Islam, the two elements are potent enough to generate fear, both from insider and outside perspectives. Dialogues about the perceived abuse of the Internet have also emerged, which may or may not have contradicted Islamic teachings. Some of these dialogues are about the nature of content and dialogue, while others are simply suggestions that the distractions of the Internet are damaging businesses: "Internet abuse by employees is costing Saudi businesses millions of riyals per year, according to a survey conducted in the Kingdom. Some 30 percent of small and medium enterprises (SMEs) are losing more than a day's work each week due to employees' misuse of the Net."[57] The report does not make clear whether this abuse is simply employees surfing the Internet, chatting online, or visiting more contentious and explicit zones associated with the Internet.

The positive and negative potential of the Internet in Muslim contexts has been explored by a number of writers and columnists. In Pakistan, Razi Azmi noted: "Like dynamite and nuclear power, the Internet can be used constructively or destructively, positively or negatively. It is an instrument, a massive force multiplier, which can be employed to proliferate and assimilate knowledge or to propagate ignorance, distortions and half-truths."[58]

The tendency to blame the Internet for societal ills has been subsumed in some quarters by a realization that complaining and blaming is not enough; the challenges had to be met online.

The impact of the Internet is felt differently in varied sectors of Muslim beliefs, and there are inherent limitations in some social, cultural, and economic contexts. Carl Ernst notes:

> The vast majority of participants in the Sufi tradition in Muslim countries are still from social strata that have very little access to the most modern forms of electronic communication, and many are indeed illiterate. Lower-class devotees who attend the festivals of Sufi saints in Egypt and Pakistan are not represented on the Web. The effect of the spread of Internet technologies is likely to be "the reinforcement of the culturally dominant social networks, as well as the increase of their cosmopolitanism and globalization." As might be expected, the authors of Sufi websites tend to be members of the cosmopolitan and globalizing classes: either immigrant Sufi leaders establishing new bases in America and Europe, immigrant technocrats who happen to be connected to Sufi lineages, or Euro-American converts to Sufism in one form or another.[59]

This developed awareness of iMuslims is a significant one that tempers any rush into assumptions about the immediate transformative powers of the Internet. As I have discussed elsewhere, many sectors and sects remain unaffected or unconcerned about the role of the Internet in association with Islam, with some going so far as to eschew the use of technology.

The concept of a "virtual *ummah*" thus presents some inherent limitations in terms of users and impact. This *ummah* is defined as representing the worldwide community of believers (across space and time) and has its origins in the Qur'an and in the statements of the Prophet Muhammad. The idea of an *ummah* being constructed online has been explored by Olivier Roy: "The virtual *ummah* of the Internet is the perfect place for individuals to express themselves while claiming to belong to a community to whose enactment they contribute to the enacting of, rather than being passive members of."[60]

I would suggest that, rather than a single *ummah* idealized as a classical Islamic concept, in fact there are numerous parallel *ummah* frameworks operating in cyberspace, reflecting diverse notions of the concepts of community. This reflects online conceptualizations of Muslim identity and authority that mirror similar ideas in the nondigital world but which can also nurture new networks of understandings in cyberspace. It is a natural phenomenon for a net-literate generation to seek out specific truths and affiliations online when they cannot be accessed in the local mosque or community context. This can be through formal channels of information, including Islamic portals belonging to major players in CIES. Equally, it can involve access to discussion lists and forums, where questions can be posted, often to peer groups.

The Internet has become a primary networking tool for many Muslim communities and individuals. The Internet has exposed individuals and communities to new interpretations and influences, fulfilling a need for those searching for knowledge unavailable in their domestic contexts. This goes beyond simple paradigms of majority and minority contexts. It can, for example, involve actors disenchanted with the majority interpretation of Islam—often state sponsored in a country with a Muslim-majority population. New frames of reference, for those who consider themselves disenfranchised or ill-served by the status quo of the real world, have led to the development of new cyber networks of Islamic understanding. These often draw on alternate readings of Islamic source materials outside of "orthodox" and state-controlled influences.

All have not necessarily welcomed these developments, especially those seeking to preserve a status quo of knowledge and interpretation based on the development of artificial barriers inhibiting communities and individuals from exploring alternative understandings of Islam. For example, those who previously consulted the Sunni "orthodox" *'ulama'* (scholars) based in their communities, who were trained in Islamic sciences at institutions such as al-Azhar, might now approach a "scholar" based in cyberspace lacking in these qualifications. The backgrounds of a cyber *'alim* (scholar) may be rooted in skills other than recognized training in the principles of Islamic jurisprudence, or *usul ul-fiqh*. This may not delegitimize that individual in the eyes of the person accessing the *'alim*'s site. He (the scholar is usually male) may possess other attributes, linked to family lineage, leading back to a significant relative with an innate religious/sacred charisma or power (*barakah*) or association with a specific religious or/and political organization. He may also feature highly in key-word searches on Google. This phenomenon is not restricted to cyberspace, but the medium has become one obvious focus for such developments. Conventions of religious authority have been challenged by those networks, organizations, and individuals intent on redefining Islam for a digital age.

Constructing models of interpretation and understanding relating to

CIES is an inherently complex activity, as observed by Eickelman and Anderson: "The role of new media in expanding the public spheres of Islam, in Muslim-majority societies and for extended transnational Muslim networks, is as complex and multi-dimensional as the connections of these spheres locally and internationally. If it is unpredictable, the consequences are not; eroding social distance and multiplying role models are reshaping the meanings of *local* and *global*, and new media are their means."[61]

The unpredictability of networks is a significant factor, with rapid mutations of technology and adherence emerging in response to events within local and global spheres. I would agree that we have to reconsider what is meant by "local" and "global." I think, in relation to iMuslims, that this reconsideration is both an inward activity of site owners and Islamic service providers reassessing their networks and an outward activity for observers (Muslim and other) seeking to chart and interpret this rewiring of the House of Islam. Those operating within CIES that constantly reappraise their networks and content can have the edge over those whose output and affiliations remain moribund. In the dynamic, evolving, and intersecting spheres of Islamic cyber communications, both local and global, there is a Web-literate audience au fait with cutting-edge Internet developments that embraces the white heat of online technological innovation in the name of Islam. They see no contradiction between Islam and the Internet and view the Web as a reinforcement tool for the proselytizing and networking of their Muslim worldviews.

This reshaping has an emphatic ideological and interpretative emphasis. On the Internet, a number of sites have been influenced directly or indirectly by aspects of authority and interpretation emerging from broad definitions of Wahhabi, Salafi, Qutubi, and synonymous political-religious interpretative contexts.[62] Sites do not necessarily come with clear indicators as to who is financing, supporting, or writing their content.

This comes into particular focus when exploring websites that present online translations and commentaries (*tafsir*) of the meaning of the Qur'an. These may be presented online as mainstream, but they can reflect any aspect of the matrix of Islamic interpretation without necessarily being clearly labeled. This was highlighted to me during my teaching of Islam, when students presented interpretative content about the Qur'an in their papers. This material had been derived from translated online sources representing specific Islamic political-religious views, which has been classified on the sites as "orthodox," "traditional," or "Sunni." It clearly was not.

Part of my teaching process was to highlight to these students that such commentaries had to be analyzed to determine their religious, social, cultural, and political framework before they could be used within papers. In some cases, this analysis demonstrated that the interpretations were drawn from content from "hardline" Islamically oriented political sources, which would not be counted as majority opinions. This does not negate the validity of an interpretation, necessarily, but it does strengthen the need for an awareness of the affiliations of website content providers.

In relation to this point, a significant proportion of online interpretative content relating to the Qur'an can be derived from sources that *some* might define as "Wahhabi-influenced" in orientation. These include a number of sites that have emerged from, or been funded by, Saudi Arabian religious foundations and agencies. These provide "fatwas" and authoritative opinions to local and global audiences. These may represent themselves as being part of the mainstream and indicate that theirs is the only Islamic model to follow, but in truth they represent one aspect of a more complex spectrum of Islamic understandings. Some scholars have talked about a "Sunnification" of Islam, drawing on this Wahhabi model, which frequently negates or condemns other Muslim religious perspectives. The combination of financial muscle and sophisticated communications strategies has enhanced the aims of Islamic missions based on Wahhabi-influenced interpretative ideals. It has also influenced those alternative models of Islamic understanding seeking to ramp up their online activities to counter the domination of these influences in CIES.

Wahhabi-influenced material has emerged in diverse online contexts from a variety of cultural and linguistic sources. There are a number of sites authored in Pakistan and Malaysia, for example, that contain materials that some might label Wahhabi or Salafi but which their authors would simply describe as Islamic.[63] This also raises some important issues on how Islam is propagated and marketed globally—not just through digital media, particularly in non-Muslim contexts. Roy perceives a homogenization of Islamic Internet content: "If you go to the Internet—in English or in modern Arabic—you find all the literature which has been produced by the [radical] Salafis, the Wahhabis and so on. It's very important to the extent that young educated Muslims who are going to other countries for studying and so look at these websites. They exchange information. And I cannot say the same with liberal Islam, [whose ideas are] less circulating [*sic*]."[64]

While it is difficult to justify such a statement on quantitative scientific grounds, and the term "liberal Islam" requires some unpacking, there is a sense that Wahhabi and Salafi discourse has a prominent role in cyberspace. These are essentially umbrella terms that can be broken down into multiple and not necessarily complementary definitions, reflecting a range of religious and political interests. Other shades of opinion also play an important role, however, as will be seen later in this book.

A number of Islamic movements have made Internet media integral to their communication culture, especially as a means to propagate their worldview, but also to network and obtain funding. Certain typologies associated with the interpretation of Islam do lend themselves conceptually to the notion of space and communication facilitated by the Internet. Roy alludes to this point in his discussion of "neofundamentalism."

> It looks at globalisation as a good opportunity to rebuild the Muslim ummah on a purely religious basis, not in the sense that religion is separated from culture and politics, but to the extent religion discards and even ignores other fields of symbolic practices. Neofundamentalism promotes the decontextualisation of religious practices. In this sense it is perfectly adapted to a basic dimension of contemporary globalisation: that of turning human behaviours into codes, and patterns of consumption and communication, delinked from any specific culture.[65]

The extent to which such a framework of neofundamentalism succeeds in neutralizing and decontextualizing religious practices is open to question, although superficially this may appear to be the case for a casual observer to some Internet sites. Unpicking the combinations of allegiances and influences, perhaps buried in the hypertext, can still reveal specific cultural and political links. The sense of the universal may be projected in cyberspace but betrayed by the subtext underneath the coded human behavior. There is no such thing as pure neutrality of allegiances within interpretations, even according to the Qur'an, which points out that the paradigm of a single tribe is challenged by the reality of human nature: "People, We created you from a single man and a single woman, and made you into races and tribes so that you should recognize one another."[66]

However, the Qur'an also notes that the concept of a "single *ummah*" can operate within this framework, a factor brought out in some translations and interpretations more than others: "Verily this Ummah of yours is a single Ummah, and I am your Lord and Cherisher: therefore serve Me (and no other)."[67]

A "single *ummah*" might be able to incorporate the diversity suggested under its banner. The extent to which that has manifested itself within the globalized context, especially in cyberspace, is quite different to that articulated in the seventh century in the Common Era, when Muhammad received the Revelation of the Qur'an from God via the Angel Gabriel.

Whether it is a single *ummah* or not is beyond the scope of this book. What one can state is that within this community (or interrelated network) that *may* be defined as an *ummah*, the Internet is facilitating communication that could make the *ummah* more cohesive; but it also represents and exposes diversity of expression and understanding, which can facilitate fractures rather than heal the divisions within Islam.

When exploring this issue, consider the dynamic ways in which chat rooms, Internet applications, and e-mail lists have been applied to represent varied, but not necessarily mutually compatible, Muslim interests. It should also be stressed that "liberal" and "progressive" Muslims have applied the Internet in dynamic ways, especially in minority contexts.[68]

Add to this equation the impact of diverse forms of religious authority. These can be in the guises of actors and institutions presenting their worldviews in ways that can circumnavigate traditional forms of knowledge transmission, entering diffuse spheres of communication. Roy observes:

> Many clerics are reaching out to a new audience by leaving the closed corporate space of *madrasas* and religious seminaries to speak on radio or television, write in non-religious journals, serve as a kind of chaplain to lay associations (for example, Amr Khaled in Egypt), or teach at state universities. Thus they become participants in the contemporary blurring of lines between the religious and secular spheres. They leave behind the clerical world (and often clerical garb, as did Amr Khaled) to address a lay audience, not as representative of any religious institution but as individual thinkers and writers.[69]

The cult of the individual certainly has a viable zone within CIES. As with other sectors of the Internet, space has been provided online to facilitate the reach-out process for individual points of view, which through the "Long Tail" (discussed below) can obtain a market. In truth, in the case of Amr Khaled, he is an individual backed up by substantial resources in order that his populist message can reach a global audience. A blurring of the lines of religious and secular spheres enables individuals to establish reputations for themselves and their opinions in "alternative" spaces.

These spaces transcend traditional boundaries and controls. They can provide a context in which opinion can be exchanged in places of relative safety for their protagonists. Some of these dialogues may be anonymous or undertaken by participants exercising online security measures. Some opinions contravene legal frameworks in different contexts (Muslim and other). They represent a challenge to conventional political authority frameworks in a way that goes outside of control options for state and governmental agencies. This may be beyond the boundaries of nationality and religious-cultural frameworks, entering into a new form of discourse.[70] This reflects what Mandaville discusses as evidence of "a new breed of Islamist intellectual whose political programmes are more likely to be found on an audio cassette or printed in a pamphlet than heard in the mosque. The populist discourse of this new intellectual is often explicitly anti-statist and emanates from spaces and places beyond the reach of institutionalised, formal political power."[71]

Linking into this is the phenomenon that has emerged of relatively low-status imams and scholars (from areas not usually associated with being central to Muslim authority) attaining a high global Internet profile and eclipsing the status of more conventional, mainstream scholars. The dedication of such cyber *'ulama'* to the creation of high-volume, user-friendly Internet content on central and topical issues has generated a higher level of awareness for a variety of Islamic perspectives that were previously obscure or off the radar.

Approaches to the development of content and its presentation have been crucial in this regard. Simply placing materials online that have previously been available in print, with no regard for design or navigability, has not been a successful approach to the medium. Attention to the views of Jakob Nielsen and others on Web design considerations should form a crucial part of the syllabus for those cyber *'ulama'* learning the application of HTML.[72] In line with other areas of the Internet, the creative application of tools such as search engines, RSS, navigability, and page clarity has to be coupled with site reliability. Does a page load correctly? Can it be viewed on a mainstream browser, especially via a conventional telephone line on a low-specification computer? Is it interactive with its readership? These are critical questions to ask of any Islamic Internet site in an already saturated zone of cyberspace. Regular Web visitors will be familiar with the phenomenon that attention spans of readers can quickly wander if the content is not easy to locate or navigate.

The impetus to go online in the name of Islam has intensified. The growth in materials other than English, previously the dominant language of Muslim online discourse, is particularly significant.[73] Coupled with improved access to the Internet, cheaper technology, and enhanced software, it is easier for individuals to not only be passive readers but also to go online and disseminate their own opinions. Those with basic technical skills and access can create a website, blog, or e-mail list. They may add Islamic symbols to it, such as quotes from the Qur'an, photos of Mecca, or images of spiritual leaders.

Some sites present pages that suggest that they are religious authorities. They may not be traditionally trained in Islamic sciences. This does not necessarily delegitimize them, as the Internet reflects a wider debate that was a precursor to the expansion of the medium, namely the nature of religious authority and the legitimization of the power to interpret Islamic sources. The Internet has exposed some Muslims to interpretations of Islam outside of the mainstream, away from their own religious-cultural outlook. They may have gone looking for these opinions or found them "by mistake." The influence of search-engine algorithms and parameters may have an ideological effect. This challenge of alternative influences has represented a problem for conventional authorities, especially some who initially chose to ignore the Internet. Some sites can present challenges to securely held notions of religious identity and knowledge.

The Internet demonstrates a fluidity and at times a fragility of Islamic and Muslim identities, where diverse associations and interpretations express and adjust themselves in different contexts and frameworks. This includes forms of discourse, interpretation, and political-religious authority in and between the strata of societies. CIES offer iMuslims exposure to alternate ideas and concepts and roots/routes into traditional networks of knowledge and religious power.

The awakening of cyber-Islamic activity has taken place over a sustained period, with spikes in activity emerging concurrently with significant events, in particular 9/11 and the second Gulf War. Gilles Kepel perhaps overestimates the impact of this campaign in cyberspace: "Through its coverage on the Internet, the Iraq War erased the geographical boundaries of Dar al-Islam (the domain of Islam) and Dar al-Harb (the domain of war) that had structured Muslim geopolitics for fourteen centuries."[74] It is dangerous to generalize on this on a number of levels, as these domains were certainly fluid and subject to multiple definitions many years before this war commenced. However, Kepel is correct to assert that the Internet has had some impact on how Muslim geopolitics are structured within the fifteenth Islamic century. This reflects the ways in which varied approaches toward the Internet have been utilized in the name of Islam.

Profiling iMuslims

The growing sophistication in the ways that multimedia has been applied within CIES parallels Web 2.0 development. These represent sustained investment of time and resources, reflecting the growing availability of high-quality equipment for mainstream domestic use, including editing software and production hardware such as digital cameras. Their popularity is linked to the growth of broadband ADSL and access to resources capable of hosting large files and substantial site traffic. The application of religious symbolism and iconography in these Islamic digital contexts demonstrates the extension of traditional media into cyber constructs.

Given the fluid and random nature that surfing the Internet can take, measuring the impact of any one site raises a number of issues, especially the type of data that is relied on in order to ascertain impact. The number of page impressions or hits on a website counter is not indicative of how a page is read or used by the visitor or the amount of time that is spent absorbing content. The date is open to manipulation by website owners. As any user of the Internet knows, the navigation of webpages can take numerous approaches. Quantifying the unique visits and page impressions is inherently problematic, especially in the field of CIES, in the absence of extensive user surveys conducted at a grassroots, user-end level. Privacy would be a key consideration for any user of such content, especially when it transcends their religious and cultural norms.

One has to consider how readers apply religious materials, as there will be considerable diversity of approaches. For example, models could be constructed in which individuals use the Web as their sole source of knowledge about Islam. Others may draw upon a comparative approach, visiting several sites for information. That knowledge may have a life-changing impact on an individual's life. Readers may only rarely use the Net for acquiring information about Islam. Some may just be curious about, or entertained by, the content of CIES. They may visit for a minute or stay several hours; a visit may be unique or part of a regular surfing pattern, incorporating regular checks on sites for updates.

There are flexible parameters associated with Internet usage in all contexts, not just CIES. Piety and a sense of obligation can form part of the overall online-knowledge equation. It can interlock with other technological developments. One example would be the integration of Qur'an applications within cell phones, PDAS, and other media.[75] Questions arise not only of how this technology is applied and used but also of how reliable and authentic source materials are.

Models of Internet use in a cyber-Islamic context could be constructed in various ways. I have drawn upon adapted business models of user relationships of products to consider the types of readers of a website as part of a relationship pyramid. This would include hierarchical categories of leaders, champions, active supporters, reliable users/supporters, casual users/supporters, and potential users/supporters.[76] This pyramid can, in the context of Web 2.0 in general and CIES in particular, be seen in a variety of ways. There may be a hierarchy of leaders and champions that represents a more traditional model of knowledge diffusion. However, it might also be feasible to use the categories within a horizontal model in which the users, supporters, and champions are intermeshed in a reconfiguration of the Islamic knowledge economy. The model could also be adapted, since on various sites different users would seek different types of relationships. For example, there are differences between long-term and short-term users: some are intimately involved with the site and related activities, while others keep a (geographical and religious) distance.[77]

Levels of knowledge about Internet use might also restrict surfing activities, as would technical limitations of equipment used and language barriers. Readers may seek different forms of "benefits" from their use of a site. A website may be the exclusive source of information about Islam for a reader; others may take a comparative approach or be a rare user of a site and its facilities. Issues of whether a site is visited for reasons of guidance, information, obligation, and/or entertainment also apply. Readers may lurk on a site, or they may actively participate. This introduces issues of identity of users and anonymity. iMuslims are multifaceted, have diverse motives, and cannot be stereotyped in terms of their Internet use. On reflection, these have a correlation with models of religious leadership, articulated by Max Weber and others within fields associated with the study of religions.

Traditional media outlets in Muslim and other contexts felt challenged with the increased popularity of news and information sources outside of their control. The growth impacted on other integrated technological developments, in particular new generations of cell phones and related products and services with Internet interfaces. These could all usefully tap into a growing market of Islamic products and services.[78]

Questions may also be asked on the locations of a surfer, an Internet Service Provider (ISP) and related computer services, the owners and author(s) of a site's content, and any ideologue or figurehead. Does the iMuslim approach cyber-Islamic material in a private space, a personal space, and/or one unmonitored by family or a wider society? Using an Internet café has different implications relating to privacy, especially in contexts where on-line material may be filtered and identities required for use of a computer.

The ways in which the Web can offer opportunities for marginalized individuals to access new channels and interpretations of Islamic knowl-edge have to be seen in a broader context. Such influences impact on the readership of all websites, but especially those containing sensitive mate-rials associated with religious values and cultural expectations associated with being Muslim. It may be relevant to avoid a clichéd understanding of this: it could be that the surfer is operating in a secularized context, where obtaining knowledge about Islam is seen as a suspicious activity. Or it may be that they are surfing in a physical context where governmental or soci-etal restrictions make visiting some websites a dangerous and/or illegal activity.

Web 2.0 and iMuslims

The technology itself is also shifting into a position where users are able to shape content provision and direct the "market," especially through spe-cific applications such as video diaries and blogs. The term "Web 2.0" was overhyped in some quarters as the dawning of a new Internet era, although some might say that Web 2.0 is now passé and another suffix is more appropriate. However, it has become a convention within discourse about online activities, so for the purpose of this book, the term Web 2.0 will be applied with extreme caution. I had considered including a "+" after the 2.0 to indicate the sustained online developments that have occurred since the term was first coined, but I have decided that this was implicit. I have also resisted the tendency in some technology circles to enter into further iterations (Web 3.0, etc.).

Web 2.0 integrates diverse tools and facilities, many developed with a collaborative element and based on peer-to-peer interaction. As such, its emphasis has been on social-networking sites, user-generated content, and enhanced and evolved information-retrieval systems. Podcasting and other alternate online data-delivery systems, innovative methods of online functionality and collaboration, and the development of social-networking communities are also part of the Web 2.0 framework. What is clear is that these elements of Internet media increase the options for iMuslims who choose to express themselves online.

There is a connection, too, with what are described as "convergence perspectives": these "range from looking at 'industry convergence,' to medium convergence, to convergence of individual media technologies."[79] This can incorporate "technological convergence," where content is delivered through alternate media, to the "functional convergence" of media types.[80] This is relevant in relation to CIES, as Islamic content can now be delivered through diverse digital media.

Web 2.0 extends to CIES. This latter term, which I first introduced in *Virtually Islamic*, now requires adaptation. This is in line with content providers diversifying their provision in response to perceived reader need and utilizing a broad platform of content formats. It is also a response to the intensification of peer-to-peer networking in Islamic contexts, a shifting online knowledge-transmission economy, and the reconfiguration of notions of hierarchies in response to Internet interaction. Changing formats of content are not necessarily distinctly Islamic but may crossover from other forms of content provision. For example, there are elements of MySpace that present a Muslim identity but are part of the broader social-networking service. There are news-service providers, such as Google News, providing RSS feeds that can be fine-tuned to have Islamically nuanced content. The tagging of data using flickr, Technorati, Del.icio.us, and similar tools can also present material with an Islam-focused identity. GoogleAds and similar services present links to Islamically themed products, although detractors may also link to material of an anti-Islamic nature through sponsoring various keyword searches.

Some Islam-related sites only have small groups of readers and limited links. These can fall off the map of mainstream searching. The phenomenon of the Long Tail, as defined by Chris Anderson, has a resonance in CIES, although it is based on a business model concept: "The Long Tail equation is simple: 1) The lower the cost of distribution, the more you can economically offer without having to predict demand. 2) The more you can offer, the greater the chance that you will be able to tap latent demand for minority tastes that was unreachable through traditional retail. 3) Aggregate enough minority taste, and you'll often find . . . a big new market."[81]

The Long Tail is analogous to the lower end of a business graph, where demand tapers out but indicates that there is still a market for a product over time. While the term is now entering the mainstream and is perhaps over-used, I was struck by this concept when Chris Anderson defined it in *Wired* magazine in 2004 as possessing a resonance when talking about Islam in cyberspace.[82] Anderson discusses how, when visitors visit Amazon.com for a specific product, they might be influenced by the recommendations of other related products on the specific product's page. The hyperlinks on one page can expose readers to a range of other materials that fall inside their interest areas but which they were previously unaware of. Those websites outside of the mainstream, with a limited number of links, may have a greater impact and cumulative market share over time than some of the key players. Of course, in the context of CIES, it is not necessarily a market for goods but a market for ideas; and in particular, the concept of the Long Tail might apply to some websites on the margins of Islamic interests and identities.

The Internet can reflect the nuanced interests of specific Muslim groups, which can reach down through the Long Tail into micro areas. The Latino site Piedad, for example, sought to provide support for female converts from this particular cultural-linguistic grouping.[83] Jews for Allah provided forms of support for people of Jewish heritage who become Muslim. Jews for Allah emphasized a Jewish edge to their actions, with personal accounts of conversion and a detailed listing of Israel-related links to human rights organizations and sympathetic religious groups.[84]

The reinforcement of identities and connectivity can be reflected at local levels for iMuslims. While it is something of a cliché to suggest transformative powers in relation to the Internet improving societies, enhanced opportunities to go online may benefit some sectors of Muslim societies who are perceived by some observers to be disenfranchised because of barriers of gender and/or wealth. Reflecting global trends, more Muslims log online daily, and the extension of access now incorporates the creation of cybercafés inside some mosques. Not all applications of the Internet in the name of Islam will necessarily be interpreted as benign to all observers, especially those within the myriad zones of political activism and violence in the name of Islam.

While the Internet certainly facilitates a wider cross-section of Muslim perspectives to be articulated, a number of areas remain "missing." New elements emerge regularly, and information management has become a crucial area for some Muslim perspectives. Not all sites maintain accessible archives of previous webpages or documents or preserve digital materials such as news services. There is an absence of sophisticated central libraries of Islamic knowledge online. These are areas that may see a change, reflecting growing sophistication of databases and their users, with materials preserved in accessible formats for future users, engendering a cohesive sense of identity and networking online that may filter into "offline" life.

Readers may be drawn into a core element of a website. For example, they may reach a Qur'anic commentary through a keyword search engine. Through this, they could be encouraged to visit other areas of a site to further develop their religious knowledge and experiential base. This might include opportunities for interaction and affiliation building with site organizers and other readers. As with other areas of the Web, a site that applies professional design considerations and frequently refreshed content may have a better opportunity of acquiring reader loyalty and return visits, becoming a "sticky" site.

The ways in which a website is designed to reflect its Islamic credentials is an intriguing issue. In some cases, this means combining elements of traditional Islamic understandings of arts and calligraphy with a dynamic and consistent symbolism, drawn from a rich variety of contexts and sources. What makes a site Islamic is perhaps in the eye of the individual surfer, especially when content is open to criticism or reflects views that some Muslims might describe as profane, heretical, schismatic, or otherwise against their interpretation and concept of beliefs.

Elements of identity and authority can be shared within the design aesthetic and graphical interface between sites, which otherwise vary considerably in terms of their ethos. For example, there may be an emphasis on green, that being the Prophet's favorite color. There may be the application of universal Islamic motifs. I hesitate to use the term "icons" in its Internet sense when discussing Islam, as the Qur'an pronounces emphatically against icons (when the term is applied in its religious sense).

There are some key identity markers that could be applied in a model of an Islamic website. Page designs might include specific reference images, such as photos of the Ka'bah, Mecca, Medina, al-Quds (Jerusalem), and other famous Islamic sites. Associated factors may include Qur'anic calligraphy, often drawn from famous examples of style or representing key names, terms, and phrases (in particular, "Allah" and "Muhammad"). Illustrations of the Qur'an, showing calligraphy or the book open on a stand, can frequently be found in CIES.

Islamic color schemes combine with themes specific to individual affiliations and interpretations. In some cases, this can be the depiction of particular leaders, even though some Muslim interpreters condemn the depiction of human form. Alternatively, a site may feature a particular regional sacred place, such as the shrine of a saint. Definitions of ownership and Islamic identity vary, representing conflicts and ideas of difference in the nondigital world. The sustained presence of minority opinions, outside of the mainstream, has suggested that in some cases, cyberspace can offer a relatively secure space for religious expression.

There is no such thing as a typical cyber-Islamic environment, but there are some common factors, particularly on top-level sites and portals. These may include reference to the pillars of Islam when introducing an interpretation of Islam to readers. One might expect a site to feature links to a Qur'anic source, related interpretative material, and information on the individual or organization behind the site. Well-resourced sites link to elements of specific Islamic activities online, such as chat rooms, moderated discussions, sermons, lectures, and multimedia content. These elements represent patterns of knowledge acquisition that have a complex relationship with long-standing and traditional concepts of education. I have represented the facets associated with CIEs in a diagram, which can also be viewed in detail on virtuallyislamic.com.

Networking: Connecting Islam 2.0

The diagram demonstrates that new forms of Internet media associated with Web 2.0 are impacting CIEs. Networking through chat rooms, blogs, video-upload sites, podcasts, and social-networking services can be integrated, in various degrees, into conventional cyber-Islamic contexts.

This diagram maps the dynamic and evolving series of connections across time and space, itself interlocking with other frameworks and interpretative approaches toward Islam and the Internet. In terms of a collaborative exercise, readers are invited to suggest their own amendments to the diagram via a wiki located on the virtuallyislamic.com website. These will be incorporated into an open-source shared document, in a number of versions, which will hopefully represent a contribution to our understandings of the Islamic digital worlds. The diagram itself has to be seen in reference to the contemporary developments associated with iMuslims' participation in the Islamic knowledge economy.

Prominent Islamic websites have maintained an online presence for several years, cultivating a web-literate audience for whom they represent a natural environment for dialogues on religious expression and authority. The ways in which the mediation of these materials occurs represent difference but utilizes familiar patterns. Every event within or about an Islamic

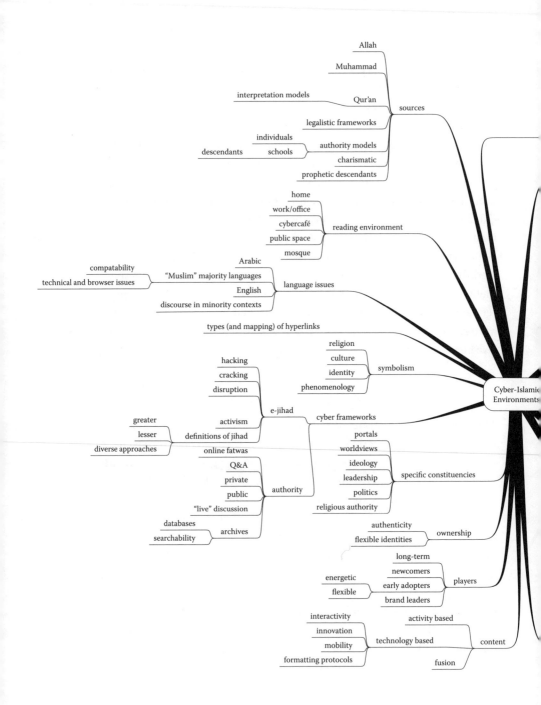

A diagrammatic representation of CIEs (Gary R. Bunt)

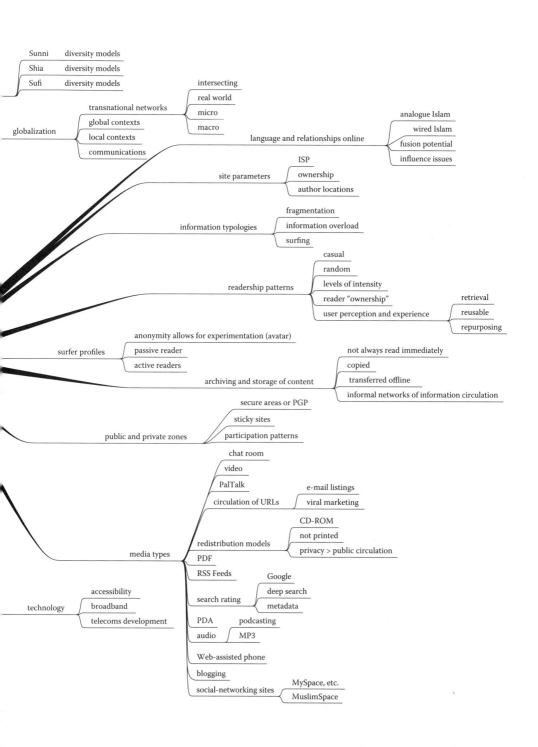

context can create an Internet ripple effect, as it resonates in blogs, video blogs, podcasts, news sites, chat rooms and other areas of the Web.

The proliferation of social-networking websites introduced into this equation offer a quick and easy way to create a website or blog, distribute multimedia, network with peers, and integrate other electronic and digital tools. Howard Rheingold, a prominent observer of online developments, coined the term "smart mobs" to define such activities: "To their users, social networking sites fill a number of functions: part diary, part shareable contacts book, part social club. For a generation of teenagers, they are increasingly becoming as important as ownership of a mobile phone."[85] This was couched in a positive tone, although for some observers smart mobs can also have a negative edge to them as well, emphatically placed on the "mob" element of the term.

Prominent examples of social-networking sites include MySpace, spaces.MSN, Bebo, Facebook, flickr, Second Life, and Cyworld US (based on a popular Korean network).[86] These all perform different functions, and an individual may have pages on several types of social-networking sites that are linked to each other. Reading personal pages of Muslim participants demonstrates that they were not necessarily afraid of posting a minutia of detail for readers to consume, or that they were unaware of the implications. These details included birthdates, locations, schooling, personal tastes and preferences, and, in some sites based on templates, the answers to over fifty personal questions.

Some social-networking sites have a propensity toward a high use of graphics and lurid backgrounds; some take advantage of increased bandwidth to present multimedia, often obtrusively. The concept of accessible Web design beloved of professional Web designers may be ignored on social-networking sites. Pages provide links to various "friends," who share similar interests.

Of the many tens of thousands of possible choices of such sites, I have taken only a random sample. It indicates that the profiles of iMuslims can be wide in scope. Within MySpace, one sixteen-year-old "Saudi Arabian born American—Pakistani" based in Texas provided extensive contact details, photos, and videos; she listed her friends, school, and activities. On another MySpace page, its hijab-wearing author Zahra linked to the blogs of others who followed similar dress codes.[87] Muslima Ilana's MySpace page included family photos and a photo of a veiled woman playing electric guitar from the Burqa Band, an Afghan rock group.[88]

A complex mixture of cross-cultural and religious influences is at work.

Another MySpace page provided links to hadith and Qur'an materials, Sufi-oriented discussions (featuring material on the prominent Sufi Nazim Adil Al-Haqqani), a booklist that included the Kama Sutra, and a photo of the writer in hijab with captions stating: "Do you think I'm hot. So is Hell. Lower your gaze!"[89]

"Hijabi" presented herself in cartoon form on MySpace, wearing a hijab and carrying a peace flag with a CND (Campaign for Nuclear Disarmament) symbol. The site linked to a page that opened with Qur'anic recitation in English and Arabic. Hijabi's page showed photos and information associated with Muslim Palestinian issues; discussed favorite punk bands; linked to TV programs such as *Crime Scene Investigation*; and listed key books, including novels by Anne Rice, alongside the Qur'an and other Islamic texts. Hijabi noted: "I am looking to meet new friends that are interested in Islam. Particularly sisters who are hijabis. Good Friends Are Hard to Find! I DO NOT WANT TO ADD ANY MEN TO MY SITE!!! I AM MARRIED AND DO NOT WANT TO HAVE MALE FRIENDS!! Please respect this guys! Sorry. If you aren't interested in having an active friendship, leaving comments, messages etc., do not add me."[90]

In terms of Internet etiquette, the capitalization represents "shouting" online, just in case visitors did not get the message. The gender separation is explicit and based on norms of practice derived from the Qur'an and other Islamic sources.

On MySpace and other social-networking sites, there are high levels of interactivity between "friends," the notion of frequent chat and updates being particularly relevant. The amount of personal detail raises some intriguing ethical problems for researchers and writers on the subject of Islamic cyberspace, reaching a point where there is a danger of such activity becoming voyeuristic. Clearly, this information is in the public domain, being published online, but there comes a time when one might feel that the "lurking" presence of a researcher is intrusive. However, MySpace is not a closed area of the Web. Does this mean that Muslim participants on MySpace are challenging and adapting concepts of personal space in relation to religious values? It is a possibility. However, it is as likely that it represents a fun activity motivated by peer-to-peer communication.

MuslimSpace, an Islamic social-networking site, emerged in 2006 with similar format to other networking sites, albeit with a halal edge.[91] MuslimSpace was founded by Mohamed El-Fatatry, who was based in Finland but of United Arab Emirates and Egyptian origin. In 2006 MuslimSpace claimed nearly 20,000 users, the majority based in the United States.[92]

Social-networking tools of MySpace and other sites suggest one form of interactivity that will have an impact on CIES. There can be some inherent or implied restrictions: MySpace is youth oriented, and older users may feel uncomfortable for religious and other reasons for networking in such an adolescent setting. The issue of age demarcation within cyberspace is an interesting one to consider, with no real equivalent to MySpace for so-called silver surfers. The exponential growth of Facebook in 2007, when it extended its user base, introduced new considerations in relation to CIES as micronetworks of Muslim interests and information channels started to emerge.

As the concept of social-networking sites extends into other media and expands user participation, these issues will become increasingly important within CIES. Virtual environments also had Islamic zones. Second Life featured a mosque and, in 2007, a Ramadan tent sponsored by the Islam Online website in which cultural and religious events were organized. The tent was attacked by two male avatars, who harassed Muslim women avatars present at the time. Despite this, Islam Online intended to increase its Second Life activities.[93] There were also other mosques in Second Life, which offered the opportunity to pray and, in one case, undertake ritual washing (*wu'du*). While visiting one Second Life mosque, it was clear that gender separation was not an issue. My casually dressed male avatar was asked on several occasions to chat by a veiled female, while exploring the precincts.[94] "Prayer" in the Cordovan-influenced Chebi Mosque included the gift of a digital Qur'an, but it was something of a solitary activity.[95] Visits on the night of Eid in Ramadan to the Islam Online tent were also quiet affairs. Clearly the online interaction had not replaced the need for "real" social networking, or perhaps potential visitors had business in other areas of the Internet.

YouTube featured a number of clips with an Islamic focus. Through the cutting and pasting of HTML code, videos on YouTube can be directly inserted into other sites. Top rated was "The Miracles of Islam," essentially a photomontage. It included plants and clouds shaped in the name of Allah in Arabic, juxtaposed with photos of Muslims in diverse contexts.[96] A number of videos with a proselytizing emphasis had been uploaded onto YouTube. On MuslimSpace, preacher Amr Khaled nestled among the popular *nashid* artists 786 and Shaam.[97] Many hours of Khaled's popularist preaching could also be found on the site, integrated into his supporters' wider media strategy. Individuals could also find a wide audience for their interpretation of Islamic issues through YouTube. Ummah Films gave an outlet to a number of speakers on popular issues via YouTube and other film sites, which generated interest through their populist and at times humorous approach to contemporary issues.[98]

DigitalHalal's portal contained a number of services, integrating MuslimSpace and including video and audio distribution, blogging, photo albums, and chat. These services feature collaborative and collectively produced content and indicate a way forward for Web 2.0 material associated with CIES. This slick and innovative set of sites, supported by advertising and donations, has continued to evolve since its inception. Its centerpiece is IslamicTorrents.com, essentially a service for uploading and downloading video and audio content similar to the BitTorrent movie-sharing site.

IslamicTorrents makes sustained disclaimers about the copyright issues associated with materials uploaded to the site, especially relevant to commercial products. This does not prevent such material from being uploaded by users, who effectively shape the nature and output of IslamicTorrents. The range of content includes Qur'anic recitation, film of sermons, and documentaries. Some of these are derived from copyrighted broadcast material, while a proportion is user generated. On IslamicTorrents, the onus is on users to upload as much content as they download. The process may be seen as technically complex for the average user, perhaps limiting the number of users to this service.[99]

Less technically complex is IslamicVideos.net, which included a number of recitations and video clips. Among the most frequently downloaded clips was "Sheikh Passes away in a Mosque," a video of an imam's death while giving a sermon. On one level, the film may appear intrusive; on another, it indicates the sheikh's religiosity and virtue, in that he was engaged in his Islamic obligations as he died. This could be viewed as the equivalent of those individuals who die while undertaking the *hajj* and are viewed as "martyrs." Visitors to IslamicVideos can upload and download short clips, e-mail their friends about favorite clips, and search for videos on specific topics.[100] A clip such as "Extremely Cute," a young Moroccan boy in Germany reciting short *suras* from the Qur'an, received exposure elsewhere on the Web. The proliferation of video camera phones meant that further expansion of this type of site was inevitable.

The photo album Muslimr essentially takes the initiative of the flickr photo blog and adds a halal twist. The portal is fully searchable, user-friendly, and easy to navigate. Information on updated pages can be obtained through RSS feeds. There is cross-fertilization between the sites, with banner advertising interlinking related areas. DigitalHalal provides a model for other sites to follow, enabling a high degree of networking and interactivity. Essentially, this was an early stage in the development of an Islamic social-networking model, which had the potential for rapid expansion. Founder Mohamed El-Fatatry was planning to integrate his sites into one package, entitled "Muxlim."[101]

Podcasting can also be integrated into the equation of CIES. In 2006 Islamic podcasts were limited to a small number Qur'anic recitation and an advice site, with MP3 downloads of recorded sermons. One exception to this model was alt.muslim, which produced specific magazine-format podcasts on a regular basis. These were presented and produced by Shahed and Zahed Amanullah, respectively based in Austin, Tex., and London. Current events, interviews, and lifestyle commentaries featured in the programming. This format, especially when podcasts can be automatically downloaded and updated via RSS, provide a template for other media providers in CIES.[102] London's Q-News Magazine was developing its own podcast service, drawing on archive materials.[103] The Radical Middle Way, cosponsored by Q-News, featured podcasts on its website drawn from Muslim scholars. Many had participated in a tour of the UK in 2006, during which time their speeches were recorded.[104]

Mainstream media also entered the sphere, when the *Guardian* newspaper introduced their Islamophonic podcast.[105] I established a podcast listing on my website but was restricted to about twenty sources in 2007. Given the relative ease with which audio productions can be produced and syndicated, and with editing packages being integrated into software, this format will expand in the future. I was aware of other organizations and individuals preparing Islamic podcasts.

References may also be given to on-site commercial links (for example, to Amazon), extending the discussion into the marketplace and perhaps introducing a trickle of financial support for a content producer. Although few would want to blog for a living, many clearly spend several hours a week or, to put it another way, hundreds of hours a year maintaining blogs or websites. Blogging tools can be simple, but the sheer quantity of potential information can make blogging a labor-intensive activity. Some sites are high maintenance, especially for the initial setup but also throughout their existence, when they might require management of readers' comments and technical supervision.

Online encounters take different forms. Audiovisual interaction is increasing online, suggesting new dynamics for relationship building between iMuslims. An example of interactivity could be engaging with a scholar from a different context, culture, or language group, introducing new understandings and possible influences. As with any medium, readers may draw from several sources and not necessarily be susceptible to the first opinion they encounter. Some may not find the process enlightening or beneficial. Others may test the environment and go back to conventional dialogues and relationships with authority.

An online Islamic experience might incorporate and combine religious sources, esoteric factors, intangible elements, religious experiences, liminality, rites of passage, religious opinions, and notions of authority. It may present motivation for religious activities through forms of online guidance, exhortation, encounter, sermons, and/or study resources. Open-source information about Islam would be useful to many surfers. This can already be located in a variety of sources and contexts, including Wikipedia. An Islamic version of this was introduced in 2006, entitled OpenIslampedia.[106]

In time, some readers become participants and writers on online content themselves or have multiple roles on the Net. The development of blogging has eased access to Web publishing for thousands of commentators on these and many other issues, although naturally some bloggers have a greater profile than others. There is a proliferation of low-content sites, blank pages, and even "splogs" ("Spam"-centered, advertising-dominated blogs) within this zone, making reliable calculations of participation and content problematic. Amidst all this, voices in the Islamic blogosphere can present alternative and critical perspectives on religious authority in a variety of languages, focusing on grassroots interpretations.[107] It cannot be suggested that all of these bloggers are necessarily writing directly or indirectly about religious issues or with Islam as the foremost motivation in their minds.

Concluding Comment

Like the Internet, Islam is neither Western nor Eastern. Global digital networks provide a natural outlet for communication, developing out of other forms of Islamic discourse. CIES demonstrate that a sense of the spiritual is entwined with the political, reflecting the historical patterns of Muslim understanding. The power of the Qur'an has been channeled through innovative digital constructs that do not diminish the profound sense of the sacred, articulated as much online as in the mosque.

Islamic symbols and notions familiar to previous generations, stretching back to the first Muslim community, have a dynamic digital religious space that, while innovative and evolving, continues to reflect the central pillars of Muslim beliefs. iMuslims or cyber Muslims connect to their heritage of knowledge and networking, but they apply an electronic interface to facilitate their communication with and awareness of each other and perhaps, in some way, with the divine.

The following chapters will explore the inherent complexity of Muslim networks online—in terms of their rapid evolution and diffuse interactions —through a number of different filters and approaches. They represent the fact that Muslims in many contexts are responding to the ways in which the knowledge economy of Islam is shifting through the evolving systems of connectivity, peer-to-peer collaboration, and shifting Muslim networks.

{ 2 }

Accessing Cyber-Islamic Environments

Bridging the Digital Divide

This chapter provides an overview of issues associated with how CIES are accessed. The "digital divide" is a critical issue, as the absence of Internet access has been interpreted as being part of the "problems" of some Muslim societies. This opinion often neglects consideration of the economic, cultural, social, *and* religious factors behind that issue, or indeed any appropriate solutions. When approaching the subject, applying a statistical analysis of Muslim usage becomes problematic. Alongside factors that include the absence of telecommunications infrastructures and the relatively high cost of computers, literacy issues and cultural constraints have inhibited growth in ICT, and consideration should also be given to the urban-rural digital divide.

Despite these limitations, reports from the United Nations, governments, and independent sources have highlighted the digital divide between countries and also within them. This has a clear impact in Muslim contexts and for Muslim networks. Telecommunications are the driving factor in access issues. The opportunity for access is significant in terms of motivating intellectual enquiry and analysis and collaboration across social networks. Determining the measure of "improvements" in Internet access vary in different contexts. This can range from the establishment of a telephone line, enabling simple dial-up access, to the establishment of high-speed ADSL connectivity, integrated with wireless technology and 3G cell phone access.

Muslim networks may connect online, but this connection is not a universal one, being bound up with factors associated with the telecommunications industry and the demands for Internet access. The digital divide widens further when discussing the international coverage of broadband services: "There are more than 1.1 billon of the world's estimated 6.6 billion people online and almost a third of them are not accessing the Internet on high-speed lines. According to the Internet consultancy Point Topic, 298 million people had broadband at the end of March [2007] and that is already estimated to have shot over 300 million."[1]

Point Topic's report noted developments in a number of contexts with Muslim-majority populations: Indonesia was reported as having the highest growth in the quarter for broadband access, at 28 percent, although the figure was skewed because of a late starting date by the operator. Morocco had 6.7 percent penetration (418,000 users) and Egypt 1.55 percent (240,000). This can be compared with Sudan, with 0.05 percent penetration, and a number of sub-Saharan countries with no figures at all.

Clearly, the trumpeting about social networking and wikinomics in relation to CIEs has to be seen within this context. What the statistics do not indicate is who those with access are, but one can assume that the figures relate to individuals and institutions with the substantial income (in relative terms) to pay for the facility.

A 2007 report in *Wired* compared the costs of broadband based upon per capita income, using measurements based on the price per Kbps (kilobytes per second) of broadband access. In Pakistan, broadband users were charged an average of US$106.98 per 100 Kbps, estimated as twice the average income. In Saudi Arabia, the cost was US$571.82 per 100 Kbps, about 58 percent of an average monthly salary; in Kazakhstan the price was US$52.68 per 100 Kbps, estimated as one-fifth of an average monthly salary. Compare this with the price of broadband access in the United States, at an average of US$0.49 per 100 Kbps, and Japan at US$0.06 per 100 Kbps.[2] The relatively cheaper cost of wireless broadband is a further driving factor when charges are based on usage rather than fixed monthly billing.[3]

There are a number of other indicators relating to Information and Communication Technology (ICT) access that can have an impact. While governments collect data in many countries, the International Telecommunications Union (ITU) states that acquiring data on more recent technologies is problematic in comparison with acquiring data on basic ICT equipment such as telephone lines, with regional differences relating to indicators making the data inconsistent. These include two primary indices for analysis. The Digital Opportunity Index (DOI) is linked to factors associated with Opportunity, Infrastructure, and Utilization, and the ICT Opportunity Index (ICT-OI) is based on factors relating to Density of ICT

Networks and Skills and Information Use Uptake and Intensity.[4] According to the ITU, analysis of these figures requires consideration of the DOI in relation to the development and economic status of a country. The classification of fifty Least Developed Countries (LDCs), which represent 11.9 percent of the world's population, includes a number of countries with Muslim populations.[5] Within these classifications, consideration should also be given to the spread of income groups.

The DOI for 2005–6 makes for illuminating reading in relation to CIES. The Republic of Korea is ranked first on the listing, with a DOI of 0.80. I have surveyed the listing (while conscious that the data requires a great deal of further unpacking) in order to determine how Muslim-majority countries are rated according to the DOI. Findings are presented in the table below (rankings according to the overall ITU listing are in parentheses).

There are some inherent difficulties with this data in relation to CIES. For a variety of reasons, including conflict situations, some countries are missing from the survey (Afghanistan, Iraq). Countries with substantial Muslim minority populations, such as India, are also not included in my listing. The DOI does not illustrate the gender divide. There can be especially low levels of access among Muslim women: the United Nations Economic and Social Commission for Western Asia suggested in 2005 that only 4 percent of Arab women used the Internet.[6] While "Arab" is not synonymous with "Muslim," this provided one regional indicator.

Despite inherent problems associated with such data, it does give some indications as to why access is a critical issue in several Muslim contexts. Infrastructural improvements, enhancing digital opportunities, will inevitably result in shifts in this index. In particular, in areas such as sub-Saharan Africa, the impact of Internet-enabled cell phones since the data was compiled will also impact the DOI.[7]

The ITU noted the impact of reforms of ICT policies in raising DOI scores, in particular in a Muslim context in relation to Senegal, where its score was raised from 0.22 in 2004 to 0.37 in 2006.[8] Senegal, alongside Morocco, achieved two of the top-ten gains in the DOI.[9] Morocco's own DOI growth was associated with sustained investment in ICT and competitive commercial cell phone coverage.[10]

It is significant that no Muslim-majority country appears in the top thirty countries in the DOI. Wealth per capita is one driving factor, with relatively buoyant economies such as Bahrain, United Arab Emirates, Qatar, and Brunei Darussalam appearing in the top sixty alongside developing economies such as Turkey and Malaysia. The most populous

Digital Opportunity Index (DOI) for Muslim-Majority Countries, 2005–2006

Rank	Economy*	DOI Score	Rank	Economy*	DOI Score
1	Bahrain (35)	0.60	24	Libya (109)	0.36
2	United Arab Emirates (37)	0.59	25	Indonesia (116)	0.34
3	Qatar (38)	0.58	26	Uzbekistan (123)	0.31
4	Brunei Darussalam (43)	0.56	27	Pakistan (127)	0.29
5	Turkey (52)	0.52	28	Yemen (128)	0.28
6	Malaysia (57)	0.50	29	Djibouti (132)	0.26
7	Bosnia (64)	0.48	30	Bangladesh (134)	0.25
8	Morocco (68)	0.47	31	Kyrgyzstan (135)	0.25
9	Maldives (72)	0.46	32	Sudan (136)	0.24
10	Saudi Arabia (75)	0.46	33	Turkmenistan (139)	0.22
11	Jordan (79)	0.45	34	Tajikistan (143)	0.22
12	Oman (81)	0.44	35	Gambia (144)	0.21
13	Algeria (83)	0.42	36	Mauritania (154)	0.17
14	Tunisia (87)	0.41	37	Nigeria (155)	0.17
15	Egypt (91)	0.41	38	Comoros (156)	0.17
16	Lebanon (93)	0.40	39	Guinea (161)	0.15
17	Kazakhstan (94)	0.40	40	Burkina Faso (165)	0.14
18	Palestine (98)	0.40	41	Mali (169)	0.12
19	Azerbaijan (101)	0.38	42	Sierra Leone (171)	0.11
20	Syria (104)	0.37	43	Eritrea (177)	0.07
21	Iran (105)	0.37	44	Chad (180)	0.04
22	Senegal (106)	0.37	45	Niger (181)	0.03
23	Albania (107)	0.37			

* DOI overall ranking in parentheses

Source: Table compiled by Gary R. Bunt, based on data contained the *World Information Society Report 2007: Beyond WSIS*. Population proportions were crosschecked with related data within the *CIA World Factbook 2007*.

Muslim-majority country, Indonesia, is lower on the index. This may reflect the dispersal of the population across hundreds of islands, each requiring an ICT infrastructure, as well as other issues relating to education and income.

When analyzing this data, it is not possible to distinguish Muslim from other religious affiliations in terms of Internet application. Consideration has to be given to whether reference is exclusively focused on personal computer use or other forms of interfaces, such as 3G cell phones.[11] This is particularly important when approaching Web 2.0–related developments, with the multitude of evolving approaches associated with accessing and contributing toward Internet content. These developments have the potential to offer greater access to CIES, which could have a variety of effects within different contexts.

In certain circumstances, especially in those economies that feature in the higher areas of the DOI, access to technology is integrated into new building projects, such as hotels or mosques. Such conspicuous technological consumption is not typical of the majority of Muslim contexts. There has been enthusiasm for many aspects of high-tech developments in affluent areas of the Middle East; the United Arab Emirates was said to contain the most enthusiastic wireless hot spotters in the region.[12] Cybercafés have emerged within the fabric of cities across the world with Muslim populations, often within the shadows (if not the structures) of mosques and other religious buildings.

In less-affluent economies, and for those lower rated on the DOI, Internet technology has also been seen as significant. Governments such as that of Iran have encouraged the private sector to develop high-speed ADSL services.[13] The motivation for this has more to do with business and enterprise than accessing CIES. The loss of Internet connections or bandwidth could be catastrophic in Muslim contexts, even those lower down the DOI. When Pakistan's Internet connection broke in June 2005, 10 million users had low-speed access, and infrastructures reliant on the Web resorted to traditional means of communication (at least temporarily).[14]

Corporate access and software initiatives may fuel information technology development, but this does not necessarily trickle down to the broader population. Many Muslim populations remain poorly served in terms of Internet access, although innovative solutions have been considered: "A tiny percentage of Africa's 800 million people own computers. And since few fixed-line operators can afford to roll out telephone lines across the continent's often inhospitable terrain, wireless connection is one way of delivering mass Internet access."[15]

There has been an exponential growth in the telecommunications sector in some Muslim contexts, even those territories perceived by some as being lawless or unregulated. Somalia is a case in point here, although its data did not feature on the DOI. The growth of Internet access in urban contexts is associated with the diaspora of Somali people, primarily using e-mail and online chat as a means to keep in contact with families and friends. As the Somali language can be written in Latin script, this facilitated rapid adoption of e-mail by Somalis as a cost-effective method of communication.[16] Somali language content has also emerged through YouTube and a variety of blogs, including a profusion of music.[17]

Cost continued to be a significant barrier inhibiting Internet access in other countries, such as Yemen: "Despite the liberalization of the Internet market in Yemen, the Arab Advisors Group believes that the market has high entry barriers. The low tariffs of the governmental ISP, Yemen Net, compared to its rival, Y.Net, which has majority government ownership as well, and the substantial difference in their market shares may hinder new entrants from seeking to operate in the country."[18] These limitations meant a relative lack of competition in Yemen in the commercial sector, with the Ministry of Communications exerting a strong hold on the industry.

The Internet resiliently functioned, albeit in limited fashion, in Muslim contexts in which there was political and military turmoil. The value of information technology was quickly recognized in Iraq, particularly following the removal of Saddam Hussein, although there was no representation on the DOI during the turbulent period in Iraqi history. Many Iraqis were keen to take advantage of computer training as part of a dynamic growth sector: "With the assistance of foreign companies, the country is getting ready to leapfrog much of the technology that has been implemented in the region, and some commentators see IT going straight to cutting-edge solutions—Iraq is moving from a crawl to a sprint, and could overtake many of its neighbours in the process."[19] This would suggest that further DOI reports will feature Iraq in some form.

Internet cafés became popular in Iraq, with a growth in café start-ups, because they provided better-quality connections than domestic telephone systems.[20] More significantly, perhaps, after a protracted custody battle, the ".iq" domain was launched by Iraq and the Internet Corporation for Assigned Names and Numbers (ICANN) in 2005.[21] However, the domain could only be registered to businesses and institutions rather than to individuals.[22]

Expansion of IT connectivity can be stimulated by political factors and conflict. For example, there was a substantial increase in efforts to enhance connectivity between and within the international Palestinian communities, especially in the refugee camps and across the Palestinian Authority: "Internet lease lines are bought from Palestinian ISPs and re-sold to several households in the camp, using the same bandwidth and server, according to the head of one local ISP. The households then open makeshift Internet cafés, where they rent out their line at a rate of two new Israeli shekels per hour ($0.45)."[23] Palestine's DOI ranking may not incorporate those users who have bought into other users' systems but do not register on data-gathering exercises. Internet penetration is relative to affluence, with only 7.5 percent of residents in the Palestinian Territories online in 2005 compared with 52 percent of Israeli households.[24]

This forms part of an overall pattern of restricted access. In January 2006 a report from the Mardar Group noted in a discussion on the relatively low levels of Internet penetration in the Middle East that "the Middle East needs to purchase six million more personal computers to keep up with global PC sales figures as the level of PC penetration is much below the world average. Consumers are collectively purchasing only one-third the number of the PCs they ought to have bought."[25]

Cheaper computers offer one solution. The development of the One Laptop Per Child program, promoted by Nicholas Negroponte at Massachusetts Institute of Technology, could, if it attains its objectives, impact on Muslim contexts.[26] In 2007 it was announced that recipients of the first mass-produced versions of these computers would include children in Afghanistan.

It was suggested that the general reach of the Internet in "Arab," including Muslim, contexts was relatively low. This does not negate the impact of the technology on the minority of those who are connected. This issue was raised at the World Telecommunication Development Conference in Doha, Qatar, in March 2006: "The Arab world is lagging behind in the digital revolution, with Internet users making up less than four percent of its population. . . . 'The Arab presence on the Internet is almost zilch . . . not more than a few websites providing information or personal sites,' said Syrian Telecommunications and Technology Minister Amr Salem."[27]

This assessment of impact is perhaps conservative, drawing on figures from 2004: "According to statistics compiled by the UN's International Telecommunications Union (ITU), a co-organizer of the week-long Doha conference ending on March 15, the 22 Arab League members had only 11.7 million Internet users out of a total population of 316 million in 2004."[28]

Solutions for the reduction of this digital divide also relate to when hardware and software become cheaper and more accessible, as well as available in local languages. Software for the Linux Operating System is open and free for users to develop, unlike systems such as Microsoft Windows or Vista. An example of this was the Ubuntu software system, free to download and based on Linux.[29] A Muslim edition of Ubuntu was also developed. In addition to the conventional Ubuntu operating system and Arabic support, it incorporated "Islamic" features in this package. These included a parental control tool for safe Internet browsing, although it was not clear what the specific technical parameters were for this filtering technology or how they were configured in comparison with other filters. Other components included Qur'an recitations, prayer-time software, an encyclopedia, and various Islamic wallpapers and themes. While much of this was open source or freeware (and thus available via the Internet), the advantage with this particular package is that everything is preinstalled, which is particularly useful for anyone with limited access. From this basic platform, given its open-source nature, there is also potential for this software to be adapted to different forms of Muslim expression and language. The integration of databases, including religious opinions, which could be searchable and limited to one particular religious perspective, could also be a future development within an open-source package of this nature. Qur'anic commentary based upon particular worldviews and religious outlooks might be integrated into such software packages, together with specific translations and interpretations representative of political and religious worldviews. An officially sanctioned software package of this nature might encourage forms of Internet access and also circumnavigate the issues of control and censorship that some religious authorities feel significant. One scenario would be that all computers sold in specific religious and cultural contexts would, through legislation, be forced to have a particular set of software included inside. This would have implications for computer manufacturers and software providers. So while open-source software offers opportunities for the Internet access in a cost-effective manner, especially in regions where access is currently limited, there are also potential issues associated with freedom of expression and censorship. One can imagine a future dialogue between religious authorities and computer developers in which such packages are negotiated. Elements of Ubuntu have been developed collaboratively through forums and the sharing of data. The portfolio of Ubuntu applications is the open-source equivalent of Microsoft or Apple software, without the need for paid licenses. This represents the removal of one significant barrier to access.

The availability of open-source Arabic software—which is free or less expensive to install, use, and develop—offers one way of enhancing access to the Internet in Muslim and other contexts.[30] Unix/Linux–based Arabeyes launched a free open-source Arabic product in 2001, which it continued to refine.[31] Handasa Arabia also presented an alternative open-source product.[32] Such developments, in conjunction with an increase in the creation of Web applications with Islamic interfaces, encourage Internet access as well as economic and knowledge development in some Muslim contexts. A member of Linux-Egypt predicted that open-source software could have a profound effect on education in Egypt and beyond.[33] The software initiatives are important when seen in conjunction with the development of products in a broad range of languages. The relative absence of materials in "Islamic" languages was an inhibitor for Internet access. In the early days of the Internet, English was the natural language for many early adopters of technology, including those producing cyber-Islamic content. This reflected the educational background of software and site developers, as well as the available applications.

There have been levels of change in this as the Internet market adjusts. There is now substantial material in Turkish, Indonesian, Somali, Malay, Farsi, and Arabic but still a relative absence of material in Urdu and Bangla. Other markets, including sub-Saharan Africa and Central Asian republics, are also demonstrating growth in Islamic materials.[34] The Internet also became a space for marginalized, minority languages in Islamic contexts. For example, the Berber Amizigh networked and collaborated using the Web and promoted the use of their language, although this did not necessarily reflect "Islamic" content.[35]

The utilization of Web 2.0 interfaces within these contexts may bring elements of Muslim networks up to speed rapidly, with exponential growth in DOI being a driving factor. It has to be stressed that Muslim networks traverse international political boundaries associated with nation-states. It would be an intriguing piece of research to consider the DOI of specific nodes within Muslim networks. There are some micronetworks associated with specific belief patterns that rely heavily on ICT as a driving factor to facilitate collaboration and networking across political boundaries. These may be "minorities-within-minorities"—for example, the offshoots of smaller branches of Shi'ism such as Dawoodi Bohras (which itself has its nodes). Their Mumineem.org site contains detailed technical discussions within a blog, discussing Java script, databases, streaming, and software issues. Members of the network collaborate on aspects of this at various levels, which can be seen as a religious duty.[36]

A further significant issue was the absence of top-level domains in the characters of principal "Muslim" languages not written in Latin script, such as Arabic, Urdu, and Persian. The system at the time of writing requires the input of Latin characters for a Web address. A campaign by the Multilingual Internet Names Consortium sought to challenge what was perceived as a significant barrier within the "digital divide."[37]

Reflecting Varisco's and Anderson's comments in the first chapter, the rapid expansion of software and online content in (other) "Muslim" languages raises particular issues associated with the monitoring and analysis of content. Even though the digital divide remains, sheer information overload from existing CIEs introduces issues and difficulties. As research on CIEs becomes more specialized, it is envisaged that every language (and context) will form a separate line of research.

Islam Inside: Toward the Pray Station

In conjunction with accessibility and software issues, a number of Islamically oriented products appeared on the market. These include cell phones with integrated features such as the call to prayer (*adhan*), Islamic ringtones, Islamic calendars, and the Qur'an. Cell phones and PDAs can also be adapted through the downloading of Islamic software. Some of this is fairly basic in nature; for example, SMS alerts can be obtained that remind subscribers about prayer times, and similar services may also offer Qur'anic quotations. While there were no known plans for an Islamic BlackBerry and Islamic iPhone in mid-2007, Islamic applications could be used on them.[38] Islamic PDA packages shared some of these features.[39]

Islamic computer software has been available for several years, including varied Qur'an software applications and language-learning tools. A range of Islamic games for PCs was also developed. One Syrian game company presented an interactive game associated with the early history of Islam.[40] The representation of Islam and Muslims in gaming has, at times, had a negative hue, so this represented an important development. One CD of Islamic games included Islamic variants on traditional gaming, with a "Shoot the Idol" game. Lower-tech Islamic games also had a place online, including word searches and puzzles based on Islamic sources.[41] Games players such as the Nintendo Wii, DS, and Sony PS3 offer Internet access as part of their package and conceivably could be interfaces for accessing CIEs.

Some Web-enabled products raised the ire of authorities and commentators. Cell phones that rang during congregational prayers became a particularly "hot topic": "As Dhuhr prayer commences, the imam calls the devoted to stand in line and fill any gaps between them. The mosque is a near-perfect atmosphere for peaceful, quiet self-reflection and piety. Suddenly the ambience of the holy place is shattered by the hip-hop beats of Los Angeles rapper Snoop Doggy Dogg. The worshippers turn their head to look at the offender. Tsk-tsk. Once again somebody didn't turn off his cell phone."[42] Disturbing the congregational prayer unnecessarily in such a way would be seen as a disrespectful act of the highest magnitude, with analogies to the ramifications of "idle talk" in the mosque, possibly requiring the restarting of prayers. There was a sense that the "silent" function on cell phones was becoming a *sunnah* (obligation).

Cell phones and associated technology also have an addictive quality, which may be detrimental to family life. In a discussion on BlackBerrys, one commentator noted: "At a recent Jewish-Muslim dialogue, a Muslim businessman told me his wife referred to the hated gizmo as his 'mistress,' demanding he lock it in a drawer from Friday night till Sunday evening, so badly had it disrupted their weekends."[43] This could also be related to the issues associated with Internet addiction, which have a currency in Muslim contexts as well.

Despite such concerns, the popularity of cell phones, including those with built-in Web capability, extended to individuals owning two or more phones. One commentator noted that "the trend in Saudi Arabia is to have at least two mobile numbers and perhaps three—one for work, one for family and then a third one for 'significant callers.' "[44] The third category had a somewhat ambiguous meaning. The enormous growth in mobile communications was not without detractors, although their protests were limited.

Specific applications that were perceived to breach Islamic values were targeted. For example, Sheikh Abdul Aziz al-Sheikh issued a proclamation against phones with integrated cameras: "Saudi Arabia's grand mufti has prohibited as un-Islamic trading in camera-equipped mobile phones which can take 'illicit' pictures. . . . Such phones 'could be exploited to photograph and spread vice in the (Saudi) Muslim community,' Al-Madina quoted Sheikh Abdul Aziz al-Sheikh as saying. Camera-equipped mobile phones are ostensibly banned in the kingdom, but they are apparently very much in use and are often the centre of controversy."[45]

Despite such statements, there is no doubt that cell phones have been embraced and are big business in many sectors of Saudi Arabia: "Some 18 million mobile phone text messages in Saudi Arabia wished Muslims happiness at the start of their holiest time of year, the fasting month of Ramadan."[46] In 2007 it was reported that Egyptians spent US$2.1 million sending 40 million Ramadan text messages.[47]

Clearly, there are levels of "appropriate use." There was controversy in some Islamic contexts attached to the use of Bluetooth-enabled computers, phones, and PDAS. These allowed for informal communication, which may have traversed traditional and religious barriers, leading to "abuse": "On a recent warm night, Abdullah Muhammad sat in front of his laptop at a sidewalk café waiting for his computer's Bluetooth to pick up nearby users. 'I use Bluetooth to meet girls,' said the 24-year-old businessman. 'The religious police cannot catch me.' His long, dark hair combed back, Muhammad said when he sees a woman walking past, he presses the search button in the hope her phone's Bluetooth is on."[48]

Cell phones were the subject of other concerns associated with morality, including their use to photograph unveiled women at weddings and schools.[49] One Saudi merchant noted: "It's a pity that our youth abuse this technology in an immoral manner. . . . People abroad use the camera to capture good moments within friends and families without abusing its use or using it to scandalize someone or take revenge. It's the same thing with Bluetooth; you can use it to transfer data for work or school, not just as a new flirting trend."[50]

This could be linked to a comment from Sheikh Abdullah Al Manee of the Saudi Council of Senior Ulama. He suggested that Saudi society had been harmed by the introduction of such technology, a claim that might be contested as idealistic: "Until recently, Saudi society was clean and innocent. Unfortunately, it has changed due to several factors. Among these is the household staff that has come from different societies, also, the spread of satellite television and Internet, which has introduced pornography."[51]

Asharq Alawsat noted that Bluetooth had caused particular difficulties among some sectors in Saudi society: "Bluetooth has disgruntled many Saudis such as Layla Al-Majid who believes 'that modern technology will cause a transgression in social norms and traditions as it has facilitated the establishing of friendly ties between members of the opposite sex.' Similarly dissatisfied with this technology, Fadwa Al-Jahni expresses her frustration with 'ridiculous messages and scandalous pictures' that she receives causing her to turn her mobile phone off."[52]

In 2007, in what was perhaps a surprise move to counter such activities, the Riyadh Branch of the Commission for the Promotion of Virtue and Prevention of Vice adopted Bluetooth technology. They started sending out messages in public places in an attempt to prevent Bluetooth "transgressions," while emphasizing that they were not against the technology per se.[53] This could be seen in light of the plans to develop Riyadh as a "digital city."[54]

The perceived impact of the Internet on religious and cultural values may, in fact, cloak other influences. The Internet becomes one particular target articulated by commentators, an approach that ignores other factors. This was raised by commentators discussing an apparent "addiction" to the Internet in the United Arab Emirates, in particular the availability of "cybersex." One person noted: "Cybersex in online chat rooms is a disease. . . . My divorce recently was due to the Internet. My husband had become addicted to the Internet and used to spend the whole night in chat rooms. Suddenly, I found that he was receiving sexual solicitations over the Net and on several occasions, he asked women to meet him. He also called and sent them regular mail, money, or gifts. Sometimes, I found pictures of naked women on the computer, so I filed for divorce in Dubai Court and they ordered him to divorce me. This was considered [a] new type of marital infidelity."[55] This is significant on a number of levels, not least the element that offers an Internet-driven cause for divorce. However, without ICT, the husband, sufficiently motivated, may simply have utilized other channels of communication and connection.

As software applications diversify and improve in technical quality, they generate new discussions within Islamic contexts. Disquiet was raised in Saudi Arabia at a perceived invasion of privacy from Google Earth, the mapping and digital-imaging application that provides satellite photographs from across the world. This did not appear to inhibit Google's plans to upgrade the imagery available.[56] I took a look at the images of Riyadh, Jeddah, and Mecca. Given that these images are not "real time," and that they possess a pixilated quality, at this stage it would not suggest that personal privacy would necessarily be invaded. Real-time, high-intensity satellite images would be another matter. This might be an issue for consideration as the service, and those of its competitors, becomes upgraded and the picture quality enhanced in some regions. Perhaps greater concern should be focused on the quality of these images available to the military security sectors and their application by jihadi platforms.[57]

Generic products also required adaptation for Muslim markets. An atypical example emerged with the introduction of a "virtual girlfriend" that was being marketed in Malaysia. This application could be downloaded for use on a 3G cell phone:[58] "The problems have ranged from the cosmetic—Vivienne is being reprogrammed not to bare her navel or display body piercings in conservative Muslim countries like Malaysia—to the technological."[59]

This represents a commercial decision, but it is necessary to point out that those consumers wishing to observe something more explicit would have few difficulties, even allowing for firewalls and other barriers put into place by governments and ISPs.

Major computer corporations established themselves in markets with significant Muslim populations and adapted their products, marketing, and technical support accordingly. In 2006 a manufacturing facility in Dubai promised the assembly of 100,000 PCs a year.[60] Intel planned an information technology education center at the Islamic University of Gaza in an attempt to stimulate trade and education.[61] The impact of the Internet on regional infrastructures included the development of Dubai Internet City, which became a brand as it sought to export the concept to other locations, including India.[62] It could be compared with the Multimedia Super Corridor in Malaysia.

The computer industries have placed themselves firmly within Muslim contexts: Bill Gates met with Middle East businesses and government officials in conjunction with Microsoft's Government Leadership Forum Arabia (GLF Arabia). A number of Middle Eastern states proposed e-government infrastructures—notably Bahrain, which adopted open standards for e-government.[63]

Searching for Islam

The commercial sector has also been responsible for the development of search technology for diverse language and regional markets. Transformations in the wider Web structure have had an impact, a significant one being the establishment of Arabic-language search engines. Araby.com and Sawafi provided competition for established search engines and facilities, such as Ajeeb, Ayna, and Naseej.[64] Google's Arabic search engines had an important profile, enhanced with the news that Google was establishing business in Egypt, a further indicator of the financial potential of Arabic-language search engines.[65] The British University of Dubai and FAST Search launched an Arabic search-engine project in 2006.[66]

Enhanced searchability will have an impact on the access of Islam-related content in Arabic across the Middle East and beyond. The ongoing availability and development of search engines in other "Islamic languages" will also resonate in CIEs. This raises complex issues associated with censorship, as some governments do not wish their subjects to access specific forms of spidered content or related caches. Given that only a relatively small percentage of the entire World Wide Web is logged by search engines and found on databases, there are also issues of data mining to consider. Despite the issues of information overload, vast amounts of knowledge, including that relating to CIES, lie undiscovered in areas of the Web that are not part of the top level for search engines. This influences research and knowledge of Muslim networks and understanding of CIES.

Islamic Firewall

With the growth in Internet access, and its attendant infrastructure, comes the often inevitable issue of censorship. The sustained growth in Internet censorship in Muslim contexts is a complex issue. It is not the intention here to make specific value judgments as to what (if anything) is worthy of censorship or somehow subversive in nature. A number of different models apply where censorship has been deemed relevant.

Transgressions of religious values and/or attacks against state policy are dominant motivating factors for some forms of censorship, even by those who otherwise claim that they uphold "freedom of speech." The parameters for such freedom may vary in different Muslim contexts, with some critics suggesting that the concept is a misnomer. The freedom-of-speech platform embraces a number of different themes and causes, not all of which are mutually compatible within an Islamic context. This is, of course, not just an Internet-related issue. The aftermath to the publication of Salman Rushdie's *The Satanic Verses* (1988) was a precursor to many of the contemporary discussions about censorship.[67]

Advocates of freedom of Islamic political and religious expression may seek censorship of those espousing support for values that are not deemed to be compatible with their worldview. Channels of control have been subverted. Eickelman observes, in the Middle Eastern context: "The frontier between banned words and images and those that are tolerated in the Middle East has never been fixed, but access to new technologies has multiplied the channels through which ideas and information can be circulated and has enlarged the scope of what can be said and to whom. It has eroded the ability of authorities to censor and repress, to project an uncontested 'central' message defining political and religious issues for large numbers of people."[68]

The issue itself is indicative of an intensified awareness of the potential and realized impact of the Internet on Islamic values and societies, as well as its application as a means of fulfilling a variety of political-religious agendas. While the Internet may be opening up in some Muslim contexts, inherent restrictions of access apply in certain areas of content. The opportunities for collaboration and networking are restricted or, in some cases, rerouted through other channels. Web 2.0 has facilitated alternate forms of dissemination of materials, with interactive elements that can be problematic to monitor—no matter how much time and money is invested into filtering and censorship protocols. Authorities have specific difficulties keeping up with the quantity of data published in domestic and international contexts about them.

Censorship has manifested itself in a number of ways. In Kuwait, for example, government agencies attempted to block jihadi websites.[69] In some contexts, simply placing hyperlinks to banned websites within a webpage or blog could lead to prosecution.[70] Within other Islamic contexts, or locations with Muslim-majority populations, there were further examples of the inherent restrictions and possible dangers of using the Internet as a means of self-expression.

Defining what is hostile and in need of censorship is another issue. In Saudi Arabia, it may be fatwas, sermons, and/or interpretations that "deviate" from state policy. Some interpretations of Islam (including so-called Wahhabi-influenced and others) are censored, where possible, by Saudi Arabian authorities because of perceived incompatibility with national religious interests. Concerns are raised about uncensored chat rooms or those out of the censorship reach of Saudi Arabia.

Of course, censorship can take many forms. Closing down or strictly controlling a local ISP hosting hostile content may be easier than filtering content hosted abroad. Certain content may require passwords to access, or it may shift rapidly across different Internet locations, making it difficult to censor. In some cases, the original source of dissent may be beyond censorship control. The anti-American sermons of the late Sheikh al-Shuaibi continued to proliferate online after his death, causing his followers to be prosecuted in Saudi Arabia.[71] In other cases, "dissident" opinions have been circulated through content masquerading as "mainstream" authoritative sources, damaging reputations in the process.[72]

In Saudi Arabia, the Internet Service Unit sought to censor "those pages of an offensive or harmful nature to the society, and which violate the tenants [*sic*] of the Islamic religion or societal norms."[73] This includes the utilization of content-filtering technologies, developed in conjunction with software companies that are frequently located in Western contexts.

This raised concerns for anticensorship organizations, as well as "hacktivists" promoting freedom of speech. Web users in Saudi Arabia and elsewhere were able to get around the censorship issues and access content through other means. Reporters Without Frontiers observed: "Saudi Arabia has created one of the world's biggest Internet filtering systems. The authorities have officially announced that they block access to nearly 400,000 webpages, with the aim of 'protecting citizens from offensive content and content [that] violates the principles of Islam and the social norms.'" Reporters Without Frontiers also noted that gay-oriented sites, such as GayMiddleEast.com, which had previously been filtered, were examined for pornographic content. Restrictions were subsequently lifted after pressure from activists abroad.[74]

On occasion, militaristic jihad-oriented organizations have claimed that governmental agencies have conspired to block their websites. Islamic Jihad suggested that the Pentagon was blocking four of its websites "because they contained news and pictures supporting the Palestinian resistance against Israeli occupation."[75] Censorship was a two-way (or more) process, with the U.S. government being accused by the Iranian Republic News Agency of blocking various Iranian government sites, including the Universities Jihad Movement, which claimed academic status.[76]

The Committee to Protect Bloggers devoted campaigns on the perceived persecution, prosecution, and imprisonment of bloggers in various Muslim-majority countries. The committee was proactive in their campaigning efforts to free imprisoned bloggers, including those who had spoken on religious issues.[77] Amnesty International also launched a similar campaign.[78] Reporters Without Borders issued the *Handbook for Bloggers and Cyber-Dissidents*, offering advice on retaining anonymity and getting around censorship.[79] Such censorship may be a domestic issue, involving pressure on the author of a contentious site. The attempts by governments in Muslim contexts such as Saudi Arabia, Iran, and Tunisia to censor or restrict Internet access have met with varying levels of efficiency.[80]

Political platforms and their supporters have found creative ways to circumnavigate restrictions, at times adjusting or cloaking the online location of sites in order to frustrate those seeking to close them down or using friendly or unsuspecting ISPs. Censorship is a live issue within the Internet in general, and in relation to CIEs in particular. It opens up the question of controlling the Internet, and the parameters of "freedom of speech." Whether filters are self-imposed and based on Islamic principles and/or government imposed and based on political values is an important consideration. The setting of a browser's filtering to "safe content" may represent an Islamic virtue.

The protests that some governments in Muslim contexts are indexing and filtering political opposition, drawing on software from international corporations, brings in complex attendant issues associated with the information flow emanating from jihadi and other potentially destabilizing forces online. Filtering does not detract the Net literate, and it may enhance the excitement of following the "forbidden." It will be interesting to observe how religious authorities of varying persuasions choose to react to such issues as the digital divide is reduced in some contexts and the "threat" of contentious material intensifies.

Ministers responded in various ways to censorship and other forms of pressure. In Iran, this led to a former minister developing his own blog.[81] President Mahmoud Ahmadinejad also launched a blog in 2006, although the extent to which he was personally inputting and posting content appeared limited. Iranian governmental agencies attempted to restrict access to certain types of Web content and in 2006 blocked websites containing content deemed detrimental to the republic's interests, such as the BBC Persian Service.[82] In an effort to promote a specific Islamic formulation of blogging and presumably an element of control, the Iranian government launched an International Qur'anic Blogging Festival. This offered advice and tools for creating blogs. The festival had a competitive element, which attracted 800 entries:[83] "Dr. Boutorabi who heads the Blogging Services Provider, Persianblog, says that weblogs are means for revealing human identity at the cyberspace and a powerful means of communication. . . . Since blogging is so widespread in the world today, it can be used for holy purposes as Muslims around the world did by protesting against the publication of insulting cartoons in Danish and other western Media through their weblogs."[84]

Iranian officials often made complaints about the nature of the Internet but were restricted in how they might control it, at least outside of Iran: "Too often, the Internet is used for the 'propagation of falsehoods,' said Mohammad Soleymani, Iran's minister of communication and information technology. . . . Soleymani called for the elimination of the California-based Internet Corporation for Assigned Names and Numbers (ICANN)—which approves new top-level domain names—in favor of United Nations control."[85]

The efforts that were made in Iran at some form of control of the Internet, in a somewhat belated reaction to evolving technological innovation, included the filtering of blogrolling.com.[86] This application is a system for the rapid compilation of lists of the URLs, which can be inserted into other blogs as a "blogroll." Thus, a blogger can indicate favorite other blogs and sites with the possibility of the links being reciprocated.

There were numerous protests—articulated online and in physical demonstrations—against the censorship of the Web. In 2003 protests against Iranian censorship were made at the un's digital summit in Geneva.[87] Human rights activists and Internet campaign groups have been documenting for several years how Internet censorship has been enacted in Muslim (and other) contexts. It is not the purpose here to discuss every case that has emerged. A few further examples will suffice.

In Libya, writers using the Internet to publish their thoughts were arrested. Internet journalist 'Abd al-Raziq al-Mansuri, arrested in January 2005 for his writings in Akbar-Libya, was granted a pardon in March 2006.[88] Reporters Without Borders noted numerous cases of imprisonments and abuse of writers and journalists. Writer and journalist Daif Al Ghazal, who wrote for the London-based online newspaper *Libya Al-Youm*, died in prison. His critical articles were not always focused on exclusively Islamic content.[89]

According to human rights organizations, a number of people in different Muslim contexts were jailed for Internet activities.[90] Each case has subtle differences. One focus was on Tunisia, where eight Internet users received heavy jail sentences in 2004.[91] The presence of the World Summit on the Information Society in Tunis in 2005 highlighted that country's alleged practices. These included the closure of some Internet cafés and a requirement that café users present identification cards.[92] The U.S. Department of State observed: "Security forces routinely monitored the activities, telephone, and Internet exchanges of opposition, Islamist, and human rights activists and sometimes harassed, followed, questioned, assaulted, or otherwise intimidated them, their relatives, and associates."[93]

Governments applied the Internet to observe dissident activities online.[94] More sophisticated encryption programs meant that control of many aspects of the Internet becomes problematic for government agencies in Muslim and other contexts (for example, in censoring e-mail exchanges). Advice is made available online on how to evade controls of Internet usage, such as retaining anonymity.[95]

Complaints emerged from diverse Islamic perspectives relating to apparent anti-Islamic materials published online. Not all objectionable materials were necessarily produced and/or published in the complainants' own countries, making censorship and restrictions problematic. For example, the emphatic and growing influence of Internet content reached Pakistan's political-religious milieu, prompting a flurry of correspondence, if not e-mail:

> Deputy chief Jamiat-ul-Uloom Al-Islamia and deputy prayer leader of Lal Mosque, Islamabad, Allama Qari Abdur Rashid Ghazi had written a detailed letter to federal minister of information technology, Awais Khan Leghari, some four months back in which he appealed to him that some Internet websites contain objectionable material about the Islamic creed, injunctions, the Koran, the personality of the Prophet and his sayings [hadith] in order to misguide the Muslim youth.
>
> He demanded that immediate action be taken to either block such websites through firewall system, as is practiced in other Muslim countries, or to completely ban them.[96]

This request for the instigation of a ban reflects limited awareness of the potential for circumnavigating Internet barriers, even with firewalls in place. This does not allow for the offline circulation of content through DVDs and other means. Technologically literate individuals, especially those who have grown up using the Internet, have no problems subverting restrictions if they wish.

Some "offensive" Islamic sites were controlled through sustained online and offline campaigning attacks. Threats or other forms of abuse may act as a deterrent to publish, especially if the Muslim credentials of an individual are being challenged. Iranian expatriate author Ghazal Omid found that her critical assessment of the Islamic Republic of Iran, contained on her website livinginhell.com, led to abuse and death threats: "'Yes, we could trace them [the death threats]. Most of them came from Turkey, Pakistan and Iran,' Ghazal said in an almost upbeat fashion. 'Many said things such as—you'll roast in hell.' The implication being when they killed her, God will send her to the devil."[97]

As will be seen in the discussion on blogging in chapter 4, political-religious criticism found a ready audience in Syria, despite the state's censorship mechanisms: "Savvy cyber rebels who have broadened the political debate could be preyed upon at any time and thrown in jail for proselytizing to Syria's burgeoning Internet audience, thought to number more than 500,000 people."[98] With the general growth in Web content come not only products that might be deemed un-Islamic, but also the perceived dangers of information overload. This was even recognized by heads of state: "Syrian President Bashar Assad has said the media and technological revolution sweeping the region and the world is helping his country's foes to undermine and crush the Arab identity. Assad told the congress of Syria's ruling Baath Party on Monday that a media influx had left Arabs 'swamped by disinformation' about themselves."[99]

This "influx" is surely dependent on how information is managed, censored, and filtered, especially within a Syrian context. Assad was not necessarily discussing Islam-related content. However, Assad does make a valid point about the quantity and quality of information available on Arab issues. These are not necessarily synonymous with Islamic issues, but it is simply impossible to keep up with every online development.

Considerable attention has been paid to the representation of Islam and Muslims, both online and offline. The subject received sharp focus during the 2005–6 "cartoon crisis," when protests were mobilized across diverse Islamic contexts, resulting in attendant demands for censorship. The controversy arose when the Danish newspaper *Jyllands-Posten* published cartoons that were deemed (by some) to be detrimental to Islam. Pakistan telecommunications organizations blocked a number of sites believed to contain related contentious materials, including blogs. This meant that several significant Pakistan-based or Pakistan-oriented blogs could not be accessed in that country or updated by their Pakistani authors, although inevitably there were ways around the blocking.[100]

Concluding Comment

Governments in Muslim contexts have had to adjust to the Internet as a phenomenon. Many have recognized the importance of going online and have done so with varying degrees of effectiveness, developing websites both for domestic and international audiences. Censorship can take many forms as attempts are made to prevent apparent transgressions in societal and religious norms. Many of these issues are universal; for example, pornographic content represents a significant proportion of Internet content, and its impact is an issue in Muslim contexts as much as elsewhere.

Access in general remains a crucial area, not just in regard to CIEs but also to acquiring knowledge and services that reduce the issues associated with the digital divide. The increase in access through cheaper hardware and open-source applications will have a profound effect on how Islam is articulated and Muslim networks are shaped in the twenty-first century.

These might not necessarily be interpreted as benign, especially if jihadi-oriented groups enter the present vacuum of the knowledge economy. There is also potential for there to be an impact on the formulations and understandings of the sacred within Islam, which is the subject of the next chapter.

Decoding the Sacred

Islamic Source Code

Approaches to Islamic Phenomena Online

The source code for CIES relates to the essential beliefs and values articulated in the name of Islam. In order to interpret the factors, which drive the multifaceted dialogues and interactions, it is important to explore the aspects of sacred phenomena associated with Islam and Muslim beliefs as represented online. This element of CIES has a profound impact on forms of networking and collaboration. The Internet may offer a personal and dynamic religious space for iMuslims. They can network, share experiences, and feel a sense of community with others occupying the same virtual space.

The combination of these elements into a single portal can offer the essential components of a Muslim religious experience, which may for some reflect aspects of "offline religion." The mosaics of Islamic religious lives are represented online through websites offering resources for festivals and rites of passage. These may focus on materials related to specific cultural, religious, political, and/or linguistic interests. Connecting to the divine online provides numerous possibilities and aspects of experiential and ritualistic life. The human element on a one-to-one level can also be located through linking up with other members of a religious affiliation online, via mailing lists, social-networking sites, online video and phone conversations, and/or e-mail or chat-room dialogue with a religious scholar.

This chapter looks at the digitization of many long-standing essential concepts and practices associated with Islam, including ideas of the sacred, within Muslim frameworks. It focuses on the elements of the sacred, in terms of Muslim practice and values, as they are enabled through the Internet. It looks at the types of intersections between real-world practice and online interaction and again opens up the questions relating to online religion and religion online. In the concluding section, this chapter determines how the frameworks for their articulation continue to expand, mutate, and evolve, especially in relation to aspects of Web 2.0.

A key element that has driven my study of Islam and the Internet to date relates to a phenomenology of Islam as presented in cyberspace. I have been particularly interested in how the symbols, rituals, and conceptual frameworks of Muslim belief have been presented online within diverse Muslim networks. It is my opinion that on some levels, the Internet can also offer a digital glimpse into the shared religious experiences of Muslims.

I can relate in particular to the approach toward Islamic Studies of Annemarie Schimmel. Her book *Deciphering the Signs of God* (1994) presents a phenomenological approach to the study of Islam that draws on key sacred concepts and understandings. Schimmel was prescient—she mentions computers within her discussion. Her breakdown of Islam into specific areas of ritual and symbolism crosses many intra-Islamic divides and is something that I apply when teaching Islamic Studies.[1]

Among numerous other sources, John Renard's approach to the study of Islam is also relevant within this context. He references a broad range of Islamic sources within a framework encompassing Foundations, Devotion, Inspiration, Aesthetics, Community, Pedagogy, and Experience.[2] This helps us when interpreting different forms of Muslim information exchanges and networks within historical and cultural knowledge economies. Although Renard was working on what were then more traditional Islamic visual and literary sources, they apply as critical factors to consider when exploring Islam on the Internet.

Within a religious studies context, Ninian Smart is a further influence on my approach toward this subject matter. While I have not followed his "Seven Dimensions of Religion" to the letter in this chapter, there are certainly aspects that fit into a phenomenological categorization model applicable to CIES. Smart discusses his approach in numerous works, essentially applying the headers of Practical and Ritual Dimension, Experiential and Emotional Dimension, Narrative or Mythic Dimension, Ethical and Legal Dimension, Doctrinal and Philosophical Dimension, and Material Dimension.[3]

These have a resonance within many of the applications within CIES, with different degrees of emphasis. Questions arise as to the extent to which experiential dimensions of Islam translate into cyberspace, and if they can generate an emotional effect. Whether this has an equivalency to the real-world interaction is difficult to measure in practical terms, but my conversations with users of CIES would suggest that in some cases, they generate a strong emotional and experiential reaction. Perhaps it does not have to be comparable, but just different. A cyber interaction may open the individual up to other forms of interaction with religious values and beliefs, with resultant "benefits." They may also generate reactions between communities online or those collaborating toward a shared religious purpose.

While the emotional and experiential categories are perhaps difficult to pin down in cyberspace, the other dimensions are easier to approach. Ritual and practice, and the ethical and legal dimensions, can be found on many sites, especially portals seeking to impact upon Muslim values and patterns of life. These aspects of the Islamic knowledge economy may act as "one-stop shops" for surfers seeking to discover Islam.

Islamic Dimensions of Cyberspace

Many dimensions of Muslim worldviews can be observed online, including what might be regarded as the essentials of belief. Computer programs provide information on the precise direction and prayer time from any location in the world. This is important, given that the precise degree of orientation toward Mecca is required. Prayer times change throughout the year because Islamic calendars are lunar based, and some prayer times rely on knowledge of the position of the sun throughout the day. In mosques, this information may be posted by the entrance and adjusted slightly for each variation throughout the year. While human observation and calculation still have a role in many contexts, obtaining accurate information on these factors may be an essential obligation, especially for travelers.

Traditionally, the call to prayer may be made from a minaret or other appropriate space, performed by a designated muezzin. Muhammad appointed his companion Bilal as the first person to call the prayer, recognizing his qualities, including clarity of diction. Today, in order to counter urban noise, the *adhan* is amplified. The call echoes throughout Muslim environments, not always in a synchronized form, reminding worshippers of their obligations. There is a sense of competitiveness between mosques in some places, relating to which *adhan* is the loudest.

The amplification and broadcast of the *adhan* and other aspects of Islamic invocation and recitation represented a significant historical challenge to some authorities, some of which identified such practices as unIslamic innovations. While these practices have now been integrated into many Muslim contexts, further challenges emerged with the appearance of Islamic sources on the Internet. The online presentation of these most basic elements of ritual and practice take many formats, especially Qur'an recitation, which comprises the central element of prayer.

Numerous recordings of the *adhan* and the *takbir* (the pronouncement of *"Allahu Akbar"*—God is Great—before prayer) can be sourced, viewed, or listened to in real time. There are many versions available for download for use on a computer, an MP3–4 player, or a cell phone or to be burned onto a CD/DVD. They may come with commentaries and translations or be available to view on YouTube or MySpace.

Many exponents of Qur'an recitation, or *mujawwid*, can be heard online. In some contexts, these are the "pop stars" of the Muslim world. Their works have traditionally been broadcast on the radio or TV or sold at stalls and shops. Racks within some CD and cassette stores are devoted to the latest releases. Their sound resonates through Muslim neighborhoods and markets, and they are played on buses and cars as a soundtrack to everyday life. While there is no copyright for the Qur'an, those who previously benefited from the sales of its recordings have had to adjust their marketing strategies. They are now sold online, but also, in disregard to copyright considerations, freely available to copy and distribute through the Internet.

Qur'anic ringtones can also be downloaded from the Internet, a practice that has become popular but is not without controversy. A number of edicts have been issued refining approaches to this practice, notably in 2007, when the Saudi Arabian Islamic Jurisprudence Council issued a fatwa banning the use of Qur'an verses as ringtones: "It is demeaning and degrading to the verses of the Holy Book to stop abruptly at the middle of a recitation or neglecting the recitation, as happens when they are used as ringtones in mobile phones. On the other hand, recording the verses from the Holy Qur'an in phone sets with the intention of recitation and listening is a virtuous act," the scholars attending the council said in a statement.[4]

This call was echoed elsewhere, amid concerns regarding the promotion and marketing of these tones. The discussion reflects other long-standing debates about the sanctity of the Qur'an, albeit with a digital gloss. Some religious scholars now learn hypertext markup language alongside classical Arabic in Islamic institutions such as Qom and Al-Azhar, developing online interfaces, interpretations, and commentaries in a variety of other languages.

I have assembled several collections of Qur'anic recitation via Internet sources, which I have placed on my iPod and cell phone. These present different styles of recitation and *sura* (chapter) choices. Outside of straight audio delivery, there are alternate interfaces available to enhance one's understanding of the Qur'an. These have drawn upon recent developments in ICT, and they have also been effective demonstrations of collaborative projects in relation to their distribution and production.

Multimedia programs now demonstrate prayer methods and recitation, with video clips showing what is deemed appropriate religious practice. These are intended for newcomers to Islam and for those whose ritual practice may be rusty. Sermons from different imams and scholars can also be found online, sometimes uploaded immediately after their initial presentation in a mosque. In the presence of such developments, commercial Qur'an products available on CD and DVD are now less competitive in the dynamic Islamic knowledge marketplace.

Computers can become a sacred space for Muslims. The presence of the Qur'an online can have an evocative effect on the listener and provide immersion in Islamic religious sources. This may produce the emotional and experiential reaction discussed in other contexts by Ninian Smart. *Sura al-A'raf*, a chapter from the Qur'an, states: "So pay attention and listen quietly when the Qur'an is recited, so that you may be given mercy."[5]

Can humanity's relationship with God take on a digital interface? How does it relate to other, "conventional" forms of liminality? In what ways does it apply traditional conventions, and in what ways are innovations utilized to interact with the divine? The Qur'an has a format that may appear complex to "outsiders." Its content is not presented thematically nor in relation to a chronological pattern or context.[6]

If I want to read the Qur'an, outside of looking at one of the many texts, translations, and commentaries on my bookshelf, I am now faced with numerous options through various interfaces offering different potential experiences and results. This can range from an online resource providing a searchable database to an RSS feed regularly updated with a new extract from a *tafsir* commentary source. Some provide potentially time-saving devices to get an individual "up to speed" with the Qur'an, especially for those unfamiliar with the text or who have not committed it to memory.

Whether the experience of reading the texts on-screen is equivalent to reading or reciting a portion of the Qur'an in the mosque is open to question. When accessing the Qur'an through the Internet is the only option, then it might represent a virtuous act, or even a way through which an individual can get closer to Allah. I have frequently played Qur'an recitations derived from online sources in my lectures, often accompanied by the music visualization software available through Real, Windows, and iTunes players. Students from various backgrounds, including Muslims, have been visibly moved when listening. Some have also been encouraged to seek out further Qur'anic materials through printed copies and online resources.

The Qur'an and its multiple-format presentations offer a way into understanding different expressions of Islam in contemporary contexts. Several sites that contain Qur'an resources have become key players in CIES, especially those early adopters of technology, who placed the sacred text at the center of their online activities.

Even before the development of Web interfaces, college students in the United States in the 1980s were placing Qur'an materials online. These could be accessed through File Transfer Protocol (FTP) and were generally small, low-tech files designed to cope with limited bandwidth and Internet access. Sites hosted on university servers offered student societies opportunities to register an early profile for their religious perspectives and a chance for programmers and "geeks" to demonstrate their abilities.[7]

This was an exciting time for those that recognized the potential of the medium. I can remember spending several hours a day for weeks on end, searching for and downloading Islam-related materials. Even in the early days of the World Wide Web, there were possibilities of information overload. During this period, I was responsible for a university server meltdown through the sheer weight of Islam-related Internet traffic arriving into my e-mail account while I was absent on a field trip.

As the Web has evolved, approaches to the Qur'an online shifted to accommodate the enhanced access opportunities for readers, the developed knowledge and experience of site developers, and technological shifts and improvements. This integration of material gave new possibilities for studying the Qur'an. The tools also created new questions of method, practice, and approach toward the Qur'an. The emergence of a variety of resources highlighted the issues surrounding the "validity" of translations. Arguments were amplified related to translations produced from specific political-religious perspectives.

Online translations are a competitive area. Various site developers seek to present their translations, commentaries, and interpretations, attempting to expound the meaning of the text. One prevalent Muslim view was that the Arabic source is the definitive divine Word of God, which could not effectively be translated into another language. This did not stop many software developers from collaborating and wrestling with the concepts surrounding the production of user-friendly Qur'anic interfaces.

Digital interfaces demonstrate imaginative ways to make the divine text accessible for a variety of users. Qur'an materials online are often searchable, multilingual, audiovisual resources. They demonstrate different approaches to the Arabic content of God's Revelation, which according to tradition was given to the Prophet Muhammad via the Angel Gabriel between 610 and 632 C.E. The Arabic Qur'an is immutable and fixed in time. It has been preserved in a consistent format through human memory and by its writing on various media. The emergence of print revolutionized practices surrounding the preservation of the Qur'an but did not negate those original methods of ensuring the safety of the divine script.

Questions surround how Qur'an information is acquired and processed through searchable hypertext. The utilization of metadata in page construction and the diverse ways in which the content is read and navigated are significant when considering the approaches of iMuslims to source materials. While some digital resources are similar to conventional CD-ROMs of the Qur'an, others have been designed, formatted, or edited specifically with Internet users in mind.[8]

Accessibility is a key issue in exploring Qur'an sites. It is one filter that can be introduced when discussing Qur'anic interfaces. Issues that are relevant include the design, color, and format of Qur'an pages. Are pages easy to read online? Can they be navigated effectively? Many surfers are dissuaded from using a website when it is difficult to locate information quickly. Fortunes have been won and lost in relation to good Web design. These factors are as true of CIES as of the commercial sector. I know many users of CIES who will migrate to another Qur'an page, which may contain different commentaries and interpretations, if they cannot find the answers they seek immediately from a site appearing at the top of a Google listing. Sites that disappear or relocate without advising their readers quickly lose their appeal.

Susceptibility to reading an online text as a "definitive" translation, edition, or version is a major issue. The ways in which *tafsirs* or commentaries on the meaning of the Qur'an further add interpretative meanings to the Revelation represents a further layer of potential difficulty for a reader. Reproducing a print version of the Qur'an is not enough. A Qur'an interface has to be user-friendly if it is going to reach its intended audience and present its specific interpretation of Islam to readers with different levels of familiarity. Sites are designed for a variety of readers, ranging from those iMuslims fluent in classical or Qur'anic Arabic to those who have limited knowledge of Arabic or who can only approach the Revelation in a language other than Arabic.

The providers of some Qur'an resources have the propagation of the faith as their central mission. They seek to engender greater interest in Islam, often from a particular religious perspective among Muslims, or to encourage others to adopt their worldview. Others simply seek to develop a sympathetic comprehension of Islam outside of the Muslim world, tied to a specific set of interpretative and cultural values.

IslamiCity provides an example of a Qur'an resource that features highly on related Google keyword searches. Its premium membership channel offers a Qur'an Memorizer, which features recitation by Siddiq Minshawi and simultaneous Arabic text and English translation and transliteration. Its Devotion section contains a library of information central to Muslim faith, including prayer times, recitations of the Qur'an from noted reciters, and a recitation competition featuring children and young adults. The Qur'an link presents a hyperlinked list of verses; through selecting a portion from the Qur'an, its page appears in Arabic, with options to view an English translation and/or to listen to the verse recited. Other Qur'an resources on IslamiCity include phonetic textual search facilities, translations in twenty-two languages, and topical indices.[9]

A further significant site that has set a benchmark in this field is that developed by the Egyptian company Harf Information Technology for the Saudi Arabian Ministry of Islamic Affairs, Endowments, Da'wah, and Guidance. This site owns the high-level domain al-islam.com. Its centerpiece is a comprehensive database on the Qur'an, including a multilanguage translation of the meaning from the Arabic script and recitations. The database is searchable by subject, *sura* and *aya* (verse) number, and interlinks to numerous other resources. It also links into various Saudi ministries. Harf delivered a separate Qur'an site for the King Fahd Complex for the Printing of the Holy Qur'an, which also had download options from various reciters and alternative-language translations.[10]

Minnesota-registered Al-Islam introduces its perspective on religious leadership and interpretation of the Qur'an (from one Shi'a perspective). The Qur'an resources feature a number of translations and commentaries and demonstrate how resources can be shared and produced collaboratively, drawing on content produced in Iran. The Multilingual Qur'an offers a choice of Windows Arabic and Karbala Arabic, the latter in particular being associated with Shi'a tradition.[11]

Qur'an index, Ministry of Islamic Affairs (Endowments, Da'wah, and
Guidance), Saudi Arabia, on al-Islam.com, December 2006

The levels of guidance and advice provided by site developers about how
to use a Qur'an website, and from content providers about the Qur'an itself,
varies considerably. There are some paradoxes, such as major Islamic institutions with technically poor Qur'an sites and minority perspectives with
highly usable resources. Casual visitors may seek user-friendly interfaces,
unaware that there are perhaps less well-presented alternative and nuanced
perspectives online. A hadith of the Prophet Muhammad stresses the importance of acquiring knowledge about the Qur'an: "Narrated 'Uthman:
The Prophet said, 'The best among you (Muslims) are those who learn the
Qur'an and teach it.'"[12] Presumably, this now applies to those who learn
and teach the Qur'an through the Internet.

While the mass market is covered with various versions of online
Qur'ans, there are also degrees of specialization within the Islamic knowledge economy. Some preserve and transmit traditional scholarship to
a wider audience, including rare Islamic manuscripts, and that activity
crosses over into the commercial sector. The International Hadith Study
Association Network brought together users of a Hadith Encyclopedia
through a members-only searchable database.[13] In a separate develop-

Extract of the Qur'an, *Surah al-Munafiqun*, Al-Islam.com

ment, Tradigital presented versions of the Qur'an in digital format.[14] Al-Azhar launched an Islamic manuscripts database, including copies of the Qur'an. Secularized institutions also played a role: the British Library presented rare copies of the Qur'an online as part of an exhibition of the sacred.[15]

The digital preservation of Islamic resources became a conference topic, focusing on the preservation of Islamic manuscripts through digitization processes.[16] Qur'an and other sources, especially rare manuscripts in diverse cursive scripts, could ultimately be made available to a wider public through Internet channels. Some of these areas might only be in the interests of academics and specialists. They do offer a window for others seeking to enhance their understanding of the range of historical Islamic materials.

The source code of Islam has become searchable and dynamic, while retaining its intrinsic nature and values. Approaches to the sacred text are nuanced toward different types of readerships. Imaginative approaches take online Qur'an resources beyond reproducing the text and translation in hypertextual format. Integration of multimedia formats, combined in some cases with sponsorship that has allowed investment of time and

Index, Al-Azhar Library (*http://www.alazharonline.org*), 2005

money, enhances the potential access toward the Revelation in its written and recited forms.

Throughout Islamic history, and via various Muslim networks, the intrinsic merit of the printed and written Qur'an as an entity has been promoted. The Qur'an holds its own power of *baraka*, or blessing, for listener, reader, and beholder, which has seen portions of the text used as talismans and cures. Perhaps it can offer a similar power within CIES, with its mere presence on a website and within cyberspace infusing cyber networks and their readers with their own *baraka*. An electronic Qur'an may need to be accorded the same respect as its traditional equivalents. Just as a hand-calligraphed or -printed Qur'an must be protected and kept clear of impurity, there may be a place on a separate portion of a believer's hard drive, apart from other forms of content of a nonreligious nature, for a digital Qur'an.

Islamic Dimensions of the Sacred in Cyberspace

The rewiring of the House of Islam facilitates interaction and allows iMuslims to participate in the basic principles and practices of Islam. The ideas expressed by Smart and others have a resonance in CIES. There are many possible approaches toward understanding Islamic dimensions of the sacred in cyberspace that are articulated by iMuslims in different formats and interfaces. Some take full advantage of Web 2.0 and increased bandwidth to promote their messages, often collaborating and participating across networks and continents. The concepts associated with sacred time, space, and ritual, for example, find a place within the online expression of the five pillars of Islam, or *arkan al-islam*: *hajj*, *salat*, Ramadan, *shahada*, and *zakat*. These basic principles offer an aide-mémoir when first approaching Islam, encompassing many significant principles that form part of Muslim religious life. They have a consistency across Muslim networks. The question can also be asked of how their virtual manifestations impact on non-digital world practices.

Shahada ◆ The essential proclamation within Islam, the *shahada*, is: "There is no god but God and Muhammad is the Messenger of God." Literally, the term *shahada* represents "bearing witness" (to One God). As well as being a central tenet of prayer, this proclamation is applied when individuals convert or "revert," in the language of some, to Islam.

The *shahada* is a phrase interwoven into the textures of CIES. In its starkest form, it is when surfers "embrace" or convert to Islam via the Internet. Through this process, an individual becomes an iMuslim. IslamiCity maintains a log of the numbers of "online *shahada*," observing that online conversions increased tenfold after 9/11.[17] Many have found their path toward Islam through reading online content:

> When I was living with my mom I had attended my grandmother's church and sung in the choir but then Sept. 11th happened and my dormant interest in Islam reawakened and I started doing research, I went online and chatted and went to sites, I bought an English translation of the Qur'an and a book on Islam and I was convinced by these literature [*sic*] that I took my shahadah online on January 7th at 11:45 pm, I took it again in person three weeks after that, I have never felt so . . . spiritually lifted!![18]

This 9/11 effect was replicated elsewhere, where curiosity toward Islam in general opened up following the attacks of September 11, 2001. It would be naive to consider that all responses concluded in this way, although a number of sites reported conversions online. Like other areas relating to Islam and the Net, this is an innovative practice. Some felt that it required a scholarly justification and response in order that it be recognized as Islamic and permissible.

This was especially appropriate for those whose focus and understanding of Islam had an edge tempered by forms of Islamic jurisprudence. In part, this may be because of the ways in which Islam has often been represented online—by actors whose motivation is inspired and dominated by the opinions from various schools (*madhahib*) of Islamic jurisprudence. These were founded in the centuries following the emergence of Islam and have a dominant role to play within the development of varieties of Islamic scholarship and doctrine. Many of the precedents established during this formative period in Islamic history have a role to play in interpretations of Islam in contemporary society, hence the reliance on Muslim scholars trained in Islamic sciences.

With adoption of Islamic practice to the digital age in mind, Islam Online, linked to the scholar Yusuf al-Qaradawi, discussed the "permissibility" of an online *shahada* as part of an online fatwa. It was the opinion of Sheikh Ahmad Kutty that

> it is very good to use the Internet in fields like calling people to Islam and even offering them the *Shahadah* online. However, there are some rules to abide by if we want to give the *Shahadah* to a person who wants to accept Islam on the Internet:
>
> "The man has to say the *Shahadah* by his tongue and it is not enough to write it[, believes Kutty]. Proficiency is not a condition as we bear in mind that the one who accepts Islam has no background of Arabic. If the website has an audio system that allows people to have voice conversation, then it is easy to ask the person to say the *Shahadah* by repeating it. If there is no such means of voice conversation, then we can transliterate the words of *Shahadah* and ask the person who wants to embrace Islam to say it to himself. We can write it as follows: *La 'illaha 'illa llah Muhammad rasoolul Allah* (there is no god but Allah; Muhammad is the Messenger of Allah.) If the person says the translation only, it does not count."[19]

Some very clear principles are put in place here in the form of a religious opinion or fatwa. The language of the Qur'an, rather than a translation, is stressed. The integration of Voice over Internet Protocol (VoIP), in which real-time conversations (and conversions) can be facilitated over the Internet, is also significant. Webcam use could offer another avenue for such activity. A significant Islamic rite of passage, through which an individual undergoes an irrevocable transition of religious status, now has a legitimized online precedent of ritual space and practice.

There are a number of online guides detailing how to convert to Islam.[20] The Internet offers that most basic of requirements for all Muslims and potential Muslims: the declaration of faith. This has its precedents in the practice of the Prophet Muhammad himself. He encouraged members of his family and community to convert to Islam, after he received the initial Revelation from God via the Angel Gabriel on Mount Hira in the year 610. That same proclamation has now been digitized but retains its sacred essence and continuity.

Salat ◆ Following *shahada*, the next duty for a new Muslim to learn is that of *salat*, or prayer. This takes many forms online, demonstrating creativity amid the practice that takes its principles from the actions of Muhammad. According to tradition, the Prophet was taught how to pray by the Angel Gabriel. The practice was refined, in terms of the number of prayers, during Muhammad's miraculous Night Journey (*Isra'*) from Mecca to Jerusalem and his ascendance to the heavens (*Mi'raj*). This occurred some twelve years after he first received Revelation. During the ascendance, he encountered previous prophets and led them in prayer. After some negotiation, Muhammad then received the prescribed number of five daily prayers from Musa (Moses). This sequence of events has been interpreted in a number of different ways from diverse Muslim perspectives. Some place greater emphasis on its esoteric dimensions than others.

The principles of prayer have been carried through generations, cultures, and Muslim networks. There is a consistency that now has continuity in CIES. It is possible for an individual to learn how to pray and recite specific prayers online while observing the appropriate sequential actions (*rak'a*). There is information on the appropriate state of body and mind and the requirement of intent within prayer. While a mosque may be preferred for prayer, it is not obligatory. It is recommended, however, for the Friday *Jum'a* congregational prayers and at significant Muslim festivals.

Whether participation online provides the ritually appropriate space for *salat* is an issue of conjecture. It certainly offers the ritual dimensions of the sound of prayer and the sense of belonging in a community. Using webcams, individuals could pray with each other online. Other rituals

Flash object, "The Right Way
to Pray" (for beginners),
Islamway.com (*http://
english.islamway.com/
prayer/BegSound.htm*),
May 2008

are performed in this way. However, perhaps its greatest attribute is facilitating access to materials giving advice on Islamically appropriate behavior. The Internet enables the facilitation of the dimensions of the sacred for
those who do not have access to traditional resources or who seek an
alternative perspective.

Islam is based around a lunar calendar, in which prayer times and festivals are calculated based on the position of the sun and moon. Numerous
computer databases provide applications providing accurate calculations of
salat and the necessary direction toward Mecca from any point in the world.
Some can be downloaded for use on cell phones, PDAs, and BlackBerrys.[21]
Moonsighting.com is a long-standing and comprehensive resource that
details aspects of calendars and prayer calculation. This includes detailed
discussion on the mathematics of such calculations. These are complex but
essential for understanding the accurate timing of prayers, Ramadan, and
festivals—including *Eid al-Adha*, the feast that marks the conclusion of
hajj. It pays attention to the different methodological approaches to calculation, based on varied religious interpretations and traditions. This is a
contentious subject, generating online debates about the timings of festivals, which can vary between different schools of interpretation.

There are many sources associated with the principles of prayer available online. Sometimes, less usefully in a computer-mediated context,
these are simply reproductions of books.[22] Others extend their content in a
more constructive manner; MuslimConverts.com provides audio clips and
advice on how to perform basic prayers and augments this with video clips
for teaching the Qur'an's opening *sura* (*al-Fatiha*), drawn from a secondary
source.[23] There is a breakdown of the prayer line by line, transliterated for
non-Arabic speakers, together with detailed explanations of the appropriate actions.[24]

There are numerous examples of this application of multimedia. The
Islamic Center of Raleigh, North Carolina, provided a detailed online

guide, illustrated by photographs, breaking down aspects of prayer into user-friendly segments. Jannah.com provided links to Macromedia Flash presentations on how to pray and perform ablutions. "Prophet Moham-mad's Manner of Doing Prayer by His Eminence Sheikh Abdul Aziz Ibn Baz" used animated graphics and photos, together with audio recitation and transliterated Arabic. The late Ibn Baz was a senior religious scholar up until his death. There is evidence of his so-called Wahhabi perspective in this presentation.[25]

iMuslims cannot be categorized according to a single paradigm, es-pecially when discussing the ritual dimensions of Islam. If one wanted to compare different approaches to prayer ritual, then exploration of a prominent Shi'a site offers not only contrast, but also an indication of any commonality. Prominent Iraqi scholar Ayatollah al-Sistani is the focus of Sistani.org. Ayatollah al-Sistani's organization promoted his interpre-tations of Islam in the languages of Arabic, English, French, Farsi, and Urdu.[26] The Shi'a cleric's views on ritual issues, law, and contemporary issues can be found through Sistani.org, including reproductions of print publications and an interactive section for questions and answers. It was intriguing, but not surprising, to learn that one of al-Sistani's sons-in-law runs an Internet company in Qom.[27]

Sistani.org features many of his statements relating to the situation in Iraq, as well as general advice for Muslims across the world, according to a specific Shi'a approach. This can be seen in the way Sistani.org discusses *salat*. There are detailed explanations of the "correct" approaches to prayer and the elements that are obligatory and specific to particular occasions.

While complex to the outsider, this advice is described as "Simplified Islamic Laws for Youth and Young Adults." It gives insight into practices specific to this form of Shi'ism. Particular laws associated with personal hygiene and clothing appropriate for prayer are detailed. These are impor-tant to ensure that prayer is ritually valid. It describes the role of mosques and the duties requiring Muslims, especially males, to be present in them. While providing information online, it emphasizes that attendance is a necessary part of Muslim ritual practice. The site ostracizes those who fail to attend prayer without a good reason.

After giving all the recommended practices prior to prayer, specific sequences of the declaration of intention of prayer, standing, prostrating, and recitation are illustrated. Each element is described in detail. Advice is given on the portions of recitation required, the specific circumstances leading to differences in practice, and the responses for when a mistake is

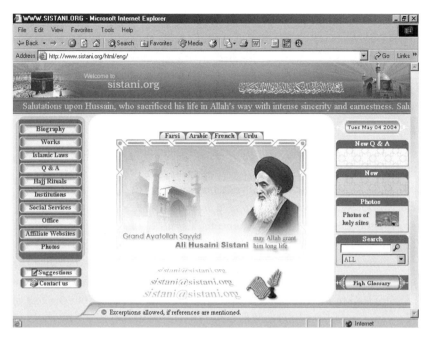

Index, Al-Sistani.org, May 2004

made in prayer.[28] Greater detail on prayers, with specific rulings for all aspects of ritualistic practice, is also provided on the database (divided into specific areas for ease of access).[29]

In many ways, this is a reproduction of legalistic printed texts on aspects of Shi'a decision making. The application and following of religious authority (*taqlid*) specific to Shi'ism through a *mujtahid* is explained in detail. This includes how to identify a *mujtahid*, the required qualifications and abilities of *mujtahid*, how an individual should respond to a fatwa or a verdict, and the different ways religious information can be transmitted. Presumably, the presence of these books and sources (including al-Sistani's) online makes the Internet part of the authority equation. They open up this particular perspective on Islam to other Muslims. This does not necessarily evoke a sympathetic approach, given the virulent online dialogues that have occurred between some Sunni and Shi'i factions, reproducing friction in real-world contexts.

Daily prayers and recitation are one reaffirmation of the covenant between humanity and God. Islam has always provided many channels to the Divine. The duties of prayer can be represented at the most basic level through reproducing the practice of Muhammad, which is more than sufficient in the eyes of Allah and guarantees those who pray with sincerity a place in paradise. For some, they have sought to go beyond these traditional parameters—often to the disdain of orthodox scholars—by seeking out a mystical path. Whichever route an individual might follow toward Allah, it seems that in part its facilitation can be accommodated online.

Hajj ◆ The *hajj* represents the major pilgrimage to Mecca, seen as one duty for all Muslims to undertake if they can afford it. Historically, this could be a hazardous undertaking, taking several years in some cases, and the rigors of the journey become part of the spiritual process. The honorific epithet *hajji* was seen as a mark of devotion for those who completed the pilgrimage. Numerous accounts of journeys are part of Islamic literature across Muslim networks in a variety of languages.[30]

In some ways, the hazardous element of the *hajj* diminished with the emergence of modern transportation, from the steamship to the jet airplane. Despite the efforts of the Saudi government, including the use of ICT as an organizational tool, pilgrims have continued to die on the *hajj* in tragic accidents. The victims are seen as martyrs for their demise while on a sacred quest.

The meetings of scholars on the *hajj* profoundly influenced the knowledge economy of Islam. Through the centuries, knowledge was transmitted and networked through the *hajj*. The pilgrimage became a meeting point for the exchange of information about Islam. Travelers from various parts of the Muslim world gathered to share in the sacred ritual established during the time of Muhammad, which held a link to pre-Islamic practices. The *hajj* has continued to be a place where scholars and others come together, offering political and religious cohesion at times and status for those sponsoring pilgrimages or providing secure passage on the hazardous routes. The *hajj* still has a significant role in the knowledge economy, although some of the scholarly interactions that have historical precedents in *hajj* meetings now take place online.

While the *hajj* can have a place in cyberspace, a virtual *hajj* lacks the dangers of its historical precedents. It does not offer participants any honorific title. Whether a virtual pilgrim might receive any form of spiritual sustenance from their online journey is clearly in the eye of the beholder. It can offer knowledge of practice, accounts of the experiences of *hajji*s, logistical information, and insight for those unable to make the journey. (This may be because of expense or because they are not Muslim, the latter being a requirement for entry to Mecca.)

The extent to which the *hajj* can be fully represented online is debatable. One "has to be there" in order to fully comprehend the enormity of the pilgrimage. For an online observer, the Internet does offer one way of attaining some comprehension of the impact of this pillar of Islam. In terms of ritualistic practice, the *hajj* is represented online in many ways. *Hajj* information hubs provide associated information, organization, representation, and substantial advice on aspects of ritualistic practice.

Hajj websites incorporate pilgrimage instruction, both for *hajj* and for the minor *umrah* pilgrimage. This includes links to related Islamic textual sources. Sites can have a commercial edge, with links for making airline, hotel, and package bookings.[31] The logistical elements of *hajj* are facilitated through visa assistance and health-care advice. Immersion in the *hajj* experience also becomes a luxury lifestyle: IslamiCity offered deluxe and special packages for American pilgrims, complete with online booking.[32] This information is presented alongside photographs, step-by-step guides, and related commercial products such as software and videos.

Technical information on the Ka'bah, the focus of prayer within the sacred precincts of Mecca, is contained on the Islamic Gateway.[33] Highly detailed plans relating to key areas in Mecca can be found on the site, alongside a glossary of *hajj*-related terms. Key concepts and places are linked to various sound and image files, giving further advice to assist the prospective *hajji* and the armchair pilgrim. The pilgrim's *Qurbani* sacrifice can also be facilitated online through the use of a credit card, while satisfying (to some) the requirements of the ritual.[34]

There are other ways of approaching pilgrimage via the Internet. Google Earth offers a distant satellite view of the Ka'bah in Mecca. More detailed is the 3D Kabah WebPage created by Abid S. Hussain. It represents a long-term project, applying three-dimensional computer modeling to produce animated video clips, including a flight through the Ka'bah precincts.[35] This site has developed over several years, with updated computer imagery, unique angles on the holy precincts, and files downloadable for use on an iPod. This open-access content introduces a new dimension and understanding of the Ka'bah, devoid of pilgrims and with a computer-enhanced aesthetic.

Media coverage has a role in how the *hajj* is represented online. Coverage is intense on many broadcast channels, relaying live feed that is available online. Awsat al-Islam links to multimedia resources on the *hajj*, some drawn from external resources such as PBS, CNN, and ABC

Index, Islamicity.com, December 2006

News.[36] Channel 4's coverage of the pilgrimage, produced by Lion Television and entitled "The *Hajj*—The Greatest Trip on Earth," included a "Virtual *Hajj*." They described this as "the closest thing to being there."[37] The site included the prayers for every aspect of the *hajj*, with recitations in English and Arabic. Scholarly opinion provided guidance on ritualistic practice. An archive of film coverage and day-by-day reports presented the perspectives of five pilgrims from different social and cultural backgrounds.[38] These dynamic eyewitness accounts of key elements in the *hajj* "experience" were presented in documentary format, with videos and interview transcripts.

Personal accounts of pilgrimage can be found throughout CIEs. Irshaad Hussain describes in journal form the experiences of *umrah* and her circumambulation of the Ka'bah—the *tawaaf*. Her account was based on an e-mail composed in a Meccan cybercafé.[39] Personal technology will offer further glimpses into *hajj* experiences. 3G cell phones with video cameras allow for photos and clips to be posted online directly from Mecca, apparently avoiding restrictions on photography evident for *hajj* in the past. Authorities are not necessarily sympathetic to this practice. Pilgrims have been seen using cell phones while performing *tawaaf* in order to share their experience with relatives back home.[40] It could be that there is some religious merit in this real-time "sharing" of the *hajj* experience (no doubt a scholar will furnish a fatwa on this), although a counterargument would suggest that such technology would be distracting when applied during a *tawaaf*. Certainly it could be linked seamlessly into a webcast.

There is greater scope for personal *hajj* blogs and other personal accounts, presented with immediacy online.[41] There have been pioneers who endeavored to log their thoughts in a blog format. CNN presented a video/blog in 2005 by journalist Zain Verjee as part of annual *hajj* coverage.[42] In 2007 CNN reporter Mohammed Jamjoom was blogging "almost live" via mobile phone from the *hajj*.[43] Abu Eesa's Islamiblog offered a less slick, more personal diary. It gave an indication of the enormity of the *hajj* and its impact on the pilgrim, as well as recording the tribulations in the pilgrims' way: "As we struggle over walls, highways, rocks, and sand, everyone is just focused upon one thing—Du'a! [prayer]."[44]

Such personal *hajj* experiences reflect the personal and community dimensions of *hajj* in terms of ritual and the sense of sacred space. Mecca can now be accessed online, and experiences posted via handheld ICT. Clips from broadcasts are also posted on YouTube. A further level of experiential expression is facilitated through elements of Web 2.0. Whether this sharing of religious experience and enhanced familiarity with the *hajj* takes away any sense of the numinous within the pilgrimage, especially if it becomes intrusive, is something one might observe as access to ICT increases.

Ramadan ❖ The Islamic month of Ramadan can be interpreted as a period of spiritual renewal, particularly on the night during the month when the Qur'an is believed to have first been revealed. The fast (*sawm*) requires abstention (*imsak*) from eating, drinking, smoking, and sexual activity—but not using the Internet. Ramadan creates an individualistic sense of Islamic identity and cohesion, both to the "outside world" and the individual community. Its physical hardships, especially when Ramadan falls during hot seasons, can be debilitating. This is from dawn until dusk.

In many ways, the Net helps bring iMuslims together during this sacred month, especially those living outside of established Muslim communities. The net facilitates the exchange of important information about ritualistic practices and timings. A prominent example of a long-term online Web discourse is about the sighting of the moon during Ramadan. This is integral to the timing of fasting, which commences and concludes according to the moon's waxing and waning. It is a subject that annually generates substantial dialogue, if not consensus, on e-mail lists and in chat rooms. The United States–based Zaytuna Institute offered Crescent Watch in 2007, which sought to synchronize moon sightings across the nation.[45] The institute also presented video and audio podcasts from their founder, Shaykh Yusuf Hanson, including reflections on Ramadan that could be downloaded as part of the institute's online output.[46]

The special requirements of Ramadan are described and catered for on a number of sites, which illustrate approaches to this pillar of Islam. For Net-literate Muslims, electronic cards for specific events mark events such as Ramadan.[47] There are many Shi'a resources relating to Ramadan available online, including lectures, sermons, and prayers. Al-Islam.org offers specific Ramadan supplications in audio format.[48] Ramadan.co.uk is a good example of a hub, co-coordinating Ramadan activities. It includes links to the various Ramadan community radio stations in the UK. These are permitted to operate on special licenses during the month, with recitations, discussions, sermons, and advice. While catering for regional audiences, through Internet broadcasts they have a potential international reach. The broadcasts, which often make up in enthusiasm what they lack in professionalism, go beyond the central theme of Ramadan.

Radio Ummah, based in East London, provided a "marriage show" in 2005: "Every week, Zahid will discuss a new matter regarding choosing your spouse, getting engaged, and married life issues all from an Islamic and contemporary perspective."[49] It is not clear what Zahid's specific qualifications were in this regard. Glasgow's Radio Ramadan offered podcasts of its marriage program in 2006. In 2007 its broadcast team was collaborating on a situation comedy based on the differences between life in Scotland and life in Pakistan, using theme music from *The Simpsons*. One episode satirized the demands of prospective marriage partners in Pakistan seeking a British visa.[50]

The intensification of online activity in the month of Ramadan is reflected in CIES internationally. They offer a chance for iMuslims to dip into the experiences of other communities in local and international contexts. Some of this potential for comparison is reflected in the RamadhanZone, which in 2007 had accounts of diverse practices in twelve international locations. These discussed some of the differences in ritualistic practices, illustrated with photos. The site also coordinated charitable donations for Islamic Relief (which distributes food parcels across the world), supported by video clips. The site featured a calculator for *zakat* (see below) and encouraged online donating. It linked to a related Ramadan site for children, integrating stories, music, games, quizzes, and explanations of Islamic Relief's activities.[51]

Zakat ❖ *Zakat* is the financial tithe incumbent on all Muslims, essentially based on a fixed percentage of individual wealth. This goes to help the less well-off within a local community or elsewhere in the *ummah*. Islamic charity has increasingly attained an international dimension, as charities seek to mirror and in some cases complement the activities of other international charities. Some causes have a specific Islamic component, such as the provision of Qur'ans, the building of mosques, or campaigns to provide specific Islamic clothing in various areas. *Zakat* is not understood as a tax but as an act of worship.

Many sites have responded to this pillar with advice and information, as well as opportunities for surfers to apply their *zakat* to contribute to specific causes. In some cases, this includes donating to help the website in its activities; building a database has become *fard* (an obligation), taking the concept beyond its original precepts for alleviating poverty. IslamiCity describes how *zakat* functions and provides calculating software, as well as a link to transfer *zakat* (via a secure Web server) to IslamiCity for distribution.[52]

The proliferation of major Islamic charities online offers new opportunities for individuals to offer their *zakat*, but this may be at the expense of other, smaller charities that do not cultivate an online presence. Some Islamic charities have become the targets of various campaigns for their alleged affiliations to causes deemed by some as being controversial in nature. There have been cases in which this has resulted in prosecutions, some of which have been based on data derived from online sources.

Sacred Time and Space

Festivals ❖ Within certain strands of Islamic beliefs, there are festivals and celebrations that do not fall within the "mainstream" or shared areas of Islamic thought. These can be significant sacred dimensions for adherents to a particular worldview whose international networks are naturally enhanced by use of the Internet. The celebration of the Prophet's birthday (known as *maulid*, or *Milad-e Nabi*) is an example of this, and it has a place online.

The long-standing Ismaili Web Shi'a portal provides poetry and music in audio format to celebrate the *maulid*.[53] It also links to other Ismaili and Shi'a specific festivals. These include Imam Ali's birthday and the birthdays of historically significant religious leaders within the Ismaili and Shi'a traditions. As an early Muslim and Muhammad's son-in-law, Ali ibn Abi Talib has significance for both Sunni and Shi'a Muslims. In Shi'ism, he is seen as the "founder" of a line of spiritual authority and leadership. This has branched out over the centuries to form the diverse nodes of Shi'a Muslim networks. Online, festivals specific to these networks can be located. On Ismaili Web, these include celebrations associated with the present Aga Khan (a spiritual-religious leader for many Ismaili Muslims) and his ancestors.

Similar expressions relating to specific religious leaders can be located elsewhere on the Web in relation to Shi'a Ismaili beliefs. A branch of the Dawoodi Bohras is centered in India. They "adhere to the Shia Fatimi tradition of Islam, headed by the 52nd Dai al-Mutlaq, Syedna Mohammed Burhanuddin." The Dawoodi Bohras present their own microcosm of networks and affiliations online in a sophisticated series of sites, including concepts surrounding festivals, ritual, meetings, and rites of passage.[54] Their spiritual leader's activities and historical networking traditions have lent themselves to the Internet. There are numerous online activities generated by the Bohras. This includes the online timetables for religious leaders' travels in local and global contexts. Specific festivals unique to this branch of Shi'ism are explained, demonstrating what is shared and what is very specific to Dawoodi Bohra beliefs.[55] The Dawoodi Bohra are firmly rooted in a top-down authority model, based on the pronouncements of the Dai. With branches across the world, they are a good example of a collaborative Islamic knowledge economy reliant on electronic networking to present their worldview.

There are other examples of ways in which CIES can focus on a particular interpretative approach within the diversity of Shi'a Islam and adapt technology to reflect specific interests. The Bahrain-registered Al-Imam portal provides Flash animation clips on religious themes, integrating music and images. "The Awaited Saviour" section refers to the "martyrdom" of Muhammad's grandson al-Husayn ibn Ali at Karbala in 680. This pivotal event within Shi'a Islam is represented by related images and recordings of the observance of *muharram*, which is the Islamic New Year and the anniversary of al-Husayn's death. The emotional outpouring around *muharram* are well represented online. Other Shi'a issues also emerge: *Ya Fatima* asks where the grave of Fatima,

Index, Dawoodi Bohra Net (*http://mumineen.org*), December 2006

the Prophet Muhammad's daughter, is. It shows the destruction by anti-Shi'a elements throughout history of various shrines and mosques associated with significant imams acknowledged as key sources of Shi'a Islamic authority.[56]

Issues of ritual also extend to the margins of Islamic beliefs, away from the Sunni and Shi'a mainstreams. This includes events specific to sects and strands of Muslim belief, not always universally recognized within the macrocosm of Islam. Prominent among these would be the Nation of Islam (NOI) coverage of Saviors' Day, which celebrates via a webcast the birthday of NOI founder Wallace Fard Muhammad on 26 February.[57] The Web offers a space for such articulation of belief and practice, integrated into the presentation of worldviews for adherents *and* observers.

Sacred Places

Beyond Mecca and Medina, other places hold a special place in the hearts of (some) Muslims. These can be based around interpretations and influences associated with specific religious and cultural perspectives on Islam. One generally accepted sacred place would be al-Quds (Jerusalem), considered a Muslim holy city. Muhammad's Night Journey to Jerusalem is seen as being a significant turning point in the fortunes of the Prophet and the development of Islam. This status is enhanced by the presence of the Dome of the Rock mosque, marking the point of Muhammad's ascendance to the Seven Heavens within this religiously significant city.

The status of al-Quds is presented online in a number of different ways. Some sites are associated directly to Palestinian Muslim issues and the Intifadas.[58] The Palestine Ministry of Waqfs (Religious Endowments) published a detailed survey of al-Aqsa mosque and its environs, copiously illustrated with photos and plans.[59] This might be utilized in conjunction with generic resources, such as Google Earth and Wikipedia, in order to build a picture of the status of al-Quds in Islamic contexts. Given that many Muslim Palestinians have difficulties accessing Jerusalem, the city's online presence is an important one.

The Internet also forms an information conduit on the many pilgrimages and religious events of specific interest to particular worldviews. For example, there are listings of pilgrimage sites of importance to Shi'a Muslims. These itemize tombs and shrines that might be meritorious for a visit. The Al-Islam listing incorporates sites in Saudi Arabia, Iraq, Iran, Syria, Jerusalem, and Egypt. The significance of each shrine is detailed, alongside maps and photographs. In some cases, further detailed information about a shrine is available, such as the History of Mashad, with its historical, architectural, and religious information.[60]

This resource-rich material can be integrated with data derived from generic sources and resources that are not affiliated with particular religious worldviews. Islamic sacred spaces at every level of significance— local, national, and global—feature in cyberspace. Details of religious sites associated with Islam are on Archnet, whose digital library shows important religious buildings from across the Muslim world.[61] Online resources such as Wikipedia feature detailed articles on these locations, including an extensive essay on the Damascus Mosque.[62] YouTube contains numerous video clips taken in mosques. It is feasible to construct a digital map of significant Islamic sites and their representation online, drawing on Google Earth and other mapping applications to form a digital map of Muslim sacred space.

Rites of Passage

From cradle to grave, the elements of (Muslim) human life are located online. The focus in this section is on three elements: birth, relationships, and death. These provide an indication of how the Net is integrated into the worldviews of some Muslims for key decision-making processes, and how it might influence, inform, and change fundamental human actions.

Birth ◆ Even from birth, the Web can influence the lives of future generations of iMuslims—potentially influencing their very identities. Parents can draw upon databases to select the most "appropriate" name for their baby based on Islamic criteria. These searchable databases allow a degree of intersite comparison. This is not to say that parents lack the wherewithal to name a child without such data by following a family tradition, the advice of a religious leader, or other criteria.

Sites may reinforce a prior choice of name as well, with relevance for converts wishing to select an "Islamically correct" name for themselves. Online resources compete with commercial products for baby-naming CD-ROMs.[63] The content hyperlinked to these sites, in terms of additional information and links to other resources, is revealing in acting as entry points to other data. Muslim-names.co.uk is a database of children's names with basic meanings.[64] Linked to this is advice on the basic ritualistic principles associated with the arrival of a child, backed with precepts drawn from the Qur'an.

Muslim-names.co.uk featured extracts drawn from Islamic question-and-answer sites from specific Wahhabi-oriented perspectives. The Islamic ritualistic process associated with the arrival of a baby was mapped out online. Clarification was given to interpretations linked with announcing a birth. These included advice on naming a baby; giving *adhan* in the ear; circumcising male babies; shaving the head; and the necessity of *aqiqah*, or animal sacrifice, which is associated with the tradition of cutting a baby's hair seven days after birth.

Sites can also issue advice that some deem as controversial, innovative, and "un-Islamic." For example, the Muslim-names.co.uk hyperlink on circumcision led to a discussion promoting the "advantages" of female "circumcision."[65] This is not a universally agreed-upon Islamic practice. Otherwise known as female genital mutilation, it has been the subject of sustained international preventative campaigns.

Less controversial but still potentially provocative is the practice of *tahnik*, which is recommended on the Sunni Path site. *Tahnik* requires a "pious and God-fearing scholar or a venerable saint" to chew a date or an alternative sweet food, which is then given to the child.[66] This is not something that would be endorsed by all Muslims, yet it is represented as a significant practice on this popular site. Clearly, there is scope for a multitude of opinions in CIES, as with other areas of cyberspace. Caution is also necessary when receiving advice without critical consideration. Determining the extent to which such online advice is acted upon is difficult, but clearly its place on a website opens up the application of particular worldviews to iMuslims who choose to follow a particular line.

Relationships ◆ This section focuses on traditional Muslim marital relationships and their formulation in cyberspace, which can be seen from commercial, political, religious, and emotional angles. This is not to imply that Muslims do not form other kinds of relationships and friendships that may have various degrees of "permissibility." These, too, may be facilitated through cyberspace. This represents a further example of shifting Muslim networks and the ways in which online issues have a practical resonance as real-world issues. These developments introduce specific mapping issues, often being invisible transactions, hidden in many cases to researchers or outside observers. This is understandable, given the potentially sensitive nature of male-female dialogues and the parameters for discourse articulated in the Qur'an and other sources.

The types of relationships that can be engineered online between men and women can transcend cultural restrictions and religious values. Often, such activities are private and hidden within cyberspace. They are low-profile and discreet, and they usually do not generate headlines, except when it comes to technical innovation and real or assumed "breaches" of interpretative models of authority.

This is particularly true in the areas of dating, marriage, and matchmaking. The acceptance of technology into conventional models and practices suggests an inherent practicality and flexibility, based on pragmatic religious and cultural norms. On another level, such practices reinforce traditional practices. In the context of Pakistan, for example, "Islamic devotion and Internet dating are emerging as dual signatures of some Pakistani communities where matchmaking has long been a family affair."[67]

This suggests a complex relationship between paradigmatic religious practices and technical innovation. Inherent cultural-religious concepts associated with male-female relationships—including *purdah*, engagement, and betrothal—are challenged, adjusted, and compensated by technology. They retain an implicit, familiar, deep-rooted Islamic core.

The development of online marriage bureaus, giving matches based on established religious and cultural norms, emerged from a variety of contexts. These have been supported at the highest levels. The Iranian website (and marriage bureau) Ardabili.com was endorsed by several senior clerics. Organizer Jaffar Savalanpour Ardabili, himself a cleric, established the website to encourage marriages and circumnavigate traditional barriers to the development of relationships.[68] This was in conjunction with his blogging activities. Similar activities were not without risk: in 2003 the Basij arrested users and operators of an Internet dating service in Iran under charges of "unlawful actions."[69]

While it is dangerous to generalize across Muslim networks, there is a sense of implicit endorsement by religious authorities of at least some marriage sites. The inclusion of links and articles provided by particular religious perspectives is one good indicator. As the following excerpt indicates, the subject has also appeared in online chat rooms and question-and-answer sites.

> Imam Yahya Hendi, Muslim chaplain at Georgetown, said he has received many requests to serve as an intermediary for Muslim couples who have gotten to know each other through the Web, and he has rarely heard anyone in the Muslim community object to the online courtships.
>
> "There are few other ways to be intimate without being inappropriate, no doubt," he said. The websites "give opportunity for people across the spectrum from all backgrounds, from all locations to meet and engage in an open, honest discussion without violating what they believe would be the rules of Islam."[70]

Dating sites are not just altruistic; they often have a commercial edge. London-based MuslimMatch.com boasted "90,353 registered Members have exchanged 351,514 Mailbox messages."[71] MuslimMatch.com links to SpeedIntros.com, where "speed dating" could be booked online (although the meetings took place in real time at a real location): "We provide all this in stylish, upmarket yet [M]uslim-friendly venues! We provide you with excellent customer service and attention to detail, with prayer facilities made available on site! With so many people attending, the only person missing is you! . . . Book Online today before your Muslim Match is snapped up by someone else!"[72]

This is something of a hard sell. The site acted as a hub for other information and services, such as webcasts from Islam Channel and Islam Radio. The database is searchable, based on varying criteria of location, age, ethnicity, and Islamic branch. MuslimMatch also provides "success

stories" of couples that have married via their service. These are interesting, in that they provide examples of the types of approaches to the Web that can be made while retaining Islamic value systems.

> I opened a standard account on 26th January 2004 under the nickname kahati__takwa and she opened hers on 21st January 2004 under the nickname of galb. (We come and stay in different countries). In only three days I had spotted her. I contacted her by email on Arafat day (Saturday) and wished her a happy Idd [Eid]. I also declared my intentions to have a serious relationship with her. She instantly accepted and replied to my email after Idd. In the next week, we had a flurry of emails to each other and without any procrastinations made marriage vows to each other. She has already informed her parents about her decision. They have no objection. The same applies to me.[73]

This appears to have been something of a quick decision. Others may take longer to find a partner. MuslimMatch.com provides advice on

netiquette/*adab* (customary interpretative practice) when seeking a partner. This indicates a fusion between traditional practice and awareness of
the role and potential "pitfalls" of the Web. Attention was focused on
the levels of caution to be exhibited when communicating online with
strangers, linking into evolving concepts of Islamic netiquette:

> Take a relatively conservative approach to trusting anyone you meet
> online. If you think someone is lying, it is likely that they are, so act
> accordingly. Move on to someone you can eventually trust. Conduct
> yourself and your romances in a responsible manner. Don't fall in love
> at the click of a mouse. Don't become prematurely intimate with some-
> one, even if that intimacy only occurs online. . . .
>
> The beauty of meeting and relating online is that you can gradually
> collect information and then make a choice about pursuing the rela-
> tionship in the real world. You are never obligated to meet anyone,
> regardless of your level of online intimacy.[74]

Adaptation of traditional with digital practice establishes precedents for
others to follow. Other advice from MuslimMatch included an "11 Point-
Plan for Marital Bliss," "Female Safety: Putting It First!," and "Etiquettes for
Marriage" by Al-Albaani. This gives aspects of the marital relationship,
such as when to pray after marriage and "What to say at the time of making
Love." This advice is certainly comprehensive, although one presumes that
the couples also turn off their computers at the appropriate moments. The
author of some of this content, Muhammad Nasiruddeen al-Albaani, was
accused elsewhere of being an "innovator" and a "salafi," the term being
applied in a derogatory sense.[75]

Many have recognized the commercial potential of this aspect of CIES.
Similar services have emerged. They do have different features and perspectives, drawing on Web 2.0 in some cases. For example, muslimintro
.com includes XML and RSS feeds, allowing members to be instantly
updated when new people join the service. Presumably, cell phones and
BlackBerrys can also be used for such updates. Somewhat pessimistically,
perhaps, the Zawaj marriage-arrangement site included links to Islam-
Online articles citing Yusuf al-Qaradawi on "triple *talaq*" (divorce).[76]

Some "mainstream" Internet dating services recognized the commercial
potential of the Muslim market and now provide "Muslim areas"; these
include singles-bar.com and other sites focusing on people with links to
particular regions, such as Mehndi.com.[77] ShiaMatch.com catered for a
niche Shi'a market and had an active membership of over 9,000.[78] Within

many success stories, it noted parental approval of its services: "Alhum-dollilah [praise be to God] I have found a girl for my son from your site. I cannot thank you enough. All I can do is pray for all of you to Allah (SWT)."[79] The notion of appropriate "manners" and behavior were also highlighted within this Shi'a context. It emphasized that members from across the world were networking and interacting "appropriately" online: "Thank you very much for your services. I have met my future husband through your site. It is filtered, sheltered and decent. I would encourage anybody who is seriously looking for a mate to try your site. Once again, thank you."

Families could draw on Internet services to "upgrade" prospective mar-riage partners, as well: "Myself and my family are very thankful to you because you are the only one through whom we found a better and nice guy for my younger sister." The socially inhibited were also able to utilize online space: "We both agreed that the Internet was a very good way of getting to know someone as it cuts out the initial awkwardness."[80]

There is a sense in these comments that the Internet offers a greater choice for potential partners. Surfers can attempt to match specific educa-tional, ethnic-cultural, and linguistic interests, as well as particular re-ligious orientations. These examples do not indicate a radical change of mainstream practice necessarily, but they illustrate ways in which conven-tions might be digitally challenged and channeled. This is particularly ap-posite in the case of the Web being applied as a means of conveying the cultural-religious practice of parental consent for marriages. Perhaps this replaces other communications practices, such as letters, and could be seen as having greater "reliability" to reinforce traditions.

These "innovations" have been contested elsewhere in the Muslim spec-trum. The Institute of Islamic Understanding Malaysia "urged Malaysian Muslims to look for love in the mosque, not on the Internet."[81] It did not suggest how that process might be facilitated. Perhaps this was a panic response or an indication that local community-cultural norms were threatened by Internet dating options. Within a more secularized society, in particular, it may be a means through which lip service can be paid to religious practices and cultural traditions.

The application of the Web can be extended to include rites of pas-sage, such as marriage ceremonies: "Shabnam, the 26-year-old bride, said Qubool hai (I accept) to groom Abdul Kalaam in front of a web camera on Friday. While Shabnam was sitting in a cybercafé in Lucknow's walled city, Kalaam positioned himself before a webcam thousands of miles away in

Makkah in Saudi Arabia. And it was not as if the two had struck a chord while accidentally browsing the Net."[82]

The developments on the Web have forced institutions to reflect on their own services and offer alternatives, either on- or offline. Such proclamations do not necessarily have an impact: "On the Internet, Arab, Persian, Kurdish, Aramaic, and other love and music chat rooms attract ten times the al-Ansar-crowded [jihadi] rooms. There, you read and hear discussions of love; they seek, not decadence, but the early stages of a romantic revolution."[83] This comment suggests that romance-oriented sites conquer jihad chat rooms.

Technical innovation can take many forms in different stages of relationships. The notion of *talaq*, or pronouncement of divorce, itself can be interpreted in diverse ways; it has been taken as being appropriate by some when delivered by e-mail or cell phone (so called "SMS divorce").[84] "Amid the controversy over triple talaq," read one news story, "a man has reportedly used e-mail to divorce his wife in Bareilly district. Rahat Iqbal, living in the U.S., is reported to have given triple talaq to his wife Rubab Anwar through e-mail."[85]

Potential for disaster is also apparent within online relationships: "A budding romance between a Jordanian man and woman turned into an ugly public divorce when the couple found out that they were in fact man and wife."[86] In other contexts, some also determined that the Internet held a negative influence within personal zones. When Londoner Abdul Gaur's daughter fled home to India to marry a Hindu she had met on the Net, Gaur's reaction was predictably bitter: "The girls are teenagers and were not allowed out after school or college and certainly not near men. But we could do nothing to protect our daughter from the evil of the Internet. While we slept this evil came into our home and has led to our daughter running away and marrying a Hindu boy."[87] Film of the marriage was broadcast across India and inevitably appeared on webcasts and blogs from all perspectives.

A significant amount of advice is offered for establishing and maintaining relationships. This includes fatwa-type responses to particular questions and information for those in various stages of relationships. The discussion of sex and sexuality online in Islamic contexts raises important questions within controversial subject areas. "Islamic-style" sex education briefly emerged on the lovebeaches.net site, whose content was organized by the Qatar Welfare Association and the Family Counseling Centre: "In an address on 'Islam and sexuality,' British-based psychologist Maamum

Mubayedh said that 'Islam bans homosexuality, which should be fought' and from which people should be protected. . . . Aisha, a computer special-ist who has been married for two and a half years, said she had 'learned methods' that drew her closer to her husband."[88] The site featured music and links to themes on sex and sexuality. Visiting such sites may offer an Islamic gloss to material that could be viewed by others as prohibited or salacious. Similar issues emerged with elaph.com, organized by an Egyp-tian doctor, although this was more "Arab" than "Islamic" in orientation.[89]

United States–based Muslim WakeUp created a column called "Sex & the Umma." In one entry, columnist Mohja Kahf essayed the experiences of women in mosques in a piece of fiction. It contained an array of color-ful language speculating on the rewards for women in paradise—which were not, perhaps, for the traditional religiously sensitive reader.[90] Several women readers responded positively to the column, suggesting it reflected their own experiences. It led to a detailed online discussion about the nature and rewards of heaven. Amina Wadud stated: "Bravo for MWU for bringing to light such a small thing with such a BIG taboo surrounding it. Maybe we can bring a few more of us out of the closet of our own sexual masquerades."

Others condemned the online publication of the article, while the con-troversy no doubt led more readers to its pages.

> It is fine and nice to create an atmosphere of freely discussing sexuality between spouse and between parents and their children within certain limits, but what you have done and advocate is to open forums whereby the fundamental principles of Islamic modesty and ettiqutte [*sic*] are thrown out of the window and acceptance of the perverted western concept of sexuality, which has done more harm than good in the relationship between men and women.
>
> You would be wise to seek repentance for what you have done and entirely correct yourself when again dealing in matters of sex.[91]

A protracted dialogue ensued between this critic and the article's writer. Elsewhere, the site provides other accounts of sex and sexuality in an Islamic context. These include, in Kahf's piece titled "Wedad's Cavalry," two Meccan sisters dialoguing on their sex lives and former husbands.[92]

This type of expression regarding sexuality is not representative of CIES in general. It indicates that the Web gives access to materials beyond traditional authoritarian models associated with relationships. The enve-lope is pushed further in "Sex & the Ummah"—its title clearly indebted to the television series *Sex and the City*. This contained an article on the gay, bisexual, lesbian, and transgender Muslim scene in the UK, exploring dimensions of barriers facing this group.[93] The Internet became an important arena for such discussions to emerge from all perspectives. Within some interpretations, these could also form part of CIEs. These are well beyond the pale for orthodox Muslims but a significant area of Web discourse.[94]

In relation to gender issues, concepts associated with sexuality have received a great deal of attention in relation to CIEs. Diverse gay, lesbian, transgender, and bisexual (LGB) individuals and communities who identify themselves as Muslims have had an active presence online, utilizing the Web as a dynamic campaigning tool.[95] Brian Whitaker observes that "in countries where public discussion of homosexuality is still taboo, it is often the most accessible source of information and provides comfort for many whose sexuality has made them feel lonely and isolated."[96]

This comfort takes many forms. There are a number of long-standing LGB sites, such as al-Fatiha and Queer Jihad, which have been joined by others promoting regional and cultural agendas associated with LGB issues, facilitating specific campaigns.[97] LGB websites are educational and activist resources but also act as social and economic hubs for some iMuslims. This can be seen in the variations of the online dating/matchmaking phenomena, significant in some LGB Muslim contexts.

The Web has also been a means of entrapment in countries where homosexual activity is deemed illegal and/or against Islamic values. Through arranging assignations online, police in some contexts have captured and prosecuted "illegal" homosexual activity. This whole issue is rife with controversy. Some scholars would state, based on their interpretation of the Qur'an, that homosexuality is un-Islamic and deserving of severe punishment, and therefore it would be impossible to be "gay" and "Muslim." The website of Irshad Manji, a "lesbian Muslim," highlighted this perceived controversy. Manji maintained a website to discuss her thoughts on the perceived need for a "reformation" of Islam and to promote her writings.[98]

The Web was applied as a research tool on sexuality issues in Muslim-majority contexts, although this was not without danger for respondents. New York–based director Parvez Sharma constructed a film documentary entitled *A Jihad for Love* on LGB issues, primarily on the basis of e-mail interviews.[99] It highlighted the risks facing some LGB Muslim Internet users who were seeking to express themselves, their religion, and their sexuality.

Death ◆ CIES extend to the deceased. This can be presented in the context of advice of appropriate burial rituals, mourning periods, counseling, and wills, all located in online advice forums.[100] Much of this is drawn from interpretations of Islamic sources. Some communities apply the Net to announce the deaths of members, such as the World Federation of Khoja Shi'a Ithna'asheri Muslim Communities, which has for several years maintained a listing of their deceased members.[101] The related Shi'a Ithna'asheri Community of Middlesex keeps a local listing of Muslim graves.[102]

In Karachi, the Wadi-a-Hussain cemetery took this one stage further. It produced a website with memorials and film clips of funerals. These include a database of clips from funerals, which feature all aspects of the ritual.[103] The database is fully searchable by grave number, name, and month/year of death. Each grave reference has a photograph and details of the deceased. The site also has a commercial element, advertising associated funeral services to the public.[104]

In a completely different context, the concept of online memorials for the dead, in relation to CIES, came to prominence with the development of martyrs' memorials for "jihadi" activity by organizations such as Hizbullah and Hamas.[105] The identities of Muslim victims of conflict were also placed in cyberspace: victims of Saddam Hussein's regime had an online memorial.[106] The numbers of civilian casualties of the war in Iraq and its aftermath were recorded in Iraq Body Count and updated regularly. These developments were a natural adjunct to other online activities for iMuslims.[107]

Interpreting Islam

Sacred People ◆ Those Muslims, living and dead, who have a sacred status within their communities' histories hold a prominent place in cyberspace. Most prominent of these would be the Prophet Muhammad, whose biography, sayings, and life are charted in detail online. The caliphs that followed him in ruling the proto-Muslim community, responsible for the rapid spread of Islam, also have a prominent place online. An online picture can be drawn up of those individuals linked with Muhammad's life, not all of whom might be classified as sacred; these include Muslim protagonists and the Prophet's family members, early followers, companions, authorities, and supporters.

To this online historical environment can be added (depending on an individual Muslim's perspective) interpreters of shari'ah, including the founders of the Sunni schools of jurisprudence and their Shi'a equivalents. Interpreters of Islam across the generations have their supporters in cyberspace, if not elsewhere. The debates of philosophers and political thinkers across historical Muslim networks continue in the digital context.

The terms and classifications for such individuals are diverse. The various "holy people" could include saints, *pirs*, and *murids*, who add to this picture of dialogue, disagreement, and exploration of the divine. Within contemporary contexts, prominent descendants of these individuals have their place on the Net, and some are proactive participants in Web activities. Manifestations of religious authority in its different forms are presented online.

Religious authority differs among Muslim sects. The legalistic model offers one approach but is by no means universal. A leader's divine inspiration may be more significant for some Muslims than the number of degrees (if any) that a "scholar" has derived from Islamic institutes of learning. The legal model often appears to dominate cyberspace. The tracts of opinions, sources, and knowledge have a textual basis that can be reproduced and enhanced online. The purpose of a religious opinion may be as part of a religious duty and/or for a political campaign. Each opinion should be taken on its own merits and assessed accordingly.

This reflects the pragmatic and contextual nature of aspects of traditional Islamic decision-making processes. Some of these were only meant to be one-off opinions and statements rather than produced for wide circulation. The development of question-and-answer sites, and the constant online petitioning for responses, is interpreted by some as evidence of "too many questions" from surfers with excess surfing time on their hands. However, it could be said that it represents an opening up of knowledge online—albeit for a Web-literate elite with access to the medium and the time and inclination to go online.

With Web 2.0, the forms of authority transmission incorporate podcasting, video blogs, and social-networking sites. The extension of Internet-technology access (for example, in sub-Saharan Africa) is opening up new markets for specific forms of religious authority, challenging traditional norms. In part, this might represent a reflection of real-world activities but also to some extent an acceleration of competing processes of propagation. Whether presenting the Qur'an or other forms of knowledge, the digital intermediaries who seek to present God's Word online will compete for surfers' attention with other distractions, some more worldly than others. CIES can incorporate cutting-edge approaches to the medium, but all link back to a primary ethos of religious knowledge and expression that, in the eyes of believers, transcends the digital and connects the individual with God.

Analysis of Islamic religious authority, both on- and offline, requires accommodation of ideas of spiritual and legal diversity as well as acceptance of common threads of Muslim understandings.[108] New concepts associated with the transmission of knowledge introduce traditional models of interpretation and understanding and integrate them into digital frameworks. For technologically literate Muslim surfers, there can a specific and intimate relationship between technologies and their religious beliefs, with a liminal or transitory element in between. Clearly there is the potential for it to impact on real-world understandings, one that has increasingly been recognized by Islamic authorities.

The mundane concepts and religious understandings found in cyberspace—but frequently difficult to track and interpret—may be as significant as any headline-generating fatwa, a term that itself is open to interpretation. In the context of CIES, an opinion may be publicized on a website for a couple of days and then disappear from view. Hidden e-mails, lost caches, deleted files, encrypted data, shredded folders, and sheer information overload in a variety of languages mean that certain opinions are lost to the outside observers, as well as adherents to and readers of online Muslim perspectives.

A range of Islamic opinions proclaiming themselves as authoritative is located on the Internet. They have a variety of agendas. These range from tackling the mundane issues of everyday life to providing commentary and inspiring action in relation to world affairs. Generalizations can be difficult, as the formats of the sites vary. Some encourage petitions and questions from readers, with high levels of interactivity, including personal counseling. Others prefer to pronounce on specific issues, perhaps via the presentation of sermons.

Religious authority does not have to be embodied in a scholar or ideologue. God's Revelation through the Qur'an is the authoritative Islamic voice on the Internet. Other voices resonate online, from the Prophet Muhammad to generations of authorities, spiritual leaders, imams, and *murshid*s (religious guides). Added to these voices are those without traditional Islamic science backgrounds, who use the Internet to present their own personal perspectives. Some have sought to promote different forms of Islamic interpretation, ranging from so-called liberal and progressive Islam to the concepts of militaristic jihad.[109]

There was a period where institutions such as al-Azhar or Qom played "catch up," investing resources to develop multilingual resources. The imagination could generate the image of a senior imam, ayatollah, or sheikh sitting at his computer, constructing hypertextual responses across the Net to petitioners. In reality, it is likely to be his intermediaries inputting data, constructing pages, and managing databases.

This raises issues of how content is mediated, translated, and adapted linguistically in its journey into hypertext. In some ways, these dialogues have a historical continuity with traditional modes of interaction and networking. These integrated scholarly and conceptual frameworks date back to patterns of consultation and knowledge transmission established by the Qur'an and the practices of Muhammad.

The shifting nature of Islamic religious authority has been attributed in part to the application of the Internet. This has been in conjunction with other forms of media, such as satellite television: "Many Saudis contend the House of Wahhab's iron grip is slipping with expanded access—partly through the Internet and satellite television—to more-moderate Islamic preachers elsewhere in the Arab world."[110]

Adherents to a specific perspective may be able to establish whether in their eyes a site is legitimate. These include applying sophisticated searching techniques, such as looking for a specific scholar's name, as well as insider knowledge derived from their own communities. Some sites are less transparent in this regard. They may draw in general readers to a perspective that is presented as a definitive interpretation of Islam.

This raises questions on how readers approach and mediate digital media and the sacred Net, especially identifying which dimensions are legitimate. In some cases, that image of imams and scholars directly typing religious opinions or fatwas into a laptop has become reality. This counters the emergence of other "authorities" online, whose training does not necessarily reflect traditional schools or learning. There is a long-term discussion on the legitimacy of "fatwas" and the qualifications to lead online debates. These ideas integrate associated paradigmatic forms and models of dialogue; these could include diverse definitions of the pragmatic interpretation of Islamic sources in the light of contemporary conditions (*ijtihad*) and consultation and consensus with other scholars (*shura*). Scholars, perhaps challenged by such new notions, obliquely suggested that "fatwas, or religious edicts, should only be

Index, Al-Qaradawi.net, May 2004

issued by clerics with religious authority."[111] There remain issues as to how that authority can be defined.

The traditional paradigm of religious authority in Islam has been associated with the training of individuals, usually males, to varying degrees in Islamic seminaries and *madrasas*, often associated with specific *madhhab* or schools of Islamic law. Although there is no equivalent to "priesthood" in Islam, a qualified individual might lead a community in prayer as an imam and become a source for solving religious questions for various levels of society. The role of the traditional imam has not been negated, but now authorities are increasingly emerging online, individually or as part of wider organizations. This reflects, in many ways, the fact that sacred authority is multifaceted and can at times become what Piscatori and Eickelman describe as "one *kind* of authority among others."[112]

Counseling can also emerge through forums beyond the controls of imams in the form of online social networking. Such wiki counseling raises further issues, as readers attempt to assist others in their problems to varying degrees. Load-Islam provided one such service, where readers sought advice on diet, image, religious issues, friendship, and identity.[113]

These perspectives can be seen in conjunction with, and in competition

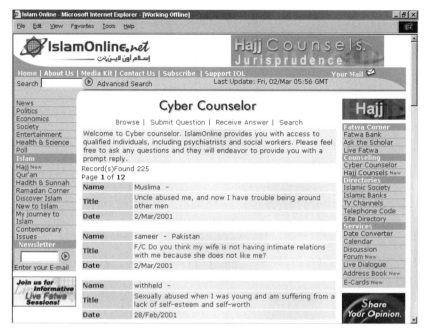

Cyber Counselor, IslamOnline.net, February 2001

with, the major personalities permeating ideas associated with sacred authority in CIEs. Two of the most prominent authoritative voices online are Shaykh Yusuf al-Qaradawi and Ayatollah al-Sistani—high profile Sunni and Shi'a voices, respectively.[114] They are both backed with media outlets to promote their messages and ideas.

As al-Sistani's output was discussed earlier in this book, the focus here is on Qatar-based al-Qaradawi. His supporters made the Internet part of broader media strategies in conjunction with his TV work. The online translation of his works and the reproduction of his materials on affiliated websites has been extremely influential. Qaradawi's supporters were behind Islam Online in both English and Arabic. This features interpretations and religious opinions, including live interaction with scholars for question-and-answer sessions.

Islam Online's cyber counseling and fatwa database focuses on responses to contemporary issues affecting Muslim communities.[115] Questions in some cases are of a highly personal and life-changing nature, particularly those in relation to issues of human relationships and sexuality. These can be highly charged, emotional, and provocative areas, challenging traditional Muslim norms. Questioners adopt pseudonyms. Respondents are counselors and/or scholars, presenting their specific brand of interpretation to a global audience and drawing on aspects of Islamic sources and sciences in the process. Qur'anic precedent is applied where appropriate, and answers are couched in a religious framework.

The Web is also a channel through which such scholars are criticized; for example, the blogger "Mahmood" wrote about al-Qaradawi: "I am at a loss in trying to reconcile his effective edict, for a very renowned scholar, a supposedly learned person, how can things be so black and white in his mind?"[116] Al-Qaradawi's opposition to the Iraq war aroused further online ire when he signed a proclamation issued by the Muslim Brotherhood (and signed by a number of scholars) condemning American action in Iraq.[117]

Shopping around for a religious opinion on a topic is an activity that I recall discussing with Islamic scholars in Pakistan and Malaysia in a period that predated widespread Islamic question-and-answer sites. The phenomenon has now become a dominant one in online discourse. There may be different answers to similar questions, depending on which sites the surfer visits. While the status and profiles of some scholars have increased, questions arise as to whether greater clarity has been achieved for those seeking advice within this knowledge economy.

The recognition of the validity of the Internet as a means of presenting religious discourse and authority has gone beyond conventional geographical, religious, and cultural barriers. Many authorities have entered this dimension of CIES, demonstrating some intriguing networking possibilities. Syrian Grand Mufti Ahmad Kuftaro launched an official site in 2005 that included translations of sermons in several languages, linking to Qur'anic commentaries derived from a Pakistani source. The site is regularly updated with lectures, a biography, and other materials in Russian, Spanish, German, Japanese, Turkish, French, Arabic, and English. This takes Kuftaro's authority far outside of its traditional sphere of influence.[118]

Religious authorities are not inflexible to the application of the Web in specific contexts. Mohammed, a young Saudi preacher, told *al-Hayat*: "The most efficient means of preaching nowadays are the Internet and satellite channels, even though some people tried to spread other teachings by pretending to be them, and hence ruin their reputation."[119]

Equally significant has been the emergence of religious opinions from outside of conventional frameworks. This opens options for those able to challenge and tackle "mainstream" religious opinions via the Web. This can range from imams in "minority," "western" contexts to jihadi authority figures (these are not synonymous) that have applied the technology to boost their profile and the footprint of their authority. These activities are not without risk for their instigators, who may face prosecution.[120]

They have applied technical innovation to galvanize an audience unsatisfied with convention, for which the Net is a natural place to acquire knowledge and converse with peers. It is essential to incorporate understandings of Internet use that go beyond the Middle East into diverse Muslim cultures and frameworks. New models of religious expression have emerged rapidly into the mainstream in tandem with growths in Internet access.[121]

Within this dramatic shift in religious authority models, all forms of Islam are encompassed, some with an emphasis on presenting forms of online religion. From Jerusalem comes a site centering on Shaykh Abd'ar-Rahman as-Shadhili, the spiritual mentor of the Sufi Shadhiliyya order.[122] His significance, in the view of the site's authors, is emphasized online through a website that incorporates an account of a meeting with the Shaykh and discusses his role as one who can draw followers closer to God.

Diversity of Sufi religious authority can be seen in the representation of Naqshbandi International Sufi order, with distinct regional Web spaces, and in sites that represent followers of the Senegalese Shaykh Ahmadu Bamba.[123] Esoteric dimensions of Islam have a digital manifestation, providing online indicators of religious perspectives, philosophies, and symbols, connecting to wider networks of associated understandings. Such materials may contrast with legalistic, political, and jihadi frameworks of Islamic interpretation presented elsewhere on the Internet. They connect, drawing on a technological edge, with long-standing Muslim traditions, historical knowledge frameworks, and diverse ideas of the sacred. Linking into such ideas associated with religious authority are the sermons that can be found online. These form part of a complex media process. Sermons are featured on the radio, TV, print, and CD-ROM recordings—part of the development of what has been described as *al-Islam al-sawti*, or "voiced Islam."[124]

The Egyptian preacher and al-Azhar graduate Amr Khaled adopted an integrated-media strategy for *al-Islam al-sawti*.[125] Khaled's website contains transcripts from many of his "lectures"/sermons. Subjects are varied and provide a populist edge. He offers content for those Muslims living in minority contexts with discussions on Muslims in Britain and a strategy for getting Muslim players into the England soccer team for the 2010 World Cup.[126]

This focus on "popular" subjects is not beyond criticism and was the subject of lively discussion on forums: "Amr Khaled is what I like to call a 'gateway' into religious ignorance (or extremism, take your pick)," stated one commentator, "much in the same way people call marijuana a gateway drug. He tallks [*sic*] about the life of the sa7abi, embelishing [*sic*] as much as possible and then compares them to 'today's youth' and makes you feel essentially unworthy to call yourself a muslim. In addition to this he tries to address the youth in their language and relates to them well, making himself sound like a reasonable person."[127]

Despite such comments, Khaled retained a high level of popularity. His organization applies the Web as part of an integrated multimedia approach, backed by substantial resources in order to deliver his message and enhance his profile(s). While many have been receptive to his Internet message and image, there was a conflict between Khaled and al-Qaradawi in 2006, played out in part over the Internet, over approaches toward the "cartoon crisis."[128]

The capacity of the Internet as a dissemination tool has led to increased focus on its output. Attempts to control and/or counter Web pronouncements have intensified. Certain Saudi clerics, for example, became the focus of authority's ire in their alleged support of militancy and were encouraged to reverse their positions, as articulated in sermons placed on the Web.[129] Other "scholars" made substantial changes to the tone and content of their public pronouncements and themselves became the targets of online abuse.[130]

Many surfers log into fatwa zones online for a variety of reasons. In one case, Muslims applied the Internet to issue a fatwa against Osama bin Laden, via the FEERI website.[131] More "controversial" fatwas have attracted greater publicity and criticism when they have been published online, notably one from Sheikh Yousuf al-Ahmad prohibiting women from working as pilots.[132] Equally contentious was an online statement supporting "militaristic" jihad, signed by "scholars" in Saudi Arabia in November 2004.[133]

Grand Mufti Sheikh Abdulaziz bin Abdullah Aal-al-Sheikh reacted to this and similar fatwas by proclaiming (in a widely circulated statement that appeared online) that "Islam does not tolerate blood shedding, and subsequently it prohibits random killing of people either Muslims or non-Muslims."[134] Confusion over a perceived profusion of fatwas, and in some cases their content, led to the Grand Mufti seeking the imprisonment of some online scholars.[135] He stated, after a prominent case in which fatwas promoting jihad in Iraq were circulated, that "whoever intends to make a mockery of the edicts mocks the faith and scholars. Such a person deserves to be punished in accordance with the Shariah rules in order to deter others from giving misleading edicts usually transmitted on the Internet."[136]

The whole issue of online fatwas and the status of scholars generated heated debate in Saudi Arabia, especially from those concerned about the opinions emerging from outside the influence of official Saudi Arabian muftis. One reaction to this decision was a general discussion on the efficacy of fatwas:

> Over the years, and since the Internet came to the Kingdom, fatwas by people who claim to be sheikhs have been published left and right, poisoning the minds of the younger generation and also taking people's intelligence for granted. Last year, a colleague in Arab News told me of a fatwa by a unpopular sheikh on the Internet who said that it was sinful in Islam for a woman to log on the Internet on her own without a male guardian. Such a fatwa, in my opinion, is sickening. That a person who claims to be a student of Islam doubts the intentions of all Muslim females who log on to the Internet and judges them for misdeeds, is pure prejudice. The Internet, as any other tool, can be used for good or bad. Males are just as responsible as females are when they log on the net. Why should females be doubted only? This fatwa coincides with other nonsense we hear from sheikhs, some of them on our national radio and television, who say that "women are the core of all evil in the world. They should be subdued and looked after carefully."[137]

Sermons, commentaries, and fatwas are central elements of CIES, with many sites offering regularly updated resources. Alminbar.com, a Mecca-based site dedicated to sermons, organizes them thematically and by area of origin in a searchable Arabic and English databases. Alminbar is keen to identify and include the credentials of its contributors: "When we go through the Islamic sites on the Internet, one notices that many sites fail to introduce those who run and supervise the site. This is despite the fact that these sites generally have well balanced and objective material, which is of course praiseworthy and something that we ourselves take pride in at our site."[138] Khutbah.com features sermons, categorized according to Societal Issues, Seeking Knowledge, Islamic Beliefs, and Returning to Allah. The material has a distinct Sunni orientation; it also contains articles, a discussion forum, and an e-mail list. Khutbah.com linked to emanrush.com (which broadcasts audio materials and promotes alMaghrib seminars)

AlMinbar.com, May 2008

and to an educational institute, the alMaghrib Institute, and its founder Ustaadh Muhammad Alshareef, based in Ottowa, Canada.[139] This was a striking example of a single scholar in a minority context presenting his sermons to an international audience in French, German, and English. His work can be accessed through the community forums, which focus on the "tribes" of alMaghrib followers established in North America and appear to be particularly youth oriented (as evidenced in the posting, "AlMaghrib in MEMPHIS: Everyone's Sayin' Yyyyyeaaahhhhh!!!!"[140]).

Online sermon production and circulation has become a global concern, from the largest international institute of Islamic learning to the smallest mosque. Productions transcend international boundaries and integrate a wide range of interests. The impact of sermons in Muslim-minority contexts is significant in that they present a voice or voices demonstrating that Muslims are proactive in addressing specific regional and cultural concerns, which may be very different to majority contexts.

Other Religious Obligations

As can be seen above, iMuslims can find advice and explanations relating to aspects of many elements of Islamic interpretation through Internet channels. This is significant when the Internet is the first point of call for information in many contexts. Provision of online information encompasses the basic necessities of life, with many sites endeavoring to present definitive resources on Islam. The following section explores some of these elements in detail as a way of approaching different aspects of the online knowledge economy and its relationship with sacred dimensions of Islam.

Food ❖ One example of this specialization of CIES is linked to issues surrounding food. There are strict criteria as to what is permissible (halal) or not within Muslim diets. This includes clear prohibitions on certain foods (such as pork) and drinks (such as anything with alcohol content). Specific processes for the production of foods are required, including "appropriate" methods of slaughtering animals. These criteria are based on the Qur'an and other Islamic sources and are topics discussed in detail online.

Some sites have dedicated themselves to this task, such as the Canadian Eat Halal site. This contains information on specific foods, advice on animal-slaughter methods, recipes, a restaurant guide, health advice, and a product directory. Commercial links are incorporated for products such as halal meat and vitamins.[141]

It is also possible to search for an appropriate restaurant online. The term *zabihah* is linked to animal-slaughtering methods. Zabihah.com contains a searchable database of restaurants, reviews, and advice. Zabihah.com claimed "13,960 reviews of 3,614 establishments," primarily in North America and Europe.[142] Organized regionally, it links into Eat Halal's database. Travel issues are also included within the reviews of airline meals based on various Islamic criteria.

The site demonstrates how CIES can link to other resources and tools through the integration of Google maps into reviews. It also offers readers the chance to provide feedback and their own reviews on subjects that occasionally go beyond food issues. Site creator Shaheed Amanullah received "angry e-mails from owners of halal markets and restaurants, who complain about bad reviews, and sometimes they even threaten lawsuits."[143]

I examined the eat-halal.com database for East London in the UK, being familiar with several restaurants in that area. This is a region with a high percentage of Muslims, especially in the boroughs of Tower Hamlets and Newham, which have strong links to Bangladesh and Pakistan, respectively. The website raised controversial issues. Online critics discussed how "cheap meat" was being used in some of the restaurants, with related health implications. Others were critical of halal restaurants in which alcohol was served, as consumption of intoxicants is prohibited within Islamic sources.[144] "Some of the non-muslims [*sic*] customers were drunk," one critic complained. "How could a nice muslim family or sisters in Islam could attend a restaurant like this. They should set an example but they are merely interested making large profits in the haram [forbidden] way. Another fact is there are [*sic*] behind East London Mosque (Masjid) and London Muslim Centre, why does any muslim brother from that masjid, check and correct on them."[145] This stimulated a sustained online dialogue, although one reader believed that the Web was an inappropriate forum for discussing the intoxication issue. What is significant here is how the Web has become a place for everyday and mundane (on one level) issues such as eating out and not just major life-and-death concerns.

Financial Transactions ◆ Muslim networks throughout history were often formed on the basis of trade, through which the reach of Islam extended. As Islam expanded from its Arabian origins, merchants had prominent roles in the conversion of people along many global routes. Traders took Islam along the Silk Road to China, following Muslim conquests in the Indian subcontinent and commercial opportunities throughout Southeast Asia. Trade is also a significant element within contemporary online Muslim networks, with trade routes acting as conduits for religious ideas as well as goods in the electronic marketplace.

The Internet has become a *souq*, or marketplace, not just for ideas but also for products with an Islamic ethos. Areas of eBay sell Qur'ans, hijab, and other Islamic clothing, as well as software, multiformat recordings, books, calligraphy, food, prayerbeads, and other products for Muslim online shoppers.[146] The application of halal transactions and availability of Islamically appropriate products across frontiers has enhanced the position for businesses selling Muslim goods and opened up new networks of communication and commerce.

Isolated communities and individuals can lock into any Muslim-oriented product available on the Internet. This product may be a book that provides a specific interpretative understanding of the Qur'an, in line with ethnocultural-political-linguistic interests. It may be an item of clothing, including the latest hijab fashion. It may be music from a *nashid* group in Malaysia, or devotional music from Senegal. This concept also extends to download options, such as music material available through iTunes or movie downloads via BitTorrent.

Islamic goods can be located though mainstream electronic marketplaces. Amazon.com stocks a wide range of books, music, and DVDs that could be classified as Islamic. Cinematic releases with Muslim themes and actors and/or from Islamic contexts can be purchased online. The transaction may be conventional, using credit card and Paypal, but it equally may apply the use of the electronic dinar ("e-dinar"). This is a system of currency, advocated by some Muslim interest groups, based on weights and measures from the time of the Prophet Muhammad and his early community.

The financial sector is a significant element of the integration of Islamic Internet applications into the lifestyles of iMuslims. This is especially relevant for those who use Islamic banks, whose financial management and control is based on diverse Islamic principles. In general terms, the concept of *shari'ah*-compliant banks integrates concepts of ethical investment and observance of financial management that does not seek interest on loans or investments. Integrating electronic-banking elements into an Islamic interface has required observance of the basic banking principles, along with conventional banking issues of security and use. Services are now available in a variety of languages, tailored to specific markets and cultural-religious groups in the personal and corporate sectors. Mainstream banks have also started offering electronic Islamic banking to their customers.

In some contexts, Islamic banking principles extend to ideas of space to include gender-segregated service options, such as separate queues, tills, and staff-customer interaction. Countries with long-established Islamic banking services and a record of information and communication technology investment (such as Malaysia) have seen substantial increases of growth within this sector. The Islamic element of a banking site may be subtle rather than overt: Bank Islam Malaysia, for example, has prayer times discretely placed on its entry page, but other than its name it has no other specifically Islamic identity marker. In many ways, this reflects the experience of entering a real Islamic bank branch, certainly in the Malaysian context. Their clients also include people who are not Muslim but perceive the services as advantageous from their personal financial perspective.[147]

The concept of online banking with an Islamic ethos allows for halal transactions in the marketplace and acts as a significant undercurrent to the economy of CIES. This can be extended to a variety of financial concerns and businesses operating under a Muslim framework at both global and local levels. It is inconceivable that there would be resistance to the concept of the integration of information technology to assist in Islamic banking and financial processes. Many banks employ their own religious expertise, with scholars on boards and in advisory roles. However, there may be objections to the ways in which businesses present themselves as "Islamic" and their interactions with supposedly corrupt governments and institutions. At a grassroots level, the popularity of the *halwa* system of currency exchange, where money can be immediately transferred from one country to another electronically, has had a profound impact.

Living an Islamic life online has extended into many new opportunities. These may mirror different forms of customary practices to a degree, but Muslims have also engineered new forms of Islamically appropriate behavior, especially in terms of transactions. Muslim merchants now seek good star ratings on eBay or advertise through banners on Islamic websites or through services such as GoogleAds. The variety of products and services advertised through GoogleAds range from links to sites containing online Islamic Studies courses and requests for donations to Islamic charities to the marketing of Islamic software.

Such developments have interested a number of scholars, some of whom have active roles within Islamic banking. They have also necessitated the development of fatwas associated with online practices relating to finance. Islamtoday.com has issued fatwas associated with affiliate programs, the use of cookies, and Internet referral services.[148]

Defending the Sacred

The Internet has also been applied as a tool to defend perceived Muslim values. Perhaps the most significant example of the application of the Internet as a mobilization tool by Muslim interests followed publication of a series of cartoons in the Danish newspaper *Jyllands-Posten* in September 2005. This led to controversy and international reactions—eventually.

The twelve cartoons, featured on a double-page spread of the print edition of the newspaper, illustrated an article on "freedom of expression." Different artists devised the cartoons on the page, which was entitled "Muhammeds-ansigt" ("The face of Muhammad"), and at least five of the cartoons appear to present a caricature of the Prophet.[149] The article was associated with the difficulties a writer had found in locating illustrations for a book on Muhammad: artists had been reluctant, for fear of drawing the ire (literally) of certain Muslim parties. *Jyllands-Posten*'s editorial discussed this issue, and showed the series of cartoons commissioned in response. The cartoons were also published in the online version of the newspaper, and subsequently copied by readers onto other sites and blogs.

The representation of Muhammad in the cartoons received a specific focus within ensuing comments in CIES. Depicting the Prophet in any pictorial context raises specific problematic concern, especially because representing the human form in any illustrative manner is condemned by some religious authorities. This has been the focus of conjecture, as the history of Islamic arts (and art produced by Muslims) demonstrates that figurative art has a prominent role in some Muslim cultural contexts.[150] Partially as a response to the confusion surrounding this issue, the ethos of the Muslim arts has historically focused instead on other forms of expression, such as calligraphy or geometric arts.

The Internet was applied by some Islamic and Muslim interests in order to communicate reactions and coordinate protests associated with the cartoons. It became a tool for mobilizing Muslim opinion(s) across borders and continents, while being utilized as a means of articulating causes for concern to wider audiences. The cartoons themselves retained their place online, despite hacking attempts, but cyberspace itself was not a specific target for protests. Few attempts, at least by formally constituted bodies such as Islamic institutions, were made to shut down sites that were "offensive" to Muslims, although other forms of pressure, filtering, and deterrents might apply. This was in contrast to the SuraLikeIt controversy in the late 1990s, when al-Azhar University attempted to have a website closed for purporting to present "new" Qur'anic verses, a campaign that generated further publicity for the forgers.[151]

The cartoon controversy may have taken place without the Internet and computers, but it would have been more difficult to coordinate and disseminate viewpoints and source materials. It might be compared with *The Satanic Verses* controversy in the late 1980s and the attendant Iranian "fatwa" on Salman Rushdie, condemned for his fictionalized representation of the Prophet. This campaign relied in part on fax machines for the dissemination of materials and logistical arrangements, alongside "traditional" telephonic exchanges, but it lacked the "feedback" and input from ordinary observers and participants. There were still demonstrations in relation to *The Satanic Verses*, and selected and edited images from demonstrations were transmitted across the world through the world's print and broadcast media.[152] Of course, the impact of these media forms in their more technically refined twenty-first-century manifestations on the cartoon controversy and its aftermath cannot be questioned. The images first appeared in a single newspaper; news of local protests in Denmark spread elsewhere through newspaper and broadcast reports.

Anyone downloading *Jyllands-Posten*'s cartoons in a domestic Muslim context—for example, in a public space such as a cybercafé—might have been taking some risks unless it was for the purposes of campaigning or criticism. What is significant is that, throughout the cartoon controversy, the Internet became a natural place for a myriad of discussions on the topic. While it is not the first issue to be taken on in this way, it represented a significant milestone within CIES. There was integration between real-world issues and contexts, narrowing the gap between the digital Islamic interface and traditional Muslim communications, magnified when defense of the sacred was the primary objective.

Concluding Comment

No interpretation of CIES is complete without understanding the basic principles of Islam as articulated in cyberspace. The Internet can touch upon the dimensions of the sacred and give surfers insights into Muslim diversity of expression and understanding, often far away from the daily headlines generated by other media. The key principles of Islam have a digital representation that closely links to the real-world understandings while also taking on new facets that relate to ideas of online religion.

In some areas, the impact of CIES on Muslim practices is more explicit than others. Generalizations are impossible, but clearly there are individual cases where services have a life-changing nature. Elements relating to online marriage services and financial transactions have an obvious impact. Microareas of lifestyle preferences and choices influenced either directly or indirectly through exposure to online content cannot be quantified. For other elements of ritualistic behavior and practice, the impact is more subtle and difficult to measure. The empirical evidence has to be observed and recorded in order that a more complete impression of contemporary Muslim life can be constructed.

We may never know the impact of online fatwas in terms of individuals or the number of people who follow them, but they can form an influential source of searchable materials for surfers seeking discrete answers to difficult questions. The fact that so many organizations and individuals make sustained effort to publish fatwas regularly would suggest that they believe the content is having an impact, which may be cost-effective and comparable with other media in some contexts.

Assessing the impact of material is always problematic, and from my phenomenological approach, it presents a different set of challenges from the need to gather and record Islamic activities online. As will be seen in other chapters, the impact of online news media and blogs can have a formative effect on the development of trends and the creation of new forms of online Muslim networks. The anecdotal evidence generated in forums and blogs, as well as my personal discussions with a range of contacts, suggests that great attention is paid to all elements of this evolving discourse on Islam that can be found on the Internet.

While significant access issues apply, CIES can touch the phenomena and experiences of people at the grassroots level while also offering an approach toward the different forms of decision-making guidance provided by the Internet. For some scholars and organizations, the Internet has become a natural outlet for the rapid dissemination of religious dialogue and authority, facilitating access to a variety of readerships. New loyalties can be generated, and Muslim network models are developed and enhanced. All can trace their loyalties back to the Qur'an, which remains the dominant theme in CIES.

{ 4 }

The Islamic Blogosphere

Blogs have become critical adjuncts to the Islamic knowledge economy. This chapter shows how they draw upon many facets associated with Web 2.0 to open up a dynamic space for iMuslims to participate in online collaboration and forms of information gathering and exchange. The discussion provides an overview of the Islamic blogosphere, showing many of its significant nodes and hubs. This is identified as a key area relating to Islamic and Muslim discourse online, and it also provides a sense of how further developments in Web 2.0 social-networking tools might impact on cyber-Islamic environments.

Awareness of the significance of blogs has increased exponentially in the contexts of CIES, given the enormous number of Islam and Muslim-related blogs that have emerged in various forms online. For the purposes of managing the megabytes of blogging data, I have organized Muslim blogs on a regional basis. As discussed in chapter 1, I drew upon a range of RSS feeds, aggregators, blog rolls, and other sources to visit sites.

There was a core group of long-standing pages that were checked on at least a weekly basis. During the writing of this chapter, some of these blogs had relocated, disappeared, or undergone technological enhancement. New blogs also emerged, which have also been placed into the discussion. This provides an opportunity to highlight distinctive elements as well as similarities and to explore specifically Islamic-related elements that they contain.

It is not possible to generalize on the social profiles of bloggers in CIES because there are limitations in terms of acquisition of data. Given the implicit imperative factors relating to access, it would appear that many of the bloggers discussed are either in higher education or have finished it. Some are professionals, including IT specialists and scientists with high levels of Web literacy. There are also a number of journalists, using blogs where other channels are more restrictive or to promote their other output. Those working within political-religious offices, including presidents and imams, have also found the concept of blogs appealing.

Narratives range from the politicized to the personal. Some seek to comment on interpretative issues, linking into Islamic sources and networks. Content may have a formalized structure in which discussion is backed up by quotes from the Qur'an, Hadith, and jurisprudence sources. The format of the blog may be a convenient method of imparting content that would otherwise have emerged on a more "conventional" website. Others draw on the diary nature of weblogs, posting about their daily activities and responding to the news with commentary and links to other online sources. There are, of course, many points in between. Some bloggers do not post regularly; others appear to be "always on" and blog with a serious intensity.

This has been facilitated, in particular, with the expansion of Web access and wireless, as well as interfaces for blogging made available through cell phones and BlackBerrys. Their output, which may be the result of collaborative networking that can transcend national boundaries, rivals the content of traditional media sources. A blog may translate, edit, plagiarize, and/or hyperlink to other materials. Increasingly, this includes video and other multimedia content.

In short, blogging is a dynamic and rapidly evolving sector in cyberspace that has been drawn upon by iMuslims of all political and religious persuasions. The ease of posting and opportunities for anonymity have meant that jihadi content has also emerged within blog formats. These have posted on operational activities and presented propaganda materials, including media clips. While service providers have removed some of this jihadi content, the ease of the format means that it quickly emerges elsewhere on another blog. Jihadi sources will be discussed separately in chapter 5.

New forms of Muslim networks are evident within the blogosphere, in particular those taking advantage of Web 2.0 (and its successors). Dan Burstein discusses how blogs bring together a broad range of technologies in a fulfillment of what was seen as the Internet's perceived potential in the 1990s. This is in conjunction with them being "the raw, human face of the brave new technological world":

> Blogging, in addition to being a huge phenomenon in its own right, is a key metaphor for interactivity community-building, and genuine conversation: one to one, one to many, many to one, many to many. Years

from now, the kind of blogs we know today may or may not exist
in a big way as a discrete genre, but the breakthrough principles of
community-building and genuine activity they represent will be incorporated into the way much of our media functions in the future. Blogging is the "killer app" of the current generation of Web innovation,
just as email and instant messaging were at the core of the last version.[1]

Burstein also notes how blogs were segmenting, with some becoming professional enterprises, while major media players had entered the service
provision area. CIES are part of this interaction and themselves can represent a viable element of interaction between and within political-religious
interests.

The impact of blogs reaches from the cybercafé in the *souq* to governmental offices and international media. They can be a point of protest
and/or a propagation of Islamic beliefs and values. For blogging iMuslims,
there can be little separation between online and offline worlds. Blogs have
become a significant adjunct to, if not the primary thrust of, conversation,
intellectual stimulus, and Muslim networking. They reach down into the
Long Tail of segmentation and nuanced content delivery, with highly specialized content emerging throughout sectors of the Islamic blogosphere.

This momentum intensifies as access and technical literacy increases. It
is recognized that many elements of the mundane and trivial are also located
in blogs, although these in themselves can offer insight into popular culture
and ethics, including their intersection with Islam. The personal nature of
blogs is in marked contrast to other areas of CIES. This is reflected in Zizi
Papacharissi's comment: "Viewed as the latest trend in online use and
publishing, blogs preset a personalized, self-referential and self-serving use
of the Internet, a medium first introduced as informational that then established a following based on social communication avenues it provided."[2]

This is an important distinction in our understanding of CIES: blogs
open up forms of Muslim discourse to analysis that can have an extremely
personal focus. This can contrast with those more journalistic offerings
within the information marketplace, which still fall under the banner of
blogs. In terms of CIES, these contrasts can be equally valid ways of approaching the discourse of iMuslims.

Not all bloggers discussed here would necessarily define themselves at
first (or at all) as "Islamic" or "Muslim" bloggers. Some might describe
themselves using the Arabic term *mudawin*, which has been applied in
relation to defining "blogger."[3] This is an interesting application of the

term, being derived from the verb "d-w-n," which is defined as "to record, write down, set down, put down in writing."[4] Arabic terms used for "blog" include *mufakkira*, with connotations associated with diaries and note-books.[5] Other terms will no doubt emerge in Muslim contexts in relation to other aspects of the Internet. This forms part of an overall response to technical development and the need for specific Arabic Computer Infor-mation Technology (CIT) terminology. In this regard, the Arabeyes Project was developing its own technical Arabic-English collaborative dictionary.[6]

Blogging represents a significant element in an interactive evolutionary process that entered the mainstream to inform processes of debate, knowl-edge dissemination, and authority reinforcement. Particularly relevant has been the extremely personal angle of blogging, which took it away from conventional website construction or chat-room participation, especially in the ways in which individual blogging personalities were developed and reinforced through their posting activities.

Popular notions relating to the blog genre and its status were initially often negative, it being seen as an inferior form of journalism or a place for trivial chat. These are reflected in Mark Tremayne's discussion of the myths and realities relating to the blogosphere.

> A reading of popular press and the earliest published research of the blogosphere reveals some contradictions. The blogosphere is described as a forum for political discussion or, alternately, a collection of elec-tronic diaries written by adolescents. It is described as a virtual public sphere and a place for spreading rumors. It is described as highly interactive and not. It is described as a hangout for young, educated, technically savvy and conservative men and also as egalitarian. It is described as a worldwide phenomenon and as dominated by the United States.[7]

It is apparent that these contradictions and qualities (depending on your point of view) manifest themselves in CIEs to various degrees. Blogs repre-sent a significant networking tool for iMuslim "netizens" to communicate with, and their impact continues to intensify in local and global perspec-tives. One must understand the specific dynamics taking place within and between diverse blogging zones. Some have a journalistic nature, often aiming for a mass audience, while others form part of a subgenre of online diaries and draw upon the interactive elements of Web 2.0. Blogs with an Islamic focus can represent a challenge to mainstream forms of media, with an influence in political-religious spheres that has resulted, in some cases, in their suppression by authorities and/or public pressure. Within the context of CIES, there remains an implicit negativity from other elements of the media in relation to blogs.

One key issue is determining why iMuslims turn to blogs. In a study of blog use and gratification research, Barbara Kaye explores the motivations for using blogs and introduces a framework that may be relevant when exploring the Islamic blogosphere. Drawing on a series of motivational items, these were "grouped into 10 broader motivational blocks: Blog Presentation/Characteristics, Personal Fulfillment, Expression/ Affiliation with Bloggers and Blog Users, Information Seeking, Intellectual/Aesthetic Fulfillment, Anti-Traditional-Media Sentiment, Guidance/ Option Seeking, Convenience, Political Surveillance, and Fact Checking."[8] These categories are as relevant to CIES in many ways, although if research were undertaken to analyze the motivations of those within the Islamic blogosphere, one could anticipate an overarching religious factor having greater dominance within the framework. One might also link this model with the earlier discussion in this book on reader profiles to determine whether motivations might vary when iMuslims connect to blogs. On another level, it is relevant to link blogs with other aspects of CIES and Web 2.0 contexts to which they may be integrated. Kaye's categories could be coupled to Hossein Derakhshan's suggestion that blogs could be described by applying the metaphors of "Windows (culture, information); Bridges (society, activism); Cafés (politics)."[9] This might be a useful model for other sectors of the so-called blogosphere, or networks of blogging communities.

In terms of Muslim networks, they are a response to the notion that models are fluid and responsive to technical and societal change, particularly in a frame of reference where ideas can be communicated immediately and received and responded to by literate and technologically enabled bloggers. Tremayne makes some pertinent comments relating to the blogosphere as a network. He notes the advantage of its communication being in many cases archived, and that its social ties can be tracked through a blog roll of recommended links and through links to other posts: "Links of both types are directional: I may consider you part of my social network but you may not consider me part of yours. Directionality is important in calculating the centrality of a node in a network. Collectively, these links and the blogs connected by them comprise the blogosphere."[10]

The roles of these hyperlinks are significant indicators in understanding how the Islamic blogosphere(s) function and the complex relationships between high-profile hubs and peripheral nodes within an online network. They also impact on how information is produced.

> An effect of network-based communication is to shift emphasis from information producing to an "information synthesis culture." Information synthesis only comes to be seen in disparities of power on the Internet. Some authors and websites become central focal points by their selective limiting and organizing of information; or strong personal voice [*sic*] attracts readers by providing synthesis. There may be hundreds of blogs with small groups of readers interested in the person or issue being discussed. In them, power comes to rest in a relatively limited number of sources who are compiling, organizing, and synthesizing information from across the network.[11]

It may be possible to talk about Islamic synthesis cultures in relation to cyberspace and information networking. There are, of course, many examples of analogue Islamic synthesis cultures across Muslim networks as well. Many maintain continuity online. This is apparent when exploring blogs in CIES, where there are certainly examples of selective information organization and also strong personal voices. Despite access and literacy issues, a sector within Muslim cyberspace prefers blogs as a tool for discussion and networking on issues of religion, culture, society, and politics as well as faith. There is a sense of linkage between these zones and other sectors of CIES. Blogging provides a conduit of interaction that further extends and synthesizes models of digital Islamic understandings.

In the final analysis, bloggers may not be writing about Islam or define themselves as Muslim, but they may still influence how the Islamic blogosphere is perceived. This may incorporate intra-Muslim perspectives, with bloggers and readers learning about their peers through their online articulation. Numerous Islamic blogs confront media stereotypes, particularly in Western contexts, which make them crucial to a holistic understanding of CIES. They provide readers access into the personal perspectives of individuals on critical issues. This occurs in a context that is evolving rapidly and developing new networks and nodes.[12]

Observing the Islamic Blogosphere

Monitoring blogging developments requires close scrutiny of a variety of channels. Dedicated blogging portals and aggregators, themselves based on RSS feeds, endeavor to index the blogosphere with varying degrees of success, and certainly without applying scientific or academic criteria. A number of significant Muslim bloggers used English as their communication medium in the formative period. There was a limited availability of specific software in other languages. Arabic writers were putting themselves online using conventional Web tools in the early period of blog development, but these lacked the immediacy and ease of use of specific, automated blogging tools. Popular tools such as Moveable Type and Blogger functioned in Roman script and required knowledge of the English language.

Equivalent tools became more widely available in Arabic and other languages and scripts. Arabic blogging, after a slow start, became an increasingly competitive sector for service providers and portals to become involved with. In 2005 Fastlink, Jeeran, al-Bawaba, and Maktoob launched free blog services in both Arabic and English.[13] Serdal, a pioneer blogger from the United Arab Emirates, recognized the potential impact of Arabic-language blogs in terms of social networking and their prospects for transforming Muslim society.[14]

Blogging was also seen as an opportunity to promote "democracy" within Islamic contexts by some external interests. Spirit of America made an Arabic blogging tool available in 2005, although concerns were expressed as to whether output derived through the application's use might be censored. It defended itself against charges that it was monitoring or censoring content.[15] Spirit of America supported Blog Safer: The Anoniblogging Wiki. This provided detailed information on anonymous blogging in Arabic, Farsi, and other languages.[16]

Farsi blogging was well established through the development of language applications by 2001. Urdustan.com was offering tools for blogging in Urdu as part of a community portal promoting the online use of the language.[17] Bangla (Bengali) blogging became available in 2006, with a Dhaka-based Norwegian company developing a Bangla script tool.[18]

A number of portals and resources gathered together selections of blogs relevant to CIEs. Global Voices Online became a central introductory reference point for the discussion of blogs with its country-by-country scope and network of informed correspondence.[19] Among other options, Toot selected 146 elite blogs and associated RSS feeds with a focus on the Middle East.[20]

It is only by dipping into these entry points that one can acquire a sense of the complexity within the Islamic Blogosphere. A pioneering portal in this respect was Islamic Xangans. In 2006 this listed over 200 individual pages as part of a blog community and a wider network of related services.

The blogs ranged from the extremely "religious" Talibatulilm ("student of knowledge")—focused on "memorizing the Qur'an, studying. . . . [Y]ea its a nerdy thing to say but i just love to study!!"—to Binag3e's Harry Potter–centered Islamic blog.[21] Binag3e's eclectic combination of themes is typical of the ways in which there is a synthesis of influences in this area of CIES.

Other Xangan members presented their own mélange of backgrounds and ideas. Xangan member Mike Holmes discussed his survival of Hurricane Katrina. His blog displayed family photos and explained Muslim principles. Elsewhere, his site featured a backdrop based on the *South Park* TV program. There were also photos of favorite cars, with the banner "Muslims Kick Ass."[22]

This combination of influences was not unusual. Xangans represented a strong ethos of social networking. Sites held links to other related "favorite" blogs and opportunities for community members to dialogue. Such a microcommunity can be linked through thematic tags to other related interests. The motivations for affiliating were varied, from dating and friendship to the propagation of Islamic values.

Islamic agendas are not necessarily paramount in many bloggers' minds. Haitham Sabbah, a Kuwaiti-born Jordanian national with Palestinian origins, blogged because of his disappointment about how Muslims and Arab cultures were represented in the mainstream media.[23] This is a critical point for bloggers from both Middle Eastern and wider Islamic contexts, the two not being necessarily synonymous. Blogging becomes the latest in a historical line of responses, pacific and otherwise, to the orientalism discussed and exposed by Edward Said and others.[24]

The idea that blogging can be a defense mechanism used to protect and reinforce Islamic culture—part of an overall strategy or simply a cry for help—is worthy of consideration. However, that may sound particularly negative: pride in religion and reinforcement of culture can also be expressed through the pages. The frustrations of some within Islamic contexts in relation to governments, politics, or religious issues are represented within blogs. The trickle-down impact from online discourse into offline society is a significant consideration. The separation of the two spheres is for some an increasingly redundant concept.

In 2005 Ahmed al-Omran of the Saudi Jeans blog noted that blogging was attracting Arab media attention, with introductory guides appearing in newspapers.[25] He commented on the state of blogging as it related to Arabic and English. Al-Omran, a pharmacy student based in Riyadh, suggested that users of each language were living in separate worlds, although some may have been journeying in between the zones.[26] Muslim networks are never clear-cut, especially in terms of issues of language and expression.

There is some truth in this. Accepting that not all Arabic bloggers are necessarily Islamic in orientation or write about religious issues, many of the elements of the Islamic blogosphere remain separate and not necessarily connected to one another. Significant language barriers exist between and within different zones of the Muslim worlds, and Arabic is not always a social lubricant. The evidence suggests that within Arabic and English blogging zones, there are also many separate worlds and networks based on issues relating to cultural, political, and religious factors as much as on geographical location. One has to move away from the stereotype of a single Muslim voice, especially in the blogosphere, where there can be a lively exchange of views.

Muslim blogs demonstrate capacity for openness and free expression made available through the Web, which may be appealing to some readers. But mutual understanding can be problematic on a number of levels: a synthesis of Islamic terminology and Internet slang can coexist within a blog. It helps if the reader is familiar with both and tolerant of their intersection online within this Islamic knowledge economy.

Muslim Blog Networking in the Middle East

Throughout history, the Middle East has been represented in many ways—culturally, religiously, economically, linguistically, cartographically, politically, and as a state of mind. Now it also has digital representation through the numerous voices of the blogosphere, and especially through those who define themselves as "Muslim." There are numerous definitions of "Middle East." While recognizing the inherent problems of the term, I have used it here to encompass the Arabic-speaking world, together with Iran and Turkey. Within Middle Eastern Islamic spheres, each blogger's personal motivation will vary and need not be any different to the motives of other bloggers from other contexts. Islam may implicitly inform the commentaries, content, and boundaries of what is discussed.

The Kingdom of Saudi Arabia (KSA) offers many examples in this regard. The KSA may be the "hub" of the Islamic worlds due to the presence of the Ka'bah in Mecca, the focus and direction of prayer for all Muslims. The Arabian Peninsula was the Prophet Muhammad's birthplace and the environment in which Islam was first propagated. Despite this status, the KSA is not the center of the Islamic blogosphere or CIES.

Determining how many blogs are emerging from the KSA, as with any country, is problematic for a variety of reasons, and it is not the intention here to make any precise calculations. The estimated number of blogs does not provide any useful indicator as to content, quality, orientation, or origins of bloggers. It can be more useful to look at portals and services that have gathered and categorized blogs to create their own listings and blog rolls. The aggregator Saudi Blogs provides links to over 300 recommended blogs and RSS feeds (Arabic, English, and bilingual).[27]

The KSA as a whole has many more proactive bloggers, although the activity has not been without risk. In 2003 three bloggers were imprisoned for eighteen months for their online activities.[28] It was not clear from official statements what the charges were based upon, but these prosecutions did not prevent bloggers in the KSA from being proactive and vocal in their application of the medium. These can range in quality and orientation.

The Official Community of Saudi Bloggers (OCSAB) sought to represent blogging in the KSA, although whether it was "official" was open to question. OCSAB's listing covered a range of categories. In addition to commentaries on news and current affairs, listings from the arts to technology could be found on OCSAB across the Saudi blogosphere. In 2007 OCSAB suggested that the number of blogs emanating from the KSA was 1,000, a figure that might be disputed elsewhere.[29] OCSAB's page also linked to commentaries on current affairs, demonstrating its perspective. In September 2006 this included a link to the Muslim World League's discussion on Pope Benedict's controversial comments about Islam.[30]

OCSAB's definitions of a "Saudi blog" irritated a number of bloggers in Saudi Arabia. In a series of articles outlining what constituted a Saudi blog, OCSAB demanded that all such blogs be in Arabic, except when calling people to Islam. Saudi Jeans's Ahmed al-Omran commented: "If OCSAB think those who blog in English do it because they can't blog in Arabic, are not proud of their culture and religion, or have some kind of an identity crisis, then they are wrong. And if they think they can this way overcome the leadership of Saudi blogs written in English, then they are so wrong. Content is king, and it does not matter in what language it is written."[31]

Al-Omran also believed that OCSAB was equating liberalism with secularism and believed liberalism was somehow against Islam. He wryly noted: "Well, I don't think that being a liberal contradicts with being a Muslim. I'm a liberal, and I'm damn proud of it. In the same time, I try to be a devoted Muslim, and I don't feel any contradictions between the two."[32]

OCSAB denied having any input into regulation of blogging, as did the KSA's Communication and Information Technology Commission.[33]

With the thousands of KSA-related blogs that emerged in cyberspace, blogging added a new dimension to social dynamics and discussion about Islam, Muslims, and Islamic issues in the KSA. A young and relatively affluent population guarantees that the use of Internet social-networking tools will continue to develop in significance for the discussion of political-religious issues and cultural concerns in the KSA. Opportunities for the use of multimedia and Web 2.0 applications have been seized by many KSA bloggers.

There was an intensely personal element to some blogs from the KSA, offering openness and (at times) an insight into life in the kingdom: Farah's Sowaleef was subtitled "The Everyday Natterings of an Exhausted, Repressed, and Bored 'Saudi' Arabian Chick." It offered photographs, usually taken with a cell phone, and comment in Arabic and English on issues about life and identity within the KSA. The blog's then-twenty-year-old author, Farooha from Qaseem in Najd, was based in Riyadh, having spent a formative period in Virginia.[34] In between photos of shopping malls and shopkeepers, Farooha chatted on issues of dress code in response to readers' questions, determining the potential for irony when wearing Dior sunglasses over her veil.[35]

Farooha also explored issues of religion within the KSA. This included the negative opinions of some Saudis toward converts and discussion on the restrictions placed on individuals by people in Najd: "Quite frankly, I am tired of hearing, 'but Ibn Baz said this about Shiites,' or 'but Ibn Ethaimeen said that about women driving.' Ibn Baz was a great sheikh, as was his counterpart Ibn Ethaimeen. They both had and remain to have my utter respect. Both were productive *ulema* [scholars] who contributed much to Hanbali Islam. However, they are not prophets; nor are they Gods themselves. They are human beings just as we are. If we choose to disagree with them, we are in the end of the day free to."[36]

The extent to which this opinion piece on famous Saudi Islamic scholars and the Hanbali "school" of Islamic jurisprudence (*madhhab*) was a typical view in the KSA is open to question. To find it expressed on a blog in the public domain, amid discussion on popular culture, shopping, friends, and other "twenty-something" topics, was intriguing. Farooha took care in moderating the content of many of her postings and responses. The chat/feedback software Haloscan was used, suggesting a proactive and largely sympathetic readership in the KSA. This may be because she was writing primarily in English and less likely to cause concern to Arabic-only speakers in the KSA. However, her blog disappeared. Farooha reemerged in October 2006 with Adventures of a Lipstick Wahhabi, in which she continued to comment on religious issues and popular culture in the KSA.[37]

Farooha represented a good example of how aspects of Web 2.0 have been integrated into a blog, a pattern repeated on other high-profile KSA blogs such as Saudi Jeans. One of two blogs written by Ahmed al-Omran, Saudi Jeans attained prominence in Saudi and wider blogging circles.[38] The blog kept a close eye on censorship issues, noting that a KSA agency blocked the Internet Wayback Machine and the Blogspot service. This meant that surfers could not obtain archived copies of blogs that had disappeared from cyberspace, and neither could they use a popular blogging service, although alternative options were available.

In his Saudi Jeans postings, al-Omran discussed everyday encounters with authority in different forms. This was emphasized in a discussion on the *muttawa* (religious police) in relation to religious authority and censorship. He was confident enough to provide a perspective that would be more difficult to express in another forum—for example, an opinion piece in a KSA newspaper.[39] In some of his posts, there was an underlying sense of frustration and an indication of bias over the role of some scholars.[40]

Saudi Jeans included an account of a visit to Medina, where restrictions apparently prevent people from undertaking specific ritualistic practices.[41] Ideology that has been linked to Wahhabi practices suggests in general terms that praying or making visits to cemeteries, in particular those containing the remains of significant religious figures, is prohibited or not recommended. This is in part because, in their interpretation, it represents a distraction from the focus of Islam in Mecca. Al-Omran's eyewitness account of Shi'a Muslims being harassed in the KSA is therefore potentially provocative. Shi'a Muslims are in a minority in the KSA, with a population concentrated in the Eastern Province.

In the same posting, al-Omran writes about the permissibility (or not) of taking photographs in Medina. This is where the Prophet Muhammad and members of his family were buried, although the shrines surrounding their remains have been largely destroyed. This did not prevent al-Omran from producing a forty-two-photo slideshow of his visit, published on flickr.[42] Questions that could be asked include how such blogging output influences the "image" of the KSA internationally and whether censorship of such a blog would have a negative impact on this image in some contexts. The blog Saudi Jeans remained online in 2007, with al-Omran visiting the United States at the request of the U.S. State Department.[43]

One of the most controversial perspectives on the KSA emanated from the Religious Policeman. This was particularly critical of issues associated with religious freedom—or a perceived lack of it—in the KSA. The blog's title was in reference to a fire that killed fifteen schoolgirls in Mecca in 2002, in which the "Religious Police [*muttawa*] would not allow them to leave the building, nor allow the Firemen to enter." This was for reasons associated with segregation of the sexes, based on an Islamic interpretation that is the subject of serious criticism within some sectors of KSA society. The blog claimed to be a "Saudi man's diary of life in the 'Magic Kingdom,' where the Religious Police ensure that everything remains as it was in the Middle Ages."

The Religious Policeman made critical comments about many aspects of KSA society, speaking out against the Saudi monarchy and political system. Religious authority was a further target, often made in a satirical manner. This could be seen in a report on the presence in London of a senior imam from Mecca who was opening a new mosque. This allowed the blog's author to make a comparison of different types of "religious policemen." In June 2006 the postings concluded, with the Religious Policeman signing off in order to write a novel.[44]

The KSA was not the only sector within the Middle East to engage vigorously in the application of blogs to make comments on the interpretation of Islam within society. The Religious Policeman's pseudonymous entries were relatively infrequent. Others posted on a daily basis, such as Bahrain's Mahmood al-Yousif. In Mahmood's Den, al-Yousif commented on corruption in religious leadership and interpreted the causes of "stagnation" in Muslim society.[45] He posted other regional bloggers' responses to events in Mecca in 2006, where *hajji*s died while on pilgrimage, stating: "*Hajj* should be declared optional rather than mandatory, and clerics should find other ways in which Muslims can atone themselves of sins."[46] Al-Yousif focused on CIT issues in Bahrain, posting on issues related to cell phones, freedom of expression on the Web, and Internet filtering. Al-Yousif drew on concepts associated with social networking and interactivity on the blog, dialoguing with readers from a variety of perspectives.

A further significant channel for information on Bahrain was Chan'ad Bahraini (named after a fish), posting political comment on contemporary issues associated with Bahrain. Photos of religious events, such as Ramadan and a performance of religious music (*liwa*) specific to the region, emphasized distinctive traits of ritual associated with Bahrain.[47] There were no audio files of the performance, but the photos were accompanied by a detailed explanation of the associated historical origins of *liwa*. Chan'ad also discussed and linked to photos of a local festival of *hiya biya*, in which baskets containing plants are deposited in the sea at the conclusion of Ramadan.[48]

As with many other areas, there were issues associated with censorship in Bahrain, in particular a conflict between Bahrain Online and the Bahraini government. Bahrain Online's founder Ali Abdulemam was briefly imprisoned in 2005. As the *New York Times* reported, "He [Abdulemam] laughs when he recalls his arrest and how little his interrogators knew about how the Internet works, blaming him for the content of every posting."[49]

Some of this bewilderment associated with blogs extends from a lack of awareness of the concept to an inability to interpret what is being said. This is particularly apparent in reactions to the discussions by "geeks" on technology, but it is also part of the cultural rubrics of expression with online discussions.

The use of Internet-related slang is apparent in many blogs. A good example is "Q8ibloger" from Kuwait. This is written by a researcher "of Arab descent from Quraysh from banu umayyah [a tribal affiliation]," who states he was educated in a British school. The blog combined Qur'anic language with glimpses of contemporary slang, requiring conscious levels of insider knowledge to fully interpret.

Q8ibloger was an enthusiastic writer. He noted a conflict between religious duties and his need or compulsion to maintain his blogging: "Some how i convinced my self that am doing a good thing or maybe shaytan [Satan] was tricking me and am only lying to my self."[50] Within this confusion of interests, Q8ibloger gave a commentary on a perceived "decline" in Kuwaiti society:

As i expected kuwait will be more imoralised [*sic*] and women wearing more revealing cloths,, even in the air port late night women are working !!! talking about animal rights ha,, i mean what ever,, certian [*sic*] places in kuwait are headin to dubai's way,,, but dude it just doesnt suit this country,,, many peeps [people] are trying to be westernised maadri sheno yet their failing miserably,,, now if you notice then men are more dressed up that the women,, you d see a guy dishdasha,, ghuttra and 3egal next to his wife who just came out a high school prom,, seriously maskhara and no shame,, some men just have no honor.[51]

The extent to which this colloquial commentary presents a "typical" opinion from Kuwait is open to question, with its negative comments on women working and (in some cases) styles of dress seen to transgress perceived Islamic norms. This style of dynamic chat is typical of many conversations that appear with forums.

Blogs proliferated in the United Arab Emirates (UAE), where, according to one report, Internet addiction was rife.[52] The UAE Community Blog listed over 200 sites in January 2007.[53] Some highlighted regional differences, distinguishing the UAE from other parts of the Arabic-speaking world. Expatriate blogs discussed life in the UAE and provided perspectives on Islam and Muslim culture.[54] A number of UAE blogs contained politically and religiously charged content. One issued suggestions for "Changing the Arab," including this comment on religious authorities: "All Mullahs, Muttawas, and Imams should make some real use out of themselves to society like Allah would want them to and get themselves jobs."[55]

The blog Secret Arabian commented on blogs associated with Dubai and was scathing on social mores and influences, including aspects of technological usage.[56] His commentary on the fusion between Westernized and regional identities was significant, especially in terms of the emergent archetypes and stereotypes that are within the discourse. This would suggest that these are readily identifiable among readers of the blog.

Secret Arabian evaded governmental filters to present its potentially provocative content, while exploring the issue of censorship: "From an Islamic point of view, the argument against the removal of a proxy is even more potent. As Islam is not a token religion, to block pornographic websites and similar material is viewed as a highly positive thing to do. As the UAE is officially an 'Islamic' country then Etisalat [Emirates Telecommunications Corporation] has every right to exercise levels of censorship."[57]

This delineation of censorship models is interesting in terms of its justification of at least some of Etisalat's policies. Secret Arabian weighed up and attempted to justify the merits of a nuanced, culturally specific policy associated with censorship. Secret Arabian was taken over by the author of the Sleepless In Muscat blog in January 2006 but maintained a continuity of themes.

An exploration of religious concepts and principles was presented by e3ashig, a UAE expatriate doctor based in Manchester, England, who relocated to the UAE in 2007. He focused one discussion on the feasibility of jinn. According to traditional Muslim beliefs, jinn, in general terms, are ethereal beings, at times equated with spirits and created by Allah alongside humanity and angels. Jinn are referred to several times within the Qur'an (including encounters between jinn and Muhammad), and the seventy-second *sura* in the Qur'an is named after them. As such, jinn comprise a part of popular religious understandings with varying degrees of emphasis in different Muslim contexts.

The blogger e3ashig endeavored to synthesize religious understanding with medical knowledge to explain jinn within a cultural context. He gave various examples of the presence of jinn and provided medical explanations.[58] This resulted in a networked conversation between e3ashig and his readers on the veracity of the concept of jinn. This was a discussion outside of official religious channels associated with the UAE, demonstrating that blogs can represent a candid, more personalized space for the expression and exploration of religious ideas.

In contrast to the relative calm in the UAE and a contemplation of spiritual matters, blogs provided perspectives on the harsh realities of conflict, particularly in and around Iraq. These were often journalistic endeavors that augmented or replaced traditional media sources. Iraqi blogs represented key change agents in the medium, being a reference point for blogs emanating from other contexts. The blogger An Average Iraqi noted that, in 2002, there were two Iraqi blogs; by November 2005, he calculated, there were fifty-nine active Iraqi bloggers, not all of whom were Muslims. Iraq Blog Count listed 172 at the same time, a number that had increased to 241 by 2007 (although a proportion were deemed "inactive").[59] Not all of these had an overtly religious element in their content or emerged from Muslim contexts. Outsiders (Muslim and other) produced a proportion of others. Some had a Kurdish focus and would not have classified themselves as "Iraqi."[60]

However these blogs might be categorized, there is no doubt that varied forms of blogging contributed to informing perceptions of the conflict in Iraq and its aftermath. For the privileged elite with access to the Internet— albeit limited at times by power failures and other obstacles—blogging provided an opportunity to present and access alternative perspectives on Iraqi and Muslim issues. A prominent example of this was when "unofficial" film of the execution of Saddam Hussein was uploaded shortly after his death on several blogs.[61] This cell phone footage appeared amid fevered discussion on the manner and consequences of his death, especially as its timing coincided with Eid al-Adha, the festival that celebrates the conclusion of the *hajj*.

In blogs, accounts of extreme violence were interspersed with depictions of the mundane elements of normal life. Blogs about Iraq cannot be stereo-typed: they provided many perspectives related to the conflict situation and information on political and religious issues. Some were more religious in orientation than others, in terms of language, context and content. Not all blogs emerging from Iraq were "antiwar" or anti-Western, although as with other CIES, the extent to which they were representative might be ques-tioned. Islam-related themes—including identity and, predictably, politics—were incorporated into Iraq Body Count, which grouped diverse Iraqi sources and reflective reports together. In one post, contributor "Kurdo" questioned the purpose behind blogging: "I guess in the west some people (not all) see Iraqis as masked men with RPGs [rocket-propelled grenades], and suicide bombers, and Sader [Sadr] Militias. . . . What we have to do as bloggers, is to show the positive signs of ourselves."[62] Whether such ideal-ism was matched by reality is open to question.

Just as the 1991 Gulf War coincided with the expansion of the signifi-cance of satellite television, the 2003 invasion of Iraq and subsequent con-flicts coincided with growing global awareness of the potential of blogs. Most prominent of these was the pseudonymous Iraqi blogger Salam Pax, who provided an example of how a blog can (unintentionally) become an international phenomenon. Salam's English-language blog, Where Is Raed?, was titled after a friend who had temporarily disappeared from e-mail contact. It provided a ground-level perspective on everyday life through discussions on life under Saddam Hussein and eyewitness ac-counts of the "liberation" of Iraq. Posting on the blog was clearly a dan-gerous activity, particularly as Salam was so candid in his posts on sex-uality, Iraqi culture, and war. This included writing about the factions and parties associated with the Iraq campaign, with strong views on the Ba'ath Party and the Iraqi Mukhabarat (Intelligence Service) and comments on the use of religious rhetoric by various parties in Iraq.

At this critical period in Iraqi history, Salam Pax was a distinctive insider contribution from a Muslim war zone, linking into wider historical and contemporary discourse in the Muslim worlds. The posts were networked widely elsewhere in CIES, the wider blogosphere, and throughout global news channels. The effect of this was to generate sustained comment and further boost Salam's online profile. The Google effect was to lift Salam's page rankings, perhaps to a level of attention that he had not anticipated when he started the blog in 2002.

After the U.S. "conquest" of Baghdad, Salam's identity emerged. Salam al-Janabi (his real name) was an interpreter for *New York Times* journalist

Peter Maass, who was not aware of Salam's other activities. As a result of his high profile, Salam was to produce a book based on the blog, columns for the *Guardian* newspaper, and a film script.[63] Salam went on to interview his father, Adnan al-Janabi, a member of the Iraqi Parliament, for the BBC. Salam's blogs cannot be defined as Islamic, but they did offer a commentary as an insider within Muslim societies in Iraq.[64] His original blog mutated into Shut Up You Fat Whiner!, renamed the Daily Absurdity Report, in which he continued to comment on events in Baghdad until June 2006.[65]

Further examples of Iraqi blogs emerged, in some cases as personal diaries published online from within Iraq and presenting opinions of ordinary Iraqis. They demonstrated the potential for networking, interaction, and dialogue between bloggers in Iraq and surfers elsewhere. Raed Jarrar, the eponymous target of Salam's initial blog, was to provide his own commentary on Iraqi affairs in Raed in the Middle. This included details of his personal life and travels, chronicling a visit to Egypt in which he is alarmed at a taxi driver's "ignorance" in matters of Islam.[66]

Others were to obtain a broad audience for their blogging efforts, in particular Riverbend. This was a female perspective from a survivor of the allied campaign in Baghdad. Encouraged by Salam Pax, Riverbend was twenty-four when she commenced Baghdad Burning, an acerbic commentary on events. This was described as "a girl blog from Iraq. . . . [L]et's talk war, politics and occupation." It offered opinions on political changes in Iraq and a sense of what went for "ordinary life" in the city at that time. As a computer programmer, Riverbend had access to and knowledge of the Net beyond that of many Baghdadis at the time of the invasion.

Riverbend provided an account of the immediate impact of 9/11 on "ordinary" Iraqis, fusing political discussion with references to home life. Often these were very personal observations, such as her commentary on reactions to the Iraqi constitution: her neighbor's response was to use a copy of the document to clean her wall. Elsewhere, Riverbend continued to talk about emergent political frameworks and the confusion following the conquest of Baghdad.[67]

Riverbend's observations were subsequently edited into book form.[68] She observed: "I don't think I wrote the blog for any particular audience. I simply wanted to express my emotions and thoughts and I wasn't sure who would read it. I never expected many Iraqis inside of Iraq to read it because Iraqis are far too busy coping with daily realities to read blogs or even write them. I liked blogging in English because it's a language people in many different countries understand. I would have been preaching to the choir if I blogged in Arabic."[69]

The diversity of religious and political thought within Iraq was well represented on a number of blogs. Prominent among the Shi'a blogs was Hammorabi. This was named after the sixth king of Amorites in Babylon, Hammorabi (1792–1750 B.C.E.), who was responsible for establishing a specific legal system in the region. It presented a prominent link to a detailed explanation of "The Story of Imam Hussein."[70] Hammorabi was critical of "insurgent" activities and also disparaging of the Al-Jazeera and Al-Arabiyya television channels' coverage of Iraq, especially when the latter placed background music onto "propaganda" film showing attacks on U.S. forces.[71]

Blogging added a further level of danger—as if it were needed—to life in Iraq. Khalid Jarraf, a blogger associated with Salam, Raed, and Riverbend, was arrested and held by the Mukhabarat after visiting an Internet café at Baghdad University. An online campaign launched to free him was ultimately successful. He posted on his experiences, including being assaulted while under arrest and his interrogators' lack of knowledge about the Internet. This account included Jarraf explaining the concept of a blog to a judge, who possessed some computer knowledge. In various postings, Jarraf discussed the oppressive conditions in which he and others were held; he used the blog to highlight the cases of other prisoners he had met and publicize their presence to their families, who had not received information on the prisoners' location.[72] The type of personal information conveyed by Jarraf in his blog provided experiential insight into real-life issues, with an intensity lost on much of the traditional media emerging from Iraq.

Politically edged blogs such as Iraq the Model and The Mesopotamian gave insights into diverse opinions about the impact of foreign-policy decisions in Iraqi society, and their content was circulated widely on other blogs. Iraq the Model commenced in November 2003, written by brothers Mohammed and Omar. It was founded as a discussion point for presenting an archetypal Iraqi society.[73] The suggestion was that the blog would act as the reader's eyes in Iraq, clearly from a very specific angle, which was reflected in Omar's revelation that his favorite political figures included Tony Blair, then the British prime minister.[74]

Iraq the Model discussed many aspects of life in Iraq following the downfall of Saddam Hussein. This ranged from the impact on dentistry patient care (Omar being one of several dentist bloggers) to the effects of violence: "insurgents" killed two of Omar's friends, alongside seven

Spanish troops.[75] Iraq the Model covered political developments but also gave details of religious-cultural activities, such as photos of Eid ul-Fitr in Iraq. It did not present an overtly religious identity or message within its content.[76]

Alaa of The Mesopotamian presented a perspective similar to that of Iraq the Model, couched in more detailed religiously oriented references. It confidently asserted its position regarding the war in Iraq and the emphasis that al-Qaeda and its advocates had on obtaining media coverage.[77] As with other Iraqi blogs, Alaa made specific accusations against Al-Jazeera, suggesting that it was "pro-terrorist."[78] Alaa attempted to analyze reasons for this, alleging that the Qatari government's sponsorship of Al-Jazeera was influential in this editorial line and that it was motivated by anti-Shi'a "sectarian prejudice." The Mesopotamian articulated a pro-American and pro–George W. Bush stance.[79] Within his dialogue, Alaa utilized religious language frequently; posts during Ramadan were punctuated by ritual references; Alaa tried to explain Islam and offered an alternative Islamic perspective from Iraq to readers.[80] The blog gave the complex perspective of a critical, devout, pro-American Iraqi Muslim, utilizing religious language and depiction of ritual within its analysis.

The use of photos was important in several other Iraqi blogs, despite the inherent dangers in their publication. Healing Iraq, written by another dentist, had a photo blog documenting Shi'a *muharram* rituals in villages south of Basra.[81] Other offerings were blogs written by Iraqi teenagers in between power cuts: Nabil's Blog combined news on Iraqi sports with comments on cultural life in Baghdad and his progress through examinations.[82]

Iraqi blogs included those with journalistic interests, such as 24 Steps to Liberty. Commencing in August 2005 and positioned as "secular" in orientation, 24 Steps was not afraid to confront controversial issues. Following a restaurant bombing in November 2005, 24 Steps wrote a passionate commentary against the bombers. He also posted on a trip to a journalist seminar in Durham, North Carolina, addressing the dangers of his job in Iraq and how he reports on devastating stories.

The personal and societal quest for a normal life is an underlying theme of 24 Steps. The blogger wrote about how children were damaged because of the conflict.[83] 24 Steps, working with various journalists as they sought to cover stories associated with Iraq, developed a strong profile within this sector of the blogosphere, but the critical question might be asked: could 24 Steps to Liberty be classified as Islamic? A second question might be: does it matter? The blogger gave a commentary on issues relating to religion, such as terrorism in the cause of jihad and the role of religious authorities in Iraqi society. 24 Steps subsequently obtained a visa to study in the United States.

Baghdad Treasure was a further journalistic endeavor illustrating a grassroots "secular" perspective of life in Iraq.[84] He engaged in a critique of Riverbend, who was accused of allegedly being against Shi'as and Iranians.[85] Baghdad Treasure presented diary entries on everyday activities such as the end of Eid, drawing on reports from stringers elsewhere in Iraq. This sought to represent the optimism of people in Baghdad despite adversity, detailing Eid celebrations and people filling the streets.[86] The blog continued from a distance, when its writer moved to Philadelphia in 2006 to undertake post-graduate study.[87]

As another angle on the situation in Iraq, several U.S. military personnel wrote their own war blogs. With the Iraq 2.0 blog, this also formed part of the cyber-Islamic equation. A reservist sergeant in the U.S. Army, Mohammed Omar Masry, wrote Iraq 2.0 during his six-month tour of duty.[88] Omar noted: "I think I'm the first Arab or Muslim-American soldier who's blogging, and it's funny how sometimes I feel like I'm delving between amateur war correspondent and social studies teacher within my writings."[89]

Masry's experience in Iraq included preparing a briefing on Islam for army chaplains. He discussed his upbringing, and how as a Muslim from America he was experiencing life in a Muslim country for the first time.[90] Masry's experiences were documented in photos, including an account of a visit by George W. Bush to Baghdad and his meeting with U.S. officials. On Masry's return to the United States, he was interviewed in the media. His experience had caused him to reevaluate his position on America's role in Iraq, believing that he "was now 'fixing the mess that former leaders had made,' . . . and trying to gain the trust that America had 'ruined.'"[91] He was no longer blogging but continued to be consulted for media interviews.

There were some unconventional blogs emerging from Iraq. Baghdad's Mistress was an occasional blog, apparently written by a woman from the Iraqi capital city.[92] Her first post set the tone for other entries: "Do you think I really care about Osama son of bitch?! That is the Yankees problem not mine. . . . What? What was my job? I was a mistress. A proud mistress. Yes I used to sleep with married men to get money because my university degree could not get me Channel [*sic*] clothes."[93] While online for a brief period in 2005, she discussed her clients and gave insights into life in Baghdad. This included the sourcing of Chanel clothes and the different forms of marriage available in the country. There was an apparent biographical edge to the blog, as Baghdad Mistress relayed her story about her failed marriage, the death of her parents, and how she started work in the "business." If there is no such thing as a typical Iraqi blog, then Baghdad's Mistress also demonstrates that not all bloggers apparently living in a Muslim context had religion immediately on their minds.

In contrast to Iraq and other countries in the region, Syria presented itself at a relatively early stage in the blogging evolutionary process. Sasa of the Syrian News Wire observed a rapid growth of blogs in 2005, from two to over fifty: "The Internet is much freer in Syria than print media. That's probably because of the President's background. He was president of the Syrian Computer Society, and pushed for wider use of the Internet in Syria. He even promised every school child their own computer."[94]

Damascene Blog listed nearly 100 Syrian blogs on its pages in 2006.[95] There was evidence of critical blogging apparently emerging from Syria; "Karfan," whose name translates as "disgusted," was critical of the Assad regime. His Syria Exposed blog sought to present a true picture of Syria, however subjective and authentic that may be.[96] The blog contains opinions that may not be representative but which is certainly provocative. The extent to which it was aimed at a Syria-based audience is open to question. Karfan deconstructed what he deemed to be the myths surrounding life in Syria. This included extreme criticism of the past and current presidents, especially the formers' "Sunni-fication" policy in Syria, which was deemed detrimental to Alawi Muslims.[97]

Karfan gave details of his military service (which included a period in Lebanon) and his entirely negative opinions of the Syrian Ba'ath Party. Karfan discussed the care that he, and presumably his publishing partner, took when making contentious postings.[98] However, following that discussion in June 2005, he ceased posting and remained offline until August 2006. Karfan and his publishing partner had concerns regarding personal security: "We are so raised in the culture of fear to the extent that neither I nor Karfan have even looked once to this website from within Syria in the previous year!"[99]

The blog was a strident voice within the Islamic blogosphere. Other critical voices were censored, including Syrian Domari, based on a banned satirical magazine that had published cartoons and humorous pieces via its blog.[100] "Tolerant Damascene," of The Hidden Gates of Damascus blog, posted a denouncement of so-called honor killings.[101] This linked to a Syrian women's site and a related petition.[102] Tolerant Damascene discussed the status of Syria as an officially secular state and the perceived paradox of the influence of Islam in the country at personal, local, and national levels.

Among other significant offerings relating to Syria was that of expatriate Ammar Abdulhamid, based in Maryland, who offered the self-explanatory Amarji, A Heretic's Blog.[103] The blog titled Across Syria & Inside Homs ignored politics and focused on the city of Homs, providing historical photos and commentary to contrast with current views.[104] Overall, Syrian blogging was having a serious growth spurt. This was bound to impact at the grassroots level in terms of religious expression, discussion, and understanding.

Some Syrian blogs emerged from Lebanese contexts. In Lebanon itself, Lebanon Bloggers Forum listed over 100 blogs. Broad ranges of issues were commented on from Muslim, Christian, and other angles, including political and religious concerns. There were also entries of a highly personal nature: "Linalone" wrote about sexual abuse and suicide in her blog, and in a related interview she noted: "I think most Lebanese bloggers lack a personal touch. It's politics wherever you go! . . . Leave the blogosphere? I don't think I will, just because I will never stop writing, even if I was my one and only reader."[105]

During the 2006 conflict between Hizbullah and Israel, blogs were used to communicate the experience of those under attack from Israeli Defense Force (IDF) bombs and to record the devastation in Beirut and elsewhere. This included photographs, video clips, and other documents. The blogosphere had become a natural place for discourse and a safety valve for expressing the frustration of the Lebanese at the Israeli invasion. It was a place where comments could be exchanged between Israeli and Lebanese bloggers, including on video. Photographs of the victims of conflict appeared on YouTube alongside the thoughts of Noam Chomsky, Hizbullah propaganda, and video montages showing the damage to Beirut and other urban centers.[106] Online sources produced in Lebanon were drawn upon by the world's media, highlighting in particular the way in which blogs provided a form of social lubrication between different factions and concerns in Lebanon, not all of which were Islamically oriented.[107]

Jordanian writers developed a busy sector of the blogosphere. This was informed by political, religious, and cultural issues within the region and a technologically literate, young, urbanized population represented by King Abdullah's own computing background. Haitham Sabbah's blog emerged as one of the key players in online discussions of Arab issues. Sabbah's blog translated and commented on religious-cultural issues, generating lively debate when he discussed the phenomena of "business marriages" and "holiday marriages" in the KSA.[108] One of Sabbah's most "popular" posts (in terms of site traffic) was on the "merits" of one of Osama bin Laden's nieces, Wafa Bin Laden, an American-born model and singer who was featured in *GQ* magazine.[109]

Blogs reinforce identities within specific Islamic contexts. Jordan Planet commenced in August 2004, providing an English-language blog portal. It had over sixty members and offered focal points for opinion and mourning following the November 2005 bombings in Amman.[110] However, Jordan Planet suspended its services in 2006, claiming a (somewhat ambiguous) reduction in blog quality.[111]

Jordan Planet linked to MentalMayhem, run by expatriate Jordanian journalist Natasha Tynes, and Jordan First, which promoted a music video condemning the bombing entitled "Ya Amman." Jordan First showed a flickr photo badge of vociferous demonstrations against al-Qaeda that took place in Amman after the bombings.[112] Such portals offer a multifaceted reflection on Muslim societies. The extent to which such messages filter into the wider blogosphere, Islamic or other, is open to question. Wider circulation of such materials can facilitate, in some quarters, an opportunity to counter stereotypes associated with Muslims and terrorism.

Blogging became a significant medium for discussions in Palestine and the Occupied Territories. This interlocks with a pattern associated with other applications of the Net in Palestinian contexts, specifically those associated with Muslim expression and campaigning for Palestinian Muslim causes. The growth of Palestinian blogging took many forms, including interaction of varying forms between Israeli and Palestinian bloggers.

Some blogs integrated materials from other sources: Ali Abunimah's Bitter Pill represented columns written for Electronic Intifada, which he cofounded.[113] Arjan El Fassed, a cofounder of Electronic Intifada, applied his experience with nongovernmental organizations in writing for newspapers to provide an "insider" account of Israeli-Palestine relations in Dutch and English. There was evidence of Israel-Palestinian cross-posting and exchange. Bitterlemons.org featured regular postings and dialogues edited, and in some cases written by, Palestinian authority minister of labor Ghassan Khatib and Israeli writer and strategic consultant Yossi Alpher. They published the first edition in the wake of 9/11 in November 2001, and over 200 editions of the magazine appeared online. Content was been equally split between Arab and Israeli interests associated with geopolitical issues. Religious material has not usually entered the dialogue in an overt fashion, although religious issues informed some discussion.[114]

Regionality on Palestinian blogs presented diverse coverage. Reports from Rafah contained insider coverage,[115] and Rafah Pundits focused on content relating to Hamas, featuring reports and photos of funerals. Rafah Pundits, for example, covered the 2005 story of "top Hamas fighter" Amjad Al-Hinawee being "assassinated" by Israeli troops.[116] Another story, which drew on reports from *Ha'aretz* and the BBC, detailed the killing of twelve-year-old Ahmad Al-Khateeb by IDF troops; his family subsequently donated his organs to Israelis.[117]

Bethlehem Bloggers featured cultural-religious issues associated with Palestine and specific concerns faced by those living in Bethlehem. A prominent issue was the problem of marriage between West Bank and Jerusalem Arabs (Muslim and other) because of difficulties in obtaining rights of residence.[118] Bethlehem Bloggers's accounts of everyday activities included the tribulations of passing through checkpoints and visiting the Jerusalem Zoo.[119] The religious element is not apparent in this blog, and Bethlehem has a substantial Christian population. It represented a significant opinion from a Muslim milieu, and the issues it covered would profoundly affect many within the Muslim population.

The blogs Raising Yousuf and Living in Gaza City posted insider accounts of life in Palestine. This included the difficulties when attempting to leave the area in order to go abroad (and indeed to enter Gaza) and images and accounts of "normal" life. "Imaan," a Swedish convert to Islam, wrote Living in Gaza City. She described herself as an "opinionated journalist-wannabe who is trying to manage motherhood and marriage and life in general." Her posts contained numerous insights into life in Gaza. They also explored issues associated with being a convert to Islam, a theme that continued on Imaan's return to Sweden in 2006.[120]

Raising Yousuf, by Laila el-Haddad (Um Yousuf), "is about raising my son Yousuf in the occupied Gaza Strip while working as a journalist, and everything that entails from potty training to border crossings."[121] El-Haddad had links with Durham, North Carolina, where her husband had a medical residency. Her posts included accounts of filmed reports she had worked on for Al-Jazeera. Neither Imaan nor Laila could be described as typical residents of Gaza, or indeed typical bloggers. There is no such thing. Both provide a perspective into life in the region and the pressures that went unreported elsewhere. They gave greater insight into everyday issues, including those affecting religious life and culture, than many politically oriented blogs on the region.

Sites such as Umkahlil, Global Voices Online: Palestine, and Palestine Blogs ReBlog are portals into diverse pro-Palestinian areas of the Web. These synthesized feeds in different languages provide exchange points for information and publicity on specific causes. They do not have a specific Islamic emphasis or Muslim authorship; many are hosted outside of Palestinian territories or, as in the case of Global Voices, form part of wider international blogging portals. There were specific infrastructural and access issues relating to Palestinian cyberspace. This does not seem to be in parity with other sectors of Palestinian cyber activism and expression hosted outside of the region.

Turkey is a particularly energetic Muslim zone for blogging activity. This is reflected in the growth in blogs emerging directly from Turkey and from those located outside of the country who described themselves as Turks. The Turkish blogging milieu is significant in its presentation of identities that are not necessarily Muslim or Islamic, European or Asian, but instead are focused specifically on Turkish culture and politics, with comments on domestic issues and wider issues with an Islamic emphasis.

One of the long-standing blogs was Ugur Akinci's Turkish Torque blog, which commenced in 2002 (in succession to an e-mail list). It explored a wide range of political and contemporary issues associated with life in Turkey, including topics with a specific emphasis on Turkey's secularized identity and on the politics of the country's borders.[122] The Turkish-American blog Talk Turkey focused on the achievements of the Turkish-American community.[123] Bilgiedinmehakki surveyed freedom of information issues, especially those relating to the Internet, from a Turkish perspective.[124]

Journalists utilized blogs to expand their readership. Mustafa Akyol provided seminars "on issues of faith, science, religious tolerance and issues relating to Islam."[125] Extracts from Akyol's writings appeared on the White Path, relating in part to Islamic interpretation. The application of the Web was particularly important in Akyol's writings as he entered potentially controversial areas of shari'ah, Qur'anic interpretation, and religious freedom. With regard to terrorism, Akyol condemned terrorists for their "defective" interpretation of the Qur'an.[126] The blog was also significant in igniting a debate on "intelligent design," which Akyol supported from a Muslim perspective, prompting him to link up with certain Christian groups in the United States. He received substantial media coverage, contributed to online discourse on the subject in Islam Online, and generated further interest in his blog through presentations at international conferences.[127] In turn, his posts were drawn into Christian intelligent design online discourse and that of its detractors.

Again, issues of identity and religiosity apply when defining Muslim and Islamic blogs. These are central themes across the blogosphere, particularly in Iran, a key node in CIES. An estimated 700,000 Persian blogs were in cyberspace in February 2006, but this figure did not indicate how many were active.[128] Statistics retain their problematic status when approaching the subject of blogs from and about Iran.

An influential turning point in Muslim blog discourse was the creation of Farsi-script blogging tools in 2000. Hossein Derakhshan, an Iranian journalist based in Canada, had an important role in developing a Farsi-compatible blogging tool. Blogs had previously only functioned with Roman (Latin) characters. Although he was not the first "Iranian blogger," Derakhshan's innovation resulted in tens of thousands of Iranian voices emerging into cyberspace.

The rapid development of Iranian blogging was celebrated in Farsi Blog Festivals.[129] By 2006 the Iranian Qur'anic Society was proposing a festival to promote blogging on religious themes. The center of the Iranian Shi'a religious knowledge economy is based in the city of Qom, where a program for blogger training was announced.[130] The infusion of popular culture, chatting, fashion, sports, and commerce dominated many areas of the Iranian blogosphere. Qom's initiative sought to present traditional opinions into cyberspace as a counter to other content.

The development of blogging in its myriad forms was also having an impact on the Farsi language, in particular "a mix of Farsi and English—known as 'Pinglish'—which has angered some traditional Farsi speakers."[131] This could be a factor within other CIES, especially with the media innovations associated with Web 2.0. Whether they were talking "Pinglish," Farsi, English, or another language, a number of Iranian bloggers sought to tackle policy issues. Their subjects included the nature of religious leadership in Iran and the changing political language and landscape. The emergence of these bloggers caught the Iranian authorities off guard. In Iran and in exiled Iranian communities, the vibrant development of blogs coincided with a vigorous discussion about Internet censorship, which reached the top levels of government.

Derakhshan's own site, Editor: Myself, along with pages such as Mitra and Pedram Moallemian's Eyeranian.net, became dynamic focal points of discussion and analysis during the 2004 Iranian general elections. Farsi and English blogs gave "eyewitness" commentaries of events as contributors conveyed their personal experiences of visiting polling booths and provided a sense of the mood on the streets.[132] By 2005, during the presidential elections, candidates "gave out free Internet access cards and posted campaign ads on web blogs."[133] These were to encourage people to visit the campaigning websites.

A number of bloggers in Iran were arrested and jailed for their online activities; student Omid Sheikhan was imprisoned in 2004, suffering torture and solitary confinement before facing trial on charges of "having unlawful relations" and "insulting Iran's leaders." According to the Committee to Protect Bloggers, there was evidence of other Iranians being jailed or on trial on similar charges.[134] Mojtaba Saminejad was jailed on charges of reporting the arrests of three other bloggers in 2004.[135] The charges were criticized on other blogs, which monitored the imprisoned and threatened bloggers.

Some Iranian authorities suggested that there were "conspiracies" shaping Internet activities. In September 2004 *Kayhan*, an Iranian newspaper, featured opinions from Qom clerics "about accessing, hosting, and filtering websites which 'insult sacred concepts of Islam, Prophet and Imams, publish harmful and deviated beliefs to promote Atheism and irreligiousness publish and promote sinister books.' . . . Ayatollah Macramé Shiraz has responded that accessing these websites is a religious taboo and ISPs should not facilitate such access, and if filtering or blocking them is possible, people in charge must do that."[136] The potential for blocking and filtering of various sites, facilities, ISPs, and forums was clearly of interest to Iranian authorities, especially after the emergence of Mahmoud Ahmadinejad in June 2005. At that time, Ahmadinejad had a website with an "email the President" feature; he was later to become a blogger.[137]

The concept of blogging reached those who had held a religious status within governmental offices. Mohammed Ali Abtahi's webNevesht.com recorded daily activities in Farsi, Arabic, and English.[138] Significantly, Abtahi also held an Orkut account; this international social-networking portal was popular in Iran, although authorities endeavored to block its use.[139] Abtahi was a vice president in parliamentary legal affairs under President Khatami but subsequently resigned in 2004, apparently under pressure from conservative factions in Iran. Abtahi presented himself as a reform-oriented cleric who used the Web to answer religious questions from readers and disseminate his own opinions on local and world affairs. Abtahi noted: "I am the only window of the government that people can open freely. That kind of contact between society and a cleric is very important and very unusual."[140]

As an advisor for President Khatami, Abtahi wrote about the meetings he held with various local and international figures. Posts included photographs of his activities, including informal shots (taken with his cell phone) of key governmental and religious figures.[141] Abtahi was not afraid to comment on turbulent domestic and international events.[142] He criticized parts of the speech by President Ahmadinejad made on the annual al-Quds Day, in which the president called for the destruction of Israel.[143]

There were attempts to shut down Abtahi's blog, notably when his original Web domain was "stolen" after he wrote a story about bloggers being tortured in Iran.[144] Abtahi's profile may have allowed him leeway in making oblique critical comments on Ahmedinijad and others. Abtahi changed his Web domain's name and shifted his ISP to the United States. He had become a high-profile blogging imam, able to challenge the judiciary when other bloggers were imprisoned during 2004.[145]

Abtahi's writings focused further international condemnation on Iran and forced a temporary policy retraction by Iranian authorities: " 'There's been a change in the atmosphere,' Abtahi said. 'Now instead of the webloggers being under pressure it's the judiciary which is feeling the heat.' "[146] A number of other clerics emerged online.[147] Given the success of Abtahi's online activities, it was not surprising that the blog apparently written by Ahmadinejad emerged in August 2006. Although it promised regular postings, there was only one long article during the blog's first two months of online life. Postings then became more regular in Farsi and were subsequently translated into French and English. Following controversy surrounding Ahmadinejad's speech at Columbia University in 2007, a number of Americans sent supportive e-mails to the president through his blog. However, criticism from readers of Ahmadinejad for denying the existence of homosexuals in Iran also featured on the blog.[148]

Equally significant to high-level blogs such as Ahmadinejad's were the number of personal blogs that emerged from Iran. Iranian Girl, authored by "Fatemah," provided an insider perspective on Iranian culture. The blog commenced in August 2003 and focused on the writer's position as an educated professional within Tehran society. Fatemah commented on issues of religion, which would have attracted censure had she not retained her anonymous status. She noted that her opinions would attract her friends' disapproval.[149]

Fatemah drew controversy for presenting a cartoon entitled "How to Build a Mullah," in which a stage-by-stage illustration of a man having his brain removed and replaced by an imam's turban was presented.[150] Elsewhere, she noted that she was the only person in her family not to fast during the period of Ramadan[151]—a comment that was particularly provocative in the context of Iran: "It makes no difference if you believe in 'fasting' or not, you must be hungry and thirsty because GOD wants so!! this is what living in ISLAMIC REPUBLIC means, this is what stupidity means!"[152] Within netiquette, capitalization is synonymous with shouting, giving added cadence and emphasis to Fatemah's opinions.

The momentum attained for Iranian bloggers in a relatively short period suggests that it easily fitted into an information and knowledge gap in the market.[153] Religion is one strand in a wider discourse occurring both online and offline in Iranian contexts. The role of the medium during a volatile and transformative period in Iranian politics has been a significant one.

The Maghreb and North Africa also developed a dynamic if less-populous sector of the Islamic blogosphere, representing diversity between and within countries, as well as the development of new networking connections. Prominent among these activities were the vibrant blogging networks that emerged in Egypt. Egyptian Blog Ring had nearly 500 members registered on its system in 2005, but by the beginning of 2007 this number had risen to 1,481 (with 900 more awaiting approval). Of these, nearly 60 percent wrote in Arabic, 40 percent in English, and the remainder in French. Within these calculations, the majority were described as "personal" blogs, with politics, art, and culture being other significant categories.[154] This blog ring did not contain all known Egyptian bloggers, and this classification would not be exclusively Muslim in orientation nor necessarily contain fully active blogs.

Egyptian Arab Street Files and Issandr el-Amrani's weblog, the latter written by the former editor of the *Cairo Times*, represented important elements within this sector of the blogosphere. There was an interesting spat between the two blogs in 2003 over the issue of homosexuality and the "Queen Boat" case; el-Amrani described a post in the Arab Street Files as "sickeningly homophobic" and used this issue to discuss blogging etiquette and human-rights abuses in Egypt.[155]

The writer of the provocatively titled Rantings of a Sandmonkey presented himself as "an extremely cynical, snarky, pro-US, secular, libertarian, disgruntled sandmonkey. If this is your cup of tea, please enjoy your stay here. If not, please sod off."[156] His profile indicates that he spent five years in Boston as a student before returning home to Egypt, which he describes as "dysfunctional." The blog made comments on Islamic-related issues, being vociferous in its opposition to jihadi activities.

Sandmonkey, also known as "Sam," provided an impassioned document on religious tolerance, fearing for the lives of Coptic Christians if there was to be an Islamic Brotherhood government. He discussed the impact of technology on Egyptian society, exploring e-mail etiquette and the Egyptian "fetishes" of cell phones and religion.[157] Sam made critical reflective comments of protests relating to the alleged "desecration" of the Qur'an in Guantanamo Bay, suggesting: "Maybe we need to stop blaming the world, take some personal responsibility for our shortcomings and start fixing the problems in our countries that make us so backwards."[158] In a series of consistent postings, Sam gave an interesting take on the political scene in Egypt and indicated the opportunities for critical debate that the blogosphere offers in terms of country-specific and regional issues (with their various infusions of Muslim/Islamic conceptual influences).

One Arab World gave Kamim Elsahy's journalistic perspective relating to Egypt. The blog's ethos was emphasized in the posting titled "No more self gratifying lies," which stated: "Believe me, as a Muslim, I would love nothing more than to take comfort in an idea that it is all about the western media's portrayal of us. That kind of self denial is the first thing we need to administer."[159] This confrontation of media stereotypes via blogs, and the critical reflection of Arab and Muslim identities, distinguishes such blogs from other more mundane and everyday sections of the blogosphere. They are particularly significant within a changing political and religious framework in Egypt following the successes of the Muslim Brotherhood in regional elections during 2005.

Muslim Brotherhood supporters and members also developed blogs, including journalist Abdou al-Monem Mahmoud, whose blog continued after his arrest in April 2007.[160] Commenting on current affairs in blogs was not without risks. In 2007 blogger Abdel Kareem Nabil Suleiman received a four-year sentence in Egypt for "insulting Islam" (and also insulting President Mubarak).[161] New York–based commentator Mona Eltahawy noted: "It is at once sadly pathetic and oddly gratifying that the regime of Mubarak—who has ruled Egypt for 25 years—felt it necessary to convict a young man 'armed' only with a keyboard and access to the Internet. Frightening as his conviction might be, surely it is a victory for the brigade of the young and determined who populate the Egyptian blogosphere and who like Nabil have known no other leader than Mubarak."[162]

Nabil's appeal failed, and the twenty-two-year-old faced four years in prison. A vigorous online international campaign sought his release. He continued to "blog" from jail, with postings being drawn from his letters.[163]

Blogging was also not without inherent difficulties in adjacent Libya. Blogger 'Abd al-Raziq al-Mansuri was jailed in Libya for eighteen months in November 2005. This was apparently for possession of an illegal pistol rather than statements placed into his blog.[164] Al-Mansuri's website became the venue both for his articles, which attracted greater publicity after his arrest, and for campaigns seeking his release. He had been critical of the Libyan regime and subsequently suffered injuries in prison.

There was discussion between bloggers with Libyan interests about establishing an aggregator to feed in the increasing number of Libyan-related blogs emerging online from both inside and outside the country.[165] From the Rock, formerly a project charting the history of a Libyan highland village, made comments and updates on several blogs, and its writer also participated in the 2005 Tunis Conference. Ly-Hub presented itself as "a place for Libyan bloggers, or those with interest in Libya, to connect, share their blogs, thoughts, and more" and sought to fulfill this remit through drawing on posts from its (relatively small) membership.[166]

The extent to which Islamic issues pervade the Libyan blogosphere is open to question. There can be essential differences between the posts of exiles/expatriates and those located within Libya. Personal blogs such as Tripoli Girl gave the perspective of a fifteen-year-old in Libya but was confined to discussions on family and nature.[167] Dunia presented an assertive Muslim identity with a "blog of a muslim arab (libyan to be super-specific) female—with all the opinions that implies."[168] This included a selection of poetry and cultural information that transcended Libya in its origins, as well as information on family events. The blog had two female contributors as its team and commented on media, journalism, and styles of Arabic.

The Maghreb demonstrates diversity in terms of blogging themes and styles. Maghreblog, written primarily in French and English, presented itself as a collective effort between several different authors, commenting on activities associated with the blogosphere in Algeria, Morocco, Libya, and Tunisia. Each author ran their own blog as well as contributing to Maghreblog.[169] There is considerable online diversity in the blog, both between countries and within the same country. Several blogging communities emerged that were associated with the Maghreb.

In 2005 Tunisie Blogs held an aggregate of over 120 blogs in Arabic,

French, and English from authors based in Tunisia and other locations. Not all had a direct Tunisian affiliation. This number had tripled by the beginning of 2007.[170] The extent to which Islam and Muslim issues are dominant themes is open to question, with many blogs focusing on information technology, culture, arts and history. Tunisian bloggers inaugurated an annual Tunisian Blog Awards with eight categories in 2005.[171]

Tunisian blogging networks also provided an example of an ex-imam turned atheist, "Labidi Karim Mohamed," who discussed his perspective on Islamic sources and figures in Islam La. Faith Freedom stated that Labidi had trained as an imam in Iran, was the subject of a Shi'a fatwa, and had had his Internet and phone access cut.[172] Islam La featured cartoons and commentary, together with a striking montage of the author with his head replaced by photos of mosques. This was accompanied by an explanation of why Labidi had chosen a path that would be deemed "dangerous" within many Muslim contexts, at least in terms of public expression.

The cartoons in Islam La are on themes that some Muslims would find offensive, including images of Muhammad and Jesus. However, Labidi stressed that he respected the right of others to believe in God while opposing the concept of a deity himself.[173] This blog led to related websites of "atheist" Muslims.[174] Labidi's identity became a source of heated debate elsewhere in the blogosphere, with questions as to how he could maintain such a blog in Tunisia and whether his identity would emerge in a "live dialogue" over PalTalk. Islam La was subject to censorship in Tunisia beginning in February 2006. There were concerns that those leaving comments on Islam La had their IP addresses recorded, which could lead to the disclosure of their identities.[175]

Moroccan cyberspace contained hundreds of blogs, with a significant proportion of them located in France. Larbi.org listed over 300 blogs from a range of perspectives and subjects, although it contained few specific examples relating directly to Islam. This was not necessarily indicative of any "religion vacuum," but it may reflect the interests of Larbi's founder(s).[176] The listing included blogs established in response to specific events, such as the taking of Moroccan hostages in Iraq.[177]

Algerian blogs were dominated by expatriate contributions from France. Hchicha's Blog described itself as a blog of an Algerian living in Paris "for the best and for the worst." It incorporated political commentary with experience of living in France as a minority ethnic person, especially pertinent during the 2005 period of urban rioting in the city.[178] Algiers-based blogger Rabah focused on technological issues associated with Algeria. He noted the presence of 1.5 million surfers and 5,000 Internet cafés in Algeria, according to government sources. He was critical of a governmental plan for "1 PC per family," suggesting that the scheme was linked to the government charging an exorbitant amount of interest for a loan even though the scheme may have "looked good on paper."[179]

The Moor Next Door featured the output of seventeen-year-old Khalid Nourediene, an American Algerian based in the United States with a Shia/Sufi/Christian/Quaker heritage. Nourediene, who stated that he was a "secular Muslim," proclaimed: "I do hate chauvinist Muslims. But I do not hate Islam." Perhaps it was easier for Nourediene to make such a statement in the United States than in Algeria.[180] The blog provided insight into the multiple identities expressed on- and offline by Muslims of mixed heritage, especially pertinent in bridging generational gaps associated with understandings of identities. Nourediene introduced transcripts of conversations with friends in Algeria. A discussion in December 2005 between Nourediene and a friend asked why Algeria had not become like Afghanistan during its Taliban-ruled period.[181] This kind of dialogue is an indicator of the range of possibilities online in terms of dispersed "communities" presenting an openness of opinion about political-religious issues. Particularly striking is a post in defense of Algeria as a liberal and progressive society, written in response to an article about police storming a gay wedding ceremony in Algeria.[182]

Muslim Blogging beyond the Middle East

The Islamic blogosphere is more than a Middle East–related Islamic phenomenon. It is associated with numerous other Muslim zones, some with limited Internet access. The following section explores some of this Muslim blogging diversity, commencing with sub-Saharan, Horn of Africa, and East African contexts. Migrants, expatriates, and students are particularly proactive in blog production; Somaliland, Somalia, Ethiopia, Zanzibar, and Eritrea provide typical examples of this pattern.

Prominent among online communities that emerged from Somali contexts is Qarxis, which generated a great deal of traffic when showing a variety of video clips. One, via YouTube, allegedly showed jinn "possessing" a young girl.[183] The video generated thousands of viewings and considerable excited discussion within the online Somali community. Reader "Slick__Horsie" articulated his reaction in a colloquial English style:

Maaan that clip scared the crap out of me! When I was watchin it, it was ok I mean I wasn't scared or anything, coz I'm a man an that I ain't scared of no video clip. Afterwards though, whoa! Everytime I went into a room I thought as soon as I open the door I'll see that gal recitin those words in that fkd up voice, staring at me. This sorta thing should be banned!! . . . I've witnessed an actual posession back when I was a kid, it was some scary ordeal. . . . I think I got one in me. I'm serious man. Well not in me but I think one keeps whisperin bad things to me coz I keep doin things I shouldn't, must be a jinn I'm tellin ya.[184]

The clip was certainly unusual. It was significant that, in between the discussions on popular culture(s) with a Somali twist, there would be a sustained discussion on aspects of religious experiences and expectations associated with popular religion. This brought together opinion from diverse Muslim blogging contexts. Qarxis contains other material pertaining to religious beliefs, acting as a central point for information associated with diasporic Somali culture.

The output of Ahmed Quick, a migrant from Somaliland, was also significant in this area. He produced the English-language Voice of Somaliland Diaspora–Ottawa, which was a clearinghouse for information concerning this part of the Horn of Africa with numerous links to related blogs. Religious concerns formed a subtext to this blog, unsurprisingly dominated by political discussions on Somalia and Somaliland.[185]

Bloggers operated in other African Muslim contexts. Nigerian blogging was lively and informed, but it was difficult to determine a specific Islamic Nigerian presence. Nigerian Blog Aggregator developed a system of feeds from a variety of Nigerian-related blogs from residents of the country, expatriates, and their descendants.[186] It had not categorized its system along religious lines. Overtly Christian content could be found but there was little associated with Islam.

Representation of Muslim blogs in minority contexts was also limited, although there is great potential once access increases. In South Africa, among the Muslim-oriented blogs, Na'eem Jeenah blogged on Islamic issues, including his activities as a journalist and community leader. He commented on alleged "Islamophobic" remarks and reproduced statements made by Muslim platforms against efforts by the U.S. government to indict two South Africans on terrorism charges.[187] Representation of other African-Islamic perspectives in blogs was expanding as the digital divide grew smaller, especially from West African contexts such as Senegal. This reflects the diasporic cultural shifts associated with labor migration (in particular to Western Europe) in which ICT offered a significant channel of communication for political-economic refugees and their points of origin.

Many blogs with Islam-related themes could be found in Asian contexts, which transcend religious and cultural boundaries. High levels of Internet use and access have facilitated a developed blogging culture, especially among students and graduates. I can recall during a visit to Malaysia in the mid-1990s that the Internet was already penetrating Muslim organizations and being applied by activist platforms. Blogging has enabled an extension of an already highly developed social discourse online, encouraged in Malaysia in particular by the Wawasan 2020 ("2020 Vision"). This was a strategy developed by the Malaysian premier Mahathir Mohamed and his UMNO Party in the 1990s in which information technology played a core role in plans to develop Malaysian culture and society.[188]

Malaysia now has a highly developed Internet culture. There have also been particular issues of control and censorship in relation to blogging, which has not been without risk of censorship or prosecution. In 2004 online criticism of Prime Minister Badawi's interpretation of Islam led to the critic being threatened with jail.[189]

The notion of *reformasi*, or Islamic reform, in Malaysia resonated in the blogosphere. Campaigns associated with Anwar Ibrahim—the former deputy prime minister controversially imprisoned between 1999 and 2004 on corruption and sodomy charges—have been innovative in their integrated online activity. A successful appeal led to Ibrahim's release, after which he continued to apply the Internet to promote his political message. This online activity focused on Ibrahim's own blogs in Bahasa Malay and English, in which he posted regularly on international and regional political-religious issues. Postings included the integration of specially made video blogs, hosted on YouTube, and video of an Al-Jazeera interview in which he encouraged supporters to produce blogs and to become engaged with Internet political activism.[190] Ibrahim had pages on social-networking sites such as Facebook and MySpace, which linked to a video documentary on Ibrahim's incarceration. The social-networking site Friendster contained photos of the politician, together with links to "Anwar's groups," which included the Islamic opposition Parti Islam Semalaysia (PAS).[191]

The significance of hyperlinks as a method of demonstrating allegiances to Ibrahim could be seen in banners on his main blog linking to Parti Keadilan Rakyat (People's Justice Party), which promoted Ibrahim's reformist vision. Parti Keadilan Rakyat was chaired by Ibrahim's wife, Wan Azizah Wan Ismail. She had become a member of the Malaysian Parliament, taking her husband's former parliamentary seat after his imprisonment. International activities were highlighted in a link to Accountability, a sustainable-development charity, which had Ibrahim as an honorary president.[192]

While Anwar Ibrahim was restricted in his Malaysian political activities, he was still able to draw upon a broad Internet strategy that integrated aspects of Web 2.0 in order to promote his message. Given that technological concerns and infrastructural development were a core feature of his political manifesto when he was deputy prime minister, the promotion of a "wired" reformist politician is further enhanced through the use of the Internet in this way.

Other Malaysian politicians created blogs and linked into social-networking sites, and all the parties had highly developed Web networks. Johor Baru member of parliament Datuk Shahrir Abdul Samad had been blogging since 1999 and was keen to promote his concept of what constituted "appropriate blogging" in the interests of the Malaysian government. Samad felt that bloggers should not be anonymous.[193] "I am old-fashioned and what I say is as binding to me as what I write," he stated. "What you write is powerful and I make sure what I write is what I see as a fact or opinion, which I sign off as myself."[194]

Other sites also carried the *reformasi* message associated with Malaysia, posting commentary and newspaper articles while also networking to other sympathetic blogs. A number of PAS supporter sites featured political protest with photos and video.[195] PAS developed its own blogs, including one on parliamentary activities. This in turn linked to the PAS television site, featuring political video clips and commentary.[196] PAS represented an interesting example of how political interests seized on aspects of Web 2.0 to present their perspectives on Islam. In part, this was to counter the extensive online Malaysian governmental activities.[197]

Kickdefella featured social commentary, drawing on photos taken from within the traditional *kampung*s (villages) and encouraging readers to contribute to the welfare of economically disadvantaged individuals. The site was written by a filmmaker and contained a series of spoof movie posters featuring Malaysian political figures, juxtaposed with animated-film characters such as Mr. Incredible and Shrek. Kickdefella also contained a blog roll leading to over sixty reform-oriented sites.[198]

An aggregation of Malaysian (including Muslim) weblogs was on Project Petaling Street, illustrating that Malaysian blogging contained diverse religious, cultural, and ethnic interests.[199] Among the more prolific of Malaysia bloggers, MENJ's Critical Thoughts focused on the practice of Islam in Malaysia. Writer Mohd. Elfie Nieshaem Juferi, a student in IT and computing, described himself as "a Muslim Internet activist and student of Comparative Religions . . . dedicated to combating misinformation about Islam."[200] He may not be representative of Malaysian Muslim blogging, but he was proactive and posted on a variety of topics.

Juferi contributed to other websites and portals, including Bismiki Allahuma, a multinational portal seeking "to facilitate Muslim responses to the various mendacious polemics and distortions of Islam by the Christian missionaries and their anti-Islamic allies that are being spread over the Internet."[201] The issue of alleged prisoner abuse in Malaysia caused a furor in blogging circles when a video of an ethnic Chinese woman being strip-searched was circulated on the Internet; this, too, was discussed on Juferi's pages.[202]

MENJ included numerous references to popular culture. For example, a Malay-language hip-hop song, "Minah Tudung," which criticized women in traditional Islamic dress, was given the "all clear" (and a link to a download) by Juferi: "We need more songs of this nature, albeit in more softer language. Social criticism is sorely lacking in the arts and culture of this country."[203] He defended his position on religious identity in Malaysia, seeing Bangsa Malaysia or cohesive Malaysian multiethnic identity as "a failed concept."[204] Intriguing cross-cultural references emerged in a post titled "After a Linkin Park Album," which used a defense that included a character from C. S. Lewis's *The Chronicles of Narnia*.[205] Other blogs emerging from Malaysia suggested a dynamic discourse opening up in the federation.

High levels of Internet penetration in Indonesia enabled an information technology–literate and wired society. Blogging became a significant adjunct for self-expression within Indonesian educated circles. This was "top down" as, significantly, Indonesian president H. Susilo Bambang Yudhoyono had a blog containing political statements. The extent to which he wrote the content himself was perhaps open to question.[206]

The medium in which Indonesians expressed themselves was seen as significant, reflecting segmentation and different audience profiles. The use of English was seen as important in order to present Indonesian worldviews to an international readership. For example, Rabat-based student Dedy W. Sanusi made a switch from Bahasa Indonesia to English-language blogging to discuss his experiences as an Indonesian in Morocco.[207] Priyadi Iman Nurcahyo's Priyadi's Place blog presents a "Top 100 Blog Indonesia," which suggested a vibrant blogging scene on a range of subject areas (he was himself third on this listing, "beaten" by William Computer Blog—a technical page—and Enda Nasution's weblog).[208] Priyadi's own blog listed an additional 200 "friends" with blogs.

Blogger Indonesia was a significant portal that extended its reach through contributions that were posted onto Global Voices Online. It campaigned to increase the amount of English-language blogging emerging from Indonesian contexts.[209] The blog's owner, A. Fatih Syuhud, was a student of Islamic Studies and political science in New Delhi, India. These academic themes permeated Syuhud's posts, which discussed many aspects of Indonesian society.[210] In a posting in the Indonesian Diary, Syuhud asks, "Who is a moderate Muslim?," relating the term specifically to the Indonesian context as well as the global. After discussing moderate Muslim groups, Syuhud notes:

> There are one group called "abangan" which means a non-practicing muslim. a muslim whose islamic identity only in his/her ID card or may be in his/her conviction and belief in God and prophet muhammad but no more than that. you can find them in the bar, discotheque, singing naked in a hotel or become a nude model in some half- or full-porn magazines or a nude-porn-film-star and anything dirty and nasty like that. having said that, none of the moderate muslims (traditional or conservative) who ever despise this group and disregard it as non-muslim. the abangan still a muslim. they are part of Indonesian muslims which are unique and homogeneous.
>
> It's a bit difficult to identify them as they are ever changing. an abangan now, could be a SANTRI tomorrow. :-)[211]

The term "santri" implies a purer form of Islam, while "abangan" suggests syncretism in Muslim practices.[212] Syuhud's analysis, which was personal, subjective, and at times imaginative in its definition of "abangan," does challenge notions of religious and cultural identity and understanding.

In 2006 Syuhud included a roundup of postings discussing polygamy, referring to the second wife acquired by the high-profile Muslim preacher Aa Gym (Abdullah Gymnastiar): "So, the hottest Holy Man is now living with two wives. And that sparked the controversy among the Indonesian blogosphere as to the propriety of such an act."[213] The issue of polygamy in Islam generated substantial online comment, especially given the populist, reformist approach of Gym. It was an opportunity for Gym's detractors to question his moral stance, while others embraced his decision.

Syuhud's posting was coupled with a separate controversy relating to a sex scandal and allegations surrounding an Indonesian member of parliament who was minister of religious affairs in his political party. This scandal had a specific Web 2.0 element, as Global Voices Online reported: "His sex scandal with a singer recorded by and through her mobile phone gets out of hand and spreads like a virus among Indonesian mobile phones users and gets talked about by Indonesian bloggers."[214]

The video clip, in various versions, appeared across the Internet. It inadvertently raised the profiles of some Indonesian bloggers, who chose to post the clip onto their sites. Scandal aside, a broad range of blogs emanates from Indonesia, reflecting the republic's ethnic, cultural, and religious diversity. Religion and concepts of "reform" are a small part of this equation. However, the usual popular cultural themes found elsewhere in the blogosphere play a significant part in Indonesian online expression. The experimental approach of its proponents suggests that a distinctly Indonesian Muslim blogosphere is emerging from technologically literate elements within the most populous Muslim country in the world.

It is important to remind ourselves that religious content is not necessarily a dominant theme in a number of sectors of cyberspace associated with Muslims. The online op-ed columnists are often outnumbered by personal blogs, whose content is based on the mundane elements of everyday life or enlivened by scandal and gossip. In the future, if archives of such materials are preserved, they will offer anthropologists and cultural historians a treasure trove of raw materials.

There are specific nuances of segmented content within diverse sectors of the Islamic blogosphere, reflecting historical, cultural, and religious influences. This is reflected in Pakistani cyberspace, which includes English, Punjabi, Urdu, and Arabic blogs. Pakistan has seen the emergence of a number of significant blogs, including those organized between residents, expatriates, and people in the Pakistani Muslim diaspora. There is also a non-Muslim sector in Pakistani cyberspace. Pakistani Bloggers produced resources for bloggers "of Pakistani origin" and listed over a hundred Pakistani bloggers, including Urdu-language blogs.[215] Content in Pakistan's local languages is limited.

Many seek to engage with political and religious issues, seeing blogging as offering a level of freedom denied in other media. All Things Pakistan (ATP) is a good example of this. Founded in 2006, ATP's founder-editor

Adil Najam was part of a panel that shared the Nobel Prize with Al Gore for work on climate change policy.[216] ATP's team commented regularly on Pakistani issues while also reflecting on its history through numerous photos and articles. ATP ran blog polls on various issues, focusing on political concerns in Pakistan, where President Musharraf's leadership was "graded."[217] While news was an undercurrent to the blog, other cultural issues featured strongly. ATP was intended "to embrace Pakistan in all its dimensions," the writers explained, including "its politics, its culture, its minutia, its beauty, its warts, its potential, its pitfalls, its facial hair, its turbaned heads, its shuttlecock burqas, its jet-setting supermodels, its high-flying bankers, its rock bands, its qawalls, its poets, its street vendors, its swindling politicians, its scheming bureaucrats, its resolute people—in essence, *all things Pakistani.*"

The resulting blog featured sustained levels of moderated interactivity, especially on topical issues. This was apparent when Najam posted on the 2007 siege and "battle" of Lal Masjid in Islamabad, resulting in thousands of page views and hundreds of comments. Najam's detailed posts drew on newspaper reports and video clips derived from diverse sources, including the BBC. Female religious members from the mosque's *madrassah* apparently produced another clip.[218]

The Pakistan blogosphere had room for religious satire. Omer Alvie published a "Mad-Rasa curriculum" in the Olive Ream blog, a satirical critique of the *madrassah* system in Pakistan and elsewhere.[219] Alvie was proactive in providing an overview to Pakistani blogging in his entries for the Global Voices Online blog.[220] Blogs also appeared in response to specific events in Pakistan; for example, a series of blogs emerged following the earthquake in Pakistan in 2005. In between responses from humanitarian and religious-political points of view there was a discussion on whether the earthquake represented "divine punishment." Amir Saleem posted photos of pre-earthquake Balakot on his site, Falling Days.[221]

As with Pakistan, Bangladesh blogs utilized a variety of networking devices, feeds, and applications to develop a distinct online identity in which religious issues represented a significant role. Students were prominent players, and Bangladeshi blogs represented the distinct identities within the country. Rezwan, a Bangladeshi based in Dhakka, wrote 3rd World View. This focused on regional news, with comments from other Bangladesh bloggers following a bomb blast by "Islamic militants."[222]

From Chittagong, a blog by Rifat called Close Your Eyes and Try to See emerged in 2004. This commented on technology, gender issues, religion, and Bangladeshi heavy metal music. Rifat, an engineering student, provided information on e-mailing in Bangladesh and assessed the reactions of classmates to CIT. Early posts saw Rifat attempting to explain the concepts associated with blogging. However, he soon moved onto more controversial areas in an exploration of the contextually problematic issue of homosexuality and Islam, commenting: "You may be a gay. But don't try to make it legal by an Islamic marriage."[223] Rifat discussed premarital sex, noting that "everyone wants to get a virgin life partner, even though he/she isn't virgin anymore."[224]

It is significant that these life issues are presented within a blog with a distinct Bangladeshi Muslim identity, although the extent to which this represented an exploration or a reiteration of received "wisdom" is open to question. Diaspora issues are significant threads within Bangladeshi blogs, with networks and information exchange extending in particular to the UK and United States and subnetworks developing based on linguistic, cultural, regional, and ethnic factors.

Indian Muslim blogging networked internationally. Collective blogs touched upon (Indian) Muslim themes such as Sepia Mutiny, which focused on the "Desi" South Asian and diaspora communities across the world. Collaborative: Pickled Politics, a "progressive British Asian" blog, included input from Muslim writers. An article by Fe'reeha on the role of women, based on personal experience, elicited over a hundred responses regarding the "purpose" of the veil.[225] Unholy Wars was a product of a New Delhi−based blogging team. Its content suggested that Muslim blogging could articulate gender issues in a depth denied within other sectors.[226]

Some elements within Indian societies were substantially more wired than others. Determining a defined Muslim blogging space is problematic. Over 2,000 blogs were listed in the BlogStreet India Top 100, although few suggested much in the way of directly Islamic content. Blogging was the subject of media speculation and discussion, with questions related to the freedom of speech and responsibility of publishing. Dina Mehta, a prominent Indian blogger and cofounder of the Tsunami Blog, noted: "There is a case for more responsibility and ethics for bloggers—bloggers have been known to pass sentences in mob justice."[227]

Kashmiri-oriented blogs mobilized support following the 2005 earthquake, but in general, blogging was limited in relation to Kashmiri Muslim causes. Opinions of a 21st Century Kashmiri Nomad explored Christianity from a Muslim perspective, although the author retained an air of perplexity. The blog generated controversy from some readers, who used it as an opportunity to attack Islam.[228] The blogger discussed the specific aspirations of Kashmiris, especially those who "force" their children to become doctors. The Nomad suggested that those with such aspirations may be ignoring the specific religious injunctions of Islam and that their approach to religion is hypocritical.[229] This was a distinct voice reflecting one view of Islam from and within Kashmir that challenges stereotypes represented elsewhere on the Web, especially in relation to jihadi Islam in Kashmir.

Everyday concerns are effectively covered in blogs from diverse Afghanistan contexts. Diaspora commentators applied the Web as a significant tool on issues associated with Muslim cultures and societies. Examples include Afghan Pundit ("by an American of Afghan origin") and Afghan Voice (which commented from an "insider perspective" on news about Afghanistan).[230] The Farsi influence in Afghanistan was evident, although indicators relating to Farsi blogs produced in Afghanistan was limited.[231] The equivalent of a Salam Pax in Kabul had yet to emerge, unsurprising given the city's limited IT infrastructure. Afghan Warrior, produced by an interpreter working with the U.S. Army, noted: "People are really interested to use the Internet but it's too expensive for people to use it—only rich people can afford it."[232]

As has been seen from Francophone contexts, Muslims from so-called minority situations applied blogging as an effective alternative or adjunct to other online publications and commentaries. The lines are blurred in many cases between and within minority and majority situations, given the variety of contrasting—and at times conflicting—perspectives that can be present within any one Muslim context.

The blog Shia Pundit is one of many indications of the diversity within the Islamic blogosphere, providing a "Shi'a Fatimi Ismaili Dawoodi Bohra" viewpoint. It kept a close eye on prominent Muslim blogs, with feedback on significant issues, in particular "progressive Islam" and the writer's own community (or communities). It challenged media coverage of Muslim issues and gave a personal perspective on topics such as the difficulties of post–9/11 air travel.[233]

Muslims in minority contexts have used blogging as an effective adjunct to other publications and commentaries. As'ad AbuKhalil, a political science professor at California State University of Lebanese origin, regularly commented on world affairs in the Angry Arab. One particular focus was the American media and its negative representation of Arabs and Muslims. AbuKhalil included e-mail polls in which readers voted on contemporary issues.[234]

In contrast, Mas'ud Ahmed Khan's www.Mas'ud's Blog offered a colorful insight into one aspect of Muslim life in Britain. There was an account of a mosque-committee election, predated by a "a lot of incidents [that] occurred involving violence in the community to [the] point where an ambush was organised in the mosque itself, with sticks and boiling water."[235] Mas'ud was concerned about an erosion of values in his community.[236] He was aware that his blog was read within his community and that "controversial" postings were printed out and anonymously delivered to a community elder.

Muslim female bloggers engaged proactively in this element of the medium, commenting on significant issues of the day. This emphasis may contradict prevalent stereotypes about Muslim females, especially those found elsewhere on the Internet. As with other areas of the Internet, blogs demonstrate the potential for digital interactivity between Muslims across the *ummah*. Veiled4Allah, part of the wider al-Muhajabah series of blogs, included a Qur'an Journal and the Niqabi Paralegal section, which discussed "legal issues facing Muslims in the United States."[237] In between more personal discussions, al-Muhajabah approached current affairs from an American Muslim perspective. In 2005 she was condemning the Janjaweed's actions in Darfur and Sudan and the "silence" of Muslims on the issue.[238]

Away from worldly concerns, more mundane issues were tackled on Muslim parenting blogs. Umm Zaynab's Thoughts on Islamic Parenting discussed domestic concerns with a "spiritual" angle, including nutrition, breast-feeding, and advice for fathers.[239] In a theme that may resonate elsewhere, Umm Zaynab bemoans the absence of child-friendly facilities in her local mosque.[240] This theme was picked up by the Shi'a-oriented Ninhajaba, which discussed the impact of toddlers being present during prayer.[241] The issue of children's toys also featured in parenting blogs; Umm Mai's A Garden of Children discussed how to transform a Barbie doll (the subject of prohibition in some Muslim contexts) into a Muslim doll.[242]

Blogs are offering a voice unavailable elsewhere, as well as insight into the diverse agendas and issues Muslims faced. This may be life-changing and serious or simply reflections on popular culture. Canadian peace activist Tareq Lubani documented his journey in Iraq, including his meetings with Mujahideen. He had previously written about Palestine within his blog Occupation Kills, which continued in his prison cell when the Israeli Defense Forces arrested him in 2003; he was subsequently deported. His accounts of his treatment, and that of fellow prisoners, were harrowing.[243]

In marked contrast, Ninjas on the Loose followed the lives of five British Muslim women, "ninjas" being an ironic reference to the use of Islamic dress. The blog cited William Blake and Rumi, and flew an England football shield.[244] Such contrasting examples indicate that a complex proliferation of blogs reflecting Muslim discourse of different kinds had emerged.

Concluding Comment

The Islamic blogosphere has expanded and mutated rapidly. iMuslims are applying blogging technology as a tool for networking about issues associated directly or indirectly with religious life and/or values. It is an opportunity for individuals to place dialogue and respond to contemporary issues while enhancing and developing new forms of Muslim networks. Specific differences of beliefs and understandings are articulated and suggest an essence of dialogue and information exchange, not always at profound levels but frequently insightful. Blogging was in an early stage of development in some contexts. Appropriate language and software tools were becoming embedded into Web users' frames of reference beyond the early adopters.

Information overload pervades CIES as blogs appear and disappear with regularity. A core of sustained and engaging bloggers within the Islamic blogosphere has emerged, presenting regular posts and engaging with their microcommunities. Some provide a more journalistic focus than others, and there is a sense that these are competing with traditional media outlets (both online and offline). There are options for readers to explore issues, which may not form part of traditional media outlets for reasons of censorship as well as editorial quality. Sections of mainstream media operating in Muslim contexts are now producing their own blogs. The role of guides and portals to online content, synthesizing the output of others, is becoming increasingly significant.

The ongoing granulation of blogs, in terms of microsubject areas and interests, continues within the Islamic information marketplace. Web 2.0 was a basis for further interaction and exchange opportunities, which will expand in response to further developments in technology and wider access to the medium. The inevitable growth in the Islamic blog genre means that it is no longer possible to talk about a "blogosphere" in the singular; it may in fact be more appropriate to discuss a series of interconnected Arabesque blogospheres, interlocked with wider CIES.

{ 5 }

The Cutting Edge

Militaristic Jihad in Cyberspace

This chapter focuses on the militaristic connotations associated with jihad and their articulation online. The term "jihad" has entered Islamic and other discourse with a set of expectations and assumptions, being synonymous in certain areas of CIES with warfare and associated endeavors. These assumptions are themselves interesting. The image of militaristic jihad attracts controversy and generates excitement among readers in ways that surpass the many more sedate and spiritually oriented areas of the Web that focus on the greater jihad.

Developers in Silicon Valley have played an involuntary but critical role in propagating jihad—in many ways as significant as the motivating Muslim ideologues espousing their interpretations of war. In their promotion of Media Center PCs, a 2005 Microsoft Windows campaign was promoted under the banner "Start Anything," but that promotional blurb was not intended to incorporate jihad. The drawing together of a technology dominated by a multinational American industrial giant and a network created in part for U.S. military purposes by a jihadi platform that was named after a computer database is not without irony. As jihadi site developers utilized the latest Web 2.0 software applications, social-networking tools, film-editing packages, database systems, and WebPhone technology, their activities highlighted the symbiotic relationship between hardware and software developers and jihadi activists. This was combined with enhanced Web literacy and accessibility, cheaper and more powerful hardware, and faster and less expensive bandwidth.

It cannot be assumed that all jihadi networks intersect; networks may pass each other by for reasons of language, culture, politics, location, or the nuanced nature of content. This can be related to specific technological factors as well. Locations with limited bandwidth access are unlikely to benefit from video streaming or files requiring substantial download time. Individuals or groups lacking the knowledge or technology for secure access to materials may also be restricted within this zone, especially if their activities in public spaces and private locations are monitored in various ways.

Networks are also fragmented because of information overload. It could be difficult or unnecessary to maintain awareness of all jihad activities online. Some have made it their duty to act as information gatherers and portal providers, an act that itself might be described as an information jihad. This is particularly appropriate for computer-literate generations; the Internet is now a multigenerational and intergenerational tool, although some users are more intuitive than others.

Established players in jihadi cyberspace have been augmented, and in some cases challenged, by new entities and networks identifying with campaigns that engineer new forms of relationships and dynamics. Sites can be analyzed in terms of how their content is retrieved, searched, navigated, and archived; materials may be reused within this jihadi context in different formats and contexts. In some cases, jihadi sites are content driven, but there are examples where the technology itself seems to be the key element driving visitors to the site.

The explicit appearance of jihadi activities in cyberspace represents an intersection or interface between virtual and real conflict. This has taken many forms. The most prominent has been the application of Internet technology by al-Qaeda, for which the Net has acted as a logistical tool, a propagation outlet, and a reinforcement weapon for global brand(s) under many names, including the International Islamic Front for Jihad Against Jews and Crusaders, Islamic Army for the Liberation of the Holy Places, the Group for the Preservation of the Holy Sites, Islamic Army for the Liberation of Holy Shrines, or simply al-Qaeda ("the base").

The network has benefited to the extent that it has developed nuanced content aimed at adherents, readers, and viewers operating in a variety of contexts. It has addressed critical issues, justified campaigns, and presented news and perspectives directly to governments and opponents through the Internet. This has been undertaken through the application or appropriation of religious symbols and an interpretation of Qur'anic language and meaning. Those unwilling or unable to study a jihadi tract may be drawn into dynamic interactive multimedia presentations, which can facilitate an emotive response among some readers.

The Web offered unprecedented marketing opportunities for the al-Qaeda entity and its affiliates, which has unconsciously drawn on discernible marketing strategies associated with online sales. Sites are designed to rapidly disseminate their messages, with quick-loading pages and graphical interfaces as well as familiar logos and symbols. These include specific identifying markers associated with al-Qaeda and photos of ideologues. There are numerous opportunities for membership and participation, together with links for further information and associated sites. Content is refreshed frequently, encouraging return visits. Sites may draw on high levels of interactivity, together with the latest in cutting-edge technologies. Design considerations allow content to be accessed on alternative platforms and interfaces, away from personal computers.

Jihadi Networks in Cyberspace

Researching jihadi networks in cyberspace has necessitated the development of new approaches toward the study of Islam and Muslim networks. It is very much a multidisciplinary area, with previously unrepresented areas of academia and research contributing to the discourse. Clearly, there are varied motivations and methodologies associated with this discussion.

For example, academic work with a security focus has contributed to the field: Gabriel Weimann, an Israeli academic and a fellow at the U.S. Institute for Peace, has written extensively on the specific theme of "terrorism" within diverse contexts, including campaigns with Islamic identities and agendas.[1] Military academies, government agencies, and associates have also published their work for a global audience; the Combating Terrorism Center at West Point produced *The Militant Ideology Atlas*, which mapped al-Qaeda–oriented jihadi writings available online.[2] Daniel Kimmage and Kathleen Ridolfo produced a report for Radio Free Europe/ Radio Liberty, containing a detailed analysis of the impact of Sunni "insurgent media" emerging from Iraq, focusing on case studies from 2007. This was significant in its emphasis on media diversity emanating from "insurgents."[3]

Organizations such as the Jamestown Foundation regularly post analytical material on the relationship between the Internet and terrorism concerns.[4] Specific ideological and political treatments of online content can be found through channels such as the output of the Northeast Intelligence Network, SITE Institute, MEMRI, and Laura Mansfield.[5] Websites and blogs with specific interests in engaging with aspects of online discourse generate further resources and discussion material.[6]

Materials can also be derived from those who articulate strong senti-
ments, often away from the academic milieu, based on observation of
specific aspects of Islamic interpretation and online discourse.[7] Journalism
sources with specific regional foci can present detailed data derived from
close monitoring of Internet sources.[8] There have also been investigative
treatments of aspects of this subject area, including from private sector and
journalistic consultative enterprises.[9] A number of broadcasters made documentaries on associated issues, often with a sensationalistic approach to
the content focusing on aspects of jihad.[10] General works on jihadi platforms have also demonstrated awareness of the impact of CIT on their
strategies.[11]

Sustained technical and human resources were applied in a quantitative
approach toward aspects of CIES, which emerged in the field of terrorism
studies. The University of Arizona's Artificial Intelligence Lab (AI Lab)
benefited from U.S. government and agency investment in the development of a sustained content analysis of jihadi materials online. This included a comprehensive archive of content harvested and catalogued from
the Internet. Many aspects of the methodologies and resources applied by
the AI Lab cannot be realistically envisaged as being applied to other,
relatively more mundane areas associated with Islam and the Internet. The
AI Lab draws upon the utilization of a mass of technology, a team of
researchers in computer science and subject-specific fields, and a sustained
plan of future research.[12]

Applying software developed in Arabic and English, the AI Lab was able
to provide an analysis of a vast quantity of hyperlinks, data, and archival
material gleaned by regularly trawling the Net for specific keywords. The
AI Lab utilized stylometry, the application of statistical analysis as applied
to literary styles and syntax, as a means of evaluating what it determines as
the "Dark Web" of "terrorism." The research analyzed style markers—such
as fonts, colors, designer ability, and layout—as an approach toward determining site ownership and authorship.

The AI Lab developed automated Web-harvesting technology, including analysis of back links (the external hyperlinks linking into a site) as a
means of exploring jihadi cyberspace. These tools focus on key players,
primarily at an organizational level, which is one part of a more complex
picture. They are not necessarily as useful in picking up the finer details and nuanced statements on cyberspace, including the output of those
sites that are not focused on generating substantial numbers of page impressions for a mass market. Such sites are often concerned with reach-

ing or creating a specific, small group of adherents to a specific religious interpretation.

The organizational, methodological emphasis of the AI Lab does not leave room for our understanding of individuals or small groups, perhaps working autonomously without direct links to a specific organizational platform. The number of links or hits is one indicator of influence only; a closed site may have more impact on a community and society. As with any study of cyberspace, a machine-generated analysis is a snapshot of a particular space in time, which can evolve and change rapidly. Automatic information retrieval has been applied, including indexing algorithms, as a means of retrieving key conceptual data from vast numbers of materials. The AI Lab received a $1.3 million grant from the National Science Foundation to focus on posts made to jihadi forums, especially those relating to improvised explosives. This research was to further the development of their automated analytical application "Writeprint."[13]

The AI Lab also approached jihadi cyberspace through the development of visual software intended to enable a reader to understand the on- and offline interconnectivity between jihadi organizations.[14] They demonstrated the potential of such methods in their creation of a typology of jihadi video materials. This provided determinant categories based on whether the video was deemed to be operational, produced, hostage, statement, tribute, internal training, or instructional.[15] In the AI Lab's case, working with one dominant criteria for analysis (being an understanding of a threat level) clouds judgment of other aspects of the cyber environment. It may be that a holistic analytical approach of all aspects of beliefs as placed online would offer more granulated and complex interpretative opportunities.

The AI Lab presents substantial resources that are useful as part of an overall analysis of an enormous field of enquiry, although they are filtered in some cases by specific concerns associated with security issues and/or political interests. These and other contributions to the field are important in developing an understanding of diverse areas of concern associated with Islam and the Internet.

Viral Jihad

Manifestations of jihadi activities in cyberspace could be defined as viral jihad in the sense that aspects of Internet marketing patterns and paradigms can be located in the spread of the jihadi message. Its networking via the Web, with content copied on websites and transmitted in chat rooms and other forums, mimics the way other, more generic products are promoted online. A single message in a chat room can multiply exponentially through e-mail contact, Web links, discussion in chat rooms, references in Net broadcasts, publication in magazines, and other media online and offline, as well as by word of mouth. This bears some resemblance to the paradigm of a viral marketing strategy, which can be defined as one that "(1) gives away products or services; (2) provides for effortless transfer to others; 3) scales easily from small to very large; 4) exploits common motivations and behaviors; (5) utilizes existing communication networks; and (6) takes advantage of others' resources."[16]

Not all of these elements are required for a viral marketing strategy to be successful. However, these factors would all seem to apply within a viral jihad framework. The rapid dissemination of official statements, video clips, news, logistical advice, and religious opinions associated with jihadi platforms could all be associated with the above factors. A further issue is how representative of "Islam" these sites are. Can jihadi Web space be equated with "sacred" (Web) space? As with other zones of CIES, this might be best left in the eyes of the beholders: concepts of the sacred abound in discourse of justification for jihad. In terms of levels of liminality and the application of religious symbolism, the ritual associations of militaristic jihad as articulated online by supporters and protagonists clearly enter the realm of the sacred. To their supporters, these are popular acts played out in a religious universe in which the actors play a dynamic role validated and motivated by religious authority. There is continuity with historical and contemporary role models holding similar values, which may be transmitted by the Internet. The integration of Qur'anic language and religious values would justify participation as a religious act, either as part of discourse or in real-time action. Web activities can form part of the equation of jihad, which has been interpreted as a sixth pillar of Islam, synchronized with and analogous to prayer. It forms part of an integrated conceptual framework that goes beyond politics to become enmeshed in areas of CIES.

The justifications articulated online offer motivation to potential participants, provide solace to the families of martyrs, and strike fear in opponents. They offer little in the way of sympathy to the frequently anonymous (or rapidly anonymized) casualties of these jihadi actions, which end up part of yet another statistical equation: many of these victims are themselves Muslim. Some might ask, "Where are their websites?" and "Who speaks for them in cyberspace?"

Identifying E-Jihad

E-jihad, or electronic jihad, is a term that can encompass a wide range of understandings. The term "jihad" goes beyond the lesser militaristic models of "jihad" to include interpretations of "greater" jihad. This is based on spiritual striving to attain goals, focused on the paradigm of the Prophet Muhammad, which draws on the divine source of the Qur'an. Jihad itself is an umbrella term, encompassing many different forms of striving in the name of Islam and Muslim causes. Traditional Islamic sources go into considerable detail as to how the term is applied, but these are frequently ignored (on all sides).

The popular usage of "jihad" in contemporary contexts often makes a lot of assumptions—particularly in the popular media—and associates the term with holy war. This is one component of a wider and more nuanced application of the term; thus, we can have a jihad for peace or a jihad for prayer, and, if we adopt a wider interpretation, these can also form part of e-jihad. All the references to jihad in this discussion focus on the term and its application in conflict situations. E-jihad has been utilized in cyber contexts in combination with classical interpretations of the term "jihad," although caution is necessary as I see the term as encompassing nuanced ideas of religious understanding. E-jihad can take many forms, representing diverse platforms and understandings of Islam—and predating 9/11.[17]

Participants and supporters may represent militaristic jihadi actions as "Islamic." Some Muslim observers, scholars, opponents, and apologists have reacted by stating that they are criminal acts or forms of "terrorism" that have no connection with, or which are contradictory to, Islam.[18] There are long-standing issues associated with stereotyping of Muslims here, which came into sharp focus after 9/11.[19] Participation in militaristic jihad is a minority issue, on- and offline. Muslim individuals and organizations have expended considerable energies—on the Internet and elsewhere—distancing themselves from such acts. However, the purpose here is not to make delineations of judgments as to what is representative of Islam but to focus on the jihadi actions made by individuals who describe themselves as "Muslims" and their actions as "Islamic."

The term "jihadi" refers to any site or individual that discusses, and in some cases promotes and supports, ideas of militaristic activities in the name of Islam. This can be from a variety of perspectives and often is labeled (not always accurately) by protagonists and observers with other terms or descriptions. These may be in conjunction with regional conflicts as much as religious ideals or concepts, such as *salafi*. The term *salafi(yun)* is multifaceted and applied in diverse ways in cyberspace and elsewhere, often associated with the early community or "forefathers" surrounding the Prophet Muhammad. Depending on how it is applied, the term has associations with various "reform"-oriented movements seeking a return to the ideals of the first Muslim community.[20]

"Jihadi" has entered popular discourse online when applied to protagonists and supporters of the lesser jihad, as articulated in cyberspace and elsewhere. While theoretically the term "jihadi" could be applied across conflicts and interpretations, in this aspect of the discussion it is narrowed down to refer to those ideologically affiliated to the entity/networks known as al-Qaeda. This in itself is an amorphous concept; there is no single headquarters or structure, and, while its leadership had focused on Osama bin Laden and his immediate associates (especially Ayman al-Zawahiri), the unstructured entity mutated to develop separate but affiliated identities.

It could be wrong to talk about it in terms of region, as the globalized conceptual framework is in some ways redundant. However, significant regional nodes, which defined themselves as al-Qaeda, appeared in Iraq, the Maghreb, and elsewhere. It might be crude but appropriate to apply the metaphor of a computer network as representative of al-Qaeda: certainly, individual nodes can function independent of a central "server" and may not be aware of others within their network; certainly, communications can be rapid and secure and proliferate with ease; and certainly, the networking also offers logistical support and psychological senses of ownership through diverse methods and media.

There is also a practical affinity between al-Qaeda and computer networks: without the Internet and its associated tools, al-Qaeda could not have functioned the way that it did. This is not to say that it would not have functioned at all, but that its modus operandi and networking proliferation would have been substantially different. The stereotyping of al-Qaeda as somehow technologically illiterate impaired the work of security organizations in tracking down operatives, while a lack of knowledge about the precise application of the Internet by al-Qaeda and its affiliates was played upon by the network. Osama bin Laden was fully aware of these deficiencies, and he took advantage of them: "The Americans have made laughable claims. They said that there are hidden messages intended for terrorists in bin Laden's statements. It is as if we are living in a time of carrier pigeons, without the existence of telephones, without travelers, without the Internet, without regular mail, without faxes, without email. This is just farcical; words which belittle people's intellects."[21]

As well as the logistical implications of computer technology for al-Qaeda, one key element has been the ways in which the Internet has been applied to communicate various agendas, aims, objectives, and results to audiences in a nuanced and, in many cases, creative, structured, and professional fashion. In terms of an "activist" campaigning militaristic platform, al-Qaeda, paradoxically for some, represents a "success story" and model for others to follow.

Within the sphere of the promulgation of jihad, the al-Qaeda paradigm has been cloned and enhanced, rather like open-source software. Diffuse jihadi packages have utilized the central code and tweaked it to suit different operating systems and conditions. Adjustment may be in terms of language as much as militaristic objectives. The binary source remains a specific interpretation of the Qur'an firmly based on long-standing analogue models, synthesizing research and development from a range of ideologues drawn from historical and contemporary contexts.

Within the jihadi milieu, the influence of Sayyid Qutb (1906–66) and Abdullah Azzam (1941–89) is felt as much as Ibn Taymiyyah (1263–1328), and in some cases these deceased scholars and ideologues continue to dialogue with certain contemporary scholars (*'ulama'*) in order to justify jihad-oriented activities. These *'ulama'* may not necessarily be drawn from conventional or traditional scholarly backgrounds, but this does not negate their influence; some have enhanced their religious position online. Osama bin Laden (1957–) did not have a degree in traditional Islamic sciences but felt qualified enough to position himself (or be positioned) as one who could pronounce on issues interpreting jihad.

Similar factors apply to Ayman al-Zawahiri (1951–), Abu Musab al-Zarqawi (1966–2006), and others who felt empowered by their actions and interpretative abilities. This can be closely linked to ideas surrounding qualifications for religious authority within Islam, in particular the long-standing arguments surrounding *ijtihad*. This concept, particularly in Sunni orthodox models, can be associated with the ability to interpret aspects of the Qur'an and other Islamic sources in the light of contemporary conditions and circumstances. This ability is deemed as inherent in all humanity and not just in those who have undertaken the formal study of Islamic sciences.

The Internet has offered a direct route to developing the promotion of these specific interpretative models, which circumnavigate—and, for some, invalidate—traditional models of religious knowledge and authority. This is true particularly in the jihadi sphere, where they can be reinforced through the development of close-knit virtual communities with ideas of ownership, belonging, and religious justification. These do not replicate real-world networks but intersect with them to present their own unique phenomena and issues. In terms of understanding Islam and Muslims, both within and outside of paradigms of Muslim identities, the Internet has become a crucial adjunct for individual and group self-knowledge and reinforcement, especially within microjihadi networks. These can often operate beyond the jurisdiction of the authorities, including those linked to religious, state, and commercial interests. They can articulate solutions to popular causes in a radical way.

This is a critical distinguishing point: so-called Muslim causes such as Palestine, Kashmir, Chechnya, and Iraq have a popular currency beyond cells of jihadi affiliates, but the methods advocated and applied by jihadi affiliates do not necessarily retain that same currency. It may be, however, that their voice is loudest on the Internet. Certainly, opponents of jihadi violence had yet to present detailed manuals advocating their points of view or sophisticated video rebuttals. It should also be recognized that these causes cannot be reduced to a single model. The multitude of "Shi'a" and "Sunni" (and secular) voices that presented themselves in Iraq is an example of this, and evidence of these views can be found online to varying degrees.

In order to interpret this subject, I will focus initially on "al-Qaeda" as a conceptual entity (or entities); chapter 6 will develop these themes in terms of how they relate to the specific regional contexts of Iraq and Palestine.

Exploring E-Jihadi Networks

It is suggested that e-jihad–oriented sites are read widely by many people in Muslim minority and majority contexts. There is, however, no specific data on site hits, which would require hard data from ISPs and site developers. The transient nature of jihadi site locations, combined with the anonymity and reluctance of developers to volunteer such information, lends a speculative edge to this discussion. Does it matter that, as I noted when undertaking this research, 800 individuals downloaded an al-Qaeda–related file in twenty-four hours? We do not know who the 800 people were, or their motivations; we do not know how many copied the file and distributed or showed it to others; we do not know whether it had a substantive effect on them, or how many academics, researchers, journalists, and analysts were among them.

A single academic researcher cannot gather this evidence. State organizations and agencies have had their own difficulties extracting similar data. Any data that they may have derived is not generally open to academic researchers. Site participants are not open to interview, either anonymously or through questionnaires. Evidence of influence is anecdotal in part, with glimpses of information appearing in court transcripts as much as through conversations observed in chat rooms.

These limited forms of evidence, in a variety of forms, have suggested that some jihadis have been recruited directly from the consumption of online content. These include some of the sites and forums discussed in this and the following chapter that have the potential to act as radicalizing tools. These are simply a sample of the tens of thousands of pages of Internet content in various media and languages that have been published by jihadi groups and individuals, a significant proportion of which have had a very short shelf life (even in "Internet years"). Building a picture of such content is problematic, but there is some information that can be gleaned from existing evidence. Gradually, impressions can emerge that may contribute not only to our understanding of jihadi forms of CIEs but also to knowledge about the people behind them and real-world events.

Mapping might be useful in determining Web links between entities. The FMS Advanced Systems Group created a Threat Network Explorer that enables users to create a diagrammatic model of links between entities in al-Qaeda.[22] It is likely that any ideological mapping would reflect such linkages, but in terms of Internet mapping it would follow other patterns based on locations of servers, ISPs, and site-content writers in disparate locations. Information landscapes can appear in many ways as developed by a variety of IT specialists; the e-jihadi landscape might not be accommodated within metaphors of information cities, as represented within *The Atlas of Cyberspace* (2001).[23]

In the past, I have referred to the Islamic Internet *souq*, or marketplace, which might form part of an information medina, or city.[24] How one would incorporate jihadi materials within this marketplace is a difficult proposition; it is not at the center of the *souq* but is a noisy, potentially dangerous, and also popular back alley for some individuals with an appropriate secret map (one that is unlikely to feature on Google Maps). The mapping in this discussion will demonstrate an information-rich landscape of militaristic

Global Islamic Media Front,
Sout al-Khalifa media channel,
2005

jihad-oriented sites online—a small slice of CIES overall, which require constant specialist observation and considerable resources of time and technology to observe.

Jihadi sites present one form of religious authority, but that should not obscure the fact that the Web has been applied to present an increasing variety of forms of religious expression and understanding. It is applied by many senior figures and organizations—as well as individuals taking advantage of the medium to present their point of view, however legitimate—to a *potential* global audience. Whether it is read is another matter; the value of a statement may not be in the number of hits it receives but who is reading it.

What kind of immersion does a surfer receive if they spend several hours in jihadi areas of cyberspace? If it is associated with radicalization, then that is also a subjective term. An equivalent term is not necessarily in the minds of those who chose a jihadi path. They may prefer concepts associated with the Islamic ideals of *ummah* and connectivity with other jihadi exemplars from contemporary contexts and historical precedents. The transition from reader to activist may be a subtle or overt, gradual or rapid process. It links as much into jihadi finances, propagation, networking, activism, and religious ideals as it does into the Internet.

Diversity of Muslim issues and contexts plus specific interests makes defining a radical particularly problematic, or even unnecessary when drawing on that terminology. What the Internet helps us with is providing one of several ways of understanding processes and discourses. These incorporate psychological factors combined with the impact, if any, of hubs for jihadi resources acting as entry points to more detailed polemical materials and the potential development of proactive sympathies. This is

Islamic-minbar, 2004

not necessarily an overnight process, and again it should be stressed that the Net is one of many potential catalysts. It could be a long process of propagation, prior to any radicalization, in conjunction with other sources and media, such as viewing BBC News as much as Al-Jazeera.

To this should be added the human dynamics of conversations and networking in mosques and other local/national contexts, formal and informal meetings and discussions in the online and real world. The Internet is not necessarily a sole tool for such processes. A report produced by the General Intelligence and Security Service of the Netherlands suggested that mosque activity, rather than the Internet, had become the focus for the facilitation of "radical *da'wa*" (propagation)—albeit of a nonviolent nature.[25]

Profiling E-Jihad and Its Protagonists

A key question when exploring activism in CIES is determining the profiles of site authors and site readers. This is an issue of particular concern in relation to jihadi sites; interest may come from many quarters, especially when legislation appeared in several countries prohibiting the access and distribution of jihadi materials. Jihad-oriented groups take diffuse forms, but many have utilized the Internet to promote their specific understandings of Islam and to project affiliation, acquire funding, encourage recruitment, and develop affinities to like-minded networks.

While it is critical to avoid stereotyping readers of jihadi websites, it might be possible to construct a model containing certain parameters of use. Patterns could range from previously radicalized to those who are interested in specific issues associated with Islamic campaigns. This may include non-Muslims seeking to develop awareness of Islamic Internet activities. Different levels of interest, motivation, affiliation, and participation might form part of our surfer equation. Added to this would be issues of personal religiosity, identity, politics, culture, language, and education. The relationship a reader could form with a site could also be linked to their projection and recognition of these factors within a site's content and design; sites that have an aura of being "cool," with high degrees of Web 2.0 interactivity and a dynamic design aesthetic, could also be appropriate. This might depend on whether a reader was accessing a site for reasons of entertainment, knowledge, or, at the other end of the scale, desperation born of the failure of other channels to provide information and generate adherence to a cause.

The stereotype that a jihadi site user/member is necessarily lacking in education is one that might be avoided here. The implication is that if a user is Net literate, then, certainly in many Muslim contexts, she or he is likely to have attained a certain level of education and income not necessarily representative of a population as a whole.

Site creators would be seeking to recruit the allegiance of such individuals to benefit from their skills and knowledge, especially in jihadi activities; 9/11 is a model that some seek to follow, where the main protagonists came from middle-class social and educational backgrounds.[26] Among those involved in 9/11 were mainly university-educated individuals, with technical backgrounds and a familiarity of Western life. For example, Mohammed Atta acquired a graduate degree at Technische Universität Hamburg-Harburg and had also studied at the American University in Cairo; Khalid Shaikh Mohammed was a graduate of North Carolina Agricultural and Technical University in Greensboro.[27] Other prominent jihadis in earlier campaigns, such as Khalid's nephew Ramzi Yousef, were also well educated by the standards of their social origins. Yousef had an educational and professional background in engineering, communications, and computers.[28]

This might be contrasted with the relatively low educational achievements and social status of the foot soldiers of related activities. This category would include the "shoe-bomber" Richard Reid and some of the Madrid 11 March 2004 ("11-M") bombers, who included drug dealer Jamal Ahmidan among their numbers. Osama bin Laden's mentor Abdullah Azzam reflected that there was a responsibility for jihad at all levels in society:

> Jihad today is individually obligatory (*Fard Ain*), by self and wealth, on every Muslim, and the Muslim Ummah remains sinful until the last piece of Islamic land is freed from the hands of the disbelievers. Furthermore, none are absolved from the sin other than the Mujahideen. . . . Allah has not excused anybody to abandon jihad other than the ill, the cripple and the blind, as well as children who have not yet reached puberty, women who have no way of emigrating and performing jihad and those advanced in years. . . . Anybody else has no excuse before Allah, whether he is a professional, a specialist, an employer or a great businessman. None of these is excused from performing jihad personally or permitted to merely contribute materially.[29]

Clearly, there are issues of hierarchy within organizational levels associated with jihadi activities, whether labeled specifically in association with al-Qaeda or linked to other networks and entities. At all levels, however, it would seem that there are technologically literate individuals utilizing CIT in order to fulfill their objectives under the rubric of jihad.

The profiles of online protagonists cannot be stereotyped, given that significant amounts of information are unobtainable. Some suggestions of profiles have come to light during the trials of jihadi-oriented individuals, including those involved in producing online materials. These suggest social backgrounds incorporating relative economic prosperity and education, with a familiarity of Western societies and values. Jihadi sites, their authors, and their visitors are not amenable to structured research questioning. In time, a more scientific profile may emerge. A number of stereotypes emerge in discussions. The image of a jihadi warrior with an AK-47 propped up on his desk as he surfs the Net is one that might dominate the minds of some analysts. The site jihad-algeria.com and others in fact had just such a photo on their website in 2004.[30]

There could be a variety of possible profiles of content creators and readers, although these are not mutually exclusive categories. These could

Pdf manual, Dhurwat al-Sanam, March 2004

range from hard-core activists and jihadi geeks (using a jihad cause as a demonstration of their cyber prowess) to casual readers (Muslim and other). Some sites focus on providing opportunities for dialogue and inter-activity. Site content may be designed to tap into potential reader suscep-tibility toward jihadi content, combining the resonance of religious lan-guage with an Islamic design aesthetic.

One has to be careful in consideration of how much dialogue is going on, compared with "lurking." It should not be assumed that *all* readers will be politicized or turn into terrorists through the consumption of jihadi online content, a stereotype that suggests a lack of sophistication and an inherent fallibility among (some) readers. It can be a considered intellec-tual process, based upon an interpretation of sources and the input of "authorities." The Net literacy and media awareness of individuals, espe-cially when they are processing and seeking such "knowledge," are signifi-cant factors in determining reader profiles. Language and relationships online can be very different to those in the real world; anonymity allows for experimentation, passive and active reading, and points in between.

Another critical factor is the amount of time an individual reader might spend on one particular site—rather than making a sequence of rapid visits to various sites—of which jihadi content is a small but significant component. Online content is not read or accessed in the same ways as print media. Jihadi content may also be accessed through casual search-engine activity or links from non-jihad-oriented portals and platforms. The profile of a site on Google can be significant: typing "jihad+US+terrorism" into Google led to Jihad Unspun, which was condemned by some as an alleged "mouthpiece" of al-Qaeda, although there were also claims that it may be an alleged "honeypot" site attracting intelligence data.[31] Sites commenting upon or critical about certain jihadi sites have inadvertently become sources of information and links for jihadi supporters. It may be able to track the links between organizations and sites; determining who links to a site via a search is also another method of accessing related material.

Key elements of consistency relating to social profiles can be hypothesized, however, in relation to jihadi activists and "radicalized" Muslims. Writing in 1996, James Piscatori and Dale Eickelman noted that politically active Muslims were predominantly from urbanized professional and educated classes and had university degrees: "Mass education opens the way to 'democratized' access to sacred texts and overcomes restrictions as to who is 'authorized' to interpret them. As a consequence, the monopolistic control by elites—whether attained in fact or merely aspired to—is countered by the greater number of would-be interpreters from diverse backgrounds yet commonly possessing modern-style education."[32]

Many of these individuals would not be involved in activities that would be classified as "jihadi" in orientation. The opportunities for such interpretations have intensified in the digital age. In a discussion on Saudi Islamic politics emanating from the *Sahwa* ("religious awakening") movement, Madawi Al-Rasheed observes that

> Sahwis [followers of the *Sahwa*] include formally trained religious scholars who quality as members of the *'ulama'* class, in addition to ordinary men. Some Sahwis are scientists, doctors, engineers, chemists, writers and journalists, but may have studied religion as part of their education. They all therefore have some degree of religious knowledge that enables them to articulate opinions on religious texts. This puts them in the category of what is known as Islamic intellectuals, who constitute a category between the traditional *'ulama'* and the laymen.[33]

Al-Rasheed presents a nuanced interpretation of the Sahwis, which can have diverse political, religious, and social agendas associated with a variety of movements. A number of people from this umbrella grouping have been engaged in online activism, including at various times those who have advocated and influenced different forms of support for jihadi activities

There might be a need to distinguish such profiles with those of curious, nonparticipant surfers seeking to be informed—perhaps making a cursory visit to a site and not necessarily sympathetic or interested in a cause but still registering visitor clicks on a site meter. The technology does not identify readers in terms of their sympathies or profiles. Site creators and supporters believe the Web has sufficient influence to justify the time, effort, and, in some cases, threat toward personal security associated with developing such online material. At times they have made creative and considered efforts to present content to a global audience.

The flexibility of the al-Qaeda entity, with a perceived absence of rigidity and fluid networking, led to a number of organizations and individuals claiming online that their activities and statements represented al-Qaeda. This reflected the permeable nature of the entity and the adoption of its nomenclature in varied campaigns. For example, the bombing in Sinai, Egypt, in November 2004 was claimed online by the Brigades of the Martyr Abdullah Azzam, an organization that declared its affiliation to al-Qaeda but was previously unknown.[34]

The 11-M (Madrid) bombings led to a heightened awareness of al-Qaeda activities on the Internet, as claims were made attributing responsibility for the multiple bombings to associated organizations. The Norwegian Defense Research Establishment referred to documents associated with possible plans for the attacks, which it had discovered on the Internet but did not immediately recognize as having dangerous implications.[35] In many ways, this represents a significant problem of intelligence and information overload in association with CIES—the difficulty of maintaining the necessary resources for translating, monitoring, and recording such a quantity of online materials.

The 7 July 2005 ("7/7") bombing attacks in London were also attributed to "al-Qaeda" by some, leading to contentious statements on jihadi message boards as to responsibility:[36] "Nation of Islam and Arab nation: Rejoice for it is time to take revenge against the British Zionist Crusader government in retaliation for the massacres Britain is committing in Iraq and Afghanistan. The heroic mujahideen have carried out a blessed raid in

London. Britain is now burning with fear, terror and panic in its northern, southern, eastern, and western quarters."[37]

It was difficult at that time to determine the veracity of a statement from a previously unknown al-Qaeda affiliate. A subsequent report was unable to establish direct linkage, although clearly ideological "inspiration" was drawn from the statements of al-Qaeda associates, presumably including materials derived from the Web.[38]

The murder of Theo van Gogh in 2004 in the Netherlands also had an Internet element. Ayaan Hirst Ali and van Gogh's controversial film *Submission* was available on YouTube, and van Gogh was an enthusiastic blogger who used the Web to promote his film and his views on Islam.[39] The depiction in the film of Muslim women, and the "decorative" use of the Qur'an on an actress's naked body, inevitably generated sustained controversy online that was way outside of the film's Dutch origins: "On the Moroccan site for youngsters mocros.nl, Theo van Gogh had been threatened with death for months. Already in April 2004 a picture of the filmmaker was posted on a forum page of mocros.nl, with the text 'When it is Theo's turn?' In this poster, a target with seven bullet holes was projected over his throat, chest, and head. 'Allah will quickly get rid of this literal and figurative swine.' "[40]

Van Gogh's murderer was Mohammed Bouyeri, who used the online pseudonym 'Abu Zubair. He had been proactive on the Internet, publishing jihadi materials that included manuals, tracts, translations, and commentaries. This included works alluding to jihad by Sayyed Qutb, whose work influenced the development of the *Ikhwan al-Muslimin*, and some of the writings of Sayyid Abul Ala Maududi, the founder of *Jama'at-e-Islami* Pakistan. "Mohammed B." was also involved in chat rooms and used e-mail to promote jihadi concepts.[41]

Questions as to the authenticity of jihadi sites have to be considered. Suggestions were made that some jihad-oriented pages were the constructions of various intelligence services, used for gathering information on site visitors. Accusations circulated of certain websites being established as "honeypot" sites, constructed for information-gathering purposes such as harvesting visitor identities, e-mail links, and cross-posting references.

Scholars supporting ideas about jihad applied the Net as a means to present their opinions; an example was a statement from Saudi academics addressed to the "militant Iraqi people."[42] This originally appeared on *al-Islam al-Youm* and was widely publicized in the press and elsewhere on the

Web. Other proclamations on Islamic websites drew attention, including the fatwa allowing for an "infidel" to be mutilated.[43] One critical area has been the emergence of online chat rooms and other forums in which responses to such statements are rapidly generated and circulated, including commentaries on aspects of religious authority.

Can the Web be seen as an introduction to activism or a reinforcement tool? This is a hypothetical question, as each case has to be judged on its own merits. Some sites may be visited regularly, especially those with "sticky" or dynamic content that changes on a regular basis or features content associated with a popular contemporary campaign. RSS offers a further opportunity for site developers to allow their readers to be motivated and active on a regular basis. This is where the production merits of a site can kick in: fast-loading, high-quality, easy-to-navigate sites with attractive graphics and easy-to-read content, perhaps aimed at a particular constituency, will possibly have the ascendancy on more difficult-to-read, technical and/or poorly designed material.

Portals and entry points drawing on these considerations, when appropriately publicized through chat rooms and e-mail lists, may generate a substantial amount of hits. Language considerations also apply, together with the integration of multimedia and a sense of belonging to a community through the generation of conversation, friendship, members, and special-interest groups. Without wishing to distort the understanding, an environment where the "flaming" or abuse of readers based on their religious beliefs is encouraged may not be conducive to encouraging general readers. Marketing strategies apply here as much as a multinational corporation's presentation and image.

Some sites, however, would appear to have that undeniable edge of authenticity given the content provided, especially eyewitness accounts of militaristic activities and film clips. The content of many pages suggest that they would not be placed online by security forces. Checking and tracking URLs and determining site ownership through other channels can verify some sites. There has been discussion on methods of regulating the Net, which ignore the fact that the Net evolved precisely so that it was decentralized and effective in a conflict situation.

The question of whether the Net is a recruitment tool for jihadi groups has exercised a media hungry for sensational headlines, combining fear of Islam with fear of the Internet.[44] A nuanced response, in which consideration is given to a combination of social, cultural, economic, and religious factors—of which the Net *may* be a component—is probably more realistic when endeavoring to answer this question. The investment of time and resources in these sites indicated that the sites' authors and backers believed there was or would be a substantial return. This may be in various forms, ranging from general support to logistical and financial assistance.

Recruitment to jihadi causes via the Internet also featured within "minority" Islamic contexts, especially when evidence suggested that it drew in and radicalized a number of young people in different ways:

> The role of the "veterans" is not the only decisive factor in the development of the new recruits. Indeed internal dynamics within groups of radical young Muslims play an important role. For instance, the developing patterns of strife in arenas of conflict like Chechnya, Afghanistan, and Iraq are subjects of intensive discussions (on the Internet) among groups of young Muslims. Some members of these "discussion groups" are very young (aged 16 and 17). Indeed a few of them took their first steps towards the realization of a jihad before the age of 18. Such was the case with several young persons of Moroccan decent arrested in 2004.[45]

Online platforms may interconnect diverse "Islamic" campaigns. For example, Muslim sites that focused on Palestine (which is not exclusively an Islamic issue) may draw their readers to related content on other issues and contexts as part of a wider global dialogue on their perspective of Islam. Thus, opinions on Afghanistan, Algeria, Bosnia, Kashmir, Moros, Chechnya, Iraq, and/or Kurdish campaigns are interconnected online. Real-world networking and the ideals of the *ummah* are reflected, and in some cases created and facilitated, through the Internet.[46] According to one commentator, the "negative" experiences of jihadis recruited via the Internet also have to be taken into consideration: "The new generation, inspired by terrorist propaganda on the Internet, or in the Arab media, are being killed off so rapidly that their fate is having an adverse effect on recruiting. Young Islamic radicals are no longer running off to join the war in Iraq with any prospects of coming back alive. Those that do come back in one piece, are often not much help for recruiting. They tell of deadly American troops, and a hostile Iraqi population."[47]

Each case and site has to be considered individually. In general terms, there is no doubt that the information presented is slick and effective, in line with a digitally literate and educated generation in Westernized contexts. The diversification of sites means that jihadi materials are likely to be found in many languages. Some "innocuous" sites can draw a reader into a framework of extensive and detailed material that *could* encourage recruitment and logistical support in an individual susceptible to such material.

Susceptibility is a key theme here, and, in the absence of detailed case studies relating directly to Internet recruitment, one can only hypothesize. Marc Sageman suggests that the Internet alone is not sufficient and that face-to-face contact and social interaction via a variety of networks is an essential component of jihadi activities at various stages. The case studies he presents on "Salafi jihadis" are effective but do not present the Net as significant components of any recruitment pattern. This does not negate the logistical impact of IT on 9/11 and other campaigns.[48] Sageman's book was published in 2004; it may be that subsequent cases and information will come to light that shed greater light on this issue. I would suggest that Internet materials offer a direct introduction to jihadi materials and could induce affiliations in readers from a particular profile.

After the publication of his book, Sageman argued that the Internet had been applied to suggest greater cohesion and activity by al-Qaeda than reflected the reality, although this theory seemed to negate activities in the name of al-Qaeda in Iraq and the July 2005 bombings in London: "Sageman claimed that Al Qaeda is 'operationally dead' and has no network any more. Its operations are uncoordinated and it has been using the Internet to create chat groups and give the impression that it is still potent, but that is not true. It no longer has the ability to hurt the United States."[49]

This would depend on what constitutes a network, and it might be suggested that greater hindsight is required to posit such a bold statement. We may have to talk about generations of al-Qaeda nodes, upgrading and adapting their methods to suit specific circumstances. Whatever the situation, the determination of effect is subjective and something that could be the focus of future historians, assuming that there are intact archive materials available. At this stage and time within the analytical process, some preliminary activities can be undertaken. As with Sageman's case studies on jihad-oriented *individuals*, there is a role for a nuanced understanding of jihad-oriented *Web space* that can determine the specific levels of access, information, and affiliations that can be engendered through certain online materials.

Such materials address themes that have a resonance with Muslim audiences worldwide, although their interpretation may vary from that of "mainstream" channels. For example, a newspaper in a Muslim context may express sympathy for the perceived plight of the Iraqi peoples, including Muslims from various belief frameworks, but will not necessarily support the activities of supposed insurgents. The extra level (to use a computer gaming analogy) that jihadi sites and portals may apply is that they will, within their news and other coverage, also implicitly or explicitly support aspects of militaristic jihadi activity in Iraq and elsewhere. Campaigns across the Muslim worlds will also be connected with little distinguishing of objectives and a drawing together of language. The format is familiar. The rhetoric draws on proven propaganda and sermon models, in line with notions of a version of religious authority and authenticity and linked into a political conceptual framework. The content is high-tech, perhaps glamorous, and sticky in that it can draw a reader in to seek more interaction and knowledge.

Some portals represent a cross-fertilization of campaigns, such as the banners generated by global jihadi campaigns. Much like the rhetoric and activities of the al-Qaeda entity, it can associate common concepts of jihad and religious belief across diverse campaigning groups. The image is of a global, and globalized, campaign. Care should be taken here. These campaigns may be popular in some Muslim contexts—for example, the liberation of Palestine or Jammu Kashmir—but the methodology of achieving these aims as articulated by a narrow band of sites is not necessarily within the mainstream.

Pages supporting such objectives, using the language of jihad, can be transitory and quickly removed from servers. They are nevertheless effective, generating thousands of hits within their short lifespan before being removed from ISPs, hacked, or relocated; information about new sites is quickly circulated via e-mail and chat rooms, as well as via portals. The proliferation of such sites—and the ease of copying data from one site to another, then to offline technology, to CD, and to a printer—means that the quantity of material is difficult to track. It cannot be assumed that individuals sitting at computer terminals in fixed locations are reading or absorbing all content on a page. Wireless and broadband connections offer an ease of (re)location and possible anonymity in some contexts. Materials may be read way beyond traditional computer screens: BlackBerrys, iPhones, cell phones, and PDAs can pick up Web content. The integration of Net technologies into entertainment media, such as digital and satellite television broadcasts and gaming technology, offer an alternative interface. Drawing on Web 2.0, content can also be downloaded online for later playback and distribution through technologies such as podcasts, video sources, and "broadcasts."

Material can be found in European languages, as well as in languages from Muslim-majority contexts. Jihadi sites were contained on ISPS in a variety of localities, including one whose office was in Clifton, New Jersey: "On the second floor, an Internet company called Fortress ITX unwittingly provided access until recently for an Arabic-language Web site where postings in recent weeks urged attacks against American and Israeli targets. 'The Art of Kidnapping' was explained in electronic pamphlets, along with 'Military Instructions to the Mujahedeen,' and 'War Inside the Cities.' Visitors could read instructions on using a cellular phone to remotely detonate a bomb or ask for help in manufacturing small missiles."[50]

A United Nations panel report urged restrictions on the Internet: "The U.N. council should consider restrictions on the use of the Internet to lure people 'onto a terrorist path,' the experts said. . . . These could range from 'stemming the distribution of extremist material inciting to violence' to requiring Internet service providers to verify who their customers are to adding to the U.N. list any Internet firm providing services 'designed to promote acts of terrorism,' the panel said."[51]

The slow realization of the significance of the Internet as a logistical weapon after 9/11 resulted in a reconfiguration and assessment of security resources. Existing software and methodology was insufficient, and in the United States, the Carnivore surveillance program was quietly wound down. While many of the decisions relating to such activities remained closed to external observation, some projects were announced in public. A variety of databases were established, such as the Terrorism Knowledge Base, a searchable resource organized by the National Memorial Institute for the Prevention of Terrorism.[52] In a collaboration with the Malaysian Federation, the U.S. government's National Science Foundation announced a project observing the activities in chat rooms, where some of the most vociferous jihadi dialogues were allegedly taking place.[53] The Indonesian government employed previous affiliates to jihadi groups in order to acquire insider knowledge and intelligence.[54]

The ways in which site designers have attempted to weight their metadata in order to draw readers to their pages and causes is an intriguing issue. Some pages attempt to develop a sense of friendship and identity with readers, including membership, which offers access to hidden areas of sites as well. For some readers, there is the potential for anonymity; readers may have creative online identities way beyond their personal lifestyles. A reader of a jihadi site may be a youth in a café with an interest in weaponry and the "glamour" presented on the sites, for whom the Islamic dimension is secondary. There may even be a relationship between this kind of content and computer gaming. Readers could also be disenfranchised older individuals looking for a cause sanctioned by religion, for whom the technology and "glamour" are secondary to the cause. Sites that choose *not* to stereotype their readers or who create areas for different reader profiles may be more successful in acquiring support in various forms to their causes.

A reader might be drawn to a radicalizing source on the Web for a variety of reasons, dependent on whether we are discussing local, national, or global issues. One must be conscious of the frequently fluid boundaries of organizations and loose affiliations in association with Islamic causes. A reader could be equally attracted to a site as a reaction to a specific event or for news about a particular organization. A search engine, information in a blog, chat room, or e-mail listing might inform them of a URL. Publicity from another source could contribute, such as a leaflet handed outside of mosque or a printed poster. I have seen jihadi URLs displayed on illegally posted flyers and stickers on lampposts in London, Birmingham, and elsewhere.

Other printed media can contribute to URL awareness, such as newspapers and magazines. The influence of hyperlinks from other sites or organizations can be a subtle but significant potential factor in any assessment. This returns to the point of building maps of who links to whom and the issue of building a pattern of connectivity (and how many clicks) there may be between organizations. Is it possible to measure these forms of connectivity? And what, if anything, does it imply?

To this equation can be added the factor of religious symbolism: how influential is the application of religious symbols as a means of encouraging sympathy, participation, and adherence to a particular worldview? In many ways, symbols such as the Qur'an and the Ka'bah are part of what is shared with other CIES: there are also symbols that form distinct features of jihadi sites, such as the juxtaposition of the Qur'an and an AK-47 (or similar weapon) or images of those "martyrs" who have chosen "paradise" in a political-religious cause.

E-Jihad 2.0

Numerous local and global campaigns have promoted jihad online, justifying its use with various forms of religious authority from contemporaneous and historical sources. Al-Qaeda has effectively disseminated strategic and propaganda materials via the conduits of the Internet, including paramilitary operational manuals. Its name has also been invoked in localized online campaigns, even those outside of al-Qaeda's range of influences or interests. Islamic Studies professor Amina Wadud's leading of prayers in a mosque led to sustained online reaction: "An anonymous appeal for Osama bin Laden to issue a decree to kill Wadud was circulated on the Internet, prompting Virginia Commonwealth [her university] to move her lectures off campus—with remote hook-up—for the rest of the semester."[55]

The veracity of the appeal could not be proven and did not result in any response from bin Laden. It is interesting that his name was invoked online, and that there was an assumption that somehow, through a network of intermediaries, the message might receive some kind of reaction in the form of a fatwa. To what extent does this suggest an image of al-Qaeda as a "networked" type of organization that might react to this message? It is unlikely that the senior members of the network are even aware of Wadud or have any concerns over her activities, compared with the bigger picture. However, at a local level, such a provocative statement was perceived as having the potential to galvanize an al-Qaeda supporter into action— fatwa or not—hence the reaction of the university. With one anonymously posted statement online, the writer had achieved substantial publicity and generated a level of fear about the potential for action. This in itself represents a form of applying the Internet as a potentially destabilizing force, albeit at a local level. It reflects the influence of strategic approaches to media use articulated by al-Qaeda affiliates within manuals as part of an overarching media policy.

Al-Qaeda's application of the Internet has led to sustained attempts by their opponents to close access to their sites and resources, including through hacking and petitioning ISPs to stop hosting the sites. Hacking is a two-way process: after 9/11, the pro-al-Qaeda website al-Neda was attached through "hacking" onto unsuspecting websites, then rapidly publicized to supporters via e-mail lists, before attracting the attention of ISPs and closed—only for the cycle to commence again elsewhere.[56]

Political-religious Islamic organizations operating in other zones associated with the concept of jihad have also become proficient news providers, with content-rich and well-managed sites. Platforms such as Hamas, Islamic Jihad, and Hizbullah recognize that the Internet is an effective medium through which to present their perspectives and religious values, including those associated with jihad. Islamic activist groups locked into international issues and campaigns, sending messages to the American population during the 2004 election campaign—although whether the Americans were listening is another issue: "Radical Islamists used the Internet Thursday to vent their anger at U.S. President George W. Bush's reelection, with one accusing the American people of choosing 'the logic of war.' "[57]

There is no doubt that e-jihad in its varying forms continues to have significance in contemporary discourse about Islam and that mainstream awareness is intensifying. The *New York Times* noted: "To get a sense of the jihadist movement's state of mind, we must listen to its communications, and not just the operational 'chatter' collected by the intelligence community. Today, the central forum for the terrorists' discourse is not covert phone communications but the Internet, where Islamist Web sites and chat rooms are filled with evaluations of current events, discussions of strategy and elaborations of jihadist ideology."[58]

This awareness includes substantial media coverage in Muslim contexts as well, with a variety of local and international issues receiving coverage.[59] This was coupled with a perception that, in many cases, authorities were dealing with activists entirely au fait with electronic technology: "Each jihadi group in South-East Asia has its own website and is comfortable with mobile phones (provided they do not have a musical ring tone). What these groups envisage, then, is not the establishment of just any global caliphate, but a cybercaliphate."[60]

The Net has also been applied as a tool to regulate potential jihadis. The Saudi authorities endeavored to introduce a form of online ministerial outreach on the Net to counter "militants" through electronic dialogue.[61] This activity raises some critical logistical issues: "The anonymity of the Web makes it impossible to authenticate the identity of the 800 interlocutors the Saudi Religious Affairs Ministry is reportedly engaged in dialogues with. Nor is it possible to identify which countries the anonymous correspondents were interacting with the ministry from, nor for that matter if they were indeed whom they purported to be."[62]

Despite, or perhaps because of, such dialogues, disparate groups incorporated new technological developments into their dissemination strategy —way beyond basic webpages and chat rooms—to include multimedia. A plethora of chat rooms, discussion areas, and bulletin boards became key areas for distribution of materials. For example, al-Farouq.com's bulletin board contained many links to materials related to al-Qaeda.[63] News and propagation sites, including religious justifications for activities, form an element of jihadi online discourse; they provide "alternative," if not universally welcomed, perspectives on local and world events. They may provide data specific to a religious perspective/activist organization, including closed areas (members only) requiring subscription and approval from a forum coordinator or website owner. Sites of this nature can provide different levels of access on sites, with limited data in the public area. In many ways, this is no different than other sectors of the Web, with the same criteria of access and membership; unlike commercial services, such as pornography or gambling sites, payment is not usually required for jihadi content. There are some parallels between these other forms of online activity, however, in terms of security, membership, application of encryption, anonymity tools, and in many cases frequent updating of content.

The concept of a cross-fertilization of content management systems between jihadi sites and pornography sites seems at first an unusual paradox of the Web. Both skim areas of morality and legality; the pornography sector has driven the development of cutting-edge tools for conveying video and for Internet privacy, as well as for creating ways in which censorship can be avoided. As with areas of CIES, there are also sectors of the online pornography industry that are unmonitored. Pornography is one of the dominant reasons for the sustained growth of Internet use and content and is high on the list of priorities for some readers. Both pornography and jihadi sites are areas of the Web that some authorities would like to protect "vulnerable" readers from to varying degrees. Jihadi sites have also been found "hidden" on servers and sites with pornographic content, and allegations have surfaced of jihadi data being encrypted within pornographic photographs.

E-Jihadi Voices

Critical within the development of jihadi materials online has been the establishment of "personalities" among the providers of Web content. The following discussion seeks to outline a selection of them, both to demonstrate some of the different qualities attacked and to reveal some of the principal al-Qaeda/jihadi avatars online. Specific key players and identities emerged of significant "operatives" and voices representing al-Qaeda and related entities. In their pseudonymous form, these included Daleel Almojahid, Irhabi007, Zubeiddah1417, Abdul Aziz al-Muqrin, and Lewis Atiyyat Allah.

The application of anonymity makes establishing the "validity" of some protagonists problematic. Daleel Almojahid was one example of such an individual, threatening the United States with a nuclear countdown in 2004.[64] Another example was operating from London as Irhabi007, or "Terrorist 007." He maintained a consistency of jihadi postings, including the distribution of a video that also appeared on Al-Jazeera in September 2005. This was apparently produced by al-Qaeda's media production unit al-Sahab ("the cloud"), which claimed responsibility for the July 2005 bombings in London, juxtaposing film of one of the bombers with filmed statements from Ayman al-Zawahiri.[65] There was uncertainty at the time as to whether Irhabi007 was an individual or a collective.

The high level of output from Irhabi007 on forums and websites led self-styled Internet vigilantes such as Internet Haganah to vigorously campaign to close Irhabi007 down. Based on data analysis, one source suggested he was a resident of West London and could not comprehend why the UK authorities had not tracked and prosecuted him.[66] Following a series of arrests in 2005, Moroccan-born Londoner Younis Tsouli was accused of being Irhabi007 and sentenced to ten years imprisonment on terrorism charges in 2007. But, as the *Washington Post* explained, "Irhabi's absence from the Internet may not be as noticeable as many hope. Indeed, the hacker had anticipated his own disappearance. In the months beforehand, Irhabi released his will on the Internet. In it, he provided links to help visitors with their own Internet security and hacking skills in the event of his absence—a rubric for jihadists seeking the means to continue to serve their nefarious ends. Irhabi may have been caught, but his online legacy may be the creation of many thousands of 007s."[67]

This is a significant issue, given that the skills to place a site online are widespread and individuals can be highly motivated, although they may also be pragmatic in the knowledge that their activities could be finite. However, one requires the benefit of hindsight and historical distance to determine how many key players continued to function after various crackdowns, or whether the avatars involved were "fluid" in that several assumed a single identity.

Zubeiddah1417's sites similarly acted as a hub for jihadi information, including weapons manuals, tactical information, and propaganda. Some of this was of a generic nature, including translated guides on the use of a variety of armaments. The integration of diverse conflicts within similar graphical interfaces reinforces the concept of shared causes and affinity between jihadi campaigns across the world. The graphic banners found on Zubeiddah1417's pages drew on specific "Islamic" symbolism and images from contemporary conflicts and were designed to evoke sympathetic re-

Algerian Jihad, jihad-
algeria.com, 2004

sponses to emotive themes. They suggested that Zubeiddah1417, whether
that name represented a collective or an individual affiliated to al-Qaeda's
cause, possessed an eye for engaging graphic design in the application of
symbols, color, and format. These include a series of posters and banners
representing diverse strands of Muslim conflicts in different regional settings, featuring specific religious and military leaders, the victims of conflict, and Islamic motifs, including the Qur'an.

Zubeiddah1417 hosted sites that were clearinghouses for graphics,
manuals, multimedia, and other information for circulation and reuse.
Zubeiddah1417 was associated with the Alzerqawe Islamic Media Centre,
highlighting the statements of Abu Musab al-Zarqawi. One observer suggested in 2005 that Zubeiddah1417 was in Jordan.[68] The maintenance of
anonymity and a relatively high level of output added a discernable edge to
the appearance of certain jihadi Web space. This went in conjunction with
the design qualities evident in at least a proportion of the output of the
related umbrella group, the Global Islamic Media Front (GIMF) and its
affiliates. The apparent subterfuge and technical skills associated with the
creation of such sites provided a cachet to their writers and designers, one
that might appeal to a youthful audience enamored by jihadi geeks.

One skilled exponent of the Net was Lewis Atiyat Allah. In May 2005 a
letter written by Lewis Atiyat Allah on behalf of al-Qaeda to Tony Blair
emerged (and subsequently recirculated after the London bombings of
7 July 2005), in which he stated: "We say with all confidence, that the worst
of the incoming [attacks] hasn't happened yet, and that the West will pay a
high price for all the crimes they committed against the Muslims during
and before this century."[69]

Lewis Atiyat Allah and others used the Net to directly attack European
leaders, and they are also highly critical of Saudi Sahwi interests.[70] Israeli

commentator Reuben Paz, whose work has focused on a number of these jihadi players, described how Lewis Atiyat Allah has developed an "aura" or a "quality" that might be attributable to these and other Web personalities, and that he "has emerged as the most prominent interpreter of Al-Qaeda's strategy, and an admired scholar among the younger generation of Al-Qaeda supporters. Most of his readers are unaware of his real name. 'Lewis' has so far managed to remain a mysterious figure. This aura adds to his popular appeal, along with his talented style in Arabic and his ability to plant a lot of optimism in his readers' minds."[71]

Paz dialogued with Lewis Atiyat Allah and published the results on his organization's website. Lewis Atiyat Allah's online activities were brought to a halt, and an article in *Asharq Al Awasat* in October 2005 suggested "Lewis Atiyat Allah" was an Iraqi called Omar Hadid who was killed in Iraq and whose pseudonym lived on after his death.[72] This analysis was based on the opinion of an anonymous source. An earlier article from Adnkronos International had suggested that Lewis Atiyat Allah was in fact Yusuf al-Ayeeri, the leader of al-Qaeda in the Arabian Peninsula until his death in 2003.[73] There is no reason why the pseudonym will not reappear, whether or not the original Lewis Atiyat Allah is responsible for its output. If he is dead, then his thoughts maintain their currency online.

Elsewhere, others were applying the Net to present their jihadi messages to diverse audiences. Abdul Aziz al-Muqrin used Web space to send a statement to Silvio Berlusconi: "The message, posted on an Internet site and attributed to Abdel Aziz al-Muqrin, the head of al-Qaeda in Saudi Arabia, claims responsibility for the bloody weekend siege at a housing complex in the eastern Saudi oil city of Al-Khobar, in which 19 foreigners and three Saudis were killed."[74]

Al-Muqrin also made a related statement seeking to remove "infidels" from the Arabian Peninsula.[75] He was killed in June 2004 in a shootout in Saudi Arabia.[76] However, at least in cyberspace, this did not appear to have a profound effect on the production and publication of new materials, a substantial number of which emerged in the day after his death, together with an updated e-mail address.[77] This content emerged, despite efforts of some Saudi authorities to close down such jihadi Web space. On occasion, governmental pressures—and in some cases, fear of prosecution or imprisonment—led to the closure of websites. In Iraq, the activities of a pro-al-Qaeda website were stalled in September 2005 when site developer "Abu Dijana" (Yasir Khudr Muhammad Jasim al-Karbali) was captured by American military forces.[78]

The death in custody of Mohammed Abdel-Rahman Mohammed al-Suwailmi further impaired, at least for a time, al-Qaeda–related Internet activities in Saudi Arabia, of which he was seen as "an expert on the Internet and . . . recruitment and propaganda for Islamic militant groups in Saudi Arabia."[79] Al-Suwailmi, who was twenty-three, initially was thought to have "died" in September 2005, but he was finally killed following a gun battle in December 2005: "The Saudi authorities initially reported his death in September, giving al-Suwailmi the pleasure of releasing an audiotape on the Internet in which he said he was alive and well. The authorities then said they had mistaken him for his brother, Ahmed, who had just been killed in a shootout with security forces."[80]

Website developers and content providers became key targets for authorities in a variety of contexts. In Muslim-minority settings such as the UK, the Internet was a focus of observation by law enforcement agencies, although this did not always lead to action. Abu Hamza al-Masri made extensive use of the Internet as a tool for presenting his perspectives on jihad and conflict, including recordings of sermons. These featured in the website Supporters of Shariah (SOS).

Key factors in Abu Hamza's subsequent indictment were allegations associated with provocative online statements regarding Jews and others, together with accusations that he was supporting al-Qaeda. The SOS site included accusations that Abu Hamza had been tortured while in custody. It published complaints that the Muslim Association of Britain had occupied the former center of Abu Hamza's activities, Finsbury Park Mosque in north London. In between this rhetoric, there were question-and-answer sessions on the "permissibility" of suicide attacks and the conditions for a person to be labeled a scholar.[81]

Abu Hamza was eventually indicted by the U.S. authorities on a variety of charges related to the development of alleged al-Qaeda training camps in Oregon and using the Web as a tool to solicit funding for the Taliban. However, he was detained on remand in the UK in 2004. In 2006 he was convicted in the UK of numerous charges, including incitement of racial hatred and soliciting murder; he was sentenced to imprisonment of seven years. Prior to his arrest and incarceration, Abu Hamza's supporters placed his sermons made in Finsbury Park Mosque and other locations online, forming an archive of materials. After his exclusion from these premises by the mosque committee, a number of video clips of his lectures (in English) remained online. After closing in 2004, the SOS website reemerged in January 2005 and sporadic supportive messages appeared subsequently.[82]

Omar Bakri Muhammad, a former affiliate of Abu Hamza, closed down his al-Muhajiroun organization in 2004.[83] In January 2005 his reemergence online was noted via a sustained series of "broadcasts" on PalTalk promoting al-Qaeda's "jihad": "The *Times* monitored Mr. Bakri Mohammed's nightly webcasts in which he declared that the 'covenant of security' under which Muslims live peacefully in the UK had been 'violated' by the Government's tough anti-terrorist legislation. The Syrian-born radical said: 'I believe the whole of Britain has become Dar ul-Harb (land of war).' In such a state, he added, 'the kuffar (non-believer) has no sanctity for their own life or property.' "[84]

A detailed survey of transcripts would be necessary to further determine the context of this statement, especially when it was read in the shadow of the London bombings of 7 July 2005. Muhajiroun.com released a number of online statements regarding the situation of religious leaders being targeted for their pronouncements, with a defensive posture firmly aimed at Muslim and other groups and individuals:

> Sheikh Abu Hamza, Sheikh Omar Bakri Muhammad and many other Muslim political activists in the UK have been facing intense vilification by the media, who through lies and distortions have made them public enemy No. 1 for the British public. The arrest of Sheikh Abu Hamza today is therefore no surprise as the Blair regime gives in to the Jewish lobby . . . and the lackeys of the Blair regime within the Muslim community known as the Muslim Council of Britain (MCB). The arrest is also intended to appease the masses fearing another attack by Al-Qaeda and to deflect the public's attention away from the US and UK fascist policies in Iraq and Afghanistan.[85]

In August 2005 Omar Bakri Muhammad was denied reentry to the UK after a visit to Lebanon, which he had made in part in reaction to tightening antiterrorist and incitement legislation, although he was not charged with any specific offence. Omar Bakri Muhammad continued to broadcast via PalTalk using his cell phone, including a weekly Qur'anic commentary titled "LIVE from central London."[86]

In the case of prosecutions directly related to the production of jihadi content in the UK, the case of Babar Ahmad became a prominent example. He was alleged by governmental authorities to be associated with the Azzam Publications website in London. Ahmad was also alleged to have run websites that raised cash and recruited fighters for the Taliban and the Mujahidin. It was suspected by authorities that he operated websites that linked him to the Chechen leader Shamil Bassayev. The U.S. government attempted to have Ahmad extradited. The Home Office allowed his extradition, but this process stalled as Ahmad continued to make appeals to the UK and European courts in 2008. There was a website campaign for Ahmad's release.

Whether or not Ahmad was associated with the site, Azzam had a post office box in north London at the time when the site was active. It discussed jihad in Chechnya, jihad in Afghanistan, and associated statements. There was a transcript of an exposition on militaristic jihad based on the work of Abdullah Azzam, a declaration of war against the Americans occupying "the Land of the Two Holy Places," and a message from bin Laden. There was also very detailed religious documentation exploring the justification for campaigns and for fighting in the cause of Allah, using highly emotive language and trying to explain specific religious terminology from a very particular political religious viewpoint, combined with examples interpreted from the precedents of the practice of the Prophet Muhammad.[87] Mazen Mokhtar, a New Jersey–based imam and alleged affiliate of Babar Ahmad, was also investigated by U.S. authorities on charges relating to running a mirror site to Azzam.com.[88]

Following the closure of the Azzam site, IslamicAwakening.com continued publishing Azzam News on its bulletin board, "Just so that we do not get the old bill [the police] knockin' at our door!"[89] IslamicAwakening.com hosted associated forums, as well as "news." IslamicAwakening.com's URL resolved to billing and account addresses in the UK.[90] It was alleged that "notable participants . . . include English Nazi David Myatt, aka Abdul Aziz."[91] IslamicAwakening's jihad forum featured links to film uploaded from Iraq and Afghanistan as well as links to other video material, which included "Russian Hell 5" video from Uzbekistan; a "martyrdom operation that killed seven pigs, destroyed their equipment and annihilated their tank in [R]amadi, [I]raq"; "The Ruling Regarding Killing One's Self to Protect Info;" "terrorism is ok when they do it [to] us"; and a suggestion to post all videos to the "kaffir" site www.terroristmedia.com/nukem: "Here is the first and the BEst (it is a kaffir site but with the best video, for free)."[92]

Islamic Awakening's forums contained commentaries on forms of "jihad" from readers.

> Muslims! fight for this dunya: money money money . . . or women and more fun. . . . [P]ay thousands for cable and parties. . . .
> These muslims have no reason to wake up . . . or answer the call of

jihad, made by a few shuyookh. They like this life and feel satisfied with it. . . . Allah will reward them in due time. . . .

Never the less, a handful have answered the call. . . . [T]hey have chosen Allah over this life. . . . [T]hey go through tremendous trials. . . . that regular people would have breakdowns even thinking about it. . . . They have awoken from a deep sleep . . . and have seen beyond this life. They chose the sunnah of Muhammad (peace be on him).[93]

On the same pages, "mujahideen_85" drew on an interpretation of exemplars from Muslim history, such as Ali ibn Abi Talib (Muhammad's son-in-law and cousin), as well as Qur'an quotations in order to put his perspective across. Apparently then nineteen years old and living in India, he follows this tactic elsewhere in the post, commenting on the position of women under the Taliban in comparison with "Western" perspectives in order to justify his interpretation of jihad.[94]

Elsewhere in the jihad section, "Mansoor Ali," apparently located in Woodford, Essex, UK, presented a number of "theories" behind the 9/11 attacks. This included a nine-part (to date) discussion entitled "Israel was behind the attacks on 9/11."[95] Conspiracy theories also feature in other sections of the forum; one member made various claims against the prominent American convert Hamza Yusuf Hanson, who was castigated for "helping" George W. Bush through public pronouncements and accused of being a CIA officer.[96]

The discussion board al-Fussilat was another central point for jihadi materials. It was named after "*Surah Fussilat,*" the forty-first chapter of the Qur'an, whose title means "expounded" or "explained in detail." This contained a series of links gathering related content together, enabling readers to surf through to file-hosting sites containing audiovisual material. These download/upload sites, variously hosted on servers in North America, Europe, Japan, and Israel (!), are publicly accessible resources. The URLs do not suggest the nature of their content (often being alphanumeric codes). Al-Fussilat also linked to sites such as Archive.org, a United States–hosted archive of the Internet (with a mirror in Alexandria, Egypt), and sites observing (and criticizing) e-jihad, such as Infovlad. Material being promoted in 2007 included an Iraqi pro-al-Qaeda magazine offering operational information and a listing of campaigns to date. This was one of hundreds of magazines that emerged online in PDF format/Word containing advice, sermons, rhetoric, and strategic information nuanced toward specific readerships and markets.[97]

New websites also emerged during this period. Al-Qaeda's Committee in the Islamic Maghreb drew together related North African campaigning groups under al-Qaeda's brand.[98] Islamic Courts Union (Somalia) presented pro-al-Qaeda statements, together with video clips of operational activities in Somalia (uploaded onto YouTube) and followers declaring an oath of allegiance to regional leaders. The example of a young Somali suicide bomber was prominently displayed on the site. Islamic Courts Union published using the blogging tool Wordpress, a tactic also adopted by the GIMF on a variety of sites, in English, Arabic, and German.[99]

The GIMF announced a "Media Sword to defend the Land of Islam" on video via their site during this period. A statement by Abu Laith al-Libbi (the Khurasan commander of al-Qaeda) entitled "Confronting the War of Prisons" was published. The site was illustrated with downloadable posters, whose content suggested complicity between communism, Christianity, and Judaism against Muslim peoples. Posters promoting operational campaigns were prominently displayed on Al-Battar Media blog. There were links to a downloadable computer game entitled "[The] Night of Bush Capturing," where players could participate in a virtual battle to capture the American president.[100]

The GIMF linked to al-Qaeda activity in Lebanon, particularly Fatah al-Islam, whose webpage sought to clarify its historical relationship with the Palestinian al-Fatah movement: "It has come to the point where now she has been granted her wish from all this oppression, Shirk, and Kufr: the soldiers of Allah. . . . [Fatah al-Islam] emerged from the shackles of nationalism to the light of Tawheed when it declared its split from the secular apostates of the original Fatah movement."[101] Fatah al-Islam noted the importance of the Internet as a recruitment tool for its campaign, according to one leader: " 'The Internet is the most successful means to enlist great numbers of youths from different Arab and Islamic countries, such as Saudi Arabia, Ethiopia, Yemen, Algeria, Morocco and Syria,' Abu Musaab said. 'My job consists of enlisting new members under the pretext of training them to fight in Iraq.' "[102]

In the GIMF-branded site The Ignored Puzzle, otherwise known as *Inshallah Shaheed* ("martyr if God wills it"), explicit links were made between campaigns in Lebanon and Iraq. The Lebanon pages highlighted the roles of its "martyrs" and showed photos of operational activity, clearly presenting the religious symbolism of its fighters in prayer and holding the Qur'an. It hyperlinked to thumbnail photos and video clips provided by the World News Network and the Islamic State of Iraq, two prominent outlets for news associated with al-Qaeda in Iraq. This included film of the "trial" and execution of fourteen Ministry of Defence and Interior workers, together with a statement noting the (extrajudicial) judgment, which was in the form of a news release. In October 2007 a *New York Times* report revealed that the author of *Inshallah Shaheed* was Samir Khan, a twenty-one-year-old American living in North Carolina.[103] The blog relocated to the Muslimpad service, where it continued its activities in November 2007.[104]

Other expressions of jihad can also be found online, particularly in relation to political campaigns. Prominent examples would be Muhammad al-Massari and Saad al-Faqih. They have their roots in demands for Islamic reforms and "modernization" in Saudi Arabia in the early 1990s, which led to the foundation (along with others) of *Lajnat al-difa' 'an al-huquq al-shar'iya*, the Campaign for the Defence of Legitimate Rights (CDLR).[105]

The CDLR was forced into exile and subsequently splintered, with al-Faqih establishing his own platform, *al-Harakat al-islamiyya li-l-islah*, the Movement for Islamic Reform in Arabia (MIRA). Both applied various media channels, including the Internet, in order to present their interpretations of how Muslim society (particularly in Saudi Arabia) should "progress." In some ways, this has focused on the perceived excesses of the Saudi royal family and the ways in which interpretations of Islam in the kingdom have allegedly been presented to the detriment of religious life and values, in particular those associated with ideas of equality.

I first explored CDLR and MIRA Web space in the 1990s.[106] Since that time, these platforms have focused on "broadcasts" and the application of bulletin boards for the dissemination of various materials, some of which have been sympathetic with Salafi jihadi ideals. Diversification has been linked to increased availability of bandwidth and growth in Internet access in Muslim countries, together with creative approaches to combating censorship. These elements have been utilized by other platforms.

Muhammad al-Massari and his supporters have been long-term users of the Internet to promote their vision of "reform" in Saudi Arabia and elsewhere. The integration of the Net in these activities included live chat, discussion boards, and sermons under the tajdeed.net banner. In 2008 it continued to operate from London with a postal address prominent on its front page.

In the forums at various times, the logo had marked similarities to al-Qaeda's horse logo. Postings making claims of responsibility for the London bombings featured on the site. Although shut down several times, permutations of tajdeed.net resurfaced online. This was despite al-Massari and his family coming under close scrutiny from the authorities and the arrest in the United States in 2005 of al-Massari's son Majid al-Massari. Muhammad al-Massari's home was raided in April 2005 after film allegedly showing the deaths of three British soldiers in a suicide bombing appeared on his website.[107] Some believed the site was kept open as a means to obtain intelligence.[108]

It was suggested by some observers that Sa'ad al-Faqih owned or was closely associated with the al-Qal3ah ("the fortress" or "the castle") group of sites, including discussion boards, which have been closely associated with statements from al-Qaeda affiliates. Qal3ah contained a number of forums on politics, shari'ah, interpretation, computer advice, and the Qur'an. The output of Sheikh Hamoud bin Oqla al-Shuaibi and his followers featured on one forum.[109] Al-Shuaibi issued a number of fatwas against "non-Muslims" after 9/11 and also attacked the Saudi royal family. He died in January 2002, but his work and that of his followers continued to circulate online; his followers were deemed responsible for attacks in Saudi Arabia in 2003.[110] Qal3ah also linked to the website of imprisoned scholar Sa'ad bin Sa'id al-Zuair. He had been held since 1995 without trial because of his attacks on the Saudi royal family but was released in 2003. Subsequently, al-Zuair was again detained in 2004 following statements made on television about the Saudi royal family, but he was released after a royal amnesty in August 2005.[111]

Al-Faqih is also associated with the Islah discussion board, which has appeared under a variety of URLs and broadcasts regularly via his website.[112] There are several conflicting opinions as to al-Faqih's allegiances and perspectives, which are not necessarily clarified in his online output. Al-Rasheed asks: "Is al-Faqih a covert Jihadi? Or is he a Sahwi Islamist who calls for the peaceful overthrow of a 'blasphemous' regime? Is he a believer in 'theoretical *jihad*'? Or is he simply a cover propagator of *jihad 'amali* (practical *jihad*)?"[113]

The U.S. government seemed to think that the "covert Jihadi" definition applied: in December 2004 the U.S. Treasury identified al-Faqih as a supplier of funds for al-Qaeda and froze his financial assets. Al-Faqih, whose websites continued to be online, denied these allegations. He noted a crackdown on his supporters in Saudi Arabia: "The problem is that the Saudis are using the technology to trace and detain non-jihadi authors and contributors as well. In fact several people connected to our organization have been detained in recent months as a result of the transfer of technological expertise."[114]

Al-Faqih is careful to ensure that callers do not endorse violent acts during his broadcasts, but other materials on his sites are more problematic.[115] Islah contained regular articles associated with the "reform" movements in Saudi Arabia: it featured the address of the MIRA on its front page. Threads in Islah contained statements and photos in support of Osama bin Laden. These included a montage of hagiographic images of the "Sheikh," drawn from broadcasts and archive footage. Abu Musab al-Zarqawi also started to emerge on the Islah forums in 2004, juxtaposed with images of Osama bin Laden, Ayman al-Zawahiri, and others associated with al-Qaeda. On the same discussion board was an article on Sayyid Qutb and his "martyrdom."[116]

Pro-al-Qaeda sources presented materials on a number of locations, hosted on sites in the UK. Rightword.net was a jihadi site apparently registered to an address in Treforest, Wales.[117] It contained content in Arabic and English, although the account was suspended during 2006. For a period during 2005, the English-language pages were down, but the Arabic pages were regularly updated. The entry page was dominated by the horse symbol associated with al-Neda and al-Qaeda pages. The news pages included statements from Ayman al-Zawahiri and a satirical photograph (accompanied by an article) of Ayatollah al-Sistani dressed in the American flag. The content of Rightword included discussion boards on a variety of subjects, with a particular political emphasis. There was also logistical information, particularly associated with the campaigns in Iraq.[118] In 2003 Rightword's English pages featured Osama bin Laden on its banner, with an accompanying *nashid*, or religious song, promoting martyrdom. The news pages highlighted news from Afghanistan and Iraq, praising the "heroic" efforts of Mujahidin in killing American soldiers. A "special section" of Rightword included substantial content on jihadi activities with articles titled "Four Kinds of Jihad," "Jihad in Quran," "No Deed Equivalent to Jihad." and "Seven Gifts to the Martyr."[119]

There were also a number of sites promoting forms of e-jihad. The 3asfh.com bulletin board contained a hacker jihadi forum, amid other technical discussions, for the exchange of data and information. This included articles on anonymizing identities from Internet cafés to participate in PalTalk discussions, advanced e-mail and encryption, and anti-spyware. MSN Bomberman gave a tutorial on e-mail flooding/pinging and general network disruption.[120] One section detailed hacking protocols for defacing websites, with a case study of a hacked site, including references to a wide range of hackers.[121] While there is substantial generic hacker chat on the site, there were banners featuring Osama bin Laden and one with a photo of Adolf Hitler (stating "actions speak louder than words").

Jihadi networks share and transmit ideals through diverse interfaces online. For example, a group of four URLs shared content using tawhed.ws, alsunnah.info, almaqdese.net, and abu-qatada.com.[122] The al-Qaeda logo featured on each page, and other al-Qaeda banners dominated pages. It represented a slick and well-produced site. Pages explained the "da'wa" of the site, drawing on Qur'anic justification. More detailed statements and "educational materials" could be found through compressed files.

The application of Abu Qatada's name as one of the URLs, and its juxtaposition with the al-Qaeda logo, did not help his judicial case when Abu Qatada (Omar Mahmoud Othman Omar) was detained in the UK in 2005. The Jordanian was alleged to have close connections with Osama bin Laden and was convicted in absentia of bombings in Jordan in 1998, prior to obtaining asylum in the UK. Following his arrest in 2001 and his release without charge on terrorism offenses, Abu Qatada was detained in 2002 in London for two years without trial, and he was rearrested in 2005. Pending a possible deportation to Jordan, he was bailed under conditions of being monitored electronically ("tagged") and close supervision. The deportation was approved in 2007, but this was pending, as various appeals led to Abu Qatada's release on bail in 2008. Abu Qatada was also associated with Abu Hamza and the Finsbury Park Mosque in North London. Recordings of Abu Qatada's sermons were found in the homes of 9/11 bombers, and he was allegedly associated with the 11-M bombers and Richard Reid. He was also linked to Abu Musab al-Zarqawi. During his detention, Abu Qatada's sermons and commentaries continued to circulate on the Internet.

Jihadi portals took many forms. Kataeb Mojahdat was a typical example of a portal containing a broad range of resources associated with al-Qaeda campaigns.[123] Its front pack contains banners pronouncing jihad and association with various "brigades" (linked to al-Qaeda). The al-Qaeda logo and Osama bin Laden's photograph featured on the Arabic pages. The bin Laden link led to a recording of an audio statement, while another link featured the last moments and statement of a "martyr."[124] Kataeb Mojahdat led in turn to other sites with major sections on jihad, Iraq, and Palestine.[125]

There was certainly an element of choice between jihadi portals. Daleel Abualbukhary represented a significant entry point to pro-al-Qaeda content; hosted on free Web space, this was easily searchable through scroll-down menus, representing a jihadi directory, at least at entry-point level.

Jihadi *nashid*s greeted the surfer. There was a choice of audio content, including Qur'anic recitation and other *nashid*s. It was heavy in images and could take a substantial time to download, making it more appropriate for broadband constituencies. Photos of Omar Bakri Muhammad, Abu Qatada, John Walker Lindh, Sheikh Rahman, 9/11 "martyrs," Tony Blair, Colin Powell, and an animated George W. Bush (his head superimposed on an execution victim) featured on the page. There were also schematic diagrams of an AK-47. Over forty links in various stages of repair pointed to a broad jihadi universe, highlighting numerous campaigns, ranging from anti-Shi'a sites to Chechen pages and al-Neda sites. It also contains links to sites offering proxy surfing sites for anonymity when accessing the Net. The anti-Shi'a site was dhr12.com, apparently a Riyadh-registered site; its front page was dominated by images of Shi'a ritual practices during *muharram*, including self-flagellation, which were condemned by dhr12.com.[126]

There is a need to differentiate between Islamic and other content, a gray area when faced with iraqpatrol.com. This focused on American troop activities in Iraq, including an archive of photos of injured and dead troops and of Iraqi children who had been victims of conflict. There was no direct linkage to "religious" content on this page, having a greater focus on Iraqi identity and symbolism.[127] The Arabic content was mirrored in iraq tunnel.com, which included various "conspiracy theories" associated with 9/11 and the Iraq war.[128]

There were a number of significant hubs of information about Islam in relation to conflicts, which acted as information distribution points for the jihadi knowledge economy. Islammemo, registered to an address in al-Khoba in Saudi Arabia's Eastern Province, became a central point for news and information about campaigns in Iraq. It was also a distribution point for videos (via islamlight.net) and DVDs.[129] Islammemo was widely cited in jihadi blogs and forums reporting on the war in Iraq, such as Iraq Resistance Report. There were concerns in 2003 when the site was hosted in Canada. Islammemo became an important clearinghouse for news about Islam, Muslims, and related issues. This is linked into associated content, provided by the site and its affiliates. The design of the site was slick, utilizing flash and multimedia as well as news feeds.[130]

Ansar.net linked to dawah.ws, providing flash presentations on aspects of Islamic identity and jihad.[131] It acted as a hub to other sites, such as emanway.net, which contained a variety of multimedia, including recitations and sermons. It would be possible to construct a map of links between these sites. Alhesbah acted as a clearinghouse for pro-al-Qaeda (and affiliate) information. This was emphatically focused on multimedia, including statements from Osama bin Laden and eulogies for the assassinated Hamas leader Sheikh Yasin.[132]

Clearguidance.com gave an "introduction" to jihad, focusing on the work of Sayyid Qutb, the influential Egyptian advocate of "jihad" who was executed in 1966. Qutb emphasized the centrality of the Qur'an and *Hadith* in every Muslim and Islamic action. Any society that did not follow this particular interpretation of the *shari'ah* was condemned by Qutb, who sought a jihad to fight the "ignorance" within Egypt and throughout the Islamic world. Qutb's exhortation has had a sustained historical resonance elsewhere, especially online.

On Clearguidance, this was represented on a banner stating: "The affairs of Islaam, the Sunnah, and the Way of the Salaf." A side banner stresses that jihad is "the forgotten obligation," and stories of "martyrs" are highlighted. In 2003 its articles highlighted on the front page included work by Qutb; "The Islaamic Legitimacy of the Marytrdom Operations," by Nida'ul Islam; and "A Glimpse of the Taliban," by Shaykh Naasir bin Hamad al-Fahd. Qutb and Chechen jihadi "martyr" Shamil Bassayiev, who died in 2006, were the focus of a banner: "We will never forget you and what you did for this religion."[133]

The Clearguidance-moderated discussion board contain thousands of entries from various readers. In 2002 it responded to a memorial to 9/11 victims organized by Muslim organizations:

> They make me sick! What about the dead in Afghanistan?
>> What about our dead in Sheeshan?
>> What about our sisters raped in Kashmir?
>> What about the unarmed Muslim brother shot dead in Bosnia by
> the UN "peace-keeping" forces?
>> What about the 1,000,000 dead Iraqi babies?
>> What about the small children killed in Filistine [Palestine]?
>> What about the burnt corpses of our fellow Muslims in Gujurat?
>> And the list is incomplete![134]

Some sites focus on the personalities and output of a specific individual in the jihadi spectrum. Abu Muhammad al-Maqdisi (also known as Issam Muhammad Taher Al-Burqawi) was described as Abu Musab al-Zarqawi's spiritual "mentor." However, their relationship has not always been harmonious, with al-Maqdisi disapproving of the suicide bombing tactics of his protégé: "I say and stress that I am listening to and following the chaos that rages today in Iraq, by means of which they want to defile the Jihad and its honorable image by blowing up cars or setting explosive devices in the roads, by firing mortars in the streets and marketplaces, and other places where Muslims congregate. The hands of the Jihad fighters must remain clean so that they will not be stained by the blood of those who must not be harmed even if they are rebellious and shameless."[135] A complete work by al-Maqdisi was featured on revivingislam.com, including this statement on jihad. Al-Maqdisi was emphatic about not attacking other Muslims, and he argued that mistakes are dangerous: it is better to leave 1,000 *kuffar* (non-believers) than to kill a single Muslim.[136]

Al-Maqdisi's statements and influence, especially his perspectives on jihad, permeated many websites. His "official" website tawheed.ws shared a front page with the "official" site of Abu Qatada. Al-Maqdisi's statements, written while he was in prison, were widely circulated on the Internet.[137] He was released from jail in Jordan in July 2005 as a reaction in part to his (potential) moderating role with al-Zarqawi, but he was quickly rearrested after dialoguing with al-Zarqawi.[138]

The ethos of jihadi ideologues maintained a currency through online statements and interaction; Mustafa Abd al-Mun'im Abu Halimah (Abu Basir al-Tartusi) is a Syrian exile and influential scholar based in London. He generated controversy in some chat rooms through his condemnation of suicide bombings, primarily the fatwa *Bayan hawla Al-Tafjirat allati Hasalat fi Madinat London.*[139] His statements were also discussed in several newspapers, including *Asharq Alawsat*, which reproduced extracts from al-Tartusi's website. In a question-and-answer format, al-Tartusi stated: "I have received 1,000 questions about these operations, which are for me closer to suicide than martyrdom. They are haram (Forbidden) and impermissible, for several reasons."[140] His justification drew on hadith: "'Anyone who harms a believer has no jihad.' He said this is for someone who merely harms a believer, so imagine if he kills him, and kills him deliberately"; and, "One who kills a non-Muslim does not find the winds of paradise; its wind is to be found from a 70 years walk."[141]

The ire of several discussion groups was raised following al-Tartusi's analysis of jihad, with accusations of "selling out" because of his location in London. His fatwa of 24 August 2005, based on Qur'anic and legal sources, instructed readers that suicide operations were forbidden.[142] Al-Tartusi issued subsequent statements via his website altartosi.com (and abuba seer.bizland.com), which refuted the *Sout al-Khalifa* "broadcasts" (see below).[143] Al-Tartusi made extensive use of the Internet, presenting his opinions in compressed-format audio presentations.[144]

In some ways, London was an online and real-world hub for some jihadi activism, reflecting a continuity of Islamic-oriented activism that predated the digital age. The UK-based Saviour Sect (also identified as al-Ghuraaba, or "the strangers") was described as a "successor" to al-Muhajiroun, whose key figure Omar Bakri Muhammad had gone into "exile" in 2005. Its members were identified as heckling Member of Parliament George Galloway and others at a meeting about Iraq and allegedly seeking to disrupt the UK elections in 2005.[145] A subsequent undercover investigation by the *Sunday Times* apparently caught group members "inciting young British Muslims to become terrorists and praising the Tube bombers as 'the fantastic four'": "The reporter witnessed one of the sect's leading figures, Sheikh Omar Brooks, telling a young audience, including children, that it was the duty of Muslims to be terrorists and boasting, just days before the July 7 attacks, that he wanted to die as a suicide bomber."[146] Brooks (Abu Izzadeen), a convert from a Caribbean background, had proclaimed himself a supporter of Omar Bakri Muhammad, and he had stated that "assimilation is not an option for Muslims."[147] He was convicted of terrorism offenses in the UK in 2008.

The Saviour Sect's site initially resolved to an address in Gloucester, but it subsequently was registered to an address in Birmingham, apparently owned by Salafi Bookstore and Islamic Centre.[148] It underwent a subtle change of name, replacing "Saviour" with "Saved." The page was headed with a hadith, which explains the name of the sect: "The Messenger Muhammad (saw) said: 'My nation will be divided into 73 sects; all of them will be in the Fire except one (the Saved Sect).'" The site traffic for one week was clocked at over 35,000.[149] There was a link to news headlines generated by Al-Jazeera. The sect's website contained a banner indicating that the site was owned by followers of *Ahl us-Sunnah wal-Jamaa'ah* ("the people of [Islamic] Tradition and Community"), suggesting a direct line to the traditions of the Prophet Muhammad. This in itself is an affiliation that many Muslims would have, but the emphasis on the sect's site presented an agenda influenced by jihadi concepts. The site suggested that readers should "be aware" of "sects that may take you outside the fold of Islam or at least divert you from the Straight Path." It provided an eclectic list of those that fell into this category, including various Muslim platforms in the UK (such as the Muslim Council of Britain and the Muslim Association of Britain), al-Azhar University, the Islam-Online website, Jihad Unspun, and Hizb ut-Tahrir.

The sect's listing represented a cross-section of Sunni religious organizations and influences in the UK, Egypt, North America, and elsewhere. At this time, the Muslim Council of Britain was seeking to position itself into the "mainstream" of political life in the UK, and the Muslim Association of Britain had achieved prominence through for its protests against the Iraq war(s). Al-Azhar represents a bastion of Sunni thought emanating from Cairo. Jihad Unspun had been accused of links with al-Qaeda and of being complicit in CIA activities. In 2006 Tony Blair was seeking to proscribe Hizb ut-Tahrir as being a dangerous pan-Islamic political party, although he was unable to locate specific links between Hizb ut-Tahrir and violence.[150]

Elsewhere on the Saved Sect's site was a collection of over fifty *nashid*s, some potentially more controversial than others; "Idrib yaa Asad al-Falloojah" and "Sabran Sabran Yaa Baghdad," for example, referred to the Iraq conflict in martial verses (unaccompanied by musical instruments), suggesting forbearance and steadfastness in the face of "adversity." The latter title contained the sounds of machine guns and explosions. Another was "Nahnu Abtaal ul-Jihaad" (we are the heroes of the jihad). There were several titles associated with Palestinian issues. Many tracks featured on the Saved Sect site have featured in jihadi movie clips on other sites, and the site was by no means the only outlet for their distribution.[151]

More provincially, perhaps, the Saved Sect offered a link to a PDF newsletter described as "a new newsletter published by Muslims living in Luton [Bedfordshire]." *As Siddiqeqeen* determined that Hurricane Katrina was "the Punishment of Allah."[152] The site's series of articles included a subsection devoted to ideas associated with "jihad," with one entitled "How Islam will dominate the world."[153] Elsewhere was an article discussing the case of Shabina Begum, a high school student who sought to wear Islamic dress in school. The article castigated her motives (although it fell short of proclaiming *takfir*, or apostasy).[154] The sect did proclaim *takfir* against Sheikh Abdulaziz bin Baz, a central religious figure in Saudi Arabian culture who died in 1999. The pronouncements of bin Baz continue to dominate discussions on religious authority, including in online sites such as Fatwa-Online.[155]

This is a major condemnation of a significant sector in Sunni religious thought. The site revels in making provocative pronouncements aimed at "orthodox" organizations, Western governments, and key religious concepts. Some of these statements even disenchanted Omar Bakri Mohammed. Their existence on the Internet raises some important issues; clearly, it is easy to track down the instigators of the site and its comments, and there may have been good reasons for security agencies to allow the site to continue in order to track the activities of this group. While in a "minority," its aptitude in applying the media to boost its profile has echoes of the strategy of al-Muhajiroun, whose influence in applying multimedia pervaded other organizations and platforms, including al-Qaeda. Their application of *takfir* at a wide range of targets was particularly provocative, generating further publicity. The allegation that Al-Ghuraaba was influential on the London 7/7 bombers is a further factor that requires unraveling.

In October 2005 another al-Ghuraaba website emerged. This had been registered in May 2005 to Mizanur Rahman, whose address was not included on the registration documentation.[156] The site's front page featured a "warrior" with an AK-47; the banner proclaimed *al-Daw'ah wal jihad* (the propagation of jihad). Its content was provocative and contentious in its firm justification of its interpretation of jihad.[157] In this discussion, it applied Qur'anic justification and examples from the Prophet Muhammad's own practices to "justify" jihad.[158] It made explicit its authors' support of jihadi activities.[159]

The pages also justified bombings in various forms, including 9/11.[160] The page titled "The Enemy Within—al Munafiqeen" was aimed firmly at those Muslims who were against al-Ghuraaba's ideology and activities.[161] The site archived lectures and PalTalk materials from Omar Bakri Muhammad. It raised significant questions: How was it able to keep its online profile? Who was producing the content? Was it maintained as a "honeypot" site? Had the site not been noted by the relevant "authorities" or the ISP? It raised issues associated with freedom of speech and how legislation might approach and deal with such online content. A related Ahl us-Sunnah wal-Jamaa'ah Muntadaa discussion board also operated between 2006 and 2007, promoting forms of jihad and related interpretative discussions.[162] In November 2007 Omar Bakri's videos continued to be hosted online, linked by the Islam Base website to YouTube.[163] This led to demands that YouTube curtail the video facilities for Islam Base and similar sites.[164] An individual such as Omar Bakri might be prevented from returning to the UK, but his online manifestation and that of his sympathizers could not be curtailed.

Multimedia Jihad

The utilization of video clips in the jihadi sector has been an effective tool, pioneered by Chechen Muslim paramilitary groups in the 1990s, when grainy but graphic images of attacks and executions were circulated online. The psychological impact on viewers of execution videos, such as that showing the murder of journalist Daniel Pearl in Pakistan, heightened awareness of the potential of the Web as a tool for radicalization and dissemination of a jihadi worldview.

Investment in technology, wider and cheaper access to digital film cameras and editing software, the spread of broadband, and improved media browsing technology (including Real Player, Windows Media Player, and Macromedia Flash) impacted the growth in this sector of jihadi technology. It received a further boost through the expansion of online video distribution channels, including YouTube and Google Video. It would be unrealistic to consider that small cells and organizations would *not* apply such technology to transmit their operational propaganda with immediacy to a potential global audience. This is especially true when the results are of near-broadcast technical quality, can be copied and distributed effectively online and on DVDs and CD-ROMs, and are picked up by international broadcasters. In a 2006 interview, Iraqi "insurgents" discussed their media strategies: "Abu Abdullah outlines their late inclusion in the burgeoning global propaganda drive: 'Our leader used to object to taking the digicam on operations because he saw it as a security risk. . . . But now we record everything because the media are captives of foreign governments. . . . The camera lets us tell the world what we are doing.' "[165]

The technical quality of statements and videos, which were sent to major broadcasters in addition to appearing on the Web, became a subject for analysis in its own right.[166] Al-Qaeda supporters produced a range of materials in support of operations, including multimedia. Their impact has been significant, especially the use of video for actuality and operational reports. There are also examples of unusual approaches to presenting the al-Qaeda message, perhaps as a way to target certain audience strands and as a (relatively) "light touch" entry point to other materials. For example, in response to the U.S. deck of cards featuring Iraqi "war criminals," a pro-al-Qaeda set of online cards was produced by unitedshadeofswords.com in February 2004. These featured members of George W. Bush's administration and some of his international allies, with each individual possessing a card value.[167]

The rap/ragga track and video "Dirty Kuffar" by Sheikh Terra and the

"Dirty Kuffar" video, 2004

Soul Salah Crew was a significant example of an innovative application of multimedia.[168] A "kuffar" is a derogatory term for a nonbeliever. The video drew upon film clips taken from international broadcasters, as well as al-Qaeda sources; this was turned into a montage "narrated" by the rap of Sheikh Terra, who has a British/Caribbean accent but is heavily disguised by a headdress, or *kafiyyah*. He eulogized Osama bin Laden and the events of 9/11. This was significant in the way the track originally appeared through the CDLR website, based in the UK.[169]

The montage of various video clips presented anti-Jewish, anti-American, and anti-UK lyrics and images brought together with a rapped soundtrack. Animated photos of George W. Bush, Condoleezza Rice, and Colin Powell were included. Images of the Qur'an were juxtaposed with film of the victims of conflict. These include executions and news clips of aircraft flying into the World Trade Center. There were unproven claims in one chat room that Sheikh Terra was in fact "a well known London ragga artist (among the reggae community) that has been on the circuit for over 12 years, he even has a top 40 hit.[170]

"Dirty Kuffar" was an innovative application of the format; it was also copied onto CD/DVD and distributed outside of mosques. The video, which achieved a media footprint outside of jihadi circles, is one example of the creative way in which materials might be applied to develop empathy and sympathy from readers. Heated reaction to the video featured in chat rooms in the ensuing weeks.[171] The video did not receive universal praise from Muslims, including those in the youth target audience, given that the use of music in some Islamic contexts is controversial and rap in particular has been condemned as a genre by some commentators.

An intriguing related controversy emerged online with the distribution via YouTube of the video of a separate track from UK hip-hop activist collective Fun-Da-Mental, led by political activist Aki Nawaz, entitled "Cookbook DIY." This was taken from the album "All Is War: The Benefits of G-HAD," which had a commercial release. The track drew on detailed instructions taken from the Internet on making "dirty bombs," while contrasting this with other forms of nuclear armaments produced in the United States. The album also included a track using the words of Osama bin Laden as lyrics. The video and the complete album were available via Fun-Da-Mental's website for MP3 download and conventional CD distribution and could not be classified as falling into the jihadi genre.[172]

In July 2005 Dutch rappers Youssef and Kamal delivered a track condemning member of Parliament Geert Wilders, which was posted on a website and uploaded to YouTube.[173] Whether this rap was influenced by the "success" of Sheikh Terra is open to question, and it could be said that it lacked the sophistication in terms of production value evidenced in "Dirty Kuffar." It constituted a perceived threat to Wilders, who reported it to the police, concerned that the juxtaposition of the sound of automatic gunfire and his image could be made a reality. The track was aimed firmly at a localized audience in the Netherlands (Muslim and other) rather than the global jihadi aspirational audience. As such, it attracted limited attention in jihadi forums and chat rooms. This was in the shadow of the murder of Theo van Gogh, whose film *Submission* criticizing aspects of Islam had caused a vigorous online debate.

Another intriguing example of the application of multimedia was a "hidden camera jihad" uploaded in September 2005 by Mousslim Mouwaheed. The clip commences with a quotation from the Qur'an: "Those in sin used to laugh at those who believed."[174] It showed an animated digital video camera, in the screen of which is a GIMF logo, including the Qur'an and crossed swords. The video featured a montage of clips drawn from attacks against American troops in Iraq. A canned laughter soundtrack and "comic" audiovisual effects accompanied this in the style of TV shows such as *Candid Camera* or *You've Been Framed*. Clip titles include "Sniper Attack Survivor," "Tarzan Descendant of Monkeys," "Find Green Card," "Wounded," and "The Gladiators." This film appeared to have used a basic video-editing package and suggested it was "To Be Continued."[175]

A variety of other video materials with a "homemade" edge to them appeared. In October 2005 animated graphics showing the British Isles in flames appeared online on the al-Farouq notice board. This had been uploaded to twenty-five different websites. It featured a montage of less-than-flattering images of British troops in Iraq, including soldiers searching women in hijab and abusing prisoners, as well as images of the victims of conflict. There were also photos from Abu Ghraib prison showing the actions of American troops. There was a caption suggesting that "British citizen[s] have to take the decision now," implying they had to influence a pullout from Iraq.[176]

Film of jihadi activities in Iraq included footage of operations, accompanied by Qur'anic recitation and *nashid*s (together with participant commentaries). The technical quality of the video varied, given that a proportion of it was filmed from cars. Clips included all stages of suicide operations: interviews with participants, the technical buildup, and the delivery of a *shahid*'s martyrdom will and final prayers. Another subgenre was film of sniper attacks. This material was compiled into "best of" collections —including two "Top Tens"—and occasionally included subtitled commentaries. Images of the bodies of American soldiers, weapons caches, and U.S. military equipment acquired during operations also were featured. Such materials were not Web exclusive, as they often were delivered to broadcasters such as Al-Jazeera (although they were not always transmitted). The Jihad Media Battalion distributed a twelve-minute compilation video, including subtitled film of Osama bin Laden and film from campaigns in Iraq, accompanied by a *nashid* soundtrack.[177]

A further film showed Sheikh 'Abdullah al-Rashood delivering a speech with an array of weaponry at his desk. He paused in his invective castigating America to pull out a revolver from the back of his robe, placing it on the desk next to a missile launcher.[178] Al-Rashood was killed in June 2005 during a U.S. bombing raid on the border between Syria and Iraq. Al-Zarqawi subsequently delivered a eulogy on al-Rashood, proclaiming him a martyr.[179]

The anonymity of the Net in the production of such materials has also been effective, with authorities having difficulties tracking down members of al-Qaeda's video production team, al-Sahab. The application of logos and symbols associated with the al-Qaeda entity—together with the "professional" elements of their production in terms of editing, lighting, soundtrack, and juxtaposition of images—further appealed to a Net- and media-literate audience familiar with slick news channels. Such "jihadcasts," or broadcasts subsequently copied for online presentation, created a powerful interface to draw in viewers. This reinforced through repetition ideological religious-political messages and subtle identity markers such as logos, including those drawn from religious sources.

The process of distribution is complex. While content in some contexts can be uploaded immediately to the Web, in some locations there can be delays because of infrastructural barriers as well as security issues. For example, materials filmed in Afghanistan may be smuggled across the borders on videotape for editing in Pakistan and distribution on DVD/CD-ROM and the Internet. Cameraman Qari Mohammed Yusuf, who had been "on assignment" to film Ayman al-Zawahiri, apparently used a minivan as a mobile studio because it was inconspicuous.[180] Presumably, this tactic is to avoid surveillance and tracking of video facilities.

Propagation materials on behalf of al-Qaeda take many forms. *Al-Lewa* magazine integrated options for downloading materials on PDAS. Al-Qaeda's propaganda film *Badr al-Riyaadh* achieved a wide circulation on the Internet in 2004. It had a documentary format, showing the training of members and interviews with those involved in attacks in Saudi Arabia. "Islamic" groups such as Abu Musab al-Zarqawi's (then) Tawhid wa'l Jihad and Ansar al-Sunnah uploaded videos as a tool to publicize hostage taking and execution in the name of Islam. Al-Zarqawi drew on the Web to present statements, operational news, and religious interpretations, including the official announcement of the renaming of his organization to Tanzim Qaedat Al-Jihad in Bilad al-Rafidayn (Al-Qaeda Group of Jihad in the Land of Two Rivers [Iraq]).

Chat rooms, such as the al-Farouq.com bulletin board (organized by al-Faqih), were key areas for distribution of materials. This site contains many links to al-Qaeda-related materials.[181] GIMF's *Sout al-Khalifa* media channel, intended as a hub for all media activities, was promoted by *al-Farouq* and other channels as a prelude to its 2005 launch.[182] Abu Musab al-Zarqawi's pronouncements were widely distributed online on al-Farouq.

Multimedia was also applied to publicize the kidnapping of hostages. In the case of Paul Johnson, kidnapped in June 2004, there was also an online campaign allegedly organized by a Saudi friend, the veracity of which was difficult to determine. This did not prevent Johnson's subsequent murder, as images of his body later appeared online. Johnson was targeted specifically because he was an employee of the developers of the Apache helicopters. Messages appeared online via *Sawt al-Jihad* and other pages seeking the release of al-Qaeda prisoners in exchange for his release.

GIMF's *Sout al-Khalifa* media channel was promoted by *al-Farouq* and

Selection, Zubeiddah1417 banners, 2005

other channels. This included links to multimedia content as well as specific pronouncements by ideological leaders. An image displayed on *Sout
al-Khalifa*'s site (and elsewhere) showed the logos of international broadcasters such as the BBC, CNN, Fox News, Reuters, al-Arabiyya, and Al-
Jazeera being engulfed in flames. Another featured the words *sawt al-
khalifa* entwined with two crossed swords and a dagger whose tip was
"transmitting" in the style of a radio transmitter, derived from related logos
that appeared on al-Qaeda websites. Other logos integrated the symbolism
of the Qur'an with the words *sawt al-khalifa* and two swords intersecting
into a globe.

In September 2005 *Sout al-Khalifa* presented its inaugural "broadcast"
in the format of a news bulletin. This was not on *Sout al-Khalifa*'s main
URL initially. The presenter kept his face covered as he commented on
news events, reading from a paper script. An AK-47 rested on his desk,
next to a Qur'an (by his left hand). An al-Qaeda logo was in the left-
hand corner of the screen, and the *Sout al-Khalifa* logo was on the right.
News stories discussed Hurricane Katrina (deemed divine punishment on
George W. Bush), the "liberation" of Gaza, and a lengthy audio statement
from al-Zarqawi, accompanied by a photograph. The film clips drew on
"conventional broadcasters," including Al-Jazeera. The webcast also in-

cluded a "commercial" entitled "Total Jihad." The presentation lacked the professionalism of a traditional broadcast, and a mask muffled the newscaster's voice.[183] A subsequent and shorter bulletin was dedicated to the jailed Al-Jazeera journalist Taysir Allouni, sentenced to seven years in jail in Spain for "support" he gave to al-Qaeda—a statement that might have hindered any chances of Allouni having a successful appeal.[184]

A third webcast highlighted issues in Palestine. The program commenced with a Qur'anic recitation and an animated flash logo of *Sout al-Khalifa*—guns firing across a globe, the spent cartridges falling down into a fire—with the logos of various international broadcasters. The newsreader referred to Palestine, Chechen, and Iraqi conflicts in his introduction. The program featured an imprisoned Israeli businessman, alleged to be a member of the Israeli secret services, showing his driving license as evidence. The Qur'an was on the newsreader's desk for most of the webcast, although at one point it disappeared, suggesting that the webcast was prepared at different times. A machine gun pointed at the camera. The newsreader wore glasses, and a mask muffled his face. The background was a curtain. He spoke in measured tones, using newsreader protocols, including welcoming back viewers after a "commercial break."

The editing was slick as the reader discussed comments from Ayman al-Zawahiri, attacks in Afghanistan, and clips of attacks on American troops. This was accompanied by martial *nashid*s.[185] The Allouni imprisonment received further attention, with a video montage of photos of the journalist. The broadcast concluded with a further reference to Hurricane Katrina and a comment on the political situation in Niger. The key elements of the broadcast would be relatively easy to reproduce, not requiring any purpose-built location. The broadcasts themselves were available within in a number of jihadi chat rooms, including Tajdeed, which was organized by al-Massari.

A fourth webcast appeared in October 2005. The presentation was twenty-seven minutes long and again featured a *kaffiyah*-clad newsreader. This was slicker in its presentation through its use of graphics and transitions; the sound quality had improved as well. The desk no longer had a gun on it. Instead, there was a backdrop of a world map and a TV screen that showed graphics and film clips. The lower portion of the screen featured a rotating GIMF logo and banners in Arabic, stating, for example, *amal al-jihad*, or "work of jihad." This was a different newsreader from previous broadcasts. The broadcast commenced with a compilation of film clips from Iraq, drawn from other GIMF and related sources, including associated banners and graphics.[186] The presentation featured operational film of bombings and soldiers being trained. There was news of a female suicide bomber, including photographs, and a video of an execution.

This sequence was followed by news from Afghanistan, illustrated with maps and news film (citing Al-Jazeera); news of an election in Egypt that included film of Islamist protests; and updates from other regions. A commercial break offered viewers a blessed Ramadan, incorporating a video from Hamas, which extolled the virtues of jihad as a means of freeing al-Quds (Jerusalem).[187]

In November 2005 a talk-show format was utilized in a program entitled "The Argument Continues."[188] Another film in December 2005 showed viewers how to dismantle a Kalashnikov.[189] The impact of such material has been felt in many intelligence and military communities. Former CIA chief George Tenet pointed out that al-Qaeda "remained 'a sophisticated, intelligent organization with enormous capability.' The secondary leadership that was emerging, he added, envisioned 'a global, decentralised movement' whose ability to multiply depended crucially on the Internet, which enabled them to share information from explosives' recipes to the best ways to get into Iraq undetected. The group, he said, was 'undoubtedly mapping vulnerabilities and weaknesses in our telecommunications networks.' "[190]

U.S. Central Command general John Abizaid wanted to introduce ways of filtering Internet content to prevent such applications, but he did not suggest an appropriate methodology that could be applied. Even the suggestion at such a senior level that curbs could be applied suggested a profound lack of awareness of how the Internet functions. It was acknowledged by senior military officials that "Al-Qaeda and radical Islamists are winning the propaganda war against the United States," and that "President George W Bush's administration's policies in the Middle East, its fundamental failure to understand the Muslim world and a lack of imagination in using new communications technologies are responsible."[191]

Secretary of State Donald Rumsfeld also noted the impact of the Internet on the U.S. "cause" in Iraq: "Terrorists have skillfully adapted to fighting wars in today's media age, but, for the most part, America and the governments of the other democracies have not. . . . They know that communications transcend borders, and that a single news story, handled skillfully, can be as damaging to our cause—and as helpful to theirs—as any military attack. And they are able to act quickly with relatively few people, and with modest resources compared to the vast, expensive bureaucracies of democratic governments."[192]

The media has frequently been blamed for the failure of military campaigns in the past, but it was unusual that it was the opposition's media that was taking the rap in this instance. The success of the media strategy was naturally recognized by al-Qaeda itself. An announcement from GIMF in 2006 noted "that the Internet serves as the best alternative to broadcast television for Muslims to execute a 'kind of jihad' involving preaching and information disbursement."[193]

Online Magazines

The presence of online manuals further the cause of al-Qaeda and related organizations, becoming a de facto primary channel of motivation, knowledge, and, in some cases, religious expression—albeit through the matrix of a specific interpretive understanding of jihad.[194] Linked to this apparent efficiency in the application of communications technologies is the proliferation of online magazines, which present logistical data as well as religious justification for militaristic jihad activities on a number of fronts.[195]

The manuals are "professionally" produced, with illustrations and graphics. They appear in various online channels and forums for rapid distribution, usually in the form of portable document format (PDF) files. They are frequently available for a limited duration through free upload sites, where they are placed anonymously. Within a personal archive, I hold hundreds of different manuals and related documents, including sermons and statements in a similar format, primarily in Arabic.

The manuals themselves are presented in a choice of formats. PDF and Word are popular, suggesting different ways in which they might be read, and by different audiences.[196] A Word document might be easier for some to edit, circulate, and refine locally than a PDF. A detailed content analysis of each manual is beyond the scope of this volume. Key themes are associated with militaristic activity and organization, including criteria for membership, strategic considerations, approaches to military intelligence, and concealment. These topics are filtered with religious language and justification, drawing on precedents from Muhammad's lifetime and other figures from Islamic history but also on generic examples of "good practice."

These manuals frequently have appeared on free Web space and file-sharing services. Efforts have been made to close services providing this content. However, as part of a continuing practice, multiple copies are usually uploaded on a variety of services, limiting any attempts at closure. The formats are occasionally encrypted, but very often they are publicly available.

The use of free Web space and ease of site construction/mobility through shifting sites and IP addresses, together with potential anonymity, transcends registration issues associated with top-level domains. Clearly it is impractical to endeavor to register "al-neda.com" or a similar site. But it is straightforward to go to a cybercafé, register anonymously on a free Net service, and upload a site with jihad-oriented information. Outside of this visible range of materials, it is relevant to add that what is beyond observation may be more significant, including content published to select individuals through the use of encryption tools or closed chat rooms.

A proportion of jihadi material uses generic data, such as material on logistics and weaponry. This is combined with material specially designed for online readers. Content is easy to search, and files can be quickly downloaded for offline distribution. There are vast quantities of data available for download, but it may be one thing to hold it on the hard drive and another to find sufficient time to study it in detail. Questions remain on how manuals and other documents associated with diverse campaigns have been applied, and whether they give a virtual sense of organizations that may exceed their real-world presence.

Jihadi groups focused on Iraq, Syria, Algeria, Saudi Arabia, Afghanistan, Chechnya, Kashmir, and Morocco all had online magazines. The genre also focused on particular leaders, prominent voices being Osama bin Laden, Ayman al-Zawahiri, Abu Musab al-Suri, and Abu Musab al-Zarqawi. Some content in these magazines could be linked back to the *Encyclopaedia of Afghan Jihad*, an eleven-volume compendium detailing strategic and military approaches to a variety of situations. The manuals are well designed and detailed, containing logistical information and religious justification sermons with practical information about weaponry and tactics. An example of this was *Dhurwat al-Sanam* (the tip of the camel's hump), produced in the name of al-Qaeda in Iraq. The design was colorful and dynamic. It contained a message from bin Laden, as well as tactical information and sermon material.

Key titles among these publications are twenty-nine editions of *Sawt al-Jihad* (voice of Jihad), dating from 2002 onwards, and twenty-two editions of *Mu'askar al-Battar* (Military Camp of al-Battar), dating from 2003 onwards. There is a variety of region-specific and/or "special editions" from sources affiliated with the ethos of al-Qaeda, some of which only progressed to a couple of editions. These could frequently be sourced from a central site, albeit one that continued to shift ISP and identity. On one site, various issues of *al-Battar* and other documents could be downloaded and compared. These would often be in compressed format and available through a variety of free Web space URLs, often labeled as available for a limited time frame. Pages4free.biz, based in New South Wales, Australia, was one popular location of manuals in 2004; as with many such free sites, this was also hosting pornographic images and related live chat on its front page.

Essential religious issues were also covered in some online magazines. For example, approaches toward jihad during Ramadan featured in an edition of *al-Battar*.[197] News was also provided, perhaps as motivation for future activities and to provide exemplary models to follow. An issue of *Sawt al-Jihad* explained the "rationale" for the killing of other Muslims, including hostages.[198]

In the 2002 case of *United States v. Ahmed Abdel Sattar et al.*, selected manuals, known as the "Birmingham UK Al Qaida Manual," were translated from Arabic into English, heightening interest in this genre. Some of these materials would have been derived in part from the Internet.[199] Specialist manuals can also appear; one observer noted the appearance of a nuclear weaponry manual, produced by Layth al-Islam, or "Lion of Islam," and first presented on the alfirdaws.org forum.[200] The links to the manual subsequently appeared on other Internet forums and were discussed in depth.

A range of potential audiences was encouraged to view the magazines. Technologically literate youth were targeted by OBL Crew's site, which included features on hacking and the "rationale" behind beheading as a form of execution. It also provided instructions on how to participate in jihad; this included links to obtaining generic information on firearms training (from the U.S. Army) and advice on weapons training.[201] Another manual provided "Iraqi Insurgent Sniper Training," illustrating which were the most appropriate targets and what the psychological damage of each kill would be. The manual included a photo of George W. Bush next to several world leaders, under the headline, "Who would you shoot?" This was designed as a training exercise. The manual also noted: "Target U.S. Special Forces. they are very stupid because they have a 'Rambo complex,' thinking that they are the best in the world; don't be arrogant like them.' "[202]

There was also a jihadi magazine for women, *al-Khansaa* (for women), which ran to one edition.[203] "Umm Osama" has been the pen name of a writer also known as "al-Khansaa," who allegedly wrote on behalf of al-Qaeda in various forums. However, as is frequently the case online, all was not as it seemed: "It transpired that the real Umm Osama was an Egyptian woman in her mid-twenties living in Medina who was interested in communicating with extremists. She was arrested and released after it was discovered that she was using Internet message boards to fill time."[204] This use of avatars is a crucial issue in our "understanding" of such online activities, and it suggests that caution must be applied at all times when discussing Web content. The concept of exactly who is "representative" online remains a blurred area, especially when writers and site organizers have expended considerable energy to maintain their anonymity. Jihadi site content has different levels, some of which are secured by passwords. They contain distinct logos presenting "brands" of jihad, and certain contributors are recognizable by familiar user names or pseudonyms. Al-Zarqawi's organization used Abu Maisara al-Iraqi as a key identity.

To this compendium of online output could be added the extensive jihad manual *Da'wat al-Moqwama al-Islamiyah* (The International Islamic Resistance Call), produced by Abu Musab al-Suri (Mustafa Setmariam Nasar) and published online in December 2004. Al-Suri, a prominent member of al-Qaeda, wrote this 1,600-page document as a means of approaching strategy, logistics, *da'wa* to the jihad call of al-Qaeda, and specific arenas in which such a call would be successful.[205] Some guides draw on generic materials, as well, such as a guide to fighting ninja style.[206]

Another magazine, *Alma'sadah Al-Jihadiah*, published a guide to construction of a "dirty bomb."[207] Saif al-Adel, a senior al-Qaeda commander, wrote in *al-Battar* about tactics toward different weapons, including nuclear and biological materials.[208] Some manuals contained details of how to facilitate "identity theft."[209] Manuals that are downloaded were easily copied and circulated via other media; in 2003, Saudi Arabian security forces focused their energies on those circulating a bomb-construction guide and arrested four owners of computer stores in the Jazan region.

Key authors are also active participants in al-Qaeda, and some have been killed in operational activity. Fahd bin Ali al-Ghabalan wrote a number of weaponry manuals before being killed in a shootout in July 2004. Saud bin Hamoud al-Otaibi, a chief of al-Qaeda in the Arabian Peninsula, signed the *Sawt al-Jihad* editorial on his emergence.[210] The writings of

Yusuf al-Ayri (1973–2003) continued to influence *Sawt al-Jihad* after his death, in particular works analyzing the justification for specific acts done in the name of al-Qaeda.[211]

A variety of other Internet magazines in diverse formats have appeared, some linked to multimedia. While much of this material is difficult for intelligence agencies to close down, a UK-published journal, alsunnah.org, was the target of interest from intelligence agencies in 2005. This was for "allegedly soliciting suicide bombers to attack American and coalition troops in Iraq, as well as Israelis."[212]

One forum provided advice on appropriate "disguises" and ruses to fool security forces as part of a "recruitment" exercise for jihadis: "When travelling, wear jeans and carry a walkman—try not to look like an Islamic fundamentalist—and for precise instructions on how to link up with Iraqi groups 'contact the Salafite jihadist exponents in your own countries.' These are just some of the travel tips and suggestions provided on an Islamist Internet site for potential al-Qaeda recruits from various Arab and Western countries who have signalled their desire to go to Iraq to fight against the American troops."[213] Presumably the suggestion of carrying a Sony Walkman (a 1980s technical icon) should be updated to an iPod for the 2000s. Further Internet magazines supporting al-Qaeda continued to emerge, aimed at different readerships.[214]

Such tactics were not the preserve of those based in the Middle East. In the Moluccan conflict, Laskar Jihad formulated an online approach to propagation of their interpretation of "jihad."[215] In Indonesia, Imam Samudra, one of the "Bali bombers," published a book titled *Aku Melawan Teroris* (I Fight Terrorists). In this, he encouraged forms of "online jihad." Samudra's book (written in Indonesian) provided a basic introduction to hacking and also advice on the creation of cloned credit cards. While not necessarily the most thorough of sources, its integration into the memoir of the instigator of the Bali bombs was significant: "Tucked into the back of the 280-page book is a chapter of an entirely different cast titled 'Hacking, Why Not?' There, Samudra urges his fellow Muslim radicals to take the holy war into cyberspace by attacking U.S. computers, with the particular aim of committing credit card fraud. The chapter then provides an outline on how to get started."[216] The article noted that Samudra used the Net to obtain details on credit card fraud and allegedly asked for "religious permission" to undertake such activities.

In general terms, the themes of the online magazines can include

Qur'anic justifications for activities, political commentaries, and specific operational and logistical advice. This may incorporate manuals for weapons training and construction, often illustrated with photographs. Detailed information about Israeli Uzi machine guns was included in one guide. Tactical materials have included details of approaches to the taking of hostages, kidnapping, and assassination. Some material was acquired from generic sources, while a significant proportion has been written especially for these manuals.

Online Operations

Senior members of al-Qaeda were "sighted" at various times in Internet cafés, although many maintained a low profile, ensuring that their online activities were masked in anonymity. This did not mean that the use of the Internet was not without risk for jihadis and al-Qaeda's supporters. In Jordan, online activist Murad Al-Assaydeh was prosecuted for apparently being a threat to the kingdom by using e-mail and the Net as a way to facilitate electronic jihad.[217] Al-Assaydeh was subsequently jailed for two and a half years, having had an original five-year sentence reduced on appeal.[218]

There is plenty of evidence that lower-level operatives utilized the Internet as a logistical tool; for example, in the UK, Saajid Badat, jailed for a bomb plot, used e-mail to withdraw from his mission at the last minute.[219] Unsurprisingly, there were some indications that Internet cafés had also been used for logistical planning purposes elsewhere. One investigation noted that such a café was a key part of a planned attack on the U.S. embassy in Paris in 2001, with one cell member having a background in computer science and another being a former Internet café employee. The central figure in the attack, Djamel Beghal, devised a plan that involved the opening of an Internet café, in part to facilitate communications with other al-Qaeda members.[220] Beghal was sentenced to ten years in prison, with other participants receiving lesser sentences. While authorities were frequently unable to find the source of specific statements or the key instigators of certain sites, the Internet became the focus of a number of investigations.[221] Internet cafés became hubs for al-Qaeda–related activities. The 2003 bombings in Istanbul were apparently instigated by users of the Bingol Internet Merkezi Cafe in southern Turkey, one of whose brothers owned the café.[222]

Legislation, Indictments, and Prosecutions

Prosecutions have played a key role in developing our understandings of jihadi cyberspace. There is a sense that this is merely a small component in a more substantial technical interface of *da'wa*, dissemination, design, and readership on many levels.

Prosecution occurred in a variety of contexts. In Australia, charges were made against an airport baggage handler, Bilal Khazal, for writing a jihad book that he posted on a website.[223] The monitoring of such sites was also undertaken by the FBI and applied as a means to deport individuals who allegedly visited chat rooms and recruitment areas of the Web. Tashnuba Hayder, a sixteen-year-old Bangladeshi student living in Manhattan, had listened to Omar Bakri Muhammad's "broadcasts" on PalTalk. Despite proclaiming her innocence, she was deported to Bangladesh.[224]

Saad Ali Al-Shehri, a veteran of mujahideen campaigns, also noted the impact of the Internet on recruitment of jihadi operatives: "Shehri added that the Internet has made it easier to target susceptible youth, but also expressed optimism in the current backlash against the so-called global jihad. 'I am very optimistic that many men who went astray are coming back. Even some sheikhs are regretting their issuing violent fatwa's [*sic*] and have since corrected their position. . . . Many of them came to the right path after the royal pardon was issued.' The Mujahedeen veteran ended his interview by re-emphasizing the need for parents to play an increasingly active role in controlling their children's exposure to deviant propaganda."[225]

The suggestion that visiting and participating in jihad-linked website activities is dangerous to wider society was one drawn upon in a number of prosecutions. In 2004 a U.S. National Guardsman and convert to Islam, Ryan Anderson (Amir Talhah), was arrested in the United States for potential jihadi activity, with an indictment that included evidence of visiting "radical" sites. In 2004 he was found guilty of "attempted treason for trying to assist the terrorist group Al Qaeda" and received a life sentence.[226]

Jihadi supporter and Muslim convert Adam Gadahn attracted media attention for being "inspired" to convert to Islam after visiting chat rooms. Attention was given to his past as a former heavy-metal music fan from a rural California background. Gadahn was allegedly the masked speaker who was featured in a 2005 al-Qaeda video threatening Western cities, and he appeared unmasked with al-Zawahiri in a 2006 video.[227] Also known as Azzam al-Amriki, Gadahn was also featured in a 2006 video inviting Americans to Islam, and in 2007 he warned America to take specific actions in order to avoid further conflict. Gadahn was indicted under treason charges by the U.S. District Court in 2006, was placed on the FBI's "Most Wanted" list, and became the subject of a $1 million reward.

American student Mark Robert Walker posted statements in online forums supporting jihad "under the names of 'Abdullah' and 'Abdullah313.' Among the comments he allegedly made: 'I hate the U.S. gov't; I wish I could have been flying one of the planes on Sept. 11.' "[228] He was arrested after attempting an assignation with a "jihadi" in a Texas Internet café and subsequently received a two-year jail sentence "after pleading guilty to Attempting to Make a Contribution of Goods and Services to a Specially Designated Terrorist."[229]

The prosecution in the trial in Idaho of Sami Omar al-Hussayen highlighted his posting on jihadi materials on the Internet.[230] The case was significant, as al-Hussayen was cleared of terrorism-related charges but was subsequently deported to his country of origin (Saudi Arabia) on immigration charges. Al-Hussayen suggested that: "he was only maintaining Web sites he felt were promoting Islam and that any radical content on those sites did not reflect his beliefs. The jury cleared him of terrorism-related charges, but was deadlocked on eight immigration counts."[231]

The case raised some important issues by distinguishing between different types of Internet content associated with "jihad." Al-Hussayen was found to be the administrator of sites that included islamway.com and an alleged contributor to various forums. However, the case determined that administrative ownership did not always contribute to responsibility for uploading content, as knowledge of a password would allow anyone to access the site. A prosecution computer-forensic expert noted that, despite analysis of two computer hard drives owned by al-Hussayen, the defendant did not have full control over the content posted on islamway.com.[232]

Net literacy has been an important part of organizing campaigns and has featured in the training of operatives at camps in Afghanistan and elsewhere. Closer government monitoring of sites, chat rooms, and e-mail traffic may have had a detrimental effect on some of this logistical planning or simply driven operatives further "underground" on the Web. To ensure their personal security and confidentiality, operatives followed specific protocols.

The arrest in Pakistan of Muhammad Naeem Noor Khan, an al-Qaeda computer expert, offered some insight into the approaches toward information distribution in various regions. This included the use of couriers to deliver CDs and the application of multiple e-mail aliases with a finite life.[233] Techniques included the application of encryption, and there has been a separate indication that this and other methodologies have been taught both online and at various camps.[234] It was revealed that Khan had developed his own encryption systems that could not be intercepted.[235] It was suggested that Khan, also known as Abu Talha, was assisting U.S. authorities following his arrest by continuing to feed and monitor information into various online networks, until his cover was controversially "blown."[236]

Further examples emerged with the evidence in the trial in England of seven defendants convicted of having links to al-Qaeda and of plotting explosions. They had used code words in e-mail and regularly disposed of their computer equipment without leaving a trail. They were jailed in 2007.[237] In the same year in Scotland, Mohammed Atif Siddique was found guilty on terrorism offenses, including the distribution of jihadi videos on three websites. His computer hard drive contained encrypted and hidden videos: "Experts from Central Scotland Police e-crimes unit assisted by specialists from the Scottish Crime and Drug Enforcement Agency examined the computers, recovering deleted files and in some cases being able to read material which had been partly overwritten."[238]

Later in 2007, British airport worker Samina Malik was prosecuted in the UK under the Terrorism Act 2000 for her online poems and pro-jihad pronouncements. She posted these under the name "The Lyrical Terrorist," and their subjects included martyrdom and beheadings; she also called herself "Stranger Awaiting Martyrdom": "Police found a copy of Osama Bin Laden's Declaration of War and a passage in which she praised the al-Qa'eda leader and added: 'We will not let you have any peace. We will show no remorse, no mercy and no regrets.' . . . In one poem, called 'Raising Mujahideen [holy fighter] Children,' she recommended indoctrinating children from the age of seven, adding: 'Show the children videos and pictures of mujahideen and tell them to become strong like them.' "[239]

The poem has language that is markedly similar to statements and concepts contained on Azzam.com, such as: "Show them the pictures of Mujahideen and encourage them to become like these people at the least."[240] Malik was prosecuted for ownership of jihadi materials, including manuals and content produced and distributed by many of the sites discussed in this chapter, such as the Saved Sect, Followers of Ahl us-Sunnah Wal-Jammaa'ah, and Omar Bakri Muhammad. In this particular case, we see an individual who herself has been profoundly influenced by Internet content, developing a new generation and format of materials. Malik's nine-month suspended sentence was cleared on appeal in June 2008.

Shifts in legislation—making the development and distribution of jihadi content a criminal offense—have intensified the focus on e-jihad discourse. Governments have refined their legal understandings of the genre and presented far-reaching measures in an attempt to crack down on the jihadi network usage of the media. For example, in 2007 European Union commissioner Franco Frattini proposed legislation to criminalize any Web content that could be applied for training or incitement purposes.[241]

In the United States, the Violent Radicalization and Homegrown Terrorism Prevention Act of 2007 heralded the proposal of a Center of Excellence for the Study of Violent Radicalization and Homegrown Terrorism in the United States, to be based at a university. Congressional investigations recognized the role of the Internet as a jihadi tool as the act passed through the House of Representatives toward the Senate: "The Internet has aided in facilitating violent radicalization, ideologically based violence, and the homegrown terrorism process in the United States by providing access to broad and constant streams of terrorist-related propaganda to United States citizens."[242] Critics might suggest that this formal recognition was somewhat overdue.

Legislation and prosecutions will to some extent open up knowledge of e-jihadi networks and knowledge economies, giving a sense of their modus operandi and technical abilities. They represent an introduction in terms of developing an understanding of the ways in which diverse players are utilizing the Internet to promote their interpretations of jihad. These methods will continue to evolve in tandem with Web 2.0. However, they may drive e-jihad further into the dark recesses of cyberspace, making observation and analysis more problematic.

Concluding Comment

It is necessary to distinguish between the application of the Net as a propagation and recruitment tool and its utilization as a logistical device. Only in the passage of time will a complete picture emerge. This would require an analysis of issues associated with encryption, financial movement, "closed" membership-only sectors of the Web, and the application of the Net in a variety of fund-raising scams. Investigation is required into phishing, bank fraud, and other criminal activities that have been used at local levels to fund pro-al-Qaeda activities.

The concept of dissimilitude and secrecy has other precedents within religious spheres. Whether such activities can in this instance be described as Islamic is open to question. It does illustrate that approaches to jihadi Web space have to be multifaceted and multiresourced in nature. This requires awareness of the diversity of analytical angles as readers with various interests and agendas endeavor to match the realities of digitally evoked jihad and its real time equivalent. Given the range of content, and the intermeshing and juxtaposition of the digital and real worlds, it may not be necessary in some contexts to separate out these spheres, but rather to see them as interlocking and mutually interactive.

Some might suggest that politically motivated Islamic activities cannot be drawn into the pure zone of Islamic discourse, but that would not be the view of the protagonists online, who would seek to present to a broad readership that their activities are purely motivated by religious values. Others might suggest that this is somewhat idealistic and ignores the personal, socioeconomic, and/or political motivations that pulse beneath (e-)jihadi agendas. The "truth," which may incorporate a nuanced interpretation of these factors, is clearly a subjective issue. What is apparent is that Muslim actors, motivated by their interpretation of Qur'anic values, carry out these activities and dialogues with the application of Islamic language.

{ 6 }

Digital Jihadi Battlefields
Iraq and Palestine

The Internet has been applied by diverse jihadi platforms relating to conflicts in Iraq and Palestine. There is some continuity between this chapter and the previous one, perhaps demonstrating the interaction between the global and the local. Considerations relating to whether activities can be defined as Islamic, jihadi, insurgent, terrorist, Iraqi, Palestinian, or Arabic—or some combination of these descriptors—naturally apply, depending on the individual perspective of the observer.

As with the previous chapter, the term "jihadi" is applied here with caution to incorporate a broad range of perspectives, actions, and discourses. It is not the purpose of this chapter to document chronologically the entire online output of various platforms in these regions, but to discuss those with a specific Islamic ethos, if that can be qualified. A proportion of the websites, manuals, and audiovisual materials referred to in the previous chapter were related to issues surrounding Iraq and Palestine. Through further delineation of the main features of cyberspace in relation to jihadi activities in these contexts, this may contribute to an overall interpretative framework.

Digital Iraqi Battlefields

The Iraq digital battlefield and its real-world aftermath is a dominant issue for analysis and debate in relation to CIES. The Internet has been a critical element of diverse campaigns associated with Iraq, in particular the production of video materials that have had a global impact. These have included videos showing the executions of kidnapped hostages, Muslim and other, together with materials filmed on the front line(s). However, it is also a more nuanced area of the Web, with blogs and pages associated with particular scholars and organizations emanating from Iraq and Iraqi-oriented sources and specific political discourse that may or may not have an Islamic element to it.

Writing in the eye of the storm, many of the events written about occurred in real time as I prepared the chapter. For a time, there was a direct correlation between my blog entries and content for this chapter. Writing in 2008, a final analysis of the Iraq situation seems a long way off. One might hypothesize on possible outcomes, but the military angle is more difficult to determine. The language is loaded in any analysis on all sides, and emotions run high, particularly in cyberspace. Add to this equation the dynamics of Web-based news systems and the result has been in many ways a full conflict played out in intimate and at times horrifying detail online. When viewed on a computer screen, such content may be interpreted in a different, more personal way than it would be if viewed on television, perhaps in a group setting. Certainly the elements of interactivity cannot be overlooked, although they can also be clichéd at times.

Returning to the issue raised at the beginning of this chapter, the identity or identities of those undertaking online activities is of considerable importance. Are they specifically Islamic, Kurd, Shi'a, Jihadi, Salafi, Ba'ath, al-Qaeda, tribal, political, or a permutation of these elements—or none of them? There were variant forms within all of these umbrella terms and at times distinct shifts in identities. Some key figures in jihadi factions are not necessarily Iraqi by birth. Other figures in Iraqi-driven insurgency movements were in conflict with the modus operandi of al-Qaeda–linked operations, being more tribally focused and aware of the serious logistical and ideological ramifications when Shi'as were targeted.[1] The primary focus here is on Sunni–oriented al-Qaeda affiliates.

There were also implications here in terms of the balance of coverage, especially in terms of comparing jihadi al-Qaeda–linked activity with "insurgency" not linked to al-Qaeda. The online balance is certainly tipped in the former's favor, although sites such as Information from Occupied Iraq sought to present a Iraq-insurgency, nationalistic-centric position.[2] This is a general factor of all news coverage on this issue, one that those on the receiving end of militaristic activity would not necessarily have considered.

Another factor is whether Internet activity was representative of what was occurring at the grassroots level. This is difficult to determine. Certainly, a percentage of content was emerging from Iraqi sources, such as multimedia content and "official" statements, but it was distributed on servers and Web space located worldwide. There was no specific pattern, although free space was a popular option, and upload sites located in Japan featured heavily between 2005 and 2007. These included the productions referred to in the previous chapter as manifestations of GIMF and similar platforms. The reduction of content into a geographical sphere becomes increasingly redundant—although perhaps conventional in terms of academic process—in an attempt to provide basic categorization models of diffuse and ineffable information networks.

The Internet was a critical source for knowledge about developments in Iraq in the early twenty-first century, one that the protagonists and supporters of jihad were, certainly at the early stages of the invasion of Iraq, more aware of than the supporters of the United States–dominated coalition forces. This is not the space to contemplate strategic approaches and objectives on all sides but simply to observe how the Internet lubricated the conduits of knowledge about activities, informing and becoming part of militaristic jihad. Activists ensured that suicide bombers were videotaped before their operations; that their martyrdom was also filmed; that executions were filmed with deference to technical quality; and that statements emerged from key figures, often before mainstream media tackled a story or as a way of providing an alternative news perspective. Content was also e-mailed and otherwise distributed to media channels in the form of officially sanctioned multimedia and statements. Kimmage and Ridolfo observed that, in a two-day period in 2007, a plethora of images, statements, and videos were issued from Sunni jihadis in Iraq. These statements may have been press releases, operational statements, logistical information, religious propagation, and/or magazine-format materials. Kimmage and Ridolfo provide a breakdown of the statements according to a categorization model, providing a typology of operational activities and forms of media together with the identities of specific "insurgent" groupings publishing the content on two key sites.[3] This is only part of the complex picture, as added to this was the distribution of a massive amount of content from other parties and interests.

Operationally, the Internet also provided ways of organizing and facilitating logistics, finance, and propaganda to nuanced local, regional, and global audiences from all religious affiliations. Many, but not all, content providers endeavored to place their materials in a religious light through the application of religious symbols and language. They ensured that the content was rapidly distributed in a way that avoided censorship (at least until initial distribution) and provided it in universal formats that were quick to copy. Information concerning the locations of materials was made available through e-mail lists, discussion boards, and central servers. "Authenticity" was indicated, although not always guaranteed, by the use of specific logos and site-design parameters and through the graphic nature of content that would be difficult to fabricate. The explicit nature of videos captured the attention of not only the international media and governments but also a sector of the global Muslim audience.

Such content formed part of a wider backdrop of the depiction of violence occurring in Iraq in general, especially film of victims of bombings (from all sides). One might question how immune the television-viewing public may have been, especially when content shown on Al-Jazeera and Al-Arabiyya was generally more explicit in showing violence (and its results) than Western broadcasters. It may be that the producers of execution videos felt that they had to take the violence up a notch in order to make an impact. Their audience was not necessarily universally sympathetic to such materials and expressed as much on the Web. They may have suffered directly or indirectly because of the existence of these films and the publicity they attracted, particularly in Muslim-minority contexts.

There has been a suggestion that some potential jihadis were radicalized through provocative and violent content and driven to seek advice and even membership through associated Web space. There is also an indication that even some al-Qaeda supporters and affiliates believed that certain online content had the potential to alienate possible sympathy and support for causes, in particular when other Muslims became the victims and their demise was featured on webcasts. Web content providers and organizers became critical players in how jihadi activities were articulated to a wider world, part of an online discourse that featured their opponents as well as sympathizers and other observers. The ability of security forces to "lurk" and observe such content also forms part of the knowledge equation.

When content providers—the individual and collective authors, interpreters, copyists, designers, information filters, and technical geeks—were closed down through capture, death, or ISP censorship, this could have influenced the type of "real-world" activities that took place. The rapid placing of digital film online, in edited formats with logos and statements, required a series of intermediaries. In their enforced absence or closure, this may have had an impact on the timing of operations.

The operationally active appeared acutely conscious that their Web presence could be applied to justify activities through religious imagery and language. Providing a video for Web and other media was a significant liminal moment, offering a transition from supporter to martyr and vice versa. It was facilitated through the implementation of increasingly technically proficient (in many cases) lighting, music, sound, editing, backdrop, and placement on an appropriate website. Whereas earlier versions of martyr galleries were often retrospective in that they usually featured long-deceased activists, now they are anticipatory, with pages ready for online publication immediately after an operation.

The Iraq milieu was significant in this regard. It became a context for the informed intensification of the applications of Internet-based technologies for promoting jihad. This was in line with parallel technological improvements such as telecommunication accessibility, bandwidth, video editing, free Web space, anonymity tools, cheaper hardware, and increases in technical literacy among protagonists and their audiences. In many ways, the intensity of Web-based activities in connection with Iraq allowed for the hothousing of research and development. Some of the content may not have the high-tech gloss of multimedia productions, but certainly there were opportunities to utilize digital editing suites, animation, slideshows, and broadcast technology.

The viral marketing issue is particularly pertinent here as well, and the role of specific portals has been critical in facilitating the marketing of jihadi activities in Iraq globally and peer to peer. The linking of this material to other Islamic and/or political issues took on even greater significance with the emergence online of photographs taken of prisoner abuse by American service personnel in Abu Ghraib prison.

Following the conquest of Iraq by coalition forces in 2003, the emergence of e-jihadi elements associated with Iraq was marked through a series of violent and elaborately choreographed online pronouncements and performances. These had a direct relationship to the creation of a profile for the Jordanian Abu Musab al-Zarqawi (also known as Ahmad Fadeel al-Nazal al-Khalayleh [1966–2006]). This was in conjunction with his associated platforms Jama'at al-Tawhid wa'l Jihad (the Group of Unification and Holy War) and Qaedat al-Jihad fi balad ar-Rafidayn (the Base of Jihad in the Land of the Two Rivers [Iraq]).

The nature of these activities had a direct relationship to the existence of information technology, in particular the ways in which they offered a rapid distribution of the religious-political messages associated (by their supporters) with this form of action. Its nature and dissemination would have been impractical in the 1980s through the mid-1990s— and impossible in the 1970s. They may also have challenged other Islamic

Tawhid wa'l Jihad graphic, 2004

perspectives, especially less-vocal and politically quietest platforms seeking alternative solutions to the Iraq issue, but also those with a less-refined awareness of technology.

It should be stressed that the methodologies employed by al-Zarqawi and others were beyond the norm and frequently unprecedented in their scope. Whether al-Zarqawi, as he developed a status to some as an *'alim*, or religious scholar, through his online activities, would have qualified this as an element of *ijtihad* (in the Sunni sense of a personal and pragmatic interpretation of Islamic sources in reaction to contemporary issues) is open to question. Al-Zarqawi was not traditionally trained in Islamic sciences, which in the eyes of some would have disqualified him from delivering authoritative religious pronouncements or opinions.

It was not scholarship that propelled al-Zarqawi to world attention; it was his status as an insurgent to some or freedom fighter to others, although I do not intend to rehearse the old arguments of status here in detail. The pivotal act that accelerated al-Zarqawi's profile, online and in the real world, was the murder of Nicholas Berg in 2004. There is a certain irony that Berg was an American telecommunications engineer who had been traveling in Baghdad installing and promoting wireless hardware for the Internet. Berg's capture and subsequent execution was played out on the Internet via the uploading of video files onto Muntada al-Ansar's website.

The impact of this resonated worldwide, although it was not unprecedented. Rather, the filmed executions had precedents that must have been

Front page, Abualbukhary.org (portal for Tawhid wa'l Jihad and others), 2005

noted; the 2002 killing of journalist Daniel Pearl in Karachi by al-Qaeda supporters demonstrated the ways in which the Web could transcend traditional media outlets and open up propaganda from al-Qaeda affiliates to a wider audience, ranging from analysts to voyeurs. One account noted that "shocking video film of Pearl's murder, seen around the world via the Internet, was in fact a partial reconstruction of what had happened a few moments earlier, officers have been told. . . . The camera operator made a mistake and missed the moment of his death, which his murderers then re-enacted, before decapitating the reporter."[4]

Similarly, the filmed executions of Russian troops distributed on Chechen websites also gave the mujahidin a publicity profile that their print output had not acquired. The Berg killing, playing out worldwide, demonstrated how a relatively low-tech combination of camera, computer, and Internet connection could, when fed through the appropriate channels, acquire a global audience. The channels themselves are informative. The video surfaced on a number of non-Islamic sites of a voyeuristic and/or horror-oriented nature, including pages of a conspiracy theorist. Links to the Web links rapidly circulated in chat rooms. The rapid reproduction of the video negated attempts to close down the original channels on which it appeared: "The video is of poor quality, and its time stamp seems to show an 11-hour lapse between when the assailants finish their statement and push Berg down, to when they behead him. That suggests a delay between those two portions of tape posted on the Web site."[5]

The video established a conventional format for further murders online and inspired improvement in production values, with augmented logos, music, and higher quality sound and vision, together with enhanced streaming. The Berg killing caused spikes on traffic to a number of websites and blogs that had mentioned it, including my own pages, despite my choosing not to link directly to the URL. The original site was inundated with hits and was eventually closed by its Malaysian ISP.[6] The video provoked controversy and perhaps curiosity in equal measure.[7]

Coupled with the ways in which the images from Abu Ghraib circulated online, the Berg killing marked a significant shift in the development of CIEs that did not escape the attention of other commentators. The *Bahrain Tribune Daily* noted: "The 'live' beheading of the American hostage, whoever is behind it, is a terrible act, as heinous as the mental, moral and physical abuse of Iraqi prisoners."[8] Historian Phillip Knightley thought that it represented "a new era in wartime propaganda."[9] A number of conspiracy theories started to surface that placed doubts in some quarters upon the veracity of the video, including suggestions that al-Zarqawi was dead—a point that was picked up in discussion rooms.[10] With the benefit of hindsight, clearly this was not the case, but it did not halt a sustained dialogue on different aspects of the video, one that continues to provoke interest on the Web despite the subsequent stream of further victims. The video, and comments "celebrating" the execution, could also be found on discussion boards and blogs, frequently cut and pasted from central sites.

Other pronouncements and statements from al-Zarqawi appeared regularly on a variety of websites and forums, indicating the medium's primary role as a channel of immediacy for the presentation of his "official" statements and videos. These included recordings of suicide-bomb actions.[11] At times there was online competition for accountability for jihadi actions.[12] As a further example of technical literacy, there was also discussion of how videos were technically manipulated in order to "enhance" the audiovisual technical quality online.[13] According to one report, Jama'at al-Tawhid wal Jihad were using commercially available video-streaming technology developed by a British company.[14] This led to substantial interest in how al-Zarqawi and Tawhid wal-Jihad were applying the Web as a means of attracting more recruits and finance. The former aspect was more transparent in nature, with the Web and related chat rooms being loaded in language that would make a jihad campaign attractive to some readers.[15]

Al-Zarqawi also made statements focused on particular sectors of the Muslim constituency, such as Turkey.[16] The case of an American soldier apparently kidnapped in Iraq, who subsequently reemerged with family in Lebanon, also had an Internet element, with discussions appearing (prior to his reemergence) on Internet forums on the legitimacy of such a hostage taking.[17] Later allegations that his execution was online only added to the intrigue.[18] The kidnapping of other foreign nationals in Iraq and their subsequent reappearance on webcasts demonstrated a growing sophistication of the application of the medium and a cynical recognition of its efficiency when playing out violent images to a global audience.[19]

The realization that the intensity of a hostage taking could be heightened by the application of sequenced releases of online film manifested itself in its entirety in the kidnapping and murder of British engineer Ken Bigley. In this particular case, Bigley made several direct-to-camera statements. One was recorded just before his execution. Some of Bigley's comments were aimed specifically at (or were responses to) statements made by Prime Minister Tony Blair. These included Bigley's pleas for compliance with al-Zarqawi's hostage demand, which included the freeing of prisoners.

Bigley was one of a group of three Western hostages to be captured. The others, Americans Jack Hensley and Eugene Armstrong, were killed first. Related videos were placed online. An online campaign seeking the hostages' release, linked to statements from senior British Muslims as well as world figures such as Yasser Arafat and Muammar Gaddafi, was unsuccessful. Bigley's brother Paul had his house raided and computer data seized by the Dutch police because of alleged contacts with al-Zarqawi.[20] There were accusations that the media had overplayed the kidnapping, and that this might have fueled al-Zarqawi's activities, while British authorities were accused of doing too little to save Ken Bigley. This series of events was described as an "obscene poker game": " 'Al-Zarqawi obviously has a way of monitoring very well the international media and the Internet,' said Andrew Kain, a former SAS soldier who is now a security consultant in Baghdad. "He is picking up the reaction of the families in the country, and exploits it. This is media terrorism.' "[21]

A similar sequence of events occurred in the kidnapping and apparent execution of British-born Iraqi citizen and aid worker Margaret Hassan in 2004. Video of Hassan derived from the Internet was played in part in sections of the world media, generating a vociferous response, particularly in the UK. The protracted kidnapping of two French journalists was also played out online.[22] The murder of Egypt's senior diplomat in Iraq, Ihab al-Sherif, in July 2005 was also announced through the Internet, via an emphatic official spokesperson.[23] Al-Sherif had been "punished" for "religious crimes" and for representing a "tyrannical government."[24]

Tawhid wal Jihad's subsequent rebranding as Tanzim Qa'idat Al-Jihad in Bilad al-Rafidayn (Al-Qaeda Group of Jihad in the Land of the Two Rivers [Iraq])" in October 2004 was coupled with an increase in statements appearing online, such as those relating to the beheading of a Japanese "tourist" Shosei Koda.[25] Ansar al-Sunnah claimed responsibility for the murder of senior Baghdad officials,[26] as well as the executions of foreign workers, drivers, and members of the Iraqi security forces.[27] Sociological and psychological experts theorized on the impact that such videos might have on different viewers: "A terrorist may become a killer as a result of seeing violence happen before his very eyes or seeing it on TV, say researchers. It is a myth that terrorists are isolated, vulnerable young men with paranoid or borderline personality disorders."[28]

The nearly instantaneous circulation of explicitly violent images from jihadi sources clearly had an impact when those same images started to appear on news bulletins worldwide. Specific campaigns and "victories" were marked through the release of online videos guaranteed to attract the attention of the regional and global media, as well as a loyal audience of jihadi supporters online. The release in June 2004 of "Fallujah Volcano" was a prominent example that incorporated *nashid*s, film of attacks on U.S. military vehicles, and videos of jihadi "martyrs." It also showed the killing of U.S. contractors, whose bodies were hung up on a bridge.[29] The globalized circulation of these and related content, playing to the media, opened up conjecture as to its impact. Clearly, there are short-, medium- and long-term implications at many levels for the production and consumption of such images.[30]

It could be said that a conscious act is required to actively seek out the most violent materials online. This in itself is not always an easy process if the individual Web user does not know the usual entry points and chat rooms in which such information can appear. However, they were also distributed through other channels, being ripped and copied onto CDs and DVDs for distribution, including in *souq*s in Iraq and elsewhere.[31] Iraqi security forces attempted, at various times, to crack down on these sales, but they had limited success, as vendors relied upon them for a regular stream of income.[32] Clearly, there were no copyright concerns, and these videos would appear alongside other products.[33] These films could also filter through to other media, such as Web-enabled phones.

Examples of the types of material regularly surfaced online, proving what conventional media might ignore. These included a video of a suicide attack that allegedly killed three British soldiers, which was placed on Muhammad al-Massari's Tajdeed pages.[34] Militant groups were keen to put photos of their victims online.[35] An eyewitness report by journalist Hala Jaber recorded how fighters analyzed these videos and their supporters in Fallujah, in some cases in the same way that soccer fans might discuss the goals in a televised match.[36]

As part of this production of online materials, specific Iraq-focused magazines and communiqués appeared.[37] Jaish Ansar al-Sunnah (Army of the Supporters of the Sunnah) were proactive on the Internet, initially producing materials associated with campaigns in northern and central Iraq. They had organizational and membership affiliations with Ansar al-Islam. This was the result of a combination in 2001 of the forces of Jund al-Islam (Soldiers of Islam), led by Abu Abdallah al-Shafi'i, and Mullah Krekar's Islamic Movement in Kurdistan.[38]

In 2003 the U.S. government accused members of Ansar al-Islam of protecting al-Zarqawi; they were also accused by Secretary of State Colin Powell of having links with Saddam Hussein.[39] At times, these organizations appear synonymous, especially on the Internet, although members did not always share ideological aspirations. They frequently cross-posted and linked materials to one another on the Net, sharing platforms and content online. The dominant voice was Ansar al-Sunnah, linked to alleged speeches made online by Mullah Krekar.

Based in Norway, Krekar was a political-religious Kurdish ideologue who had led the Ansar al-Islam group prior to (and during) exile. Norwegian police reported that "Krekar had also been active on Internet discussion groups, and had broadcast speeches over the Internet to more than 100 Ansar al-Islam followers at a time."[40] Krekar was remanded into custody in Norway for alleged links with suicide bombers, with investigators focusing on his Internet broadcasts. In 2007 he was facing being expelled from Norway.[41] Ansar al-Sunnah presented itself in a series of statements, websites, multimedia, and logistical information, applying the language of Islamic discourse in justification of its activities. One prominent example was the rapid posting of video materials associated with an attack on a U.S. camp in al-Ramadi.[42]

The online media became a critical adjunct to real-world activities, with principal platforms cross-posting, sharing links, and cultivating their media image closely. The extent to which affiliates were "ego-surfing" is open to question, but al-Zarqawi's organization clearly observed other media closely, criticizing Al-Jazeera for reporting "false information."[43] They also applied the Net in order to facilitate kidnappings and verify identities. Australian journalist John Martinkus had his name entered into Google by his kidnappers to confirm his identity prior to his release.[44] The kidnapping of another journalist, Scott Taylor, also concluded when his identity was confirmed via the Net.[45] In some cases, the supporters and families of the kidnapped launched websites as an attempt to free their loved ones, thus initiating a sequence of online activities, pleas, and negotiations.[46]

The online output of jihad-oriented and related platforms in Iraq gained the attention of the world's media. Some expressed concerns about the existence of the websites, with one focus in 2005 being the use of the 357hosting company in the Netherlands as a platform for jihadi sites.[47] The role of ICT in al-Zarqawi's rise was highlighted when, in April 2005, there were suggestions that his computer had been seized, although the depth of content derived from its hard drive was not fully disclosed.[48] It did not seem to have any specific impact on his online activities or pronouncements, which appeared to have gone through intermediaries.

In the same month, al-Zarqawi launched a Kurdish website entitled Pegy Jehad, or "live jihad," associated with the Ansar al-Sunna platform.[49] He regularly posted statements and audio broadcasts, encouraging action and justifying campaigns in the name of Islam.[50] These online reinforcement activities would have an acute psychological effect on their readership by suggesting that, even after attack and near capture, al-Zarqawi was alive and active.

A sequence of execution videos was released from al-Zarqawi and affiliates, showing interrogations, statements from victims (Iraqi and a variety of other nationalities), and their deaths by gunshot or the blade. Victims included soldiers, diplomatic staff, charity workers, contractors, and civilians; there were Muslims from various religious backgrounds, as well as those from other religions.[51] Some of the victims were killed indoors in "studio" settings, with the backdrop of banners associated with al-Zarqawi. Others were filmed outdoors and even in apparent "public spaces"—such as on a street, complete with passersby.[52] These films, combined with film of suicide attacks, streamed onto the Internet via assorted discussion boards and upload sites.

Elsewhere on the same sites were photos and statements from the "martyrs" who had undertaken operations, part of the phenomena of *shahid* websites: "Through Islamist Web sites and a propaganda industry, young men like Fahd [a Saudi jihadi killed in Iraq in 2004] achieve a rock star's mythic status. Their photos are posted on the Web; their exploits are embellished; relatives and strangers write poems about their heroics. This creates a cycle of martyrdom in which other restless young men read their stories and find inspiration and purpose. They, too, decide to volunteer to die in Iraq."[53]

Statements and diaries of jihad formed a recruitment opportunity for al-Zarqawi, although there were suggestions that financial logistical support had greater importance than untrained fighters. The Web was also used as a way of attempting to dissuade participation in the "democratic" processes associated with various elections in Iraq.[54] Al-Zarqawi's output, at times, was channeled toward specific audiences. Thus, in July 2005 he issued (in audio form) a broadcast calling on women to participate in the jihad: "The one-hour-long speech, posted on Islamist Internet forums, is entitled 'Religion declines and I am still alive.' 'What have you done for this nation?' asks al-Zarqawi referring to Muslim women, 'don't you see that men get astride their horses and take up arms for the Jihad. Why do you not incite your husbands to fight in the Jihad against the infidels?' "[55]

These materials, however, have to be reviewed within their regional and global contexts, as well as within Iraq. The key players within networks such as al-Qaeda and Ansar al-Sunnah, to name but two associated entities, held an astute awareness of the global elements and opportunities offered through presenting their activities online. This might reflect their own members' experiences within different countries and personal exposure and use of computer technology. It is not to necessarily suggest that leaders were sitting down at their laptops and composing content themselves, although postings were made in their names. The growth in information literacy and access presents a generation (not just based in Iraq) completely au fait with the Internet and the opportunities it presents for dissemination and logistics.

Information literacy is reflected in sustained efforts to place logistical content online and to allow immediate access to videos, statements, and interactive content. The extent to which online interactivity through websites, chat rooms, and e-mail mutates into real-world activities, or coincides with them, is a significant question. One also has to explore again one of the principal questions of this subject area: can such activities be deemed "Islamic"? Perhaps the question can be reversed: should the online activities not be anything but Islamic in orientation, at least to their online protagonists? Some might say that they present a fusion of specific Iraqi and Islamic elements. Others would consider that they are primarily Arabic peninsula–oriented elements naturally applying Islamic-Arabic religious language as a medium alongside "pgp" and "xml." The individual religious convictions of the protagonists cannot be doubted, although many have challenged the authenticity and veracity of their interpretations. It could be deemed a narrow casting of dogma, albeit in a broadband spectrum.

When al-Zarqawi was killed after a missile strike on 7 June 2006, he was eulogized on numerous jihadi websites. In a sense, his presence continued online through a propaganda video that had been released a few weeks earlier. This had in fact contributed to him being located by Iraqi and U.S. forces. The video showing him firing a gun continued to have a posthumous circulation. Photos of his "martyred" body featured on numerous sites, together with calls for revenge and claims of his "martyred" status. The infrastructure surrounding al-Zarqawi's apparent successor, Abu Ayyub al-Masri, also known as Abu Hamza al-Muhajir, immediately ensured that his activities (including executions) and statements were widely circulated online. A laptop and portable hard drive retrieved from the wreckage where al-Zarqawi's body was discovered provided further evidence of the significance of information technology to his campaign, as well as further information for security services.

Other Voices in Iraq

It should be noted that a variety of other Iraqi voices emerged—not just online but drawing on the Web to various degrees to facilitate their agendas. These may have been no less strident, but they usually advocated other perspectives and approaches, if not methodologies, in order to tackle the issues in Iraq from a religious perspective. As with other sectors of Islamic cyberspace oriented toward asserting its presence within communities through militaristic activities, it may defy categorization.

One might have to introduce a model of segmentation with different strands responding to specific agendas and interests, such as al-Sadr militaristic, al-Sadr political, and al-Sadr Qur'anic interpretations. This still would not allow for those intersections that occur, especially when one starts to examine Web space associated with Muqtada al-Sadr (1974?–) and his Mahdi Army, otherwise categorized as the Sadriyun Movement.

The websites of the Mahdi Army include the official muqtada.com, prominent in its presentation of Muqtada's photo alongside that of his assassinated father Mohammad Sadeq al-Sadr (1943–1999) and his executed uncle Grand Ayatollah Sayyid Muhammad Baqir al-Sadr (1933–1980). The muqtada.com site contains biographical information about these figures and other "martyrs," including al-Sadr's assassinated brothers. This site offered very brief statements on news items but was regularly updated. Links to an Islamic Center presented audio Qur'anic recitation by al-Minshawi and *du'a* on a variety of subjects in audio format. A critical consideration is whether this site is considered (Shi'a) jihadi or scholarly, given the combination of influences.[56]

Al-Sadr also had a close affiliation with Grand Ayatollah Kazim al-Husseini al-Haeri, himself linked to Ayatollah Khamenei, who was based in Qom. Al-Haeri disassociated himself from al-Sadr in 2003, using his website to issue a statement clarifying this.[57] Al-Haeri is represented online with an official website, which contained fatwas opposing the U.S. occupation of Iraq apparently issued in 2004 but subsequently "denied" by his office. Followers and pilgrims had received a message when they visited Qom, condemning the United States–led forces.[58] A similar fatwa appeared in 2003, transmitted through al-Haeri's offices in Baghdad, Najaf, and elsewhere and appearing in Shi'a areas of the Web, including the Ahl ul Bayt Discussion Forum.[59]

Within Iraq, there are complex networks and allegiances, a significant proportion of which are not represented in cyberspace. These localized networks may occur in civil space, although in extraordinary times of conflict this entire notion is challenged by internal and external dynamics. If the central square of a community is represented by a hub website such as muqtada.com focused on political-religious allegiances, then the discussion boards and e-mail lists represent the cafés and restaurants where, certainly in more peaceful times, real life issues would be discussed over a nargilla and a coffee.

Into this civic space, one should highlight the factor that conventional routes of communication were damaged or had never existed. Internet access was restricted and broadband access was rare (except in the Green Zone). Within the urban poverty of al-Sadr's stronghold, further restrictions on access existed. Net access may not be a priority for some in zones of conflict, where human survival and security are paramount, and more traditional routes of information are relied upon.

Within this al-Sadr model, the mosque represented a central hub of communications, with the Internet a basic node; within an al-Zarqawi model, with a greater international emphasis in terms of logistics and participation, this model might be reversed. However, in the al-Sadr equation, one might add that there are logistical and communications elements that remain hidden from view. Much as past Shi'a movements have relied on dissimilitude and placed their imams "in occultation," information about the al-Sadr movement is similarly obscure in the real world and in cyberspace. Links with Lebanon and Iran, together with other external nodes, would incorporate cyber activity; however, there was certainly speculation regarding the networking between Iran and al-Sadr, especially given Iran's relationship with al-Sadr's rival, Ayatollah al-Sistani.

Al-Haeri's photo is on the front page of his site; he is dressed in the robes of an ayatollah. There were copies of his scholarly output, including works on jurisprudence and religious knowledge, and detailed fatwa archives. Through the front page, a *bay'at* was presented, through which a surfer might offer affiliation to al-Haeri. His organization's e-mail is available for enquiries, alongside telephone numbers to his office in Qom. Again, one might question the categorization of al-Haeri's website.

There would be a need also to distinguish between sites associated with Muqtada al-Sadr and those affiliated to other members of his family, including Muhammad Baqir al-Sadr. There are a number of sites commemorating his "martyrdom," in particular a miniportal of information entitled "Imam."[60] This provided biographical information, publications, speeches, and articles describing encounters with Baqir al-Sadr. The main page displayed prominent links to other sectors of Shi'a cyberspace, including the Aahlul-Bayt IT Center (which hosts collections of al-Sadr's writings), the Islamic Ahlulbayt Foundation of New Zealand, the Kufa Center of Islamic Knowledge (in Virginia), and the Sunni-oriented Islamic Voice portal.[61] There was little reference to Muqtada al-Sadr on these pages.

The activities of al-Fudala, a political party associated with the al-Sadr clan, can be brought into this equation.[62] The political dimensions associated with the al-Sadr family can be linked to the Islamic Da'wah Party, heavily influenced by Muhammad Baqr al-Sadr, whose photo appears on their central site. This offered news stories from international sources, as well as links to other sites and a presentation of the party's basic principles.[63] The Da'wah Party joined the United Iraq Alliance, and Ibrahim al-Ashaiqir al-Jaafari became prime minister of the Transitional Government in 2005. An official website reported on al-Jaafari's activities, speeches, and engagements, although it held little in the way of "religious" information.[64]

Al-Jaafari's successor, Nouri al-Maliki of the Shi'a United Iraqi Alliance, was represented on the Iraq government's site, detailing his speeches and activities in both Arabic and English.[65]

Between these speculative areas, one might also add the other religious authorities associated with the region, in particular the al-Khoei family. The murder of Ayatollah Abd al-Majid al-Khoei in 2003 at a mosque in Najaf, allegedly by supporters of al-Sadr, emphasized to external observers the divisions within Shi'ism in Iraq. Abd al-Majid was a grandson of Ayatollah Seyyid Abulqasim al-Khoei (1899–1992), a senior Azerbaijan-born religious authority based in Najaf who was persecuted by Saddam Hussein.

The extent to which the affiliates of the al-Khoei family should be regarded specifically as an "Iraqi" platform rather than an international platform is open to question, especially given their dynamic presence in cyberspace and relationships with dispersed Shi'a communities worldwide. For example, the Imam al-Khoei Islamic Center in New York presents itself as an "international, religious, charitable institution."[66] The al-Khoei Foundation also emphasizes its global reach, showing pictures of its centers in diverse locations worldwide. Al-Khoei organizations are global in nature, reflected online with nuanced websites focused on specific affiliations, of which Iraq is a central audience. This is evidenced in the output of al-Khoei websites with online magazines, scholarly debates, and opportunities to present questions to authorities.[67] The scholarly opinions emerging from al-Khoei sources could not be said to have influenced any specific types of insurgency in Iraq.

Another family with significant links to Iraq is the al-Shirazi clan. Several websites focused on the reputations of Ayatollah Al-udhma Haj Sayyed Abdullah al-Shirazi (1892–1984), Ayatollah Muhammad ibn Mehdi al-Hussaini al-Shirazi (1928–2001), and the latter's son Imam Sadiq Al-Shirazi, whose supporters maintain an English-language website. This contains fatwas of Muhammad al-Hussaini al-Shiraz on a database, with the promise that questions that cannot be answered are passed through to Sadiq al-Shiraqi.[68]

United Shia Alliance presented an image on Shi'a chat rooms, placing the photo of Muhammad al-Shirazi adjacent to the Hizbullah logo, a photo of Ayatollah Khomeini, and the Iraq flag with the banner, "One Shia Umma Striving for the Return." This can be read on several levels, but it suggests unity behind a Mahdi. The United Shia Alliance also quotes Ayatollah Muhammad Al-Shirazi, stating: "You are the majority in Iraq. Never be ruled by anyone other than yourselves again!"[69] This banner was pointing toward three sites: alshiarazi.com, alkarbalaeia.net, and alshiraz.no. Alshiarazi.com focused on Qur'anic commentary and related Real Audio broadcasts, including recitations relating to Ramadan.

The alkarbalaeia.net site interpreted the basic tenet of Shi'ism (according to this orientation), featuring biographical information about key religious figures and Qur'anic commentaries; it also contained a series of photos of religious sites.[70] In contrast, alshirazi.no was particularly oriented toward campaigns in Iraq, with prominent banners showing U.S. military forces and regularly updated news and commentary. It also used the domain almojaded.com and presented several links to Western broadcasters, including CNN and BBC, as well as the United States–sponsored Sawa broadcasts. There is a dynamic contrast of materials and perspectives surrounding the al-Shirazi family and their supporters, indicating how different elements drawn from their output can be interpreted "in their name" online.

Into this equation should be added the significant political-religious discourses that have formed part of the Iraqi landscape, especially since the conquest of Baghdad. In 2006 their status was still in a state of flux, with negotiations and recriminations occurring, in some cases, alongside a jostling for position and, in other cases, an avoidance of the political process. Some key players have presented themselves in a significant way. Emerging from the foundations of the Iraq Muslim Brotherhood, the Sunni Iraqi Islamic Party (IIP) appeared, initially under the leadership of Iyad al-Samarra'i. This was before control was handed to Muhsin Abd-al-Hamid, who was arrested by U.S. forces in June 2005 allegedly for refusing to participate in elections, although he later endorsed the Iraq constitution.

The IIP presented a detailed website, containing news, statements, polls, and discussion, with opportunities for affiliation through e-mail lists and membership. The extent to which this site could be readily identified as Islamic, in terms of symbols, was muted; the emphasis was on the Iraq flag and the IIP logo. There were no pictures of the Qur'an or other overt Islamic symbols. The photos on the banner, showing women and children in "Islamic dress," and a photo of the Iraq flag with the background of a mosque, offer a subtle reinforcement of identity. The Islamic identity of the party does not mean that one should stereotype how it might/should be represented on the Web.[71]

Other parties are marginal in terms of membership and/or do not recognize themselves as specifically "political" in orientation. The Muslim

Ulama Council (Hayat Al-Ulama Al-Muslimin), led by Harith al-Dari, op-posed the U.S. invasion but claimed not to support insurgency in any form. The council also includes several key Sunni religious figures in Iraq. A central element espoused by al-Dari was for a shari'ah-centered constitu-tion, which would accommodate all elements of Muslim beliefs as repre-sented in Iraq. However, its online activities were limited.

The Kurdish political-religious entities also need to be drawn into this discussion. One has to distinguish between groups that operated specifi-cally in northern Iraq and others in Kurdish regions across Iraq's borders, with whom there were some (not necessarily universal) natural affiliations and affinities. There have been allegations of links between these organiza-tions and al-Qaeda. Some of the jihadi organizations discussed above have had Kurdish members, such as Ansar al-Sunna; Ansar al-Islam had its roots in northern Turkey. Some parties have less of a religious identity. Krekar's Islamic Movement has already been discussed.

To this listing can be added the Kurdistan Islamic Group (Komal), which presented a detailed website containing news, political statements, and religious content that included audio files of recitations from the Qur'an.[72] There have been allegations of Komal's affiliation with Ansar al-Islam and Mullah Krekar. As a former member of Krekar's Islamic Move-ment of Kurdistan, Komal's leader Mullah Ali Bapir was arrested and held by the American forces in Abu Ghraib between 2003 and 2005.[73] Accord-ing to the Komal website, his policy was to "seek such fraternal relations with Islamic parties and organizations, Islamist figures, and groups that follow a Salafi tradition or a Sufi or a scientific tradition. In the Islamic Group, we believe that the group must be open-minded and seek fraternity with all those who call or act for Islam. If we see a mistake, we will try to correct it through dialogue and by creating a fraternal atmosphere."[74]

The extent to which these relationships are played out online raises some interesting questions. Many elements associated with Kurdish iden-tity have found a place on the Web. With Kurds in Turkey, Syria, Iran, Lebanon, and Armenia, as well as in substantial "exiled" communities in Europe and elsewhere, there is no single political entity of "Kurdistan." However, online there could be a sense of cohesive identity. Specific re-ligious factions have also held a place online, in particular Shi'a Kurds; the Faili Kurds Homepage had apparently been online since 1997, although it was down in 2005.[75] Sufi Kurds link into a number of international orders, such as the Bektashi and Naqshbandi, and may feed into their online activities as well. There is evidence of other religious affiliations associated with Kurd identities online, including Yezidism, Yarsanism (Ahl-i Haqq), and Alevism, or Kizil Nash.[76]

Iraq: Concluding Comment

Within the context of Iraq, the Internet has played a crucial role for a number of players, ranging from "insurgents" and "politicians" to religious scholars and all points in between. It has acted as an information point for local, regional, and global audiences within a period of insecurity. This is especially relevant for Net-literate individuals and groups who have developed realistic awareness of the opportunities the medium has presented.

At this point, while conflicts continue to rage, it has been possible to hypothesize on some initial themes and possibilities relating to cyber-Islamic contexts associated with Iraq. Content may be designed to develop affiliation, and provide logistical justification and support for individuals, groups, and organizations. At a relatively low cost, in terms of media, the status of certain parties and players has radically increased through the Net. This in turn has aided their cause, through providing religious and logistical support in the region and beyond. It may also have had a recruitment effect or provided greater funding; it will certainly have assisted in propagating a specific Islamic message, drawing on religious symbols and language in order to present a specific message. This has included the application of multimedia to present a "religious" message to a global audience that is not exclusively Muslim in identity and orientation. Much of what is presented has been designed for use by news channels and to "inform" and/or intimidate the "enemy."

To these areas might be added the impact of other Web-based media, including blogs. In time, further consideration may be given to the information on closed and secure areas of the Web, requiring membership and personal affiliation. Earlier conflicts may have had an Internet element (for example, the war in Bosnia). However, the campaigns in Iraq occurred at a time of the medium's relative maturity, when key players had an innate sense of the importance of the Web as a natural conduit for delivering information about their cause. Without the Web, the religious message(s) would have had a different path and shape. Some of the scenarios in which religious language was applied would have taken a different form if their self-conscious protagonists did not have to play to a regional or global audience in the same way; as such, it could be said that the Net-presented conflict had a different emphasis to its analogue-delivered equivalent. Significant parties would have had to choose different approaches to presenting their cause to the world and the region. The opportunity to develop rapid religious discourse on Iraq would have been muted.

Digital Palestinian Battlefields

The Internet has represented a significant channel for discourse on Palestinian Muslim issues—both within Palestine and the occupied territories and outside of them—by providing a fluid method of communicating campaigns, raising funds, and offering a cohesive sense of online Islamic identity for those with Internet access and literacy. This Islamic discourse can go beyond militaristically oriented materials into areas associated with human rights, reportage, medicine, and interreligious dialogue, reflecting the diverse agendas of site authors and owners.

The material is designed for diffuse audiences; Palestinians involved in political and militaristic activities (the two are not synonymous) may be a core audience, but there is an implicit sense that other audiences are engaged in this material. This can range from other Muslims in the Middle East and beyond, who use these sites as information tools, whether or not they support the strategies articulated online. Some may seek to engender an affiliation and support, whether it is financial, ideological, or even participatory. Other governments in Muslim contexts may utilize the sites to determine the activities of Palestinian residents, whether or not they support their modus operandi.

Then there are the varied other audiences outside of the Muslim milieu seeking to engage in Palestinian issues. At one end of the spectrum would be the Israeli government and its agencies, whose level of engagement would incorporate observation of the sites for intelligence-gathering purposes. Governments seeking an influence in regional politics and assessment of the balances of power would also observe these sites. At the other end of the spectrum would be those individuals and organizations engaging with Palestinian Muslims living in Gaza and the Occupied Territories, whether or not they support the various political, militaristic, and activist Islamic agendas (such as humanitarian organizations and charities).

I have observed that some sites have sought to engage with Israeli and Jewish people online, using sites as a lever to place political pressure on Israeli governments but also perhaps to intensify the demands of living under the threat of attack. While some sites have engaged in the militaristic

Hamas, Palestine-info.info, December 2006

message, others have attempted to present a depiction of the pressures of life in Palestine for ordinary people. The Internet has been a potent and cost-effective tool for presenting Islamic Palestinian perspectives, which are increasingly nuanced toward a variety of reader profiles. The focus of this section is on output of organizations presenting a militaristic message, including articulations of jihad.

The significant issue in relation to Palestinian Islamic cyberspace has been the application of "martyrdom sites" and the ways in which Hamas (Harakat al-Muqawamah al-Islamiyya) integrated the Internet into their strategies for their successful election campaign in 2006. The early "success," particularly of Hamas, in utilizing the Internet as a means of presenting its message has been a template for other organizations and platforms to follow, particularly al-Qaeda.[77] Several Palestinian Islamic cyber movements had websites beginning in the mid-1990s, with other content circulating electronically from the very early days of the Internet.

Palestine-oriented Islamic sites have been produced in a variety of languages, including Arabic, English, French, Russian, Farsi, Malay, and Urdu. The content has emerged on ISPs in diverse locations in the United States and Europe, as well as in the Middle East and Asia. The changing and flexible nature of these sites indicates experience at circumnavigating security restrictions placed on their content.

Discussing these sites raises particular challenges within any analysis due to their shifting nature, although a pattern of ownership and content management does emerge with particular key themes. They transverse international networks, with content emerging in one organizational office (say, in London or Beirut) being placed onto an ISP in Southeast Asia and then publicized on chat rooms hosted by ISPs in the United States. In some ways, this could reflect the dispersed natures of the Palestinian people.

Analysis of such sites in terms of content, location, and updates is a labor-intensive activity, pursued to varying degrees by assorted security operations. In particular, agencies and organizations located in Israel or supportive of Israeli causes have been proactive in observing and recording Palestinian Islamic Internet activity. This introduces issues associated with academic credibility and "impartiality," although this is also a relevant issue when discussing other online contexts as well.[78]

Determining site ownership introduces complex patterns of control and networking. In relation to Hamas, which has its roots in affiliation with the Egyptian Muslim Brotherhood, it is suggested by Israeli analysts that "the entire infrastructure is operated by Nizar al-Hussein from the office of Osama Hamdan, the head of the Hamas branch in Lebanon, himself, in our assessment, guided by Hamas' headquarters in Damascus."[79]

The Palestine-Information Center has been the key focus point for Hamas-associated online activity, with sites in several languages operating from a variety of URLS.[80] In 2006 the English-language site was dominated by a banner showing the Palestinian flag, intersected by the image of a youth throwing stones at an Israeli tank. The front page provides a clean and clear design, suggesting the authority of a newspaper in its format and tone, emphasizing the regularly updated *Daily News*.

The left-hand sidebar provides links to commentary on Human Rights, al-Aqsa Mosque, the Palestinian Question, and Zionist Terrorism. The site showed a number of other banners; one promoting a boycott of Israel crosses out the Magen David on Israel's flag; another remembers the Deir Yassin massacre. The right side of the page included the photo of Ahmed Yassin, linking through to resources associated with the assassinated Hamas leader.[81] The logos of Hamas and photos of local leaders are prominently displayed adjacent to various news stories. A facility to incorporate Palestine-Information headlines into other sites is provided. The site is fully searchable.

Aspects of the English-language Palestine-Information site can be located in its Arabic equivalent with a similar banner and color scheme, although the editorial tone and approach is less "measured" than the English equivalent. This can be found in the types of images that appear on the page, which are far more graphic in general terms. In March 2006 children were represented in cartoon form in the Fateh magazine; some were wearing masks, and one girl was wearing a sling. Fateh magazine included a cartoon-style feature describing the Palestinian situation, religious advice, a mothers' section, jokes, and descriptions of the "heroism" of various figures.

On the same site, the Palestine-Information link to "Terror" led to a page showing photos of child victims of bombings and shootings by the Israeli Defense Forces, including a listing of "collateral damage" victims.[82] Unlike the English pages, a direct link to Hamas content is provided on the Arabic version of Palestine-Information, which features news, question-and-answer sessions, and updated statements from Hamas leaders. This is far richer in content than the English equivalent, with many statements that were not translated.[83] The site used its own reporters to cover events such as a Hamas delegation visit to Moscow. It was interesting at that time to compare the content of Palestine-Information with that of the Palestinian National Authority in Arabic and English versions, which were relatively sparse in terms of online content.[84]

The logo of Kataeb IzzeDien Brigade, Aqsa FM, and a campaign supporting democratic change in Palestine were prominent on the pages. This was significant in its emergence in the shadow of the Hamas electoral victory in 2006, discussed in detail throughout these Arabic pages. Hamas continued to rely on their independent sites for their online output.

The Hamas pages linked during the election to Pal-Election.com, a dedicated Arabic electoral site that encouraged participation and the Hamas ticket under a Change and Reform banner. It featured photos of key leaders past and present and a banner showing a young girl dressed in military fatigues giving a victory salute.[85] The page linked directly to discussions on the election within the Palestinian Forum. For those Palestinians able and willing to vote, this site drew them into a variety of materials, including political-religious dialogue and content association. Prominent were posters produced by khaleelstyle.com in a variety of artistic styles. The banners and posters were suitable for utilization on a website. One emphasized the roles of women within Palestinian campaigns; another was a cartoon representing what its artists might have interpreted as an archetypal "Jewish" person, with a bomb on his head in the style of the Jyllands-Posten cartoon of Muhammad.[86]

A number of "martyrdom" sites, in particular those associated with Hamas, were models of practice for other related causes. They sought to record the deeds and images of each *shahid* who had undertaken a suicide operation on their behalf. Essentially, such pages acted as an extension of the concept of poster production. These represent a long-standing practice of rapidly printed iconographic posters of "martyrs," which are distributed in areas of the Palestinian territories and beyond. The Internet extended their distribution beyond the scope of any traditional censorship. There was always potential for ISPs to close pages, or for sites to be hacked.

Some sites show deceased operatives, not just from contemporary campaigns—which are frequently and rapidly posted online—but also from the ranks of "heroes" of earlier operations. For example, the Hamas military wing's Ezzedeen AlQassam Brigades' pages featured those who died in the early 1990s in suicide operations before the Internet was mainstream.[87] Such pages highlight fallen leaders, notably Sheikh Ahmed Yassin, killed by an Israeli bomb in 2004. Each is presented as a *shahid*, with photos superimposed with religious iconography and language.

In a significant evolutionary development pioneered by Hamas, al-Aqsa (Martyrs) Brigade, Palestinian Islamic Jihad, al-Qaeda affiliates, and other groups, martyrdom videos were produced for Internet consumption by operatives associated with various Palestinian Islamic platforms. These short films had a specific format, composed of statements by a (potential) *shahid* "justifying" an operation, background information confirming the identity of a *shahid*, and a statement presenting a "will" according to Islamic principles. These clips might be edited in conjunction with other video clips, including operational film. These were uploaded simultaneously to or very closely after an operation.

The technical quality of the films showed a marked technical improvement in terms of audiovisual quality, with purpose-built backdrops being used. Some were filmed outdoors, with operatives carrying weapons. Specific poses were applied; for example, some were photographed and filmed reading the Qur'an while cradling a rifle. Others had photos that were superimposed with images of al-Aqsa mosque. Some chose to pose, or were advised to pose, in military clothing. Not all the backdrops were "religious." Some were photographed in front of the standard screens seen in portrait photographers' galleries, with images of waterfalls, sunsets, or other natural phenomena. These may, of course, hold their own forms of religious symbolism associated with concepts of paradise and the rewards of martyrdom.

While such clips were primarily produced in Arabic, British subjects Asif Muhammad Hanif and Omar Khan Sharif recorded an English-language video. They were responsible for the suicide bombing of a bar in Tel Aviv in 2003. Their video denounced Britain's role in regional politics; it was a precedent in terms of format for other English-language, suicide-bomber videos, including those by the 7/7 bombers.

These statements were collected together on various multimedia galleries. Although there were pages of Palestinian female bombers and other "heroes" who predated the intifadas (not all of whom were operating for religious reasons), a further significant development was the appearance of female suicide bombers in the galleries in 2005.

The extent to which appearance on such pages represents a motivating factor for participants in operations is open to question. The cause is certainly vigorously promoted online, within a standardized format. It certainly implies a sealing of a martyrdom contract prior to an operation. There is limited data on how many individuals were filmed but did not carry out their operation. The emphasis in videos was in part on the rewards participants might attain after their "successful" suicide or martyrdom, which is often couched in terms associated with a "marriage" in the afterlife. This would indicate self-justification as well as incentive for others to follow.

The videos also incorporate rhetoric aimed at Israel, Jews, and Zionists (among others). The Israeli organization Palestine Media Watch translated, archived, and commented on a number of these videos as a retort to the Palestinian Authority, Hamas, and other platforms. It paid particular attention to the anti-Jewish rhetoric.[88] One clip showed two participants filmed in front of a green Islamic flag, with a rocket launcher and a gun in the foreground. Another participant was videotaped being prepared by his mother, almost in the style of a home movie, and there was actuality from a tunnel used in the operation. This operation took place in 2004, although, according to Palestine Media Watch, the video was not placed online until after the Hamas election.[89]

In some ways, one might consider that Hamas is playing directly to the Palestine Media Watch's audience, given that the speeches are transcribed into English and Hebrew and that the videos are readily available on an Israeli server. Palestine Media Watch produced a video commenting on the phenomena of suicide bombings.[90] It paid attention to what it perceived as the "romanticized" version of martyrdom portrayed in the 2005 film *Paradise Now* and the reality that it suggested was represented in its own pages. This factored in what it perceived by some as the complicity between the Palestinian Authority and Hamas in a "terror" campaign.

Particularly significant is the way in which Internet media has been integrated in a broader strategy of dissemination of ideology (and "theology") associated with martyrdom. This strategy has a nuanced approach toward diverse audiences, including younger readers. "Martyrs" also appear on children's pages, including the Fateh magazine.[91] Martyred leaders continued to expound their views via the Internet. Hamas leader Abdul 'Aziz al-Rantissi, who was assassinated in 2004 shortly after the death of Sheikh Yassin, continued to feature heavily on Hamas-related sites after his death.

Islamic Bloc(k) provided news accounts of operational activities, together with religiously motivated texts and propaganda to promote their causes. These included downloadable posters listing imprisoned operatives and photos showing publicity drives, demonstrations, and related activities within Palestinian universities.[92] The associated alkotla.com, a target for sustained "anti-jihadi" activity, contained links to al-Qaeda pages and Islam-Online on its index page.[93]

PalestineGallery.com acted as a further central clearinghouse for Hamas operational audio and video materials associated with militaristic campaigning in the region, including martyrdom operations. These were filtered with religious language, terminology, and symbolism (for example, a bomber photographed against the backdrop of a black Islamic flag). Posters included those exhorting military action with the image of a masked gunman superimposed against the background of a photo of al-Aqsa Mosque.

Alongside traditional calligraphic art, computer-generated calligraphy digitized the name of Muhammad on the site. In another page, a gunman in silhouette form faced a sunrise, which formed the backdrop to a flag with the word "Muhammad" on it. There were many examples of religious language encapsulated in the digital Islamic calligraphy. Images also related to specific events and campaigns, such as the protest against *Jyllands-Posten*'s publication of "blasphemous" cartoons.

There were echoes of flickr and other online photo services on PalestineGallery.com. Its images could be placed into a personal album for individual users, with a choice of over 1,000 image files. File formats are clearly specified. The number of hits each image received was also logged. The majority was only in double figures, although clips of Israeli forces in confrontation with Palestinians logged thousands of downloads. There were nearly 1,500 photos from demonstrations and political actions. These included prominent photos of participation in the buildup to the 2006 elections, including pictures of people placing their votes. The dates that they were uploaded suggested that a regular stream of new artwork appeared on the site. Readers could rate their favorite images and multimedia and view lists of content that had accumulated the highest scores. The photos usually indicate their sources, including photos uploaded by demonstration participants. A good example of this is a photo taken by "abbas—03—ramallah" at a demonstration, where a model of the Dome of the Rock mosque is carried through the streets by flag-waving Hamas supporters.[94] PalestineGallery was registered in Vancouver, Washington.[95]

Palestinian Forum acted as a further clearinghouse for Hamas-focused information and discussion, attracting high levels of traffic for discussions on the latest operations and their outcomes. It introduced content associated with al-Qaeda campaigns, predominantly in Iraq, and linked to significant resources elsewhere, in particular a blog containing hundreds of links to al-Qaeda–associated videos.[96] Photos of al-Zarqawi, al-Neda's symbols (including the black flag and a horse), and the images of "martyrs" dominated the pages. The use in the forum of praying, crying, and "raging" icons was also significant.[97] Palestinian Forum was registered in Beirut.[98]

Palestinian Islamic Jihad (PIJ) did not possess the same political profile as Hamas but retained its significance as a player within Palestinian politics and activism, launching numerous suicide operations in Israel.[99] In technical terms, their Qudsway site was dynamic, being fully loaded (or cluttered) with flash objects, images, and links to associated materials. Individuals short of bandwidth might have difficulty uploading this site.

The PIJ site's main banner included a photo of cofounder Fathi Shaqaqi (1951–1995) juxtaposed with al-Aqsa mosque. Its index page featured the burning flag of Israel, a flash object of children and crying women holding the Qur'an, followed by a photo of Mecca. A flash graphic showed al-Quds, PIJ fighters, and a burning Israeli flag; the pages included operational activity, prisoner information, and photos of male and female "martyrs." The PIJ site was regularly updated with news and other statements from leaders and in 2006 was dominated with campaigning against the *Jyllands-Posten* cartoons, at the expense of local campaigns.[100] Registration of Qudsway had been anonymized.[101]

At times, there could be an online information vacuum, as clearly some areas of PIJ were better resourced than others. PIJ's other cofounder, Ramadan Abdullah Shallah (1958–), has his own website, which was less

Islamic Jihad poster,
qudsway.com

cluttered than Qudsway; in fact, it was simply a domain name with a splash
page, as none of the links to statements, news, and other material led to any
content.[102] A page devoted to Shiqaqi was similarly devoid of content,
simply leading to Shallah's own vacant pages.[103]

Hamas-linked Sabiroon.org, associated with the al-Qassam Brigade,
contained details of deceased operatives and accounts of their deaths, many
that were seen as "collateral damage."[104] Sabiroon, which was registered in
Damascus, sought to provide a database of martyr details (searchable and
divided into categories), although clearly that data had not been fully organized.[105] The Arabic section of the site in relation to martyrs was more
detailed in terms of content, although there was limited parity in places with
the English pages. The Arabic pages detailed operations but also the "innocent" victims of Israeli campaigns. Other areas of the site, including news
and prisoner information, were sparse in English but regularly updated in
places in Arabic. Compared with some sites, areas of both language pages
were poorly maintained and out of date, indicating a lack of personnel and
resources. Given the market saturation, it may be felt that reproducing
similar types of material was inappropriate and that pages should be more
nuanced for particular markets. There are also issues of censorship and
attempts to close sites down, such as through ISPs and governmental
intervention as well as pressure from other Palestinian factions.

Al-Aqsa Martyrs are responsible for the Palestinian Voice pages, an
online forum heavily populated with posts and participation. Forum mem-

Qudsway.com, December 2006

bers utilize avatars that incorporate al-Aqsa logos and related images. The discussions go beyond activism issues, with poetry and personal issues included on the listings. They draw upon images, including romanticized greeting cards and animated flowers, when discussing personalities and issues associated with the Palestinian cause.[106] This site is an entry point into information about the organization and its latest statements and operational updates. There is a high level of participation and membership involved, with some posts receiving tens of thousands of hits.

Related to this site, Kataeb Shuhada al-Aqsa, the military affiliates of Fatah, had several sites with information on its activities. This included two primary Arabic sites that presented information on operational activities as well as downloads of "official" statements and information.[107] Kataebaqsa1.com was more content rich (depending on what the site visitor was looking for) in terms of providing posters, downloads, and updated information on martyrs. In 2006 martyrs featured heavily alongside the photo of Yasser Arafat on the front page. Its news section was regularly updated. Both sites offered an opportunity to pledge allegiance to the organization through an online statement, or *bayyanat*, which included a reference to the website.[108] There was substantial interlinking between the two sites. In the second site, katebaqsa.org, a gallery linked to martyrs and key figures in the organization, including prisoners. In March 2006,

Kataebaqsa's IP resolved to a Santa Monica address.[109] Kataebaqsa1 resolved to a Malaysian/Singaporean company.[110]

There were similarities in terms of design parameters between Kataeb Shuhada al-Aqsa and Fateh Falcons; this unit was associated with Kataeb al-Aqsa and presented operational materials on their site, including training-footage film clips and photos of martyrs. One operational film, twenty-five minutes in duration, was accompanied by Qur'anic recitation. This was edited with varied music clips, such as *nashids* exhorting jihad and the liberation of Palestine. A film of a falcon was superimposed over a background of al-Quds. It depicted photos of deceased members of the brigade, edited into a green field representing paradise, before showing film of military training and operations. Yasser Arafat's photo overlooked proceedings. Editing special effects had been applied throughout, and at times there was also a documentary feel to the video; a squad is shown praying, reading a prepared statement, and then firing surface-to-air missiles.[111] The gallery included an incongruous photo of the "martyr Sukrani Abu Hamid" posing on a chair in flip-flops, as if on holiday, while other operatives struck more militaristic poses.[112] The site was registered by proxy with an Arizona company.[113] There were several other examples of martyrs' galleries associated with Palestine; khayma.com held a listing of martyrs from the period 2000–2002.[114]

Gaza-based Donia-AlWatan adopts a slick news magazine approach to its content. There were items about lifestyle and popular culture among statements from political leaders and operational information. In many ways, it resembled the format of the BBC News or CNN site.[115] It also linked to the al-Mubadara pages organized by the Palestinian National Initiative. These had a basis in the ideals of the Palestinian Liberation Organization and associated itself with "democratic" systems under the banner, "For the implementation of Palestinian national rights and the creation of a durable, just peace." As well as generating its own material in Arabic and English, especially during the period of the Palestinian election, al-Mubadara linked prominently into external media organizations' coverage of the region; al-Mubadara did not have an overtly religious identity in their statements and design, focusing instead on its main banner on the Palestinian flag and protests against Israeli soldiers.[116]

The Internet is also a place where the plight of imprisoned activists is highlighted. For example, Hussam Khader—a member of the Palestinian Legislative Council who was sentenced to seven years in prison in 2005— had a site devoted to his cause.[117] In 2004 Marwan Barghouti, a senior

Fatah member and founder of the political party al-Mustaqbal, was convicted of murder and given five life sentences; the following year, he also became a member of the Palestinian Legislative Council. A Ramallah-registered website campaigning for his release was regularly updated in Arabic and English, incorporating full case notes of *State of Israel v. Marwan Barghouti*, photos of the trial, posters, and campaign links.[118] The Arabic version contained poetry about Fatah-founder Abu Nidal.

Palestinian Digital Battlefields: Concluding Comment

The Internet has been interwoven into campaigns and articulation of positions relating to Palestinian issues for a sustained period. These reflect the dispersed nature of the Palestinian peoples, some of whom have seized upon the technology as a viable way to network on a variety of issues. Not all of these perspectives are necessarily Islamic, reflecting the complex history of Palestinian movements. They might be labeled in several ways, not always mutually complementary; "Islamic" may be one label but not necessarily a priority for many people. Whether the label "Palestinian" is also applied might be open to question when discussing Arabs living in the borders of contemporary Israel. The Palestinian Christian populations play a part within and outside of these networks and affiliations.

The shifting nature of people, causes, and locations within a political-religious matrix—one that can connect to related causes and even, in some cases, is directed toward the "enemy"—makes the issue of Palestinian online dialogue a particularly complex one. It forms an important subtext to ongoing developments in the region. There is a profound consciousness of the significance of the medium for all those associated with "religiously oriented" campaigns in Palestine.

They form an alternative to traditional media forms on Palestinian Islamic issues, such as newspapers and broadcasters. Some of these may be owned by Palestinians and/or have offices and reporters in the region. These media are also now available through the Internet, although they are not all necessarily Islamic in orientation. There are also Palestinians contributing to other media forms and channels, such as satellite channels and pan-Arabic media, which may also have Internet outlets. Within this complex equation and networking of ideas and campaigns, information technology has become a critical component to those campaigning for the liberation of Palestine, especially those who have an Islamic vision for the future of the region.

Conclusion

The Transformation of Cyber-Islamic Environments

iMuslims demonstrates what happens when two of the dominant elements shaping life in the twenty-first century, Islam and the Internet, combine. Whether the combination of elements results in an explosion or simply gentle ripples is open to debate. The sequencing of such a broad range of variables cannot be generalized, but some basic patterns have emerged within the evolving Islamic Internet.

The effects are not necessarily one-way, as iMuslim activities have influenced generic forms of Internet activities and acted as a microcosm for the potential of information technology as a transforming medium for networks and societies. The innovative application of hardware and software in the name of Islam has shown iMuslims to be pushing the boundaries and creating precedents for computer-mediated activity. The medium is also generating new expectations for communications and networking in the name of Islam that go beyond those envisaged by (and for) iMuslims even at the beginning of the twenty-first century. For some, these have countered stereotypes associated with Islamic and Muslim use of technology.

One example of this discussed in this book has been the impact of blogging as a tool for commentary and information exchange. Less benignly, the Internet has also pushed back barriers for the development of dynamic logistical conduits for jihadi propagation. This reinforces Castells's search for "process of revolutionary technological change" and Eickelman's suggestion regarding the "formation of new and overlapping forms of community, trust, and association."[1]

These processes have taken place rapidly and continue to evolve. In terms of precedents, I cannot help but think of the rapid expansion and networking of Islam in the seventh century of the Common Era—from its emergence in the Arabian Peninsula, under the aegis of the Prophet Muhammad being instructed by God to "Recite!" in 610, to its expansion across continents as far as Western Europe, China, India, and sub-Saharan Africa (among other locations) 100 years later. That precedent resonated along traditional pre-Islamic networks of commerce and knowledge, combining social, militaristic, and political factors as the depth of the Message intensified through reiteration and interpretation. The contemporary expansion of Islamic discourse through the Internet has been in conjunction with external factors but is no less impressive.

I would not wish to present an idealized picture in this regard. Rewiring the House of Islam has not been without its difficulties, and there is much developmental work to be undertaken, but there is certainly a high level of functionality within iMuslim online discourse. The Internet has reshaped the boundaries of Muslim networks, created new dialogues, and presented new transaction routes within the Islamic knowledge economy. Statements and content, which previously had a short circulation in print format, now have added value through the Long Tail of electronic distribution, archiving, and searchability. Those same values have made the Islamic knowledge economy an increasingly competitive and global one for some players, while also reinforcing regional and local roles for some service providers.

In wrestling with data of an ephemeral and substantial nature, this book has sought to respond to the impact that this ever-extending Internet has placed on the issues of translocality and the forms of discourse that they have engendered.[2] This book has shown that there are numerous interpretations associated with the application and implementation of Muslim discourse online. The Islamic knowledge economy is one that has proven responsive to technical innovation, dedicated as much to its roots as its routers. Different levels of religiosity and religious language permeate CIES. Muslim networks can take many forms and interfaces, at times also attaining a commonality in some areas associated with conceptual frameworks and religious understanding. However, there can be no doubt that conflicts are also a motivating factor in some areas of CIES, whether they are inter- and intra-Muslim or directed at other targets. Despite the fact that many sectors in the Muslim worlds still do not have opportunities for access, the Internet has become a dominant tool of Islamic religious expression and a significant place for observation of shifting trends and values associated with conceptual understandings of Islam.

It is not intended in this book to suggest that previous, pre-Internet generations were necessarily unchanging or consistent in nature, as they too were influenced by shifting political, cultural, militaristic, social, religious, and technological factors. These elements also influence contemporary Muslim lives and networks. However, there is no doubt that those iMuslims who are permanently online or have regular access can now view the Muslim worlds in a different way to previous generations, and their Islamic patterns of life have adjusted accordingly. For example, prayer times and fasting may be governed by an online database. Searching a database for a fatwa, or petitioning an authority by e-mail, may influence practice. Relationships can be forged through cyberspace, whether of a personal or business nature. Allegiances can be reshaped, with the development of new affinities to religious authorities and/or political leaders. With the use of BlackBerrys, cell phones and PDAS, an iMuslim can always access data about Islam—whether that is prayer times, scholarly opinions, the Qur'an, or the location of the nearest mosque via Google Maps. The medium is responsive to change, whether technological or religious in nature, making resources "future proof" and influential in a way that traditional print media is not.

The sense of Islam being "always on" has potential to shape religious nature and personal understandings of those who choose to apply CIT in this way. The identities of iMuslims can have a symbiotic relationship with the Internet, but that does require a measure of control. An individual must make a conscious decision to switch on a device and hook up to a service before locating a site or resource of choice. Not only is there information overload in the Islamic marketplace, which has been shown throughout this book, but there is also information overload throughout the entirety of the Internet.

While I wrote these paragraphs, no doubt the number of Islamic sites and content has increased. Managing and processing this quantity of data is not just an issue for microchip developers but also for users. The "always on" Islamic knowledge economy may deprive the individual of the opportunity for reflection, although of course that can be computer mediated, as well. The multiple formats and applications associated with social-networking sites and Web 2.0 have extended the quantity, if not the quality, of Islam-related materials available in cyberspace and beyond.

Access to information technology has trickled down from the wealthy sections of communities. There are other inhibitors preventing individuals from accessing the Internet. One interesting question is whether a gap will open up, not between the "haves" and "have-nots," but between those who are connected and those who are not through choice. While devout Muslims will suggest that Islam is "always on" and that a computer interface is not required, there is now an option to be always connected via information technology to Islam. That may place particular pressures on some individuals, especially those seeking to compartmentalize religion within their everyday lives.

It is becoming increasingly difficult to find places where information technology does not have a role. For example, home entertainment centers integrate online content with on-demand satellite or cable television programming. Islamic channels have entered the choices of viewers. As with the Net, one has to ask: who is viewing and reacting to this content in such a highly competitive and information-rich environment? Computers in many homes are always on and can themselves present a range of multimedia materials that would have been unheard of in the 1990s. Those iMuslims who feel obligated to be online regularly in order to maintain and reinforce online affiliations, networks, and relationships may do so at the expense of traditional networks. The development of Islamic Internet products, such as IslamicTube, IslamicTorrents, and MuslimSpace, has added a level of safety and permissibility for some.[3]

Some critics have seen the Internet as having a harmful influence on Muslim societies through the presentation of values seen as having negative connotations relating to ethical and moral systems. This, of course, is not just an argument articulated within some Muslim circles. Topics such as the proliferation of social-networking activities and their impact on relationships, or addiction to pornography, have had a resonance among many critics of the Net.[4] Despite these factors, there is now no doubt that the Internet is here to stay, and that a level of adaptation to the media environment is required, especially given the increased access enabled by cell phones.

Internet developments have to be seen in conjunction with shifting frameworks associated with religious authority, including concepts associated with decentralization from the traditional locations of *'ulama'* power. The opportunities to present and disseminate decisions based on *ijtihad*, for example, are far greater than they were in the 1990s. Any person who deems themselves (or is proclaimed) an authority can make a pronouncement and upload it on a website. So-called Islamic reform agendas, which may lack governmental approval, have a ready audience. Those within the margins, including those seeking the implementation of militaristic jihadi religious practices, can broadcast their thoughts to a global audience while being relatively safe from censorship.

When I was researching religious authority and decision-making issues in the mid-1990s, the flow of communication was relatively restricted to cassettes, the fax machine, and print media.[5] E-mail was being used, but very much as a minority preoccupation. I interviewed several *'ulama'* whose offices were using computers, but generally only for the production of material that would then be transmitted through conventional media channels.

Some of these scholars spoke to me in offices that were adjacent to copyeditors, printing houses, and media copy shops, which played a critical role for ensuring that their thoughts and opinions attained some currency. I usually left meetings with a sack full of literature justifying their interpretative and political perspectives. This, of course, lacked the immediacy that we have today with the Internet. Those same offices now have Internet departments, focusing on online content in a way that may have eclipsed print media in some cases, with scholars in able to cut out intermediaries when dialoging online on a specific issue. The immediacy indicates in some contexts distinct paradigm shifts in knowledge dissemination and content creation, potentially with less inherent reflection than with print iterations.

At that time, there was no concept that could be related to what has been described in this book as an "iMuslim." The notion that one might interact with sacred knowledge online, and even attain the essence of a religious experience, was not one that had really entered mainstream Islamic discourse. There were individuals who were sizing up the potential of the medium, but even they probably had no idea of how information technology and Islam would interact. The technology at that time did not offer the multimedia scope now available.

Traditionally, accessing knowledge about religion required a human intermediary, such as a *shaykh*, *'alim*, *pir*, or *imam*. This person could be consulted either face-to-face or through textual sources. There were few alternative options. This does not mean that those channels have closed, but that the potential opportunities for accessing alternative routes and information nodes has expanded exponentially with the Internet.

I well recall sitting in on sessions in Pakistan where couples were petitioning a scholar and asking for a blessing and a scholarly opinion on their family difficulties. This required a face-to-face meeting. Now, a similar transaction and dialogue can be undertaken online. Similarly, I remember meeting people who were taking a religious oath of allegiance to a Muslim political-religious leader in Pakistan, an action that then required a physical meeting. Today, that same interaction can be made online. Traditional practices may not have been replaced, but alternative options for their enactment have been provided online.

The definition of an iMuslim can take many forms. Clearly, it is an individual who is connected to the Internet, but that in itself does not suggest the intensity of any interactivity or the forms of online conduct undertaken. As a consequence of writing this book, I can now offer some models of iMuslims (in no particular order):

- An iMuslim may spend several hours a day connected by high-speed ADSL, engaging with peers in chat rooms or producing pages of online content.
- An iMuslim may undertake shari'ah-compliant financial transactions via a BlackBerry.
- An iMuslim may search the Internet for information relating to an issue of religious interpretation.
- An iMuslim may visit an Islamic blog once a year to check on gossip.
- An iMuslim may be using the Internet as a propagation tool to convert others to Islam or to an Islamic worldview.
- An iMuslim may be using the Internet as a form of media and public relations to effectively put across a message to a local or global audience.
- An iMuslim may be active in a form of Islam with a political ethos and will use the Internet to propagate specific interpretations and discuss them with peers.
- An iMuslim in the field of combat may use a cell phone to upload operational activities, whose logistical base is derived from online jihadi manuals.
- An iMuslim may be translating and distributing material from one language to another, or from one format to another.
- An iMuslim may be uploading video and audio content, either self-produced or from third-party sources.
- An iMuslim may be campaigning on a specific issue, using social-networking tools and uploading video messages via YouTube.
- An iMuslim may be using the Internet to connect to a network or community and observe the activities of members or a religious leader.
- An iMuslim may not go anywhere near a computer but ensure that pronouncements or broadcasts are uploaded online by a dedicated team.

These are not mutually exclusive categories. There can be degrees of intersection. iMuslims may undertake similar activities while following completely different agendas. The definition of iMuslim will become further granulated in response to shifts in technology, more encompassing as interfaces open up to other languages, and more enabled as bandwidth and computer chips become cheaper. The people who are influenced by iMuslims also have to be brought into the equation. Whether individuals within these categories believe that their religiosity and "iMuslimness" is intensified by online activities is an intriguing question. For some profiles, this has clearly been the case, especially for those who see little separation between online and offline worlds.

One way in which the approach of an iMuslim can be further categorized is by drawing on the following diagram. The branches indicate some of the diffuse identity issues while also suggesting a commonality and interconnectivity in some areas. Each individual iMuslim might generate a specific pattern, dependent on context. The arrows represent the multidirectional flow of ideas.

Each chapter of this book could be represented in turn by numerous branches of this diagram. In truth, a diagram perhaps suggests a logic that is lacking in some of the linkages within the Internet, especially the random aspects generated by searching for content. This is especially true when clicking the "Feeling Lucky" button on Google when searching for Islamic material.

This book has sought to demonstrate that iMuslims encompass many interests, not all mutually complementary. The jihadi discourse may dominate media readings of CIEs, but this is clearly not the full picture. The study of Islam has to respond to this. There are several ongoing debates on the field of Islamic Studies and its future roles. Post–9/11 contexts have intensified interests in specific aspects of Islam and Muslim society but also challenged the role of those undertaking the study of Islam. There have been concerns at governmental involvement attempting to drive academic Islamic-studies agendas toward specific strategic interests or the promotions of specific forms of Islam.

Studies of some forms of online discourse have been promoted in university settings in an attempt to counter ongoing jihadi activities rather than simply further academic enquiry. There can be a relationship between these two zones of interest within universities, based on politics and financial inducement. There is also serious academic enquiry, unattached to agendas, with Internet sources increasingly part of comprehensive referencing on contemporaneous issues. Some agencies have attempted to derive insight and "get up to speed" through promotion of "academic"

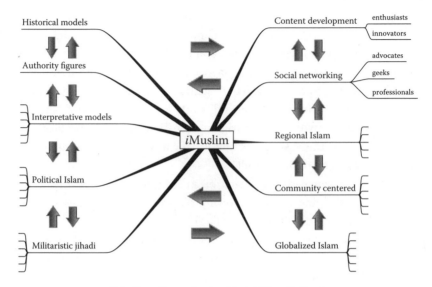

iMuslims Categorization Model (Gary R. Bunt)

conferences, although the tendency seems to be for the information exchange to be a one-way process (in the direction of the agencies). It has been a paradox to see academics, who have previously struggled to attain governmental funding, be courted by agencies seeking to draw on linguistic skills and knowledge in the fields. Some institutions have naturally benefited from seeking to fill the gaps in the academic markets to meet such subjective demands, although the reaction from some entrenched academics has been skeptical toward their new or enforced avenues of research.

Studying Internet activities relating to Islam should form part of any equation that seeks to approach contemporary Muslim discourse, and I am conscious of this from the increasing number of e-mails I receive from people seeking help on research projects. One problematic feature of this phenomena is that the emphasis of studying jihadi materials, an area likely to receive increased funding, is at the expense of understanding the relatively quieter forms of traditional and contemporary Islamic understanding online. It is important for both insider and outsider perceptions of Islam and Muslims that these elements also receive appropriate academic attention. Approaching the study of all aspects of Islam through the Internet, especially religious experience, offers materials that were unavailable before the late 1990s. The body of source material continues to expand, with an immediacy of access denied those of us seeking obscure journal articles and books in a predigital era. The Internet opens up opportunities for further access to insider perspectives and analyses from specific worldviews.

Logically, this should intensify understanding of Islam, but unfortunately in some cases this material often comes shrouded in either anti-Islamic rhetoric or in content that seeks to present a homogenized interpretation of Islam focused on one school of thought. Information overload also has a role to play in this, as does funding, with those with the deepest pockets often having the loudest online voices. This can be subverted with the use of Web 2.0 tools and the fact that grassroots materials produced on blogs and in social-networking contexts may have a greater resonance than staid official sites.

At a reader level, styles of information management might integrate curiosity for some or susceptibility for others, with content providers playing on the naiveté of some readers when espousing certain interpretations and causes. A range of players has endeavored to manipulate the interests and affiliations of readers, ranging from governmental interests to those deemed radical and subversive. This in turn is leading to new forms of research, associated with reaction to new technology and its social implications for Muslims.

It is difficult to predict which aspect of technology will be popular; in the early days of the Internet, the vision was quite different to the reality today. Few anticipated the impact of e-mail, browsers, searching tools, and social-networking sites, while a number of hyped applications bit the dust. Determining the Islamic patterns within this volatile and evolving space becomes problematic, as they do not conform to patterns that have a geometric neatness, such as the tiles found in historical mosques and Islamic buildings. Then again, the artisans and designers who created and applied those tiles themselves sought to suggest an infinite pattern and a divine order to the chaos of this world.

The Internet engagement with CIES will benefit from increased academic engagements, especially from Muslim contexts. Government engagements are assured in some form, at least in the jihadi and political zones, with some also seeking to dictate religious responsibilities and the direction of browsers. The scope for engagement also requires Muslim communities to take a closer look at Internet discourse and to determine its direction. The intergenerational digital divide is still acute in some Muslim contexts. Even Internet-literate elders cannot keep up with the range and volume of online activity, however benign, and misplaced attempts to regulate or place edicts on aspects of CIES have been met by silence or derision. In some cases, apathy and confusion regarding the Internet remains a dominant theme for elders in mosques. Those who have arranged the launch of Internet pages in the vain hope that they would reach the youth have been thwarted, as this content has been seen as poorly executed and lacking the underground ethos, social interaction, and "cool" dynamics of chat rooms and blogs.

The model of an individual rooted on a desktop has mutated, as alternate interfaces enabling mobile Internet communication have evolved in many forms. In contemporary contexts, all of these media forms can be said to be digital in many ways, and some would say there is no separation between the Internet and other media. Rather, there is an integrated media, some of which is institutionalized, official, and formal; some is within the private sector; and some is unofficial and individual. There are points in between, and connectivity between these spheres. At times, it becomes difficult or unnecessary to distinguish between the virtual and nonvirtual, as the forms of Islamic expression blur together and new ways of Islamic interaction develop. The reactions to *Jyllands-Posten*'s cartoon issue were a good example of this form of interaction. It was part of a long-standing but much broader dialogue on cultural, social, and religious issues associated with the sacred. To varying degrees, these discussions utilize a range of languages and linguistic styles, from colloquial to a measured formality.

This sense of the diffuse range of discourse, which may incorporate references to religious sources (including the Qur'an) and, in the same paragraph, street slang, is significant. Also important is the natural integration of other media forms into the discussion, in particular photographs but also other types of documentation. The use of photos and videos derived from cell phones may also be significant in providing input, especially as the technical quality of these images improves. The uploading of video content onto YouTube and related channels was becoming an integrated element of online expression, with sermons and actuality of religious expression (including recitation, prayer, and *hajj* activities) being available.[6] Web 2.0 became a natural adjunct for expression on religious issues; Ayaan Hirst Ali and Theo van Gogh's controversial film *Submission* was also on YouTube, linked to by detractors and supporters, indicating that a variety of perspectives on Islam and Muslim issues could be viewed.[7]

Technology is driving the ways in which some Muslims choose to express themselves online. Events can trigger shifts in the ways technology is applied by iMuslims. A further example was the use of blogging and integrated video during the 2006 invasion of Lebanon, including use by factions who would describe themselves and their actions as "Islamic." This content attained global audiences when drawn upon by mainstream broadcasters, including Israeli T V channels. The online chatter about issues in Lebanon were to shift perceptions of events on all sides and ensure that important issues were not subsumed because mainstream media was unable to access events at firsthand. It was clear that many significant events in Muslim spheres that had an Internet culture would immediately receive coverage via blogs, providing angles that complemented or at times contradicted conventional media.

The pronouncements of Pope Benedict XVI on Islam later in that year, perceived by some as "anti-Islamic" in their negative focus on the Prophet Muhammad, resulted in predictable chat-room and blog reaction. Less predictable was the spike in Internet defacements undertaken by hackers and crackers seeking to protest the pope's statement, with the logging of 5,000 defacements of websites in a two-week period in September 2006.[8] However, Islamic Internet chatter on the pope and on Lebanon was in marked contrast to coverage of zones in areas that generally lacked an Internet structure or general media coverage, such as Darfur.[9]

Some activism-related sites, including those with jihadi agendas, have linked into such discussions, seeing these issues as proselytizing opportunities. This included motives for hacking and cracking activities. Sites providing hacking advice are not new, but the Electronic Jihad set of pages offered an explicit and slick approach to the subject.[10] A number of scare stories about hacking and jihad were circulated in 2007, with one highly publicized jihadi campaign deadline passing without incident.[11]

The Saudi Arabia Ministry of Islamic Affairs was one of several agencies that launched a website in an attempt to counter jihadi activity of this nature.[12] Tariq Alhomayed of the *Asharq Alawsat* newspaper was intrigued that, despite such measures, al-Qaeda continued to recruit in Saudi Arabia: "One month ago, I asked a Saudi security official why and how youngsters are joining Al Qaeda despite the constant Saudi successes of countering terrorism. He answered, 'because of the Imam of deception.' I asked about the identity of the 'Imam of deception' and he replied, 'The Internet!' "[13] The pervasive influence of the Internet perceived by this official suggests that, despite the sustained investment of resources, retaining controls on the Internet remain problematic for Saudi and other governments.

Clearly, Muslim authorities and individuals remain challenged by how they might control the Internet and demonstrate awareness of how it can change both societies and individual lives. These are not, of course, exclusively Islamic issues. Jihadi sites have their equivalents in other cultural, religious, and political contexts.[14] Discussions about the impact of the Internet filter into numerous spheres away from Islamic contexts.

Even those who continue to negatively approach aspects of the Internet realize that the medium is not going to go away, and in fact it will only continue to develop and impinge on personal and community lives. The number of platforms and perspectives that have come online, or invested in enhancing their online output, indicate recognition of its acceptance within many Islamic spheres. There is a realization that the benefits can enhance religious identity, community cohesion, and the promotion of specific lifestyle choices. This was highlighted when a Tablighi Jama'at group engaged the services of a public relations company and launched a website with YouTube content in order to support the development of a "mega-mosque" in east London.[15]

This can also be an awareness that the Net is no longer a text-only medium but can operate as an effective full-media channel. News feeds, video clips, live broadcasts, downloadable tracts, forums, blogs, podcasts, flash teaching tools, and dynamic regularly updated sites have become the norm.

Muslim networking may still function in traditional nontech ways, but the social and religious pulse is digital. This has not necessarily diverted people from attending mosques, practicing Islam at home, or living an Islamic way of life. It may be that the nature of that expression has been influenced, subtly or overtly, by Internet content—perhaps by an opinion picked up in a blog, a video clip viewed on YouTube, or a fatwa solicited from Islam Online. The thread of cyber discourse is now stitched into the weave of Muslim communities. People may not be less Islamic for using the Net; in fact, it can enhance their religiosity. They may not pray less if diverted by the Net, but they may interact with religion differently, being exposed to more information and forms of knowledge about Islam.

Whether this is all seen as beneficial is clearly in the eye of the beholder, especially when the "Imam of deception" is in the picture. There are many people, including those from Muslim cultures, who indicate that their route to Islam was found on the information highway. The sector that embraced this with the greatest vigor—the jihadis—does not contain the numerical majority of Muslims. Some of their campaign subjects may elicit sympathy from a wider readership, even if their methodology is deemed abhorrent and un-Islamic.

There is a certain paradox that the online success of jihadis may have spurred other sectors to become more proactive in cyberspace and attuned to its consequences. The sustained investment in al-Azhar's online services offers one indicator of this. The relationship between other media, such as satellite television, and online services, such as those provided by supporters of Yusuf al-Qaradawi, is another significant factor to consider. How long before al-Qaradawi chooses Islam Online over Al-Jazeera as his media outlet of choice? It may give him confidence to say what he wishes, safe in the knowledge that his alternative outlet can provide streaming, broadcast media to an international audience that exceeds the footprint of Al-Jazeera.

The difference, perhaps, is that one is unlikely to see Islam Online being casually viewed in the same way as Al-Jazeera in the cafés and *souqs* of the Middle East. The mechanisms required to view Al-Jazeera are easier, in that it is a continually streaming service rather than something that has to be searched out online through multiple clicks and pages. This may change when Internet television, available through domestic sets, becomes more accessible and widespread.

When this happens, outlets such as Islam Online will be in a strategically sound position to challenge conventional broadcasts and join the range of Muslim channels that are already available. The concept of an integrated multimedia service streaming through numerous interfaces, of which dedicated personal computers are only one part, is becoming a reality. Whether these will be considered CIEs is another matter. What is true is that the smaller players will also find a voice and endeavor to enable their own expression in the increasingly crowed marketplace. However, it is one thing to place opinions and materials in cyberspace but quite another to be located and read in a saturated zone. Identifying distinctive services and voices may become more problematic. At present, deep searching or exhaustive forays into lists of URLS on portals and blog rolls are required to find some materials.

My own listing of Islamic blogs expanded rapidly during the writing of this book, even though I integrated a form on nonscientific quality control in an endeavor to stem the tide of links. Searching for new material becomes addictive; it takes time away from reading established sources. Information management distracts from the reality of the message. I base my reading on RSS feeds (which indicate headlines rather than the substance of a story) or software that tells me when a favorite blog has been updated. This suggests that a critical area in the future of CIEs is not the provision of content but the provision of guidance and information management. The online *murshid*, or spiritual advisor, pointing the disciple in the direction of sources and advice in fact has echoes with traditional Islamic scholarship going back through the history of Muslim networks. Knowing your way around the library becomes increasingly important if you are not to suffer information overload.

There is a streamlining and continual evolution in the ways in which Internet media are applied by Muslim individuals and communities, part of a growing global sophistication within other spheres. There is no reason why Muslims should react any differently to enhanced availability of technical tools such as blogging software and improved access to Internet networks. The issue itself is a specifically Muslim one, and the protagonists are to varying degrees individuals who identify with Islam.

While such dialogues are still a numerically minority phenomenon, their validity lies in the ways in which they can inform key change agents and allow opinions to rapidly disseminate into broader contexts. They also facilitate access to ideas between and within diverse Muslim contexts, and they also allow a window into contemporary Muslim issues for "outsiders."

Others feel the need to report and record and believe that it is entirely natural to utilize cyberspace in order to do that. Some seek to integrate their thoughts with other bloggers, while others appear to pursue a more solitary approach to their topic. Whether online pronouncements could act as a substitute for real-world campaigning is open to question. There is also a range of juxtaposed sources within one online document; for example, an informal blog may "naturally" be linked to a juristic fatwa. There is a sense that they comprise a new form of Islamic dialogue while also identifying that there is a link with "nondigital" discourse and issues.

This book has shown that the traditional paradigm of a Muslim community, or *ummah*, has, on one level, itself shifted online with the development of social-networking software leading to alternate forms of affiliations and friendships. A multitude of communities have opened up and developed new Muslim networks. These relate in particular to the types of online services that have been overhyped under the banner of Web 2.0 but in truth are part of a continually evolving pattern of Internet services. Their use in selected contexts allows us to consider whether forms of Islamic expression are themselves continually evolving, juxtaposed at the same time with elements of traditional Islamic values and orientations.

CIES can lock into other media spheres while retaining their own individuality and approaches relating to the interests and contexts of their owners, writers, and readers. These factors may relate to a binding point to varying degrees. It represents the relationship between the individual and a social-political-cultural-religious understanding, together with a sense of identity that may be nurtured and tangible in cyberspace as much as it is in the nondigital world.

Upgrades in software, new concepts in information distribution, and widening and improved access to the Internet were just some of the dimensions influencing CIES. The external dynamics of generic hardware and software innovation have to be coupled with the internal dynamics relating to the evolution of CIES. Many aspects of Islamic belief now have an online presence. New networks drawing upon Web 2.0 innovations show that cyber-Islamic environments continue to evolve, with iMuslims playing a proactive role in presenting Islam for the twenty-first century.

Glossary of Key Islamic Terms

adhān ◆ Call to Prayer.

ʿakīkah ◆ Animal Sacrifice, made seven days following the birth of a child; the sacrifice is given to the needy as charity. This is a practice based on the *sunnah* of the Prophet Muḥammad.

ʿālim ◆ A scholar (pl. *ʿulamā'*).

Allāh ◆ God.

al-arkān (al-Islām) ◆ The pillars or foundations of Islam (sing. *rukn*).

ʿĀshūrā ◆ The tenth day of *Muḥarram*, when Muḥammad 's grandson al-Ḥusayn was martyred during the Battle of Karbalā', 61 A.H. (680 C.E.).

ʾāya ◆ Verse from the Qur'ān, "sign" (pl. *āyat*).

āyatullāh ◆ Literally, the "sign of God"; within *Shī'a* Islam, this can denote the rank of a highly qualified interpreter of Islamic Jurisprudence.

al-Azhar ◆ University located in Cairo; literally, "the brilliant one."

baraka ◆ "Blessing," emanating from Allāh, Muḥammad, the Qur'ān, and/or an individual who can pass on this quality (through "spiritual" qualities and/or through family lineage).

daʿwa ◆ The call or invitation to Islam, associated with propagation of the religion.

dīn ◆ "Religion."

Eid al-Fitr, ʿĪd al-Fiṭr ◆ The concluding feast of *Ramaḍān*.

fatwā ◆ The opinions of specific contemporary *imāms* and *āyatullāh* (pl. *fatāwā*).

fiqh, fikh ◆ Islamic "jurisprudence."

ḥadīth ◆ A traditional saying and/or report of the actions of Muḥammad (pl. *aḥādīth*).

ḥāfiẓ ◆ A title denoting one who had learned the Qur'ān by heart.

ḥalāl ◆ A term applied to denote that which is considered appropriate or permitted within the bounds of Islam.

Ḥizb Allāh ◆ "Party of God," also transliterated as *Hezbollah* or *Hizbollah.*

Ibrāhīm ◆ Abraham.

ijtihād ◆ Independent judgment based on Islamic sources; a striving for the pragmatic interpretation of Islamic primary sources in the light of contemporary conditions. The term can be synonymous with "renewal" and "reform."

al-Ikhwān al-Muslimūn ◆ The Muslim Brotherhood, a "reformist" movement originating in Egypt in 1928 that spread elsewhere in the Muslim world.

imām ◆ The term *imām* (pl. *aʾimma*) usually refers to one who leads the prayers, not necessarily "qualified" in the sense of trained clergy. In *Shīʿa* Islam, *Imām* has associations with religious leadership *and* continuity of spiritual authority.

imsāk ◆ Abstention during *Ramadān.*

Islām ◆ "Submission" to God.

Ismāʿīlī ◆ A form of *Shīʿa* Islam, which itself fragmented to forming disparate branches, including the *Fāṭimids,* the *Nizāris,* the *Assassins,* and the *Bohorās.*

Ithnā ʿAsharīs ◆ The "Twelvers," a form of *Shīʿa* Islam following a line of twelve *imāms* descended from Muḥammad.

Jamāʿat-e Islāmī ◆ Synonymous with a Pakistani political party, the term is applied elsewhere and infers a "congregation," "collective," or "party" of Islam.

jihād ◆ "Striving" to attain an Islamic objective; the term has spiritual and/or militaristic connotations.

jihād bil-sayf ◆ *jihād*; "With the sword."

jihādi ◆ An advocate of *jihād.*

Kaʿba ◆ The "holy house" (in Mecca).

ḳalām ◆ "Theology."

khalīfa ◆ Caliph, "vice-regent," "successor" (to Muḥammad).

khuṭba ◆ Sermon, provided by a *khātib.*

Koran ◆ Qurʾān.

madhhab ◆ A "school" of Islamic interpretation, such as the broad *Ḥanafī, Ḥanbalī, Mālikī,* and *Shāfiʿī* (pl. *madhāhib*).

*mas*djid ◆ Mosque, place of prayer.

Masjid al-Quds ◆ Mosque of Jerusalem, also known as *Mas*djid *al-Aqsā.*

Mawlid ◆ Birthday of Muḥammad and/or anniversary of "saints."

Miʿrādj ◆ "Ladder," or the ascension of Muḥammad to Heaven; part of the "Night Journey."

Muḥammad, ◆ Muḥammad ibn ʿAbd Allāh; the Prophet of Islam, ca. 570–632 C.E. (active ca. 610–632).

Muḥarram ✦ First month of the Muslim calendar, associated in particular with fasting, especially for *Shī*‘a Muslims during ‘*Āshūrā*.

mudjtahid ✦ An "interpreter" (of Islam, esp. Islamic jurisprudence), a practitioner of *ijtihād*.

murīd ✦ A person on a spiritual path, or a seeker of religious knowledge, often applied in the context of *Sūfī* beliefs.

murshid ✦ A person who provides guidance to those on the spiritual path (*murīd*), often applied in the context of *Sūfī* beliefs.

muṣḥāf ✦ The definitive recension of the Qur'ān.

mutadjwīd ✦ Recitors of the Qur'ān.

nashīds ✦ Genre ranging from "sung" *ahādīth* to prayers, and popular "Islamic" music.

pīr ✦ See murshid.

qibla/ḳibla ✦ Direction of Muslim prayer (toward Mecca).

Qur'ān ✦ Revelation received by the Prophet Muḥammad via the Angel Gabriel.

rak‘a ✦ A sequence within *salāt*.

Ramaḍān ✦ Month of fasting (*sawm*) and the month in which the Qur'ān was revealed; one of the five pillars of Islam.

ribā ✦ Capital interest, usury.

ṣawm ✦ Fasting in *Ramaḍān*.

salafi ✦ (1) "Pious ancestors," applied in terms of Muḥammad's companions and the "early" Muslim community, representing an example to follow; (2) Used by Muslim "reformist" movement(s), such as *al-ikhwān al-muslimūn*; (3) Applied by a number of platforms, especially in contemporary contexts, indicating their intention to "return" to the principles of Muḥammad and his community.

ṣalāt ✦ Prayer; one of the five pillars of Islam.

shahāda ✦ The principle of proclaiming a belief in a One God whose Final Prophet is Muḥammad; one of the five pillars of Islam.

shahīd ✦ A "witness," frequently used in the sense of a "martyr."

shaykh ✦ Religious leader, leader of a *tarīqa* (also see murshid, *pīr*).

sharī‘a ✦ The body of Islamic law based on the "source" of the Qur'ān (and other Islamic sources); divine "law," as revealed to Muḥammad.

Shī‘a ✦ "Party" or "sect," the followers of the line of ‘Alī ibn Abī Ṭālib (d. 661).

Ṣūfī ✦ Muslim "mystic"; the term has broad connotations and definitions within disparate branches of Sūfism (*taṣawwuf*).

Sunnī ✦ "Orthodox" Islam, based on the *sunna*.

sunna ✦ The customary practice of Muḥammad.

sūra ◆ A chapter within the Qur'ān (pl. *suwar*)

tafsīr ◆ Commentary on, or exegesis of, the Qur'ān.

tarīka ◆ A "path," generally a term associated with *Ṣūfī* orders

taklīd ◆ Primarily the imitation of the practice of the Prophet Muḥammad and secondarily his companions and his successors (*salafi*).

ṭawāf ◆ A ritual connected with *hajj* that is associated with the circumambulation of the *Ka'ba*.

'ulamā' ◆ Scholars.

Ummah ◆ Muslim community.

'umra ◆ The "lesser" pilgrimage to Mecca.

zakāt ◆ Annual alms taxation; one of the five pillars of Islam.

Notes

All URLs are accurate as of May 2008. A webpage containing chapter URLs can be found at *www.virtuallyislamic.com*.

Introduction

1. "Wiki," Wikipedia, 18 September 2006, *http://en.wiktionary.org/wiki/wiki*.
2. Don Tapscott and Anthony D. Williams, *Wikinomics: How Mass Collaboration Changes Everything* (New York and London: Portfolio, 2006), 7–33. More information on Linux and its ongoing development can be found at Linux, *http://www.linux.org*.
3. For example, see the discussion on the hadith in J. Robson, "Hadith," in *Encyclopaedia of Islam*, CD-ROM edition, ed. P. J. Bearman, Th. Bianquis, C. E. Bosworth, E. van Donzel, and W. P. Heinrichs (Leiden: Brill Academic Publishers, 2003).
4. Gary R. Bunt, *Virtually Islamic: Computer-Mediated Communication and Cyber Islamic Environments* (Cardiff: University of Wales Press, 2000).

Chapter One

1. IslamicTube, *http://islamictube.net*; IslamicTorrents, *http://www.islamictorrents.net MuslimSpace*; "Music," *http://muslimspace.com*.
2. Sify.com, "Islamists on Net Blame U.S. for Tsunami Destruction," *http://sify.com/news/fullstory.php?id=13643663*. Also see "Jihadists and the Big Lie," Washington Post/aina.org, 10 January 2005, *http://www.aina.org/news/2005 0110135524.htm*.
3. For example, see Islamic Society of Britain, "The Islamic Society of Britain Condemns Vicious Attacks on Our Capital," 8 July 2005, *http://www.isb.org.uk/pages/pressrelease_londonattacks.htm, islamicforumeurope.com*; "IFE Media Release: Muslims Shocked by London Blasts," 8 July 2005, *http://www.islamic forum europe.com/live/ife.php?doc=articleitem&itemId=239*; "Hizb ut-Tahrir Britain Issues Message to Muslim Community in Aftermath of London Attacks," WebWire, 7 July 2005, *http://www.webwire.com/ViewPressRel.asp?aId=3249*;

MPACUK, "My Experience of the London Terror Attacks," 7 July 2005, *http://www.mpacuk.org/content/view/4/780/103/*; Islamic Human Rights Commission, "IHRC Urges Caution in Wake of London Attacks," 7 July 2005; The Islamic Foundation, "Press Release," 7 July 2005, *http://www.islamic-foundation.org.uk/IF-PR-7-7.htm*; Muslim Association of Britain, 7 July 2005, *http://www.mabonline.info/english/*; Muslim Council of Britain, 7 July 2005, *http://www.mcb.org.uk*.

4. MEMRI, "Saudi Religious Police Launch Website," May 13 2003, *http://www.memri.org/bin/articles.cgi?Area=saudiarabia&ID=SP50403*.

5. David Crystal, cited in "The Web Not the Death of Language," *Wired*, 22 February 2005, *http://www.wired.com/news/culture/0,1284,66671,00.html*.

6. Gilles Kepel, *The War for Muslim Minds: Islam and the West*, trans. Pascale Ghazaleh (Cambridge, Mass., and London: Belknap Press of Harvard University Press, 2004), 256.

7. Manuel Castells, *The Rise of the Network Society*, 2nd ed. (Oxford: Blackwell, 2000), 77.

8. miriam cooke and Bruce B. Lawrence, eds., *Muslim Networks from Hajj to Hip Hop* (Chapel Hill: University of North Carolina Press, 2005), back cover.

9. Lorne L. Dawson, "Religion and the Quest for Virtual Community," in *Religion Online: Finding Faith on the Internet*, ed. Douglas E. Cowan and Lorne L. Dawson (New York: Routledge, 2004), 85.

10. Castells, *The Rise of the Network Society*, 4.

11. Ibid., 3 (Castells's emphasis).

12. Dale F. Eickelman, "Muslim Ties That Bind," in *Religious Communities on the Internet*, ed. Göran Larsson (Stockholm: Swedish Science Press, 2006), 50.

13. David Holmes, *Communication Theory: Media, Technology, Society* (London, Thousand Oaks and New Delhi: Sage Publications, 2005), 78.

14. Ibid., 123.

15. Thomas L. McPhail, *Global Communication: Theories, Stakeholders, and Trends*, 2nd ed. (Malden, Mass., and Oxford: Blackwell Publishing, 2006), 31.

16. Ibid.

17. Lawrence Pintak, "Al Jazeera's Chief: 'We Are Not Politically-Correct,'" *Turkish Daily News*, 17 November 2006, *http://www.turkishdailynews.com*.

18. For overviews of Al-Jazeera, see the case study in Daya Kishan Thussu, *International Communication: Continuity and Change*, 2nd ed. (London: Hodder Arnold, 2006), 190–92. Also see Mohamed Zayani, "Arab Public Opinion in the Age of Satellite Television: The Case of Al Jazeera," in *Muslims and the News Media*, ed. Elizabeth Poole and John E. Richardson (London and New York: I. B. Tauris, 2006). More detailed treatments of the subject can be found in Naomi Sakr, *Satellite Realms: Transnational Television, Globalization, and the Middle East* (London: I. B. Tauris, 2001); and Mohamed A. El-Nawawy and Adel Iskandar, *Al Jazeera: How the Free Arab News Network Scooped the World and Changed the Middle East* (Cambridge, Mass.: Westview, 2002).

19. Edward W. Said, *Covering Islam: How the Media and the Experts Determine How We See the Rest of the World*, 2nd ed. (New York: Vintage, 1997).

20. For a general theoretical overview of associated concerns relating to "discourses of globalization," see Thussu, *International Communication*, 60–64.

21. Peter G. Mandaville, *Transnational Muslim Politics: Reimagining the Umma* (London and New York: Routledge, 2001), 16.

22. Ibid., 50.

23. Jon W. Anderson, "Muslim Networks, Muslim Selves in Cyberspace: Islam in the Post-Modern Public Sphere," *http://nmit.georgetown.edu/papers/jwander son2.htm*. Also see Jon W. Anderson, "Globalizing Politics and Religion in the Muslim World," *Journal of Electronic Publishing* 3, no. 1 (September 1997), *http://www.press.umich.edu/jep/archive/Anderson.html*.

24. Yvonne Seng, "Tantawi Engages with Questions of Modernity," 9 June 2004, *http://www.dailystar.com.lb*.

25. Jon W. Anderson, "Wiring Up: The Internet Difference for Muslim Networks," in *Muslim Networks from Hajj to Hip Hop*, ed. miriam cooke and Bruce B. Lawrence (Chapel Hill: University of North Carolina Press, 2005), 252–53.

26. Gary R. Bunt, "Virtually Islamic Blog," *http://virtuallyislamic.blogspot.com/*.

27. Daniel Martin Varisco, "Islam Takes a Hit," *ISIM Newsletter*, no. 14 (2004), *http://www.isim.nl*.

28. Jeffrey K. Hadden and Douglas E. Cowan, eds., *Religion on the Internet: Research Prospects and Promises* (New York: Elsevier Science, 2000); Douglas E. Cowan and Lorne L. Dawson, eds., *Religion Online: Finding Faith on the Internet* (New York: Routledge, 2004); Anastasia Karaflogka, *E-Religion: A Critical Appraisal of Religious Discourse on the World Wide Web* (London: Equinox, 2007).

29. There are a number of studies related to the representation of religion on the Internet in other contexts. In particular, see Gwilym Beckerlegge, *From Sacred Text to Internet* (Aldershot, Hants., Milton Keynes, and Burlington, Vt.: Ashgate and Open University, 2001); Brenda E. Brasher, *Give Me That Online Religion* (San Francisco: Jossey-Bass, 2001); Heidi Campbell, *Exploring Religious Community Online: We Are One in the Network* (New York: P. Lang, 2005); and Susan M. Zakar and Dovid Y. B. Kaufmann, *Judaism Online: Confronting Spirituality on the Internet* (Northvale, N.J.: J. Aronson, 1998).

30. See the findings contained in Morten T. Højsgaard and Margit Warburg, eds., *Religion and Cyberspace* (London: Routledge, 2005). Also see Göran Larsson, ed., *Religious Communities on the Internet* (Stockholm: Swedish Science Press, 2006).

31. Jocelyne Cesari, *When Islam and Democracy Meet: Muslims in Europe and in the United States* (New York and Basingstoke: Palgrave Macmillan, 2002), 113. Cesari positioned me as a sociologist; a more accurate definition is an Islamic Studies–Religious Studies academic.

32. There are several examples of such research. For example, Lenie Broewer has undertaken a study of Muslim youth in the Netherlands (in particular those of Moroccan ancestral origin), and their utilization of information technology, through close observation of a digital community center and a computer clubhouse. See Lenie Broewer, "Dutch Moroccan Websites: A Transnational Imag-

ery?," *Journal of Ethnic and Migration Studies* 32, no. 7 (2006): 1153–68. Also see Lenie Broewer, "Dutch-Muslims on the Internet: A New Discussion Platform," *Journal of Muslim Minority Affairs* 24, no. 1 (2004): 47–55.

33. For example, see Thomas Hegghammer, "Global Jihadism after the Iraq War," *Middle East Journal* 60, no. 1 (2006): 11–32. Hegghammer is a senior analyst with the Norwegian Defense Research Establishment. Also see an interview with him: UPI, "Jihad and the Internet," 14 February 2006, *http://www.upi.com/SecurityTerrorism/view.php?StoryID=20060214-032817-4513r*. The analysis of Reuben Paz, based in Israel, could also be considered in this regard: Project for the Research of Islamist Movements, "What Is PRISM?," *http://www.e-prism.org*.

34. See Philip Halldén, "Salafi in Virtual and Physical Reality," *ISIM Newsletter* 13 (2003), *http://www.isim.nl/files/newsl_13.pdf* (which discusses Yusuf al-Ayyiri and alneda.com).

35. Bruce B. Lawrence, "Allah On-Line: The Practice of Global Islam in the Information Age," in *Practicing Religion in the Age of the Media: Explorations in Media, Religion, and Culture*, ed. Stewart M. Hoover and Lynn Schofield Clark (New York: Columbia University Press, 2002).

36. Dale F. Eickelman and Jon W. Anderson, eds., *New Media in the Muslim World* (Bloomington and Indianapolis: Indiana University Press, 2003); Dale F. Eickelman and James Piscatori, *Muslim Politics* (Princeton: Princeton University Press, 1996).

37. Jon B. Alterman, *New Media, New Politics? From Satellite Television to the Internet in the Arab World* (Washington, D.C.: Washington Institute for Near East Policy, 1998).

38. In particular, see Albrecht Hofheinz, "The Internet in the Arab World: Playground for Political Liberalisation," *Internationale Politik und Gesellschaft/International Politics and Society* 3 (2005): 78–96, *http://fesportal.fes.de/pls/portal30/docs/FOLDER/IPG/IPG3_2005/07HOFHEINZ.PDF*.

39. Deborah L. Wheeler, *The Internet in the Middle East: Global Expectations and Local Imaginations in Kuwait*, SUNY Series in Computer-Mediated Communication (New York: State University of New York Press, 2005).

40. Merlyna Lim has produced a series of works relating specifically to the Internet and cyber activism in Indonesia based on doctoral research. For example, see Merlyna Lim, *Islamic Radicalism and Anti-Americanism in Indonesia: The Role of the Internet*, Policy Studies Series 18 (Washington, D.C.: East West Center, 2005); and Merlyna Lim, "Lost in Transition? The Internet and *Reformasi* in Indonesia," in *Reformatting Politics: Global Civil Society and the Internet*, ed. Jodi Dean, Jon Anderson, and Geert Lovink (London: Routledge, 2006). Further publication details can be found at Merlyna Lim, "Mer's Bites of Bytes: Publications," *http://www.merlyna.org/pubs*. Mohammed Ibahrine's doctoral thesis on the Internet and politics in Morocco presented a significant case study of political and religious discourse, backed up by Ibahrine's regular commentaries via his blogs. See Mohammed Ibahrine, "The Internet and Politics in Morocco: The Political Use of the Internet by Islam-Oriented Political Movements" (Ph.D. diss., Hamburg University, 2006). A gateway to his blogs can be found through

Mohammed Ibahrine, "Arab Blog and Political Communication," 20 June 2005, *http://arabblogandpoliticalcommunication.blogspot.com.*

41. This research on Islam and the Internet has extended to Muslims in minority contexts. Natascha Garvin's Ph.D. work on the Murabitun movement in Mexico, for example, incorporated an Internet element in its discussion of the community's websites. A report on this work was published in 2005: Natascha Garvin, "Conversion and Conflict: Muslims in Mexico," *ISIM Review* 15 (2005), *http://www.isim.nl.* This was a significant issue of *ISIM Review*, as it contained several other pieces relating to Muslims and the Internet (two of which are highlighted below). Bettina Gräf referred to Yusuf al-Qaradawi's Internet output as part of her PhD. work on his role as a "global scholar." See Bettina Gräf, "In Search of a Global Islamic Authority," *ISIM Review* 15 (2005), *http://www.isim.nl.* Thomas Pierett studied the Ahbash movement's Internet activities in Lebanon as part of his Ph.D. work on Muslim world politics. See Thomas Pierret, "Internet in a Sectarian Islamic Context," *ISIM Review* 15 (2005), *http://www.isim.nl.* Vít Sisler undertook postgraduate work on Islamic jurisprudence in cyberspace. See Vít Sisler, "Islamic Jurisprudence in Cyberspace: Construction of Interpretative Authority in Muslim Diaspora," *http://uisk.jinonice.cuni.cz/sisler/research.htm.* And Anna Piela-Ziolko was preparing a Ph.D. that was incorporating a fieldwork element; see Anna Piela-Ziolko, "Muslim Women's Online Communities" (Ph.D. diss. [in preparation], University of York, 2006–). Also see the introduction to Gary R. Bunt, *Islam in the Digital Age: E-Jihad, Online Fatwas, and Cyber Islamic Environments* (London and Ann Arbor, Mich.: Pluto Press, 2003).

42. Göran Larsson, "The Death of a Virtual Muslim Discussion Group," *Online— Heidelberg Journal of Religions on the Internet* 1, no. 1 (2005), *http://archiv. ub.uni-heidelberg.de/volltextserver/volltexte/2005/5825/pdf/Larsson3a.pdf.*

43. Göran Larsson, "Sidratul-Muntaha: An Alternative Voice for Swedish Muslims in Cyberspace?"; Ermete Mariani, "The Production of Islamic Knowledge on the Internet and the Role of States and Markets: The Examples of Yussef al-Qaradawi and Amru Khaled"; and Philip Halldén, "Militant Salafism on the Internet: 'Alneda.com' and the Legacy of Yusuf al-'Ayyiri"; all in *Religious Communities on the Internet*, ed. Göran Larsson (Stockholm: Swedish Science Press, 2006).

44. For a discussion on the veracity of this hadith (saying of the Prophet Muhammad), see Living Islam, "Islamic Tradition," 10 October 2005, *http://www.living islam.org/n/skx__e.html.*

45. Edward W. Said, *Orientalism* (London: Random House, 1979).

46. Mandaville, *Transnational Muslim Politics*, 55–56.

47. Ibid., 56.

48. Abdul-Hamid Jassat and Dilpazier Aslam, "Differentiating between Tradition and Islam," 13 May 2003, *http://www.khilafah.com/home/category.php?Docu mentID=7064&TagID=1.* Khilafah.com represents the interests of Hizb ut-Tahrir, an international political Islamic movement.

49. "Plans under Way for E-University," *Arab News*, 21 August 2004, *http://www. arabnews.com.*

50. Iran News, "IRNA Chinese Website Launched," 4 March 2005, *http://www.iran mania.com/News/ArticleView/Default.asp?NewsCode=30099&NewsKind=Cur rentAffairs*.

51. Ibid.

52. "Internet! How to Use It Right," *Milli Gazette*, *http://groups.yahoo.com/group/ islam_peace_and_understanding*.

53. Mohamed Begg, *The Muslim Parents' Guide on Responsible Use of ICT at Home* (Leicester: DeMontfort University, 2005), *http://www.ccsr.cse.dmu.ac.uk/re sources/muslim_guide_press-no-crop.pdf*.

54. Islam Online, "Fatwa Bank: Islamic Etiquette for Using Online Messengers," 3 September 2003, *http://www.islamonline.net/servlet/Satellite?pagename=Is lamOnline-English-Ask_Scholar/FatwaE/FatwaE&cid=1119503547366*.

55. Islam Online, "Fatwa Bank: Online Chatting in the Eyes of Shari'ah," 14 November 2005, *http://www.islamonline.net/servlet/Satellite?pagename=IslamOn line-English-Ask_Scholar/FatwaE/FatwaE&cid=1119503547082*; citing (with modification) Sheikh Ahmad Kutty, "Islamic Institute of Toronto, Ask the Scholar, 'I wanted to know if chatting online is haraam (impermissible) but my chats with the Muslim people only are clean and no bad intention chats,' Question number: 417," 15 June 2003, *http://www.islam.ca*.

56. Islam Online, "Fatwa Bank: Internet Chats between Males and Females," 13 November 2005; citing Muzammil Siddiqi, "Issues on Numerical Miracles of the Qur'an, Internet Chats between Males and Females," n.d., *http://www.pakis tanlink.com/religion/08202004.html*.

57. "Internet Abuse in Workplaces Costs Businesses Dear: Survey," *Arab News*, 20 February 2005, *http://www.arabnews.com*. On "Bluetooth" abuse, see Arabherald.com, "Teenagers Sinking Their Teeth into New Technology," 10 February 2005, *http://story.arabherald.com/p.x/ct/9/id/c7a3eac48b609961/cid/48f cf33f9aeb6130/*.

58. Razi Azmi, "Thinking Aloud: Too Clever by Half," *http://dailytimes.com.pk*.

59. Carl W. Ernst, "Ideological and Technological Transformations of Contemporary Sufism," in *Muslim Networks from Hajj to Hip Hop*, ed. miriam cooke and Bruce B. Lawrence (Chapel Hill: University of North Carolina Press, 2005), 203; citing Manuel Castells, *The Information Age: Economy, Society, and Culture*, vol. 1, *The Rise of the Network Society* (Malden, Mass.: Blackwell), 263.

60. Olivier Roy, *Globalised Islam: The Search for a New Ummah* (London: Hurst & Company, 2004), 183.

61. Dale F. Eickelman and Jon W. Anderson, "Preface to the Second Edition," in *New Media in the Muslim World*, ed. Dale F. Eickelman and Jon W. Anderson (Bloomington and Indianapolis: Indiana University Press, 2003), xiv.

62. Kepel, *The War for Muslim Minds*, 255.

63. Gary R. Bunt, *Virtually Islamic: Computer-Mediated Communication and Cyber Islamic Environments* (Cardiff: University of Wales Press, 2000).

64. Radio Free Europe/Radio Liberty, "Analyst Speaks about 'Globalization' of Islam," 28 May 2003, *http://www.rferl.org/newsline/*.

65. Roy, *Globalised Islam*, 258.

66. *Surah Hujurat* (The Private Rooms), 49:13, in *The Qur'an*, trans. M. A. S. Abdel Haleem (Oxford and New York: Oxford University Press, 2004).

67. *Surah Anbiyya* (The Prophets) 21:92, in *The Holy Quran: English Translation of the Meanings, and Commentary Revised and Edited by the Presidency of Islamic Researchers, Ifta, Call and Guidance*, trans. Abdullah Yusuf Ali (Medina: King Fahd Holy Quran Printing Complex, 1990). Other editions replace "Ummah" with "Brotherhood."

68. Muslim WakeUp, "Index," *http://www.muslimwakeup.com*. See the listing by Charles Kurzman, Liberal Islam websites, *http://www.unc.edu/kurzman/Lib erallslamLinks.htm*.

69. Roy, *Globalised Islam*, 15–160.

70. Bunt, *Virtually Islamic*.

71. Mandaville, *Transnational Muslim Politics*, 4.

72. Jakob Nielsen, *Designing Web Usability: The Practice of Simplicity* (Indianapolis: New Riders, 2000).

73. United Nations Development Project, "Making New Technologies Work for Human Development," 13 October 2004, *http://www.undp.org/hdr2001*; Pippa Norris, *Digital Divide? Civic Engagement, Information Poverty, and the Internet Worldwide* (New York: Cambridge University Press, 2001).

74. Kepel, *The War for Muslim Minds*, 8.

75. Gary R. Bunt, " 'Rip. Burn. Pray': Islamic Expression Online," in *Religion Online: Finding Faith on the Internet*, ed. Douglas E. Cowan and Lorne L. Dawson (New York: Routledge, 2004).

76. My colleague David Mossley of the Philosophical and Religious Studies Subject Centre discussed this concept in a marketing seminar I attended in 2005. It was adapted from the concept of a relationship ladder, taken from A. Payne, N. Christopher, M. Clark, and H. Peck, *Relationship Marketing for Competitive Advantage* (Oxford: Butterworth Heinemann, 1997), viii.

77. Mossley also discussed the concept of relationship types, based on N. Piercy, *Market-Led Strategic Change*, 2nd ed. (Oxford: Butterworth Heinemann, 1997), 242.

78. AME Info, "Islamic Mobile Phone Signals Growing Opportunity," *http://www.ameinfo.com/ news/Detailed/51870.html*.

79. Holmes, *Communication Theory*, 64.

80. Ibid., 64.

81. Chris Anderson, "The Long Tail: Universal's Long Tail Music Experiment," 19 October 2006, *http://longtail.typepad.com/the_long_tail/*.

82. Chris Anderson, "The Long Tail," *Wired*, October 2004, *http://www.wired.com/wired/archive/12.10/tail.html*.

83. Piedad, *http://www.hispanicmuslims.com/piedad*; discussed in Islam Online, "Common Grounds Lure Latinos to Islam," 31 October 2005, *http://www.islam-online.net/English/News/2005-10/31/article02.shtml*.

84. Jews for Allah, *http://www.jewsforallah.com*; Beliefnet/Religious News Service, "A Joke Becomes a Muslim's Chance to Proselytize Jews," 10 January 2006, *http://www.beliefnet.com/story/133/story_13334_1.html*.

85. Sean Dodson, "Show and Tell Online," *Guardian* (London), 2 March 2006, *http://technology.guardian.co.uk/weekly/story/0,,1720763,00.html.*

86. Their sustained growth and impact was noted by major media players, including News International, who bought MySpace in 2005 as a way to access the youthful market using this technology—to the initial derision of some observers.

87. Zahrah, 24 April 2006, *http://www.myspace.com/salafi_zahrah.*

88. Muslima_Ilana, 26 April 2006, *http://www.myspace.com/muslima_ilana.* For information on the band, see "Afghan 'Burqa Band' Creates Waves in Germany," AFP/*Daily Times*, 4 August 2003, *http://www.dailytimes.com.pk/default.asp? page=story_4-8-2003_pg9_7.* Tracks from the group can be found online at Ata Tak, *http://www.atatak.com.*

89. Diva, 5 April 2006, *http://www.myspace.com/diva11278.*

90. Hijabi, 5 April 2006, *http://www.myspace.com/nyelene.*

91. Muslim Space, 5 October 2006, *http://www.muslimspace.com.*

92. Miska Rantanen, "A Muslim MySpace Based in Espoo," Helsingin Sanomat— International Edition, *http://www.hs.fi/english/article/A+Muslim+MySpace+ based+in+Espoo/1135222538803.*

93. Islam Online, "Ramadan Tent," 19 September 2007, *http://secondlife.com*; Islam Online, "IOL Virtual Ramadan Tent Attacked," 15 September 2007, *http:// www.islamonline.net.*

94. Second Life, "Tasneem Masjid," 11 October 2007, *http://secondlife.com.*

95. Second Life, "Chebi Mosque," 13 October 2007, *http://secondlife.com.*

96. YouTube, "Miracles of Islam," *http://www.youtube.com/watch?v=Ypzpug6So9E.*

97. "Music," *http://muslimspace.com.*

98. Ummah Films, 10 February 2007, *http://ummahfilms.blogspot.com.*

99. IslamicTube, *http://islamictube.net*; IslamicTorrents.

100. IslamicVideos.net, 16 October 2006, *http://www.islamicvideos.net.*

101. Rantanen, "A Muslim MySpace."

102. Alt.muslim, "Alt.muslim review," *http://www.altmuslim.com/am_podcasts. php.*

103. Q-News, *http://www.q-news.com.*

104. Radical Middle Way, *http://www.radicalmiddleway.co.uk/.*

105. "Islamophonic," *Guardian* (London), January 2007–, *http://www.theguardian. co.uk.*

106. I-d-e-a-n-t, "Announcing the Launch of OpenIslampedia: The Open Encyclopedia of Islam," February 2006, *http://ideant.typepad.com/ideant/2006/02/an nouncing_the_.html.* Also see OpenIslamppedia, *http://www.openislampedia. org/wikis/en/index.php?title=Main_Page.*

107. AlterNet, "Building Blogs," 22 February 2005, *http://www.alternet.org.*

Chapter Two

1. Richard Wray, "China Catches Up on U.S. for Fast Internet as Africa Gets Left Behind," *Guardian* (London), 14 June 2007. This report cites the work of Point Topic; see Point Topic, "World Broadband Closes in on 300 Million Subscribers," June 2007, *http://www.point-topic.com.*

2. Frank Bures, "Access Denied," *Wired*, September 2007, 60–61; citing data from the International Telecommunications Union.

3. International Telecommunications Union/United Nations Conference on Trade and Development (ITU/UNCTAD), "World Information Society Report 2007: Beyond WSIS (3rd online version)," *http://www.itu.int/wisr* 51.

4. Ibid., 15–16.

5. Ibid., 21.

6. Bernama, 30 June 2005, *http://www.bernama.com.my/bernama/v3/news.php?id=142572.*

7. International Telecommunications Union/United Nations Conference on Trade and Development (ITU/UNCTAD), "Beyond WSIS." 44.

8. Ibid., 43. Table uses *CIA World Factbook 2007, http:/www.cia.gov.*

9. Ibid., 46.

10. Ibid., 47.

11. Madar Research produced an index of information technology use in relation to the Middle East, which offered insight into regional access issues. Mardar Research, *http://www.madarresearch.com.*

12. Khaleejtimes.com, "UAE Hotspotters Are Busiest in Region," 1 July 2005, *http://www.khaleejtimes.com/DisplayArticle.asp?xfile=data/business/2005/July/business_July11.xml&section=business&col=.*

13. Middle East Online, "ADSL in Iran," *http://www.middle-east-online.com/english/?id=8451.* Pars Online was a significant investor; see Pars Online, *http://www.parsonline.com.*

14. Reuters/New York Times, "Pakistan Internet Link Repairs to Take Three Days," 28 June 2005, *http://www.nytimes.com/reuters/technology/tech-telecoms-pakistan.html?.*

15. Rhett A. Butler, "Cell Phones May Help 'Save' Africa," 11 July 2005, *http://news.mongabay.com/2005/0712-rhett_butler.html.*

16. Joseph Winter (BBC News), "Telecoms Thriving in Lawless Somalia," 19 November 2004, *http://news.bbc.co.uk/1/hi/world/africa/4020259.stm.*

17. YouTube, "Somalia Hamiti Song," *http://www.youtube.com/watch?v=Ntovuuc Xw9U.*

18. Albawaba.com, "Yemen's Internet Market Registers High Growth Rates," 14 March 2006, *http://www.albawaba.com/en/countries/Yemen/195789.*

19. ITP, "Against All Odds," 2 April 2006, *http://www.itp.net/features/print.php?id=4104&prodid=&category=.*

20. "Iraqis Making Connection to the Outside World Online," *USA Today*, 5 January 2006, *http://www.usatoday.com/news/world/iraq/2006-01-05-iraq-Internet_x.htm?csp=34.* Also see "Slow Going for Linux in Iraq," *Wired*, 30 May 2004, *http://www.wired.com/news/print/0,1294,63638,00.html.*

21. "At Last, Iraq Finds a Web Designation," *Boston Globe*, 24 November 2005, *http://www.boston.com/news/world/middleeast/articles/2005/11/24/at_last_iraq_finds_a_web_designation?mode=PF.*

22. Marcaria.com, "Iraq Domain Registration .IQ FAQ," *http://www.marcaria.com/Iraq/Domains/domain-registration-iq-iraq.htm.*

23. Laila El-Haddad (Al-Jazeera), "Intifada Spurs Palestine Internet Boom," 11 December 2003, *http://english.aljazeera.net/NR/exeres/3707F879-1FB0-41BD-A C75-AF49B2F9F87A.htm*. El-Haddad's blog is discussed elsewhere in this book. Also see the related article on cell phones by Jehad al-Iweiwi, "Letters from Palestine: Cell Phones, Cyber-Dating, and 'Explosions of the Heart,'" Muslim WakeUp, *http://www.muslimwakeup.com/main/archives/2003/09/letters_from_pa_3.php*.

24. Internet World Stats, "Middle East Usage Stats (Based on International Telecommunications Union Statistics) September 2006," *http://www.Internetworld stats.com/middle.htm*. Also see AP/Wired News, "Palestinians Surf during Siege," 18 November 2003, *http://wired.com/news/culture/0,1284,61274-2,00. html?tw=wn_story_page_next1*.

25. Mardar Research Group, cited in ITP, "Middle East PC Penetration Still Low," 23 January 2006, *http://www.itp.net/news/details.php?id=19348&category=*.

26. One Laptop Per Child, *http://laptop.org/*; One Laptop Per Child Wiki, *http://wiki.laptop.org/wiki/One_Laptop_per_Child*.

27. AFP/Asharq Alawsat, "Arabs Lag behind in Digital Revolution," 9 March 2006, *http://www.asharqalawsat.com/english/news.asp?section=4&id=4084*.

28. Ibid.

29. Ubuntu offered an Arabic product but no Arabic support in 2006; see Ubuntu, *http://www.ubuntu.com*; and Ubuntu Muslim Edition 8.04.1, 9 September 2008, *http://ubuntume.com*. The following page updates on Ubuntu translations in various languages: Launchpad, "Translations of the Dapper Drake in Rosetta," *https://launchpad.net/distros/ubuntu/dapper/+translations*.

30. For an example of an Arabic Linux-centered project, see Arabeyes, *http://www.arabeyes.org*.

31. See Arabeyes, "Handbook," *http://www.arabeyes.org/download/documents/handbook/handbook-en/*.

32. See Handasa Arabia, *http://www.handasarabia.org/*; discussed in Waleed al-Shobakky (Islam Online), "Young Arab Engineers: Against All Odds," 1 February 2005, *http://www.islam-online.net/English/Science/2005/02/article01.shtml*.

33. Alaa, "Egyptian Linux Advocates' Replies," *Slashdot*, 12 May 2004, *http://interviews.slashdot.org/interviews/04/05/13/1346237.shtml?tid=106&tid=126&tid=185&tid= 190*.

34. Asian American Net, "Central Asia," *http://www.asian american.net/central asia.html*. For a useful portal on African-language encoding, see A12N Gateway, "A12N," 17 September 2007, *http://www.bisharat.net/A12N/*.

35. A number of online networks associated with Amazigh include an online forum, Amazigh.net, and the AmazighOnline website, which claims to be a portal to the Amazigh world. See Amazigh.net, *http://groups.yahoo.com/group/amazigh-net/*; and AmazighOnline, *http://www.amazighonline.com/*.

36. Mumineen.org, "TechBlog," 9 October 2007, *http://blog.mumineen.org*.

37. Multilingual Internet Names Consortium, *http://www.minc.org/*. Also see Jonathan Wright (Reuters/The Age), "Fully Arabised Net Has Some Way to Go,"

28 May 2004, *http://www.theage.com.au/articles/2004/05/27/1085461890581. html.*

38. See Guided Ways, "Free Islamic Softwares," *http://www.guidedways.com/all downloads.php,* for a representative selection of Islamic applications.

39. See Gary R. Bunt, " 'Rip. Burn. Pray': Islamic Expression Online," in *Religion Online: Finding Faith on the Internet,* ed. Douglas E. Cowan and Lorne L. Dawson (New York: Routledge, 2004), which contains an early discussion on this subject. One example of an "Islamic" cell phone is manufactured by Ilkone Asia, *http://www.ilkonetel.com/.* A selection of related products can be found in numerous online stores, such as Islamic Digitals, 18 September 2007, *http:// www.islamicdigitals.com.*

40. Vít Sisler, "In Videogames You Shoot Arabs or Aliens—Interview with Radwan Kasmiya," *Umelec/International* 10, no. 1 (2006): 77–81, *http://uisk.jinonice. cuni.cz/sisler/publications/Arabs_or_Aliens.rtf.* This is an interview with the director of Afkar Media: *http://afkarmedia.com.*

41. Islamic Games and Quizzes, 16 September 2007, *http://www.geocities.com/mut mainaa/quiz/quiz_game.html.* The "Shoot the Idol" game was included in Rashid Games 2.0, e-Islamic Software.

42. "All-Too-Familiar Tune: Ringtones in Mosques," *Arab News,* 27 March 2006, *http://www.arabnews.com/?page=1&section=0&article=79806&d=27&m=3&y =2006.*

43. Jonathan Freedland, "As a Reformed Addict, I Can Now See the Full Menace of a BlackBerry Habit," *Guardian* (London), 22 August 2007, *http://media.guard ian.co.uk/newmedia/comment/0,,2153801,00.html.*

44. "In the Middle East It's All Talk All the Time," *Arab News,* 28 February 2006, *http://www.arabnews.com/?page=11&section=0&article=78499&d=3&m=3&y =2006.*

45. Dawn, "Camera Cell Phones Termed Un-Islamic," 30 September 2004, *http:// www.dawn.com/2004/09/30/int15.htm.*

46. NapaNews.com, "Prayers, Shopping, and Modern Worries Mark Ramadan in Saudi Arabia," 6 November 2003, *http://www.napanews.com/templates/index. cfm?template=story_full&id=6FECA5E8-6B9C-4CE2-9C68-06E05AD96DE1.*

47. Al-Arabiyya, "Egyptians Spend $2 million on Ramadan SMSes," 24 September 2007, *http://www.alarabiya.net/articles/2007/09/24/39499.html.*

48. CNN, "Bluetooth Helps Saudis Break Taboos," 12 August 2005, *http://edition. cnn.com/2005/WORLD/meast/08/12/saudi.bluetooth.ap/index.html.*

49. Reuters AlertNet, "Saudi Arabia Takes First Steps on Path to Reform," 2 February 2006, *http://www.alertnet.org/thenews/newsdesk/L25384626.htm.*

50. "Teenagers Sinking Their Teeth into New Technology," *Arab News,* 10 February 2005, *http://www.arabnews.com/?page=1&section=0&article=58778&d=10 &m=2&y=2005.*

51. Asharq al-Alawsat, "Interview with Saudi Council of Senior Ulama Member Sheikh Abdullah Al Manee," 23 March 2006, *http://aawsat.com/english/news. asp?section=3&id=4254.*

52. Asharq al-Alawsat, "Bluetooth Increases Interaction of the Sexes in Saudi Arabia," 1 December 2005, *http://aawsat.com/english/news.asp?section=7&id=2896.*

53. Turki al-Saheil, "Saudi Religious Police Embrace Bluetooth Technology," *Asharq Al-Alawsat,* 17 September 2007, *http://www.asharq-e.com/news.asp?section=1&id=10235.*

54. ITP.net, "Riyadh Online for Digital City Status," 20 November 2005, *http://www.itp.net/news/details.php?id=18756&category=.*

55. Amira Agarib, quoting engineer Hala Hessian, in Khaleejtimes.com, "Majority of UAE Youth Addicted to the Internet," 14 January 2006, *http://www.khaleejtimes.com/DisplayArticle.asp?xfile=data/theuae/2006/January/theuae_January293.xml&section=theuae.*

56. "Google Earth Raises Privacy, Security Issues," *Arab News,* 27 March 2006, *http://www.arabnews.com/?page=1&section=0&article=79805&d=27&m=3&y=2006.*

57. ABC News/The Blotter, "Al Qaeda-Linked Group Used Google Earth to Plan Attack," 22 January 2007, *http://blogs.abcnews.com/theblotter/2007/01/al_qaedalinked_.html.*

58. V-girl, *http://www.v-girl.com/.*

59. "Sad, Lonely? For a Good Time, Call Vivienne*," *New York Times,* 24 February 2005, *http://www.nytimes.com/2005/02/24/technology/24girlfriend.html?ei=5088&en=da787b4f2249875c&ex=1267419600&partner=rssnyt&pagewanted=print&position=.* The Malaysian version is at V-girl Malaysian Version, *http://www.v-girl.com/hotlink/,* with few discernable differences at the time of writing. No male equivalent was available.

60. Khaleejtimes.com, "Dubai to Have PC Assembling Plant," 21 March 2006, *http://www.khaleejtimes.com/DisplayArticle.asp?xfile=data/business/2006/March/business_March409.xml&section=business&col=.*

61. AP/USA Today, "Intel to Open Technology Center in Gaza," 20 February 2006, *http://www.usatoday.com/tech/news/2006-02-20-intel-gaza_x.htm?csp=34s;* "Gaza Islamic University Gets Intel's IT Center of Excellence Award," *Arab News,* 15 November 2005, *http://www.arabnews.com/?page=11&section=0&article=73192&d=15&m=11&y=2005.*

62. Dubai Internet City, *http://www.dubaiInternetcity.com*; Khaleejtimes.com, "Dubai Internet City to Go Global," 5 October 2004, *http://www.khaleejtimes.com/DisplayArticle.asp?xfile=data/business/2004/October/business_October121.xml&section=business&col=.*

63. "Region's First e-Govt Solution Center Launched," *Arab News,* 17 May 2005, *http://www.arabnews.com/?page=11&section=0&article=63902&d=18&m=5&y=2005.*

64. Araby, *http://araby.com/.* On Sawafi, see "Arab-Centric Internet Portal to Be Launched This Year," *Arab News,* 28 April 2006, *http://www.arabnews.com/?page=1&section=0&article=81410&d=28&m=4&y=2006;* Ajeeb, *http://ajeeb.com*; Ayna, *http://ayna.com*; and Naseej, *http://www.naseej.com.*

65. Anna Piela-Ziolko, "Muslim Women's Online Communities" (Ph.D. diss. in preparation, University of York, 2006–).

66. "Project Launched to Extend Arabic Linguistic Research," *Arab News*, 13 October 2006, *http://www.arabnews.com/?page=4&section=0&article=88123&d=13 &m=10&y=2006&pix=world.jpg&category=World*.

67. For a discussion on reactions to *The Satanic Verses* in the UK, see David G. Bowen, ed., *The Satanic Verses: Bradford Responds* (Ilkley: Bradford & Ilkley Community College, 1992). Also see Malise Ruthven, *A Satanic Affair: Salman Rushdie and the Rage of Islam* (London: Chatto & Windus, 1990).

68. Dale F. Eickelman, "Communication and Control in the Middle East: Publication and Its Discontents," in *New Media in the Muslim World*, ed. Dale F. Eickelman and Jon W. Anderson (Bloomington and Indianapolis: Indiana University Press, 2003), 33.

69. AP/Boston Globe, "Kuwaiti Government Mounts an Offensive against Militants," 12 February 2005, *http://www.boston.com/news/world/middleeast/ar ticles/2005/02/12/kuwaiti_government_mounts_an_offensive_against_ militants/*.

70. AME Info, "Bahrain Arrests over Banned Site," 9 March 2005, *http://feeds.big news network.com/redir.php?jid=2ec092abedeb2532&cat=48fcf33f9aeb6130*.

71. AP, "Saudi Cleric's Followers Face Charges," 31 May 2003.

72. Dar al-Hayat, "Young Saudis Volunteer to Preach in 'Modern' Way," 27 May 2003, *http://english.daralhayat.com*.

73. NewsForge, "Meet Saudi Arabia's Most Famous Computer Expert," 14 January 2004, *http://www.newsforge.com/Internet/04/01/12/2147220.shtml?tid= 100&tid=49&tid=96*.

74. Reporters Sans Frontieres, "Saudi Arabia," *http://www.rsf.org/article.php3?id_ article=10766*; Jonathan Zittrain and Benjamin Edelman, "Documentation of Internet Filtering in Saudi Arabia," 2002, *http://cyber.law.harvard.edu/filter ing/saudiarabia*.

75. AP/Jerusalem Post, "Islamic Jihad: Pentagon Blocked Our Web Sites," 21 December 2004, *http://www.jpost.com*. These sites were hosted by an Ukranian ISP.

76. IRNA, "University Official: Most Iranian Internet Sites under U.S. Supervision," 22 December 2005, *http://www.irna.ir/en/news/view/line-18/05122276380031 59.htm*.

77. Committee to Protect Bloggers, *http://committeetoprotectbloggers.civiblog.org/ blog*.

78. Amnesty International, "Irrepressible," *http://irrepressible.info*.

79. Reporters Without Borders Handbook, Paris, 2005, *http://www.rsf.org/rubrique. php3?id_rubrique=542*.

80. Human Rights Watch. "The Internet in the Middle East and North Africa: Free Expression and Censorship." *http://hrw.org/advocacy/Internet/mena/*; Gary R. Bunt, *Islam in the Digital Age: E-Jihad, Online Fatwas, and Cyber Islamic Environments* (London and Ann Arbor, Mich.: Pluto Press, 2003).

81. Mohammad Ali Abtahi, "Webnevesht," 4 October 2004, *http://www.webneve sht.com/en/* (discussed in the blogging chapter of this book).

82. BBC News, "Iran Blocks BBC Persian Website," 24 January 2006, *http://news. bbc.co.uk/2/hi/middle_east/4644398.stm*.

83. International Quranic Blogging Festival, *http://207.176.218.26/quran/festival/ english/s*.

84. International Quranic Blogging Festival, "Quranic Blogging Festival Attracts Interest in Blogging," 25 February 2006, *http://207.176.218.26/quran/festival/ english/news/000121.html*.

85. CNET News.com, "Cuba, Iran Lash out at Internet Freedom," 18 November 2005, *http://news.com.com/Cuba,+Iran+lash+out+at+Internet+freedom/2100- 1028_3-5960298.html*.

86. Editor: Myself, "Blogosphere Attacked," 13 August 2005, *http://hoder.com/we blog/archives/014409.shtml*.

87. BBC News, "Iranian Bloggers Rally against Censorship," *http://news.bbc.co.uk/ 1/hi/technology/3310493.stm*.

88. Human Rights Watch, "Libya: Web Writer's Arrest Stifles Debate," 17 August 2005, *http://hrw.org/english/docs/2005/08/16/libya11634.htm*; Akhbar-Libya, *http://www.akhbar-libya.com*; Human Rights Watch, "Cyberdissident Abdel Razak Al Mansuri Released," 7 March 2006, *http://www.rsf.org/article.php3? id_article=16156*.

89. Reporters Without Borders, "Opposition Journalist Daif Al Ghazal Tortured to Death," 6 June 2006, *http://www.rsf.org/article.php3?id_article=14012*. Reporters Without Borders continued to log significant international cases and presented information in Arabic, Persian, Chinese, Spanish, French, and English. It also produced Reporters Without Borders, "A Handbook for Bloggers and Cyber Dissidents," *http://www.rsf.org/rubrique.php3?id_rubrique=542*.

90. Islam Online, "Tunisian Opposition Urges Election Boycott," 4 October 2004, *http://www.islam-online.net/English/News/2004-09/30/article06.shtml*.

91. Reporters Sans Frontieres, "Tunisia," 14 December 2004, *http://www.rsf.org/ article.php3?id_article=12080*.

92. "Tunisia: Behind the Western Mask," *International Herald Tribune*, 23 November 2004, *http://www.iht.com/articles/2004/11/18/opinion/edhroub.html*.

93. Bureau of Democracy, U.S. Department of State, Human Rights, and Labor, "Country Reports on Human Rights Practices," 25 February 2004, *http://www. state.gov/g/drl/rls/hrrpt/2003/27939.htm*.

94. A Meta Blog on Arab Blogs, "In the Arab World, a Blog Can Mean Prison," 22 February 2006, *http://arabblogandpoliticalcommunication.blogspot.com/ 2006/02/in-arab-world-blog-can-mean-prison.html*.

95. See the campaigning website Peacefire, *http://www.peacefire.org*; and Anonymizer, *http://anonymizer.com*, which has a specific toolbar application for anonymity.

96. Monsters and Critics, "Pakistan Government Urged to Monitor Anti-Islamic Websites," 3 July 2005, *http://news.monstersandcritics.com/mediamonitor/arti cle_1029188.php/Pakistan_government_urged_to_monitor_anti-Islamic*

_websites; citing BBC Monitoring, "Translation of Ausaf, Islamabad, in Urdu, pp. 8, 6," 3 July 2005, *http://www.monitor.bbc.co.uk.*

97. Human Events Online, "Iranian Women Provide Catalyst for Change," 20 December 2005, *http://www.humaneventsonline.com/article.php?id=11017.*

98. Middle East Online, "Syria's Cyber Rebels Outfox Government," 14 March 2006, *http://www.middle-east-online.com/english/?id=15985.*

99. Free Internet Press, "Syria's Assad: 'Tech and Media Crush Arabs' Identity,'" 6 June 2005, *http://freeInternetpress.com/modules.php?name=News&file=article&sid=3780.*

100. BBC News, "Pakistan Blocks Blogs on Cartoons," 3 March 2006, *http://news.bbc.co.uk/1/hi/world/south_asia/4771846.stm.*

Chapter Three

1. Annemarie Schimmel, *Deciphering the Signs of God: A Phenomenological Approach to Islam* (Edinburgh: Edinburgh University Press, 1994).

2. John Renard, *Seven Doors to Islam: Spirituality and the Religious Life of Muslims* (Berkeley and London: University of California Press, 1996); John Renard, *Windows on the House of Islam: Muslim Sources on Spirituality and Religious Life* (Berkeley and London: University of California Press, 1998).

3. For example, see Ninian Smart, *The World's Religions* (Englewood Cliffs, N.J.: Prentice Hall, 1989), 9–20.

4. "Qur'anic Ringtones Haram," *Arab News*, 9 November 2007, *http://www.arabnews.com.*

5. *Sura al-A'raf* (The Heights), 7:204, in *The Qur'an*, trans. M. A. S. Abdel Haleem (Oxford and New York: Oxford University Press, 2004).

6. Gary R. Bunt, *Virtually Islamic: Computer-Mediated Communication and Cyber Islamic Environments* (Cardiff: University of Wales Press, 2000).

7. Jon W. Anderson, "Wiring Up: The Internet Difference for Muslim Networks," in *Muslim Networks from Hajj to Hip Hop*, ed. miriam cooke and Bruce B. Lawrence (Chapel Hill: University of North Carolina Press, 2005).

8. For an early discussion on the issue of CD-ROMs in Islamic contexts, see Ziauddin Sardar, "Paper, Printing, and Compact Discs: The Making and Unmaking of Islamic Culture," in *Islam, Postmodernism, and Other Futures: A Ziauddin Sardar Reader*, ed. Sohail Inayatullah and Gail Boxwell (London: Pluto Press, 2003).

9. IslamiCity, 13 September 2007, *http://www.islamicity.com.*

10. Endowments Saudi Arabian Ministry of Islamic Affairs, Da'wah and Guidance, "Islam—Resources and Information," *http://www.al-islam.com/eng/*; King Fahd Complex for the Printing of the Holy Qur'an, 26 July 2004, *http://www.qurancomplex.org*; Harf Information Technology, "The Holy Qur'an," *http://www.harf.com.*

11. Al-Islam, "Multilingual Qur'an," 4 September 2005, *http://www.al-islam.org/Qur'an.*

12. Muhammad B. Ismail al-Bukhari, "Book 61, Number 545," in *Translation of*

Sahih Bukhari, trans. M. Muhsin Khan (USC-MSA Compendium of Muslim Texts, n.d.), *http://usc.edu/dept/MSA.*

13. Ihsan Network, *http://www.ihsanetwork.org/ihsan-home1.asp?lang=e.*

14. Tradigital, "Index," 4 October 2004, *http://www.tradigital.de*; Islam Online, "Digitized Qur'an Masterpieces to Light Frankfurt Fair," 4 October 2004, *http://www.islamonline.net.*

15. Al-Azhar Library, "Index," 22 May 2005, *http://www.alazharonline.org/*; British Library, "Sacred," 27 April 2007, *http://www.bl.uk/sacred*. The Al-Azhar Library's URL registration for alazharonline.org was subsequently acquired by a commercial company, and the library website had not been replaced by al-Azhar at the time of this writing.

16. The Islamic Manuscript: Conservation, Cataloguing, Accessibility, Copyright and Digitization, organized by the Thesaurus Islamicus Foundation (TIF) and the Center for Middle Eastern and Islamic Studies at the University of Cambridge, 2005; Ihsan Network, *http://www.ihsanetwork.org/conference.htm.*

17. "IslamiCity Gains Popularity," *Gulf News*, 11 September 2002, *http://www.gulfnews.com.*

18. Ayesha UmmAmahtullah, "My Niqab Story," *http://www.muhajabah.com/my_niqab_story/ayesha_umm.php.*

19. Opinion of Sheikh Ahmad Kutty, "Giving the Shahadah through the Internet," 10 October 2004, *http://www.islamonline.net/servlet/Satellite?pagename=IslamOnline-English-Ask_Scholar/FatwaE/FatwaE&cid=1119503545282.*

20. MuslimConverts.com, "Shahadah," 8 September 2005, *http://muslimconverts.com/shahadah/converting.htm.*

21. Guided Ways, "Free Islamic Softwares," *http://www.guidedways.com/alldownloads.php.*

22. For examples, see Domain of Islam, "Perform Salah/Namaz Correctly by Maulana Muhammad Taqi Usmani," 3 September 2005, *http://www.darulislam.info/content-3.html*; Teach Me Salaat, "Teach Me Salaat Guide," 8 September 2005, *http://www.geocities.com/teachmesalaat.*

23. MuslimConverts.com, "How to Pray," 1 September 2005, *http://muslimconverts.com/prayer/how_to_pray.htm.*

24. When Hurricane Katrina had devastated New Orleans, one of MuslimConverts's readers, evacuated from the city, posted a message requesting how to pray without a mat (or the usual facilities) in an insecure setting; see Muslimconverts.com, "Guidance on prayer," 1 September 2005, *http://groups.yahoo.com/group/muslimconverts/message/1167.*

25. Ahmad al-Megren, "Prophet Mohammad's Manner of Doing Prayer by His Eminence Sheikh Abdul Aziz Ibn Baz," 4 September 2005, *http://www.jannah.com/learn/flashprayer1.html.*

26. Bunt, *Virtually Islamic*, 35, 55, 114.

27. Newsweek/MSNBC, "What Sistani Wants," 6 February 2005, *http://msnbc.msn.com/id/6920681/site/newsweek/.*

28. Sistani.org, "Simplified Islamic Laws for Youth and Young Adults," *http://www.*

sistani.org/html/eng/menu/miscellaneous/simplified_islamic_laws/?lang= eng.

29. Ibid., *http://www.sistani.org/html/eng/main/index.php?page=3&lang=eng& part=3.*

30. See F. E. Peters, *The Hajj: The Muslim Pilgrimage to Mecca and the Holy Places* (Princeton, N.J.: Princeton University Press, 1994); and Dale F. Eickelman and James P. Piscatori, *Muslim Travellers: Pilgrimage, Migration, and the Religious Imagination* (London: Routledge, 1990).

31. For example, see Umra & Hajj Packages, 10 October 2004, *http://www.umrah tohajj.com*; 21st Century Haj & Umra Services, "Index," 10 October 2004, *http:// www.haj-umra.co.uk.*

32. Islamicity, "Hajj," 20 October 2003, *http://www.islamicity.com/travel/hajj/.*

33. Islamic Gateway, "Hajj and Eid al-Adha," 15 August 2001, *http://www.ummah. net/hajj.*

34. For example, see Qurbani.com, 9 October 2007, *http://www.qurbani.com.*

35. The 3D Kabah Website, "Index," 26 June 2006, *http://www.3dkabah.co.uk.*

36. Awsat al-Islam, "Documentary of Hajj-e-Baitullah," 19 August 2003, *http:// www.aswatalislam.net/DisplayFilesP.aspx?TitleID=50014&TitleName=Hajj,_ Mecca_and_Madina.*

37. Channel 4, "The Hajj," October 22, 2003, *http://www.channel4.com/life/micro sites/H/hajj.*

38. Channel 4, "Our Pilgrims: Live at the Hajj," October 22, 2003, *http://www.chan nell4.com/life/microsites/H/hajj/genb_pilgrims.html* Hijri Calendar, "Index," 20 October 2003, *http://members.aol.com/hmotiwala/.*

39. Islamfrominside.com, "Going around the Kaaba," 7 September 2005, *http:// www.islamfrominside.com/Pages/Articles/AroundtheKabba.html.*

40. AP/Wired News, "A Fitful Relationship with Tech," 17 January 2005, *http:// www.wired.com/news/culture/0,1284,66305,00.html.*

41. Other examples of *hajj* accounts can be found in Gary R. Bunt, "Surfing Islam: Ayatollahs, Shayks, and Hajjis on the Superhighway," in *Religion on the Internet: Research Prospects and Promises*, ed. Jeffrey K. Hadden and Douglas E. Cowan (New York: Elsevier Science, 2000), 127–52.

42. CNN, "Zain Verjee: My Hajj Experience," 25 January 2005, *http://edition.cnn. com/2005/WORLD/meast/01/19/hajj.diary/.*

43. Mohammed Jamjoom, "Blogging by SMS," 3 January 2007, *http://cnn.com.*

44. Islamiblog, 10 September 2005, *http://islamiblog.blogspot.com/2005_01_01_ islamiblog_archive.html.*

45. Crescent Watch, 12 October 2007, *http://www.crescentwatch.org.*

46. Zaytuna Institute, "Podcasts," 10 December 2006, *http://www.zaytuna.org/pod cast.asp.*

47. For example, see Rafed.net, "Islamic Occasions," 10 September 2005, *http:// rafed.net/card/islamic-occasions/index.html.*

48. Al-Islam.org, "Ramadhan," 9 September 2005, *http://www.al-islam.org/help/ ramadhan.*

49. Radioummah.com, "Marriage Show," 8 September 2005, *http://www.radioum mah.com/marriageshow/*.

50. Radio Ramadhan Glasgow 87.7 FM, "Marriage Podcasts," 29 September 2006, *http://www.radioramadhan.org.uk/*; Radio Ramadhan Glasgow 87.7 FM, "The Choudreys," 28 September 2007, *http://www.radioramadhan.org.uk/*.

51. RamadhanZone, 27 September 2007, *http://www.ramadhanzone.com*; Islamic Relief, "Hilal," 27 September 2007, *http://islamic-relief/hilal*.

52. Islamicity, "Zakat Calculator," 2 July 2004, *http://www.islamicity.com/mosque/ Zakat/Zakat_calculator.shtml*. Similar services are available; for example, see Banktree, "Index," *http://www.islam.banktree.co.uk/*.

53. Ismaili Web, "Milad-e Nabi—Milad-un Nabi—Maulid—Prophet Muhammad's Birthday," 6 September 2005, *http://www.amaana.org/prophet/milad.htm*.

54. John L. Esposito, *The Oxford Encyclopedia of the Modern Islamic World*, 4 vols. (New York, Oxford: Oxford University Press, 1995).

55. Mumineen.org, "Ahl ul-Kisaa," 6 September 2005, *http://archive.mumineen.org/ awliya/#wasi*. Also see Jonah Blank, *Mullahs on the Mainframe: Islam and Modernity among the Daudi Bohras* (Chicago and London: University of Chicago Press, 2001); and Gary R. Bunt, *Islam in the Digital Age: E-Jihad, Online Fatwas, and Cyber Islamic Environments* (London and Ann Arbor, Mich.: Pluto Press, 2003), 193.

56. Al-Imam, "Animations," 10 October 2003, *http://www.al-imam.net/clips.htm*. Also see Sabine Kalinock, "Going on Pilgrimage Online: The Representation of Shia Rituals on the Internet," *Online—Heidelberg Journal of Religions on the Internet: Special Issue on Rituals on the Internet* 2, no. 1 (2006), *http:// www.ub.uni-heidelberg.de/archiv/6954*.

57. Nation of Islam, "It's Saviours' Day," 25 February 2005, *http://www.finalcall. com/artman/publish/article_1830.shtml*.

58. For example, see Jerusalemites, "Index," *http://www.jerusalemites.org*; and Palestinian Information Center, "Index," 21 September 2005, *http://www.palestine-info.co.uk/am/publish/aqsq_mosque_0.shtml*.

59. Palestine Ministry of Waqfs, "Al-Aqsa Book," 10 July 2003, *http://www.palwakf. org/aqsa_book.pdf*.

60. Al-Islam, "History of Mashad," 4 February 2005, *http://www.al-islam.org/ shrines/mashad.htm*.

61. Archnet, "Religious Collection," 6 September 2005, *http://archnet.org/library/ images/sites.tcl?key=religious&collection_id=23&select=type*.

62. "Damascus," Wikipedia, 6 September 2005, *http://en.wikipedia.org/wiki/Da mascus*.

63. ImpianaSoft, "myName 3.0," 7 September 2005, *http://www.21stcenturymuslim. com/myname/*.

64. Muslim Names, "Index," 7 September 2005, *http://www.muslim-names.co.uk*. There are several other examples of sites providing Muslim baby names; for example, see OurBangla.com, "Islamic Baby Names," 7 September 2005, *http:// www.ourbangla.com/islam/babyname/default.asp*.

65. Muslim Names, "Islam Q&A [www.islam-qa.com], Question & Answers on Circumcision," 24 August 2005, *http://www.muslim-names.co.uk/circum.php.*

66. Sunni Path, 7 September 2005, *http://www.sunnipath.com/resources/Ques tions/qa00000231.aspx.*

67. UPI, "Devout Pakistanis Use Internet to Marry," 8 July 2004, *http://www.upi.com.*

68. "Iranian Cleric Makes Wedding Dreams Come True," *China Daily*, 25 December 2003, *http://www1.chinadaily.com.cn/en/doc/2003-12/25/content_29 3370.htm*; "Marriages Made Not in Heaven but in a Cleric's Office," *New York Times*, 11 November 2003, *http://www.nytimes.com.*

69. BBC News, "Iranians Arrested for Net Dating," 3 March 2003, *http://news.bbc.co.uk.*

70. "For Muslims, Courtship Enabled by the Internet," *Washington Post*, 6 June 2004, *http://www.washingtonpost.com.*

71. Muslim Match, 5 September 2005, *http://muslimmatch.com.*

72. SpeedIntros, "Index," *http://www.speedintros.com/index.php.*

73. Muslim Match, "Ismail and Khadija," February 2004, *http://muslimmatch.com/success_main.php.*

74. Muslim Match, "10 Qualities to Seek in a Partner (Umm Yunus)," 5 September 2005, *http://muslimmatch.com/articles_10tips.php.*

75. Masud.co.uk, "Al-Albani Unveiled: An Exposition of His Errors and Other Important Issues Compiled by Sayf ad-Din Ahmed ibn Muhammad," 6 September 2005, *http://www.masud.co.uk/ISLAM/misc/albintro.htm.* See also Bunt, *Islam in the Digital Age*, 142.

76. Zawaj, "Triple Divorce," 6 September 2005, *http://zawaj.com/articles/triple_divorce.html.*

77. Mehndi, "Index," 6 September 2005, *http://mehndi.com*; Shaadi Online, 6 September 2005, *http://www.singles-bar.com/shadi-ghar.asp.*

78. Newsweek/MSNBC, "Serious Muslim Seeks Spouse—Online," 6 February 2004, *http://www.msnbc.msn.com.*

79. Ibid.

80. Examples drawn from Shia Match, "Success," 9 September 2005, *http://shiamatch.com/success.html.*

81. "Mosques Urged to Help Malays Find Love," Straits Times, May 13, 2004, *http://straitstimes.asia1.com.sg/asia/story/0,4386,250667,00.html.*

82. The Peninsula On-line, "Lucknow Bride Says 'I Accept' Online," 25 April 2005, *http://www.thepeninsulaqatar.com.*

83. Walid Phares, "Valentine's Day Enrages Jihadists," *http://www.frontpagemagazine.com.*

84. Alt.muslim, "Indian Muslims Consider a Divorce from 'Triple Talaq,'" 19 July 2004, *http://www.altmuslim.com.*

85. "Now, Man Calls Triple Talaq over E-mail," Press Trust of India/WorldWide Religious News, 1 November 2004, *http://wwrn.org.*

86. AFP/TechCentral, "Fated: Budding Cyberlove Ends in Divorce," 8 February 2005, *http://star-techcentral.com/tech/story.asp?file=/2005/2/8/technology/1 0121275&sec=technology.*

87. "Muslim Girl Flees London to Wed Her Internet Hindu," *Times Online* (London), 16 September 2006, *http://www.timesonline.co.uk/article/0,,25689-2359903,00.html*.

88. "Qatar Battles Porn Channels, Sites by Islamic-Style Sex Education," *Arab News*, 17 March 2005, *http:/www.arabnews.com*.

89. Haaretz, "Does Allah Permit Thoughts of Sex?," 16 July 2004, *http://www.haaretz.com/hasen/spages/451281.html*.

90. Muslim WakeUp, "Lustrous Companions," 9 April 2004, *http://www.muslimwakeup.com/sex/archives/2004/04/lustrous_compan.php#more*.

91. Ahmed W, "Muslim WakeUp: Comments," 12 April 2004, *http://www.muslimwakeup.com/movabletype3/mt-comments.cgi?entry_id=2405*.

92. Mohja Kahf, "Wedad's Cavalry," 10 April 2005, *http://www.muslimwakeup.com/sex/archives/2005/04/wedads_cavalry_1.php*.

93. Yakoub Islam, "Dissident Sexualities: Muslim and Gay in the UK," 29 December 2004, *http://www.muslimwakeup.com/sex/archives/2004/12/dissident_voice.php*.

94. See Gary R. Bunt, "Mediterranean Islamic Expression on the World Wide Web," in *Islam and the Shaping of the Current Islamic Reformation*, ed. Barbara Allen Roberson (London and Portland, Ore.: Frank Cass & Co., 2003), 164–86.

95. Al-Fatiha, "Al-Fatiha Foundation," *http://www.al-fatiha.net*.

96. Brian Whitaker, "Distorting Desire," *http://www.al-bab.com/arab/articles/text/massad.htm*.

97. Bunt, "Mediterranean Islamic Expression on the World Wide Web"; Queer Jihad, *http://www.well.com/user/queerjhd/*.

98. Irshad Manij, "Muslim Refusenik," 17 June 2005, *http://www.muslim-refusenik.com/ijtihad.html*.

99. Parvez Sharma, *A Jihad for Love* (2007). Also see *New York Times*/RelishNow, "Director of Film on Muslim Homosexuals Frets over His Subjects' Safety," *http://www.journalnow.com/servlet/Satellite?pagename=WSJ%2FMGArticle%2FWSJ_RelishArticle&c=MGArticle&cid=1031779429996&path=%21entertainment%21general&s=1037645508970*.

100. For examples, see Salaam, "Index," 4 September 2003, *http://www.salaam.co.uk/index1.html*.

101. World Federation of Khoja Shia Ithna'asheri Muslim Communities, "News of Death," 26 June 2006, *http://www.world-federation.org/NewsOfDeath*.

102. Shia Ithna'ashari Community of Middlesex, "Cemetery," 26 June 2006, *http://www.sicm.org.uk/index.php?page=cemetery*.

103. Wadi-a-Hussain Cemetery, "About Us," 26 June 2006, *http://www.wadi-a-hussain.com/about.htm*.

104. Wadi-a-Hussain Cemetery, "Services," 26 June 2006, *http://www.wadi-a-hussain.com/services.htm*.

105. Also see Bunt, *Virtually Islamic*, 98–99; and Bunt, *Islam in the Digital Age*, 106–8.

106. Mass Graves, *http://massgraves.info/*.

107. Iraq Body Count, *http://www.iraqbodycount.net/*.

108. Bunt, *Islam in the Digital Age*, 135–204.

109. Manij, "Muslim Refusenik"; Muslim WakeUp, "Index," *http://www.muslimwake up.com.*

110. "In Saudi Arabia, Balancing Act Challenged by Terrorists," *Seattle Times*, 9 June 2004, *http://seattletimes.nwsource.com/html/nationworld/2001951762_saudi rule09.html.*

111. Al-Jazeera, "Muslim Scholars Move to Curb Fatwas," 7 July 2005, *http://en glish.aljazeera.net.* See the discussion in Ermete Mariani, "The Production of Islamic Knowledge on the Internet and the Role of States and Markets: The Examples of Yussef al-Qaradawi and Amru Khaled," in *Religious Communities on the Internet,* ed. Göran Larsson (Stockholm: Swedish Science Press, 2006), 131–49.

112. Dale F. Eickelman and James Piscatori, *Muslim Politics* (Princeton: Princeton University Press, 1996), 57.

113. Islamic Board, "Cyber Counselling," 10 January 2005, *http://www.islamicboard. com/cyber-counselling/.*

114. Qaradawi.net, "Yusuf al-Qaradawi," 10 January 2000, *http://www.qaradawi.net*; Sistani.org, "Grand Ayatollah Sistani," 13 October 2004, *http://www.sistani.org.*

115. Islam Online, "Live Fatwa," *http://www.islam-online.net.*

116. Mahmood's Den, "The Lesser of Two Evils," 10 February 2005, *http://www.mah mood.tv.*

117. "Preaching Violence," *Newsweek*, 30 September 2004, *http://www.msnbc.msn. com/id/6133403/site/newsweek/.*

118. Sheikh Ahmad Kuftaro, "Uniting the Human Family," 10 July 2004, *http://www. abunour.net.*

119. Dar al-Hayat, "Young Saudis Volunteer to Preach in 'Modern' Way," 27 May 2003, *http://english.daralhayat.com.*

120. Adnki.com, "Saudi Arabia: Clerics Who Justify Terrorism Face Trial," 7 July 2005, *http://www.adnki.com/index_2Level.php?cat=Religion&loid=8.0.184909 270&par=0.*

121. Anderson, "Wiring Up."

122. Sidi Muhammad Press, 8 October 2006, *http://www.sufimaster.org/.*

123. Bamba Islam-Al-Muridiyyah Official Home Page, 8 October 2006, *http://khid matulkhadim.org/Bamba.html*; Naqshbandi Sufi Way, "Index," 4 August 2003, *http://www.naqshbandi.org/chain/40.htm.*

124. Eickelman and Piscatori, *Muslim Politics*, 125.

125. "Televangelist Preaches Hip Islam," *Jerusalem Post*, 6 July 2005, *http://www. jpost.com.*

126. Amr Khaled, "An Evening of Reflection," *http://www.amrkhaled.net/articles/ articles541.html.*

127. "Saladin," March 2004, *http://www.egyptsearch.com/forums/Forum2/HTML/ 003414.html.* Original spellings retained.

128. Middle East Online, "Row between Khaled and Qaradawi on Denmark," 2 March 2006, *http://www.middle-east-online.com/english/?id=15883.*

129. AP/Sunspot.net, "2nd Saudi Cleric Rejects Violence in Name of Islam," 23 No-

vember 2003, *http://www.sunspot.net/news/nationworld/bal-te.forn23nov23,0,
2817121.story?coll=bal-nationworld-headlines*.

130. "Saudis Take Aim at Hateful Islamic Teachings," Knight Ridder Newspapers/
AZCentral, 5 December 2003, *http://www.azcentral.com/news/articles/1205
SaudiExtremism05-ON.html*.

131. "Spanish Muslims Issue Fatwa against Bin Laden," AFP/Arab News, 11 March
2005, *http://www.arabnews.com/?page=4&section=0&article=60274&d=11&m
=3&y=2005*.

132. Adnki.com, "Cleric Issues Fatwa against Female Pilot," 29 June 2005, *http://
www.adnki.com/index_2Level.php?cat=Religion&loid=8.0.181874245&par=0*.

133. Arabicnews.com, "Saudi Scholars: Al-Jihad Is a Duty in Iraq; A Call to Avoid
Sedition," 9 November 2004, *http://www.arabicnews.com/ansub/Daily/Day/
041108/2004110819.html*.

134. Albawaba.com, "Saudi Grand Mufti: 'Islam Has Nothing to Do with Terrorism,'" 27 January 2004, *http://www.albawaba.com/news/index.php3?sid=2690
64&lang=e&dir=news*.

135. Khaleejtimes.com, "Saudi Grand Mufti for Action against 'Unofficial' Fatwas,"
6 September 2005, *http://www.khaleejtimes.com*.

136. Ibid.

137. "If They Only Knew Islam's Simplicity," *Arab News*, 31 August 2005, *www.arab
news.com/?page=7&section=0&article=69330&d=31&m=8&y=2005*.

138. Alminbar.com, "Staff," *http://www.alminbar.com/staff.asp*.

139. Khutbah.com, *http://www.islamicinvitationcentre.com*. The main khutbah.com
URL was down in mid-2007. See also Islamicbookstore.com, "Accidental Reflections," *http://islamicbookstore.com/a4213.html*.

140. AlMaghrib in MEMPHIS, "Everyone's Sayin' Yyyyyeaaahhhh!!!," 26 April 2005,
http://forums.almaghrib.org/showthread.php?t=9592.

141. Eat Halal, 5 September 2005, *http://www.eat-halal.com/*.

142. Zabihah, "Index," 5 September 2005, *http://www.zabihah.com*.

143. BBC News, "Halal Site Guides Hungry Muslims," 17 December 2004, *http://
news.bbc.co.uk/1/hi/technology/4092947.stm*.

144. Zabihah, "Review by Elias al-Yafi of New Tayyab Restaurant, London, 11 April
2004," 5 September 2005, *http://www.zabihah.com/_details.php?rest_id=11 64*.

145. Zabihah, "Review by 'S' of New Tayyab Restaurant, London, 22 March 2004,"
5 September 2005, *http://www.zabihah.com/_details.php?rest_id=1164*.

146. There are numerous examples. See IKitab.com, "Index," *http://www.ikitab.com*;
Karbala Online, "Shop," *http://www.karbala.com/shop.htm*; Salsabeel, "Index,"
http://www.salsabeel.com/estore/home.php; and Talk Islam, "Index," *http://
store.talkislam.com*.

147. Bank Islam Malaysia Berhad, 10 May 2005, *http://www.bankislam.com.my*.

148. Sheikh Abd al-Wahhab al-Turayra, "Fatwa Department Research Committee;
Question: There Are Several Methods of Earning Income Online Now, and
Many People Are Profiting," *http://www.islamtoday.com/show_detail_sec
tion.cfm?q_id=1211&main_cat_id=5*.

149. "Muhammeds Ansigt," *Jyllands-Posten*, 30 September 2005, *http://www.jp.dk*.

150. Carl W. Ernst, *Following Muhammad: Rethinking Islam in the Contemporary World* (Chapel Hill: University of North Carolina Press, 2003), 184–85.

151. Bunt, *Virtually Islamic*, 123–30.

152. For a discussion on reactions to *The Satanic Verses* in the UK, see David G. Bowen, ed., *The Satanic Verses: Bradford Responds* (Ilkley: Bradford & Ilkley Community College, 1992). Also see Malise Ruthven, *A Satanic Affair: Salman Rushdie and the Rage of Islam* (London: Chatto & Windus, 1990).

Chapter Four

1. Dan Burstein, "Introduction; From Cave Painting to Wonkette: A Short History of Blogging," in *Blog! How the Newest Media Revolution Is Changing Politics, Business, and Culture*, ed. David Kline and Dan Burstein (New York: CDS Books, 2005), xxi.

2. Ziki Papacharissi, "Audiences as Media Producers: Content Analysis of 260 Blogs," in *Blogging, Citizenship, and the Future of Media*, ed. Mark Tremayne (New York and London: Routledge, 2007), 37.

3. Asharq al-Awsat, "Saudi Arabia: Blogging Continues to Gain Momentum," 18 October 2007, *http://aawsat.com/english*.

4. Hans Wehr and J. Milton Cowan, eds., *A Dictionary of Modern Written Arabic*, 4th ed. (Wiesbaden: Harrassowitz, 1979), 303.

5. Nastik, "English-Arabic Dictionary," 19 October 2007, *http://tps.edu.ee/nastik/ar-en*. Using the following database: Arabeyes, "Wordlist," 19 October 2007, *http://www.arabeyes.org/project.php?proj=Wordlist*. Also see "mufakkira," in *A Dictionary of Modern Written Arabic*, 725.

6. Arabeyes, "Wordlist."

7. Mark Tremayne, "Harnessing the Active Audience," in *Blogging, Citizenship, and the Future of Media*, ed. Mark Tremayne (New York and London: Routledge, 2007), 262.

8. Barbara K. Kaye, "Blog Use Motivations: An Exploratory Study," in *Blogging, Citizenship, and the Future of Media*, ed. Mark Tremayne (New York and London: Routledge, 2007), 136.

9. Hossein Derekhshan, "Editor: Myself," 1 April 2005, *http://hoder.com/weblog/archives/2005_04_01_index.html*. Also see Ethan's Weblog, "My Blog's in Cambridge, but My Heart Is in Accra," 31 January 2005, *http://blogs.law.harvard.edu/ethan/2005/01/31#a745*, which is reproduced in Saudi Jeans, "An American Promotes Arabic Blogs as Alternative to the Lost Democracy," *Al-Hayat*, translated by Amina Khairy.

10. Tremayne, "Introduction: Examining the Blog-Media Relationshiop," xi.

11. Evan Henshaw-Plath, "Network Technology and Networked Organizations," in *Reformatting Politics: Global Civil Society and the Internet*, ed. Jodi Dean, Jon Anderson, and Geert Lovink (London: Routledge, 2006); citing Mark Surman and Katherine Reilly, "Appropriating the Internet for Social Change: Strategic Uses of Networked Technologies by Transnational Civil Society Organizations," November 2003, *http://www.ssrc.org/programs/itic/civ_soc_report/*.

12. Tremayne, "Introduction: Examining the Blog-Media Relationship," xi.

13. Jeeran, *http://www.jeeran.com*; Fastlink, *http://fastlink.jo*; albawaba.com, *http://blogs.albawaba.com/BlogMaster_en*; Maktooblog, *http://www.maktoobblog.com/*.

14. Global Voices, "Serdal: Arabic Pioneer Blogger from U.A.E.," 16 May 2005, *http://cyber.law.harvard.edu/globalvoices/-/world/united-arab-emirates*.

15. Committee to Protect Bloggers, "Statement from Omar, of Friends of Democracy," 27 March 2005, *http://committeetoprotectbloggers.blogspot.com/2005/03/arabic-blogging-tool.html*. Details of the blogging tool: Friends of Democracy, *http://friendsofdemocracy.net*.

16. Anoniblog, *http://anoniblog.pbwiki.com*. Also see Anoniblog, "Arabic Anonymous Blogging Guide," *http://anoniblog.pbwiki.com/Arabic AnonymousBlogggingGuide*.

17. Urdustan.com, *http://www.urdustan.com*.

18. Aparna Ray, "Bring the World of Bangla Blogs to GV," 7 June 2006, *http://www.globalvoicesonline.org/2006/06/07/bring-the-world-of-bangla-blogs-to-gv*.

19. Global Voices Online, *http://cyber.law.harvard.edu/globalvoices/*. Significant among these was the output of the Middle Eastern regional editor: Amira Al Hussaini, "Global Voices Online," 10 December 2006, *http://www.globalvoices online.org/author/amira-al-hussaini*.

20. Toot, 20 March 2007, *http://itoot.net/*.

21. Talibatulim, *http://www.xanga.com/talibatulilm*; Binag3e, 23 March 2006, *http://www.xanga.com/binag3e*.

22. Asoulunique, 22 March 2006, *http://www.xanga.com/asoulunique*.

23. Sabbah's Blog, "About," *http://sabbah.biz/mt/about/*.

24. Edward W. Said, *Orientalism* (London: Random House, 1979).

25. Saudi Jeans, 1 February 2005, *http://saudijeans.blogspot.com*. Also see Jihad el Khazen, "Ayoon Wa Azan: The Blogosphere—Blogs 4," *Dar al-Hayat, http://english.daralhayat.com/opinion/OPED/01-2006/Article-20060109-afd1b883-c0a8-10ed-015e-e9e35ef74437/story.html*.

26. Saudi Jeans, "The Great Divide: Observations on the Arab Blogosphere," 17 February 2005, *http://saudijeans.blogspot.com/2005/02/great-divide-observations-on-arab.html*.

27. Saudi Blogs, "Aggregator," 21 August 2006, *http://aggregator.saudiblogs.org*.

28. Middle East Transparent, "Saudi Release Web Loggers from Prison," 1 July 2005, *http://www.metransparent.com/texts/saudi_release_web_loggers_from_prison.htm*.

29. Asharq Al-Awsat, "Saudi Arabia: Blogging Continues to Gain Momentum," 18 October 2007, *http://www.aawsat.com*.

30. Official Community of Saudi Bloggers, 10 September 2006, *http://www.ocsab.com*; linking to Muslim World League, "News," 25 June 2006, *http://www.the mwl.org/News/default.aspx?ct=1&cid=4&nid=298&l=AR*.

31. Saudi Jeans, "OCSAB: Not My Thing," 4 April 2006, *http://saudijeans.blogspot.com/2006/04/ocsab-not-my-thing.html*.

32. Ibid.

33. Asharq Al-Awsat, "Saudi Arabia: Blogging Continues to Gain Momentum."

34. Haloscan, "Comments: Farooha," 21 November 2005, *http://www.haloscan. com/comments/farooha/113136274692528943*; Farah's Sowaleef, "So I Just Turned 20," 17 June 2005, *http://farahssowaleef.blogspot.com.* The site was removed but remained available through *archive.org.*

35. Farah's Sowaleef, "Shopping Spree—The Saudi Way!," 28 June 2005, *http:// farahssowaleef.blogspot.com.*

36. Farah's Sowaleef, "On Wahabism, Najdism, and a Whole Lotta Other 'ism's,'" 25 June 2005, *http://farahssowaleef.blogspot.com/2005_06_01_farahssowa leef_archive.html.*

37. Adventures of a Lipstick Wahhabi, 17 October 2006, *http://lwahhabi.blogspot. com/2006_10_01_archive.html.*

38. Ahmed's other blog (in Arabic) is Yawmyat, *http://yawmyat.blogspot.com.*

39. Saudi Jeans, "Religious Police Bans a Play," 15 January 2006, *http://saudijeans. blogspot.com/2006_01_01_saudijeans_archive.html.*

40. Also see Saudi Jeans, "The War of Hearts and Minds," 4 March 2007, *http:// www.saudijeans.org/2007/03/war-of-hearts-and-minds.html.*

41. Saudi Jeans, "Medina Diaries," 25 October 2005, *http://saudijeans.blogspot.com/ 2005/10/medina-diaries.html.*

42. Flickr, "Saudi Jeans' Medina Slideshow on Flickr," *http://flickr.com/photos/ah med/sets/1230624/show.*

43. Saudi Jeans, "Thoughts on America," 1 October 2007, *http://www.saudijeans. org/2007/03/war-of-hearts-and-minds.html.*

44. Religious Policeman, "Saudi Schoolteacher Scandal Site (Citing the Case of the Saud Teacher), *http://www.malharbi.com/en/home.html)*," 21 November 2005, *http://muttawa.blogspot.com.*

45. Mahmood's Den, "One Erstwhile Arab Leader on Trial . . . More to Follow," 13 July 2004, *http://www.mahmood.tv/index.php/blog/678.*

46. Mahmood al-Yousif, "A Tragic Week in Bahrain and the Gulf," 16 January 2006, *http://www.globalvoicesonline.org/2006/01/16/a-tragic-week-in-bahrain-and-the-gulf.*

47. Chan'ad Bahraini, "Chanad's Day Out," 13 January 2006, *http://chanad.weblogs. us.*

48. Ibid.

49. Neil MacFarquhar, "In Tiny Arab State, Web Takes on Ruling Elite," *New York Times,* 15 January 2006, *http://www.nytimes.com.*

50. Kuwait n Islam, "Peace," 30 September 2005, *http://kuwait-n-islam.blogspot. com/2005_09_01_kuwait-n-islam_archive.html.*

51. Kuwait n Islam, "Back in Kuwait . . . What's Up," 24 July 2005, *http://kuwait-n-islam.blogspot.com/2005_07_01_kuwait-n-islam_archive.html.* Original spellings and punctuation retained.

52. Khaleejtimes.com, "Majority of UAE Youth Addicted to the Internet," 14 January 2006, *http://www.khaleejtimes.com/DisplayArticle.asp?xfile=data/theuae/ 2006/January/theuae_January293.xml&section=theuae.*

53. UAE Community Blog, 20 January 2007, *http://uaecommunity.blogspot.com.*

54. For example, see Secret Dubai, *http://secretdubai.blogspot.com*, which also maintains a list of Dubai bloggers.

55. An Emaratis Thoughts, "Changing the Arab," 28 December 2005, *http://ae thoughts.blogspot.com/2005_12_01_aethoughts_archive.html.*

56. Secret Arabian, "FCUK That," 18 December 2005, *http://secretarabian. blogspot.com.*

57. Secret Arabian, "Don't Knock the Block," 7 December 7 2005, *http://secretara bian.blogspot.com/2005_12_01_secretarabian_archive.html.*

58. E3ashig, "Jinn vs. Medicine," 15 July 2005, *http://www.e3ashig.com/2005/07/15/jinn-vs-medicine.*

59. Iraq Blogcount, 10 November 2005 and 20 March 2007, *http://iraq blogcount.blogspot.com.*

60. For example, see the long-standing blog Kurdo's World, *http://kurdo.blogspot.com/.*

61. For a summary, see BBC News, "Iraqi Bloggers React to Execution," 12 January 2007, *http://news.bbc.co.uk/2/hi/talking_point/6228785.stm.*

62. Kurdo's World.

63. Salam Pax, *The Baghdad Blog* (London: Guardian Books, 2003); Salam Pax, "Where Is Raed?," 10 February 2003, *http://dear_raed.blogspot.com.*

64. Salam Pax, "Shut Up You Fat Whiner! I'm Still Your Fag—Broken Social Scene," 26 September 2005, *http://justzipit.blogspot.com.*

65. The Daily Absurdity Report, 18 July 2006, *http://justzipit.blogspot.com.*

66. Raed in the Middle, *http://raedinthemiddle.blogspot.com.*

67. Riverbend, "Baghdad Burning, Movies and Dreams . . .," *http://riverbendblog.blogspot.com.*

68. Riverbend, *Baghdad Burning: Girl Blog from Iraq* (New York: Feminist Press at CUNY, 2005).

69. Lakshmi Chaudhry, "The Girl Blogger from Iraq," *AlterNet, http://www.alter net.org/waroniraq/21782.*

70. Hammorabi, "The Story of Imam Hussein," *http://hammorabi.blogspot.com/Imam%20Hussein/Imam%20Hussein.html.*

71. Hammorabi, "A Spot of Light," 30 August 2004, *http://hammorabi.blogspot.com*; Hammorabi, "New Recorded Voice Tape for Saddam in Al-Arabyiah TV," 16 November 2003, *http://hammorabi.blogspot.com.*

72. Tell Me a Secret, "I Found Myself . . .," 30 July 2005, *http://secretsinbaghdad.blogspot.com/2005/07/i-found-myself.html.*

73. Iraq the Model, 19 November 2003, *http://iraqthemodel.blogspot.com.*

74. Normblog, "Profile: Omar," 4 November 2005, *http://normblog.typepad.com/normblog/2005/11/the_normblog_pr.html.*

75. Iraq the Model.

76. Ibid.

77. The Mesopotamian, "Arab Media," 1 November 2005, *http://mesopotamian.blogspot.com/2005/11/arab-media.html.*

78. Ibid.

79. Ibid., 9 October 2005.

80. Ibid., 20 October 2005.

81. Healing Iraq, 9 November 2005, *http://healingiraq.blogspot.com.*

82. Nabil's Blog, *http://nabilsblog.blogspot.com.*

83. 24 Steps to Liberty, 10 November 2005, *http://twentyfourstepstoliberty.blogspot.com.*

84. Treasure of Baghdad, "Enemies!!," 8 November 2005.

85. Ibid.

86. Treasure of Baghdad, "The Killing Fields," 2 November 2005.

87. Ibid., 12 October 2007, *http://baghdadtreasure.blogspot.com.*

88. Masry's mother, Ferial Masry, born in Saudi Arabia, was a Democratic candidate for the 37th Assembly District of California in 2006. See Ferial Masry for Assembly, *http://www.ferialmasryforassembly.com.*

89. "The Front Line Online," *San Diego Union-Tribune,* 18 July 2004, *http://www.sig nonsandiego.com/uniontrib/20040718/news_blogcpy.html.*

90. Iraq 2.0, "Iraq Chaplain Briefing," *http://www.omarmasry.net/chaplain_brief. htm.*

91. Urban Journalism Workshop, "A Young Soldier Sees War and Changes Heart," *http://journalism.nyu.edu/ujw/2004/Iraq.htm.*

92. Baghdad's Mistress, 10 April 2005, *http://iraqimistress.blogspot.com/.*

93. Baghdad's Mistress, "My First Post as an Iraqi Mistress," 9 April 2005, *http:// iraqimistress.blogspot.com/2005_04_01_iraqimistress_archive.html.*

94. "Blogging in Syria," Syrian News Wire, 5 September 2005, *http://saroujah.blog spot.com/2005/09/blogging-in-syria.html.*

95. Damascene Blog, "Blogroll," 20 January 2006, *http://www.damasceneblog.com.*

96. Syria Exposed, "About," *http://syriaexposed.blogspot.com.*

97. Syria Exposed, "Syria Exposed, Myth No. 7: Alawie Is Still a Religious Sect," 28 March 2005, *http://syriaexposed.blogspot.com* (some typographical corrections).

98. Syria Exposed, "Myth No. 11: Karfan Is Important," 20 June 2005, *http://syria exposed.blogspot.com* (some typographical corrections).

99. Syria Exposed, "Myth No. 12: We Wear Suits," 19 August 2006, *http://syria exposed.blogspot.com.*

100. Syrian Domari, *http://aldomari.blogspot.com.*

101. The Hidden Gates of Damascus, "Stop the 'Honor Crime,' " 28 September 2005, *http://hiddengates.blogspot.com.*

102. Syrian Women, "Observatory Concern about Syrian Society Issues," *http:// www.nesasy.com/honorcrimes/honorcrimes.html.*

103. Amarji—A Heretic's Blog, *http://amarji.blogspot.com/.*

104. Across Syria & Inside Homs, *http://acrosssyria.blogspot.com/.*

105. Lebanese Blogger Forum, "Profile, Linalone," 23 November 2005, *http://leba nonheartblogs.blogspot.com*; Linalone, "Lebanese Female Diary," *http://afifa80. blogspot.com.*

106. YouTube, "Cooco89, Lebanon 4 Ever," *http://www.youtube.com/watch?v=vP2cu APG_3g.*

107. Reuters, "Lebanese Use Blogs to Vent Frustration at War," 10 August 2006, *http://www.reuters.com*; "Welcome to the Lebanese Blogosphere," *Daily Star*, 14 March 2006, *http://www.dailystar.com.lb/article.asp?edition_id=10& categ _id=4&article_id=22818*. Also see Sune Haugbolle, "From A-lists to Webtifadas: Developments in the Lebanese Blogosphere, 2005–2006," *Arab Media and Society, http://www.arabmediasociety.org/?article=40*.

108. Sabbah's Blog, "Mesyaf (Summer Holiday) Marriage, New Form of Prostitution in Saudi Arabia! Response, Roba," 9 June 2005, *http://sabbah.biz/ mt/archives/ 2005/06/09/mesyaf-summer-holiday-marriage-new-form-of-prostitution-in-saudi-arabia* (based on article in *Al-Arabiyya*, 29 Rabat al-Thani, 1426 (6 June 2005), *http://www.alarabiya.net/Article.aspx?v=13741*).

109. Sabbah's Blog, "Wafa bin Laden Decided to Show Her Butt, and Sabbah Pays for It!," 25 December 2005, *http://sabbah.biz/mt/archives/2005/12/24/wafa-bin-laden-decided-to-show-her-butt-and-sabbah-pays-for-it/*.

110. Jordan Planet, "About," 24 November 2005, *http://www.jordanplanet.net/About*. Also see Slashdot, "Answers from 'Our Man in Jordan,'" 22 March 2006, *http:// interviews.slashdot.org/article.pl?sid=06/03/21/2329216&mode=nocomment*.

111. Jordan Planet, "Jordan Planet Put to Sleep," 29 December 2006, *http://blog.jor danplanet.net*.

112. Mental Mayhem, 22 November 2005, *http://www.mentalmayhem.org/mental_ mayhem*; Jordan First, 22 November 2005, *http://www.jordanfirst.com/?p=35*; Laila El-Haddad, "Across the Killing Field," 15 September 2005, *http://a-mother-from-gaza.blogspot.com/2005/09/across-killing-field.html*, *http://www.flickr.com /photos/gazawia*.

113. Ali Abunimah's Bitter Pill, 10 September 2005, *http://www.abunimah.org*.

114. Bitterlemons.org, "Palestinian-Israeli Crossfire," *http://www.bitterlemons.org*.

115. Rafah.virtualactivism.net, "Report about the Child Islam Khateeb," *http://rafah. virtualactivism.net/news/special.htm*, *http://rafah.virtualactivism.net/news/to daymain.htm*.

116. Rafah Pundits, "IDF Assassinate Top Hamas Fighter," 17 November 2005, *http:// rafahpundits.com/?p=37*.

117. Rafah Pundits, "Palestinian Boy's Organs Save Israelis," 9 November 2005, *http://rafahpundits.com/?p=31*.

118. Bethlehem Bloggers, "Marriage in Palestine," 21 October 2005, *http://bethlehem ghetto.blogspot.com/2005_10_01_bethlehemghetto_archive.html*.

119. Bethlehem Bloggers, "Who Are the Bethlehem Bloggers?," March 2005, *http:// bethlehemghetto.blogspot.com/2005/03/who-are-bethlehem-bloggers.html#com ments*.

120. Living in Gaza City, "Can a Blog Be Dedicated?," 22 October 2005, *http://www. living-in-gaza.blogspot.com*; Imaan, "Profile," *http://www.blogger.com/profile/ 14438292*; Imaan on Ice, 12 October 2007, *http://www.living-in-gaza.blogspot. com*.

121. Laila El-Haddad, "Raising Yousuf: A Diary of a Mother under Occupation," *http://a-mother-from-gaza.blogspot.com*.

122. Turkish Torque, "Why Torque," 3 November 2002, *http://tork.blogspot.com/ 2002/11/why-torque-since-termination-of-my.html*.

123. Talk Turkey, *http://www.talkturkey.us/*.

124. Bilgiedinmehakki.org, "Freedom of Information Turkey," *http://www.bilgiedin mehakki.org/index_eng.asp*.

125. The White Path, "About," 5 November 2005, *http://www.thewhitepath.com/ about.php*.

126. The White Path, "Vision," 6 November 2005, *http://www.thewhitepath.com/ vision.php*.

127. Summarized in the White Path, "Darwinism v. Design Archives," 12 October 2007, *http://www.thewhitepath.com/archives/intelligent_design/*.

128. Blogherald.com, "The Blog Herald Blog Count February 2006: 200 Million Blogs in Existence," 2 February 2006, *http://www.blogherald.com/2006/02/02/the-blog-herald-blog-count-february-2006-200-million-blogs-in-existence/*. Also see National Institute for Technology and Liberal Education, "NITLE Blog Census, Languages," 15 November 2005, *http://www.blogcensus.net/ ?page=lang*. It should be noted that this census did not register any blogs in Arabic. The census uses Web crawlers.

129. Weblogfestival.com, "The First Farsi Weblog Festival," 31 May 2004.

130. "Iran's Clerics Caught Up in Blogging Craze," *Guardian* (London), 11 October 2006, *http://www.guardian.co.uk/iran/story/0,,1892562,00.html*.

131. BBC News, "Web Sparks Revolution in Farsi," 4 May 2004, *http://news.bbc. co.uk*.

132. Editor: Myself, *http://hoder.com*.

133. SignOnSanDiego.com, "Iran's Presidential Campaign Draws to a Finish with Race Tight," 16 June 2005, *http://signonsandiego.com*.

134. Committee to Protect Bloggers, *http://committeetoprotectbloggers.civiblog.org/ blog*.

135. Free Mojtaba Saminejad, *http://www.iabolish.com/campaigns/campaign.php? id=Motjaba*. See Association of Iranian Blog Writers (Penlog) for more on this issue (Penlog English, *http://penlog-en.blogspot.com*).

136. Editor: Myself, "Stop Censoring Us," *http://stop.censoring.us/*.

137. Mahmoud Ahmadinejad, "Presidency of the Islamic Republic of Iran," *http:// www.president.ir*.

138. For a useful overview of the development of Iranian blogging, see the timeline in "Iranian Blogs," Wikipedia, 15 November 2005, *http://en.wikipedia.org/wiki/ Iranian_Blogs*.

139. Orkut, *http://www.orkut.com*.

140. Reuters, "Iranian Cleric Blogs for Free Expression," 16 February 2005, *http:// reuters.com*.

141. Webneveshteha, "My Autobiography for the Internet Users," *http://www.web neveshteha.com/en/about.asp*.

142. Webneveshteha, "Jordan and Iraq Explosions and Islam's Fate," 11 November 2005, *http://www.webneveshteha.com/en/weblog/?id=2146307261*.

143. Webneveshteha, "Mr. Ahmadinejad's Speech on the Threshold of Qods Day," 27 October 2005, *http://www.webneveshteha.com/en/weblog/?id=2146307222*.

144. Webneveshteha, "The Story of Stealing My Website's Name," 1 October 2005, *http://www.webneveshteha.com*.

145. Reuters, "Iranian Cleric Blogs for Free Expression."

146. Ibid.

147. "In Iran, Web-Savvy Clerics Reach out to Shiite Faithful," *Los Angeles Times*, 7 April 2007, *http://www.latimes.com*.

148. Ahmadinejad Official Blog, 12 October 2007, *http://www.ahmadinejad.ir*.

149. Iranian Girl, 24 October 2003, *http://iranian-girl.blogspot.com/2003__10__01__iranian-girl__archive.html*. For a detailed commentary on Iranian Girl, see Michael Keren, *Blogosphere: The New Political Arena* (Lanham, Md.: Lexington Books, 2006), 51–64.

150. Iranian Girl, "How to Build a Mullah," 30 March 2004, *http://iranian-girl.blogspot.com/2004/03/how-to-build-mullah.html*.

151. Ibid., 27 October 2003, *http://iranian-girl.blogspot.com/2003__10__01__iranian-girl__archive.html*.

152. Iranian Girl, "Ramadan, Ramadan, Happy Ramadan! Hehe," 18 October 2005, *http://iranian-girl.blogspot.com/2005/10/ramadan-ramadan-happy-ramadan-hehe.html*. Emphasis/original typography kept.

153. See the overview of Iranian blogs in Nasrin Alavi, *We Are Iran: The Persian Blogs* (New York: Soft Skull Press, 2005).

154. Egyptian Blog Ring, 22 November 2005, *http://www.egybloggers.com* (updated 21 January 2007).

155. Issandr El Amrani, Weblog, Blogging Etiquette, 2 October 2003, *http://homepage.mac.com/issandr/2003/10/02/#gays-response*.

156. Egyptian Sandmonkey, December 2004, *http://egyptiansandmonkey.blogspot.com/2004/12/sandmonkey-question.html*.

157. Egyptian Sandmonkey, "Religious Tolerance in Egypt," 5 April 2005, *http://egyptiansandmonkey.blogspot.com/2005/04/religious-tolerance-in-egypt.html*.

158. Egyptian Sandmonkey, "Koran Desecration Protests," May 2005, *http://egyptiansandmonkey.blogspot.com/2005/05/koran-desecration-protests-and-other.html*.

159. One Arab World, "No More Self-Gratifying Lies," 10 November 2005, *http://onearabworld.blog.com*.

160. Mariam Fam, "'Brotherhood' Blogs in Egypt Offer View of Young Islamists," *Wall Street Journal*, 20 April 2007, *http://online.wsj.com*; Abdou al-Monem Mahmoud, "Ana Ikhwan," *http://ana-ikhwan.blogspot.com*.

161. Karem Amer, 19 April 2007, *http://karam903.blogspot.com*.

162. Mona Eltahawy, "Threats Unlikely to Silence Bloggers as Egypt Jails Youth for 'Insults,'" 9 March 2007, *http://www.diplomatictraffic.com*.

163. Free Karim, 9 March 2007, *http://www.freekareem.org*. For a fuller assessment of Western media responses to Nabil's case, see Arab Media Society, 10 September 2007, *http://www.arabmediasociety.org*.

164. Human Rights Watch, "Libya," 3 November 2005, *http://hrw.org/english/docs/2005/11/03/libya11965.htm*.

165. See the discussion in From the Rock, "Libyan Canadian Blogger," 12 October 2005, *http://lonehighlander.blogspot.com/2005/10/libyan-canadian-blogger-nuras-blog-is.html*.

166. Ly-Hub, 1 February 2006, *http://libyans.blogspot.com/*.

167. Tripoli Girl, 25 October 2005, *http://tripoligirl.blogspot.com*.

168. Dunia, 25 October 2005, *http://duniatyen.blogspot.com*.

169. Maghreb Blog, 18 October 2005, *http://maghreblog.net*.

170. Tunisie Blogs, 18 October 2005 and 20 March 2007, *http://tn-blogs.com*.

171. Tunisie Blogs, "Awards 2005," *http://tn-blogs.com/awards2005*.

172. Faith Freedom, "My Friend Karim Mohamed Labidi, the Lonely Soldier . . .," *http://www.faithfreedom.org/forum/*.

173. Islam La, "Index," 18 October 2005, *http://islamla.over-blog.com/album-38273.html*.

174. Islam La, "Islam la—critique de l'Islam," 18 October 2005, *http://islamla.over-blog.com*.

175. TuNiZien PeOpLe, "Un débat ouvert sur Paltalk me semble mieux pour éclaircir différents points," 15 December 2005, *http://tunizien.blogspot.com/2005/12/un-dbat-ouvert-sur-paltalk-me-semble.html#comments*.

176. Larbi.org, "Annuaire des blogs marocains," April 2005, *http://www.larbi.org/index.php?2005/04/13/78-annuaire-des-blogs-marocains*.

177. Rayhanenajib, *http://rayhanenajib.blogoma.net/*.

178. Hchicha, *http://www.hchicha.net*.

179. Infonet-Algerie, "Opération 1 PC par Famille," 30 October 2005, *http://infonetalgerie.blogspot.com/2005_10_01_infonetalgerie_archive.html*.

180. The Moor Next Door, "It May Take a War," 19 December 2005, *http://wahdah.blogspot.com*.

181. Ibid.

182. The Moor Next Door, "Gays Prove That Common Western Assumptions about Algeria Are Poppycock," 26 May 2005, *http://wahdah.blogspot.com/2005/05/gays-prove-that-common-western.html*.

183. Qarxis, "The Jinni(s) Inside, Post by RockSTAR," 17 November 2005, *http://www.qarxis.com/jinni#comment*.

184. Qarxis, "The Jinni(s) Inside, Post by Slick_Horsie," 20 December 2005, *http://www.qarxis.com/jinni#comment*. An avatar by the name of "Slick_Horsie" claimed to be a Bangaldeshi Muslim in a series of postings on Faith Freedom, "Forum," 20 December 2005, *http://www.faithfreedom.org*.

185. Voice of Somaliland Diaspora–Ottawa, *http://www.waridaad.blogspot.com*.

186. Nigerian Bloggers Association, *http://www.nigerianbloggers.com/*.

187. Naeem Jeenah, 10 September 2007, *http://naeemjeenah.blogspot.com*.

188. Gary R. Bunt, *Virtually Islamic: Computer-Mediated Communication and Cyber Islamic Environments* (Cardiff: University of Wales Press, 2000), 83–85.

189. Asia Pacific Media Network, "Internet Row Tests PM's Free-Speech Creden-

tials," 6 October 2004, *http://www.asiamedia.ucla.edu/article.asp?parentid=15585*.

190. YouTube, "Anwar Ibrahim—Aljazeera TV (Part 1)," 28 March 2007, *http://www.youtube.com/watch?v=jlWSuEyfAec*; Anwar Ibrahim Blog, "Habibie in Reformasi E," 26 March 2007, *http://www.youtube.com/watch?v=j7-pi-PJXPE&v3*; Anwar Ibrahim Blog, 26 March 2007, *http://anwaribrahimblog.com*; Anwar Ibrahim for Malaysia, 28 March 2007, *http://www.anwaribrahim.com/site/*.

191. MySpace, "Anwar4Malaysia," *http://www.myspace.com/anwar4malaysia*; Facebook, *http://facebook.com*; Friendster, "Anwar Ibrahim," *http://profiles.friendster.com/anwaribrahim*; all accesed 28 March 2007.

192. Parti Keadilan Rakyat, 15 October 2007, *http://keadilanrakyat.org*; Accountability, 15 October 2007, *http://accountability.org*.

193. Dato' Shahrir Abdul Samad, 15 October 2007, *http://shahrirsamad.blogspot.com/*.

194. "Be Responsible, Bloggers Urged," *Daily Star*, 23 March 2007, *http://thestar.com.my/news/story.asp?file=/2007/3/23/nation/17218822&sec=nation*.

195. Weblog Husam Musa, 15 October 2007, *http://cetusan-hati.blogspot.com*; Reformasi, 15 October 2007, *http://formerigp.blogspot.com*.

196. Ahli Parlimen PAS, 15 October 2007, *http://mppas.wordpress.com/*; TV PAS, 15 October 2007, *http://www.tvpas.com*.

197. Bunt, *Virtually Islamic*, 85–88.

198. Kickdefella, 15 October 2007, *http://kickdefella.wordpress.com*.

199. Project Petaling Street, "Directory," 10 November 2005, *http://www.petalingstreet.org/directory/*.

200. MENJ, *http://blog.menj.org*.

201. Bismikaallahuma.org, "About," December 2005, *http://www.bismikaallahuma.org/index.php/about/*.

202. MENJ, "A Nation Fumes over Video," 26 November 2005, *http://blog.menj.org/index.php/2005/11/26/a-nation-fumes-over-video/*.

203. MENJ, "'Minah Tudung,' a New Hit Song," 8 December 2005, *http://blog.menj.org/index.php/2005/12/08/minah-tudung-a-new-hit-song/*.

204. MENJ, "DeepaRaya? Sacrilegious!," 22 October 2005, *http://blog.menj.org/index.php/2005/10/22/deeparaya-sacriligeous/*.

205. MENJ, "Under Attack," 31 October 2005, *http://blog.menj.org/index.php/2005/10/31/under-attack/*; citing C. S. Lewis, *The Chronicles of Narnia: The Silver Chair* (1953; New York: Collier Books, 1970).

206. Presiden Republik Indonesia, 15 October 2007, *http://presidenri.blogspot.com*.

207. Dedy W. Sanusi, "My English," 24 October 2005, *http://dedywsanusi.blogspot.com/*.

208. William Computer Blog, *http://wpram.com/*, 25 March 2006.

209. Blogger Indonesia, *http://blogs.mit.edu/afatih*, 25 March 2006.

210. A. Fatih Syuhud, "Indonesia Journal Blogger," 18 March 2006, *http://indo-blogs.blogspot.com/* (link deleted); A. Fatih Syuhud, "Blogger Indonesia," 17 October 2007, *http://fatihsyuhud.com*.

211. Indonesian Diary, "Who's the Moderate Muslim?," 13 October 2005, *http://indo-blogs.blogspot.com/2005/10/whos-moderate-muslim.html*.

212. Discussed in Clifford Geertz, *The Religion of Java* (New York: Free Press of Glencoe, 1960).

213. Global Voices Online, "Indonesia: Polygamous Holy Man and MP's Sex Scandal," 8 December 2006, *http://www.globalvoicesonline.org/2006/12/08/indonesia-polygamous-holy-man-and-mps-sex-scandal*.

214. Ibid.

215. Pakistani Bloggers, "Forum Index," 12 November 2005, *http://pakistanibloggers.cogia.net/forum/viewforum.php?f=1#top*.

216. Dawn, "Pakistani Scientist in Nobel Team," 14 October 2007, *http://www.dawn.com/2007/10/14/nat5.htm*.

217. All Things Pakistan, "ATP Poll Results: Grading Gen. Musharraf," 1 October 2007, *http://pakistaniat.com/2006/10/01/atp-poll-results-grading-gen-musharraf*.

218. For example, see All Things Pakistan, "Laathi Raj: Jamia Hafsa's Offensive on a Divided Society," 29 March 2007, *http://pakistaniat.com/2007/03/29/jamia-hafsa-taliban-talibanization-islamabad-brothel-madrassa-mosque-hostage*; and All Things Pakistan, "Battle for Lal Masjid: Soldier Killed; Students Wounded," 3 July 2007, *http://pakistaniat.com/2007/07/03/battle-for-lal-masjid-pakistan-soldier-killed-madrassah-students-wounded*.

219. The Olive Ream, "Mad-Rasa Curriculum," 19 November 2005, *http://oream.blogspot.com/2005/11/mad-rasa-curriculum-2006.html*.

220. Global Voices Online, "Pakistan," *http://cyber.law.harvard.edu/globalvoices/-/world/south-asia/pakistan*.

221. Falling Days, *http://amirsaleem.blogspot.com/*.

222. 3rd World View, "Bangladesh Is Held to Ransom," 15 November 2005, *http://rezwanul.blogspot.com/*.

223. Close Your Eyes and Try to See, "Homosexuality and Islam," 19 October 2005, *http://iurifat.blogspot.com*.

224. Ibid.

225. Pickled Politics, *http://www.pickledpolitics.com*.

226. Unholy Wars, "Shaddan Alam, Professional Maulvis and Amateur Fatwas," 10 December 2005, *http://www.unholywars.org/entry/professional-maulvis-and-amateur-fatwas/*.

227. Indicubed, "Bloggers vs. Journalists or the Best of Both Worlds?," *http://indicubed.blogspot.com*; Tsunami Blog, *http://tsunamihelp.blogspot.com/*. Also see Darryl D'Monte, "Are Bloggers Parked?," 19 October 2005, *http://www.indiatogether.org*.

228. Opinions of a 21st Century Kashmiri Nomad, *http://kashmiri-nomad.blogspot.com/*.

229. Opinions of a 21st Century Kashmiri Nomad, "For the Love of Money and Status," 15 October 2005, *http://kashmiri-nomad.blogspot.com/2005_10_01_kashmiri-nomad_archive.html*.

230. Afghan Pundit, *http://www.afghanblog.net*; Afghan Voice, *http://www.afghan voice.blogspot.com*.

231. Herat News, *http://www.heratnews.tk*.

232. Afghanwarrior, "Afghanistan's First Blog," 8 March 2005, *http://afghanwarrior. blogspot.com/2005/03/afghanistans-first-blog.html*.

233. Shia Pundit, *http://shiapundit.blogspot.com/*.

234. A number of academics have adopted the blogging format as an adjunct to their other output, including those with an interest in the Middle East and Islam (and related subjects). One high-profile example is Juan Cole, "Informed Comment," produced by a University of Michigan history professor.

235. Masud, *http://www.masud.co.uk/blog/*.

236. Ibid.

237. Muhajabah, *http://www.muhajabah.com/*.

238. Ibid.

239. Thoughts on Islamic Parenting, *http://islamicparenting.blogspot.com*.

240. Ibid.

241. Ninhajaba, *http://www.ninhajaba.blogspot.com/*.

242. A Garden of Children, *http://www.mumsy.blogspot.com/*.

243. Tareq Lubani, "Occupation Kills," 9 September 2006, *http://tarek.org/journeys*.

244. Ninjas on the Loose, *http://www.ninjasontheloose.blogspot.com/*.

Chapter Five

1. Gabriel Weimann, *Terror on the Internet: The New Arena, the New Challenges* (Washington, D.C.: U.S. Institute of Peace, 2006).

2. William McCants and Jarret Brachman, "The Militant Ideology Atlas," 4 December 2006, *http://www.ctc.usma.edu/atlas/*.

3. Daniel Kimmage and Kathleen Ridolfo, *Iraqi Insurgency Media: The War of Images and Ideas* (Washington, D.C.: Radio Free Europe/Radio Liberty, 2007).

4. Terrorism Monitor, August 2005, *http://jamestown.org/terrorism/*.

5. Laura Mansfield, *http://www.lauramansfield.com*; Northeast Intelligence Network, *http:// www.homelandsecurityus.com*; SITE Institute, *http://siteinstitute. org*; MEMRI, *http://www.memri.org/*. Mansfield published book versions of her translations: Laura Mansfield, *Al-Qaeda 2006 Yearbook: The 2006 Messages from Al-Qaeda Leadership* (USA: TLG Publications, 2007).

6. Clandestine Radio, *http://www.clandestineradio.com*; Ciberterrorismo (e-Yihad) (e-Qaeda) y Terrorismo Islamista, *http://cyberterrorism.blogspot.com*; Counterterrorism Blog, *http://counterterrorismblog.org*; Open Source Intelligence, *http:osint.blox.pl*.

7. Internet Haganah, *http://haganah.org.il/haganah*; Dhimmi Watch, *http://ji hadwatch.org/dhimmiwatch*; Jawa Report, *http:// mypetjawa.mu.nu*; Infovlad, *http://www.infovlad.net*; Little Green Footballs, *http://littlegreenfootballs.com*.

8. Adnkronos International, 10 January 2006, *http://www.adnki.com*.

9. This includes the work of Neil Doyle, who launched a business that provides paying subscribers with alerts to jihadi materials derived from Internet sources.

See Neil Doyle, *http://www.neildoyle.com*; Neil Doyle, *Terror Base UK* (Edinburgh: Mainstream Publishing, 2006); and Neil Doyle, *Terror Tracker: An Odyssey into Pure Fear* (Edinburgh: Mainstream Publishing, 2005). This is a similar approach to that established by Rita Katz of the SITE Institute and others.

10. For example, see Paul Eedle, "Jihad TV," in *Dispatches: War on Terror* (UK: Channel 4, 2006); Peter Taylor, "The New Al-Qaeda: Jihad.com" (UK: BBC, 2005); and National Public Radio, 2002, "Islam on the Internet," *http:// www.npr.org/ programs/watc/cyberislam/*.

11. For example, see Jason Burke, *Al-Qaeda* (London: Penguin Books, 2004); Rohan Gunaratna, *Inside Al Qaeda: Global Network of Terror* (London: Hurst, 2002); and Olivier Roy, *Globalised Islam: The Search for a New Ummah* (London: Hurst, 2004).

12. Artificial Intelligence Lab, "Dark Web Terrorism Research," 10 September 2005, *http://ai.arizona.edu/research/terror/index.htm*.

13. AP, "Project Seeks to Track Terror Web Posts," 11 November 2007, *http:// news.yahoo.com*.

14. Hsinchun Chen, Jialun Qin, Edna Reid, Wingyan Chung, Yilu Zhou, Wei Xi, Guanpi Lai, Alfonso A. Bonillas, and Marc Sageman, "The Dark Web Portal: Collecting and Analyzing the Presence of Domestic and International Terrorist Groups on the Web," *IEEE Intelligent Systems Archive*, September 2005, 44–51, *http://ai.arizona.edu/research/terror/publications/ITCS_Dark_Web_ submission.pdf*.

15. Arab Salem, Edna Reid, and Hsinchun Chen, "Content Analysis of Jihadi Extremist Groups' Videos: Proceedings of the Intelligence and Security Informatics: IEEE International Conference on Intelligence and Security Informatics, 23– 24 May 2006," *http://ai.arizona,edu/research/terror/publications/isi_content _analysis_jihadi.pdf*.

16. Ralph F. Wilson, "The Six Simple Principles of Viral Marketing," 1 February 2005, Web Marketing Today, *http://www.wilsonweb.com/wmt5/viral-princi ples-clean.htm*.

17. Gary R. Bunt, "Defining Islamic Inter-Connectivity," in *Muslim Networks from Hajj to Hip Hop*, ed. miriam cooke and Bruce B. Lawrence (Chapel Hill: University of North Carolina Press, 2005), 243.

18. Rasha A. Abdulla, "Islam, Jihad, and Terrorism in Post–9/11 Arabic Discussion Boards," *Journal of Computer-Mediated Communication* 12, no. 3 (April 2007), *http://jcmc.indiana.edu*.

19. See, for example, Lawrence Pintak, *Reflections in a Bloodshot Lens: America, Islam, and the War of Ideas* (London: Pluto Press, 2006).

20. "Salafiyya," in *Encyclopedia of Islam: New Edition* (Leiden: E. J. Brill, 1960–).

21. Osama bin Laden, "Interview by Taysir Alluni, October 20, 2001, Broadcast on Al-Jazeera, January 31, 2002, Translated by James Howarth," in Osama bin Laden and Bruce Lawrence, *Messages to the World: The Statements of Osama Bin Laden* (London and New York: Verso, 2005), 127.

22. William McCants and Jarret Brachman, "The Militant Ideology Atlas," 5 October 2005, *http://www.trackingthethreat.com*.

23. Martin Dodge and Rob Kitchin, *The Atlas of Cyberspace* (Harlow, England: Addison-Wesley, 2001).

24. Gary R. Bunt, "The Islamic Internet Souq," Q-News, November 2000, *http://www.lamp.ac.uk/cis/liminal/virtuallyislamic/souqnov2000.html*.

25. AIVD General Intelligence and Security Service of the Netherlands (Algemene Inlichtingen-en Beiligheidsdienst), "The Radical Dawa in Transition: The Rise of Islamic Neoradicalism in the Netherlands," *http://www.aivd.nl*.

26. 9/11 Commission, *The 9/11 Commission Report; Final Report of the National Commission on Terrorist Attacks upon the United States, Official Government Edition* (Washington, D.C.: 2004).

27. Yosri Fouda and Nick Fielding, *Masterminds of Terror: The Truth behind the Most Devastating Terrorist Attack the World Has Ever Seen* (Edinburgh and London: Mainstream Publishing, 2003).

28. Marc Sageman, *Understanding Terror Networks* (Philadelphia: University of Pennsylvania Press, 2004).

29. Azzam Publications, "Abdullah Azzam: Follow the Caravan," reproduced on Islamistwatch, *http://www.islamistwatch.org/texts/azzam/caravan/conclusion.html*.

30. Jihad-algeria.com, 2 July 2004, *http://jihad-algeria.com*.

31. Jihad Unspun, *http://www.jihadunspun.com/*.

32. Dale F. Eickelman and James Piscatori, *Muslim Politics* (Princeton, N.J.: Princeton University Press, 1996), 111.

33. Madawi al-Rasheed, *Contesting the Saudi State: Islamic Voices from a New Generation* (Cambridge and New York: Cambridge University Press, 2006), 68.

34. "Egyptians Probe Palestinian Link in Sinai Attacks," *Toronto Star*, 11 October 2004, *http://www.thestar.com*.

35. Forsvarsnett, "FFI Explains Al-Qaida Document," 19 March 2004, *http://www.mil.no/felles/ffi/start/article.jhtml?articleID=71589*.

36. SITE Institute, " 'The Secret Organization of Qaedat al-Jihad in Europe' Claims Responsibility for London Attack," 7 July 2005, *http://www.siteinstitute.org*; "Specter Surfaces of World of Local Qaeda Offshoots," 8 July 2005, *http://www.boston.com/news*.

37. BBC News, "Statement Claiming London Attacks," *http://news.bbc.co.uk/go/pr/fr/-/1/hi/uk/4660391.stm*.

38. Der Spiegel, "Qaida-Bekennerschreiben zu Anschlägen in London," 7 July 2005, *http://www.spiegel.de/politik/ausland/0,1518,364121,00.html*; BBC News, "Statement Claiming London Attacks," 7 July 2005, *http://news.bbc.co.uk/1/hi/uk/4660391.stm*; ANSA.it, "Gruppo Rivendica Su Web E Mette in Guardia Italia," 7 July 2005; Adnkronos International, "London Bombs: Al-Qaeda Claim Emerges," 7 July 2005, *http://www.adnki.com*.

39. Theo van Gogh and Ayaan Hirst Ali, "Submission, Part 1," *http://www.youtube.com/watch?v=SXGZBs65qMs*.

40. Geert Lovink, *Zero Comments: Blogging and Critical Internet Culture* (New York and London: Routledge, 2007), xvii.

41. For a thorough discussion on this case, see Albert Benschop and Connie Menting

(trans.), "Chronicle of a Political Murder Foretold—Jihad in the Netherlands," *http://www.sociosite.org/jihad_nl_en.php*. Benschop's work is discussed by Lovink.

42. Arabicnews.com, "Saudi Scholars: Al-Jihad Is a Duty in Iraq; A Call to Avoid Sedition," 9 November 2004, *http://www.arabicnews.com*.

43. "New Violence, Old Problem: The Saudis Fight Terror, but Not Those Who Wage It," *New York Times*, 6 June 2004, *http://www.nyt.com*.

44. Susan B. Glasser, "'Martyrs' in Iraq, Mostly Saudis," 15 May 2005, *http://www.washingtonpost.com/wp-dyn/content/article/2005/05/14/AR2005051401270.html*.

45. Edwin Bakker, "Radical Islam in the Netherlands," *Terrorism Monitor* 3, no. 1 (January 2005), *http://jamestown.org/terrorism/news/article.php?issue_id=3196*.

46. UPI, "Analysis: Europe's Immigration Breakdown," 17 December 2004, *http://www.washtimes.com/upi-breaking/20041214-104044-4930r.htm*. Sfier is the editor of *Cahiers de l'Orient*.

47. Strategy Page, "Young, Clueless, and Dead," 4 January 2006, *http://www.strategypage.com/htmw/htterr/articles/20060104.aspx*.

48. Sageman, *Understanding Terror Networks*, 157.

49. "Al Qaeda Seen as Clear and Present Danger to the World," *Daily Times*, 5 December 2004.

50. "U.S. Prowls in Qaeda's 'Cyber Sanctuaries,'" *International Herald Tribune*, 29 September 2004, *http://www.iht.com/bin/print.php?file=540208.html*.

51. Reuters, "U.N. Terrorism Panel Urges Lost Passport Crackdown," 14 February 2005, *http://www.reuters.com/newsArticle.jhtml?storyID=7628451&type=worldNews*.

52. Terrorism Knowledge Base National Memorial Institute for the Prevention of Terrorism (MIPT), "Terrorism Knowledge Base," *http://www.tkb.org*. Also see "Site Tracks and Charts Terrorism Information," *Chicago Tribune*, 20 October 2004, *http://www.chicagotribune.com/news/nationworld/chi-0410100381oct10,1,5821350,print.story?coll=chi-newsnationworld-hed*.

53. "U.S. to Spy on Chatrooms," *Star* (Malaysia), 12 October 2004, *http://star-techcentral.com/tech/story.asp?file=/2004/10/12/technology/9112047&sec=technology*.

54. Malay Mail Online, "MM Focus: From Terror Agent to a Man of Peace," 20 July 2004, *http://www.emedia.com.my/Current_News/MM/Tuesday/National/20040720113248*.

55. "Breaching the Wall at Prayer," *Los Angeles Times*, 27 June 2005.

56. Gary R. Bunt, *Islam in the Digital Age: E-Jihad, Online Fatwas, and Cyber Islamic Environments* (London and Ann Arbor, Mich.: Pluto Press, 2003), 67–90.

57. AFP/TurkishPress.com, "Islamist Web Surfers Foresee World War III after Bush Reelection," 8 November 2004, *http://www.turkishpress.com*.

58. "What the Terrorists Have in Mind," *New York Times*, 28 October 2004, *http://www.nyt.com*.

59. "Reflections—The Bin Ladens of Yemen's Internet Service—Yemen Needs a Privacy Act," *Yemen Times*, 2 November 2004.

60. David Martin Jones, "The Cybercaliphate," *Financial Review*, 11 April 2003.

61. BBC News, "Saudis 'Reform Militants' on Web," 6 February 2005, *http://news. bbc.co.uk/1/hi/world/middle_east/4241391.stm*.

62. UPI/Washington Times, "Analysis: Islamic Tradition and the Web," 14 February 2005, *http://www.washtimes.com/upi-breaking/20050206-085830-7891r. htm*.

63. For example, Al-farouq.com, *http://www.al-farouq.com/ vb/showthread.php? p=6209#post6209*.

64. Discussed in Spirit of Truth, "Nuclear Terrorism," *http://www.spiritoftruth.org/ nuclearterrorism.htm*.

65. Irhaaboo7.org, "Al-Qaeda London," *http://www.irhaaboo7.org/Alqaedah_lon don.zip*. Note that there were variants in the spelling of *irhabi*. For a technical discussion on Irhabioo7's methodology, see Internet Haganah, "Great Moments from the Online Exploits of 'Irhabioo7,' Episode Number 3,432," 11 August 2005, *http://www.Internet-haganah.us/harchives/004734.html*.

66. Internet Haganah, "Communications Infrastructure of the Global Jihad: Three Players Join Forces," 1 September 2004, *http://haganah.org.il/harchives/0026 49.html*; Internet Haganah, "Yo! Irhabioo7, We'll Have a Word with You Mate," 12 August 2004, *http://Internet-haganah.us/harchives/002492.html*.

67. Rita Katz and Michael Kern, "Terrorist 007, Exposed," *Washington Post*, 25 March 2006, *http://www.washingtonpost.com/wp-dyn/content/article/2006/ 03/25/AR2006032500020_pf.html*. Katz and Kern are principal figures in the SITE Institute, which was involved in the search for Irhabioo7.

68. Infovlad, "Zubeiddah1417 Is Now in Jordan?," 21 March 2005, *http://www.infov lad.net/?p=142*. A Zubeiddah1417 page continued to operate, although many links were not functional; Zubeiddah1417, 6 April 2006, *http://www.geocities. com/zubeiddah1417/imc-final.html*.

69. SITE Institute, 16 May 2005, *http://siteinstitute.org/*.

70. For a detailed profile of Lewis Atiyat Allah, see Al-Rasheed, *Contesting the Saudi State*, 175–210.

71. PRISM, "Occasional Papers No. 3 Vol. 3 (2005)—From Madrid to London: Al-Qaeda Exports the War in Iraq to Europe," 10 July 2005, *http://www.e-prism. org/images/PRISM_no_3_vol_3—London_Bombings.pdf*.

72. Asharq Alawsat, "Infamous Al-Qaeda Bloggers' Nationalities Revealed," *http:// aawsat.com/english/news.asp?section=1&id=2137*.

73. Adnkronos International, "Profile of Al-Qaeda Figure 'Lewis Atiyallah,'" 8 July 2004, *http://www.adnki.com*.

74. Independent Online (South Africa), "Al-Qaeda Message Takes a Stab at Berlusconi," 30 May 2004, *http://www.iol.co.za*.

75. Alsaha, *http//alsaha.fares.net*.

76. SFGate.com, "Saudi Arabia Faces Internal Threat: Radicals Back from Iraq Plot Terror at Home, Experts Say," *http://www.sfgate.com*.

77. Evan Kohlmann, "Evan Kohlmann on Al Qaeda and Saudi Arabia," *National*

Review Online, 28 June 2004, *http://www.nationalreview.com/comment/kohl mann200406210820.asp.*

78. Ashraf al-Taie, "U.S. Nabs Al-Qaida Web Site Producer," 16 October 2005, *http://msnbc.msn.com/id/9720497/.*

79. AP/CNN, "Gunman Kills Five Saudi Policemen," 27 December 2005, *http:// www.cnn.com/2005/WORLD/meast/12/27/saudi.gunman.ap.*

80. Ireland On-line, "Wounded Terror Suspect Dies in Saudi Custody," 28 December 2005, *http://breakingnews.iol.ie/news/story.asp?j=167278934&p=y67z7 964x.* A transcript of al-Suwailmi's statement in September 2005 can be found at Global Terror Alert, "Audio Recording from Al-Qaida's Mohammed al-Suwailmi on Raids in Dammam," 11 September 2005, *http://www.globalterror alert.com/pdf/0905/saudi0905-2.pdf.*

81. AP, "Radical Muslim Cleric Walks Fine Line in London Sermons," 18 January 2005, *http://www.azcentral.com/arizonarepublic/news/articles/0116britain-clerics16.html.*

82. For a discussion on Abu Hamza, see Quintan Wiktorowicz, *Radical Islam Rising: Muslim Extremism in the West* (Lanham, Md., and Oxford: Rowman & Littlefield Publishers, Inc., 2005), 65–67.

83. ICBirmingham, "Muslim Terror Group Splits," 17 October 2004, *http://icbir mingham.co.uk.*

84. "Britain's Online Imam Declares War as He Calls Young to Jihad," *Times Online* (London), 17 January 2005, *http://www.timesonline.co.uk/article/0,,2-1443903, 00.html.*

85. Al-Muhajiroun, "Which One Do You Prefer—Death Penalty or Life in Prison?," 30 May 2004, *http://muhajiroun.com/.*

86. Ibid., 3 March 2005, *Al-muk.com/obm/index.html.*

87. See the earlier discussion on Azzam Publications in Bunt, *Islam in the Digital Age*, 67.

88. "Friends Say NJ Webmaster No Terrorist," AP/USA Today, 11 August 2004, *http://www.usatoday.com/tech/news/2004-08-11-nj-terror-case_x.htm.*

89. Islamicawakening.com, 22 February 2004, *http://islamicawakening.com.*

90. SamSpade, "Whois for http://www.as-sahwah.com," *http://samspade.org.*

91. Jihad Watch, "Jihad at Islamicawakening.com," 20 March 2004, *http://www.ji hadwatch.org/archives/001243.php.*

92. As-sahwah.com, *http://www.as-sahwah.com/forums/viewforum.php?f=12&sid =2d54396ccf3 d22bffe84a9445c870160.*

93. Abu Khalid, "Islamic Awakening Forum Comment," 2 March 2005, *http://www. islamicawakening.com/forums/viewtopic.php?t=539.*

94. Mujahideen_85, "Please Stop the False Call for Jihad," 13 February 2005, *http:// www.islamicawakening.com/forums/viewtopic.php?t=539* (typographical errors corrected).

95. Intissar, "Islamic Awakening Forum Comment," *http://www.islamicawakening. com/forums/viewtopic.php?t=105&postdays=0&postorder=asc&&start=225.*

96. Gag Order, "Islamic Awakening Forum Comment," 27 February 2005, *http:// www.islamicawakening.com/forums/viewtopic.php?t=386#top.*

97. Al-Fussilat, 6 June 2007, *http://al-fussilat.org*; Internet Archive Wayback Machine, *http://archive.org*.

98. Al-Qaida's Committee in the Islamic Maghreb (AQIM), 6 June 2007, *http://www.qmagreb.org*.

99. Islamic Courts Union, 4 May 2007, *http://abusayfullaah.wordpress.com*; Qaadisiya, 12 October 2006, *http://qaadisiya.com*; AlKarnee, *http://alkar nee.word press.com*.

100. Footage remained available through searching YouTube, *http://www.youtube.com*.

101. Ignored Puzzle Pieces of Knowledge, "Abu Riyaadh—Military Commander from Fatah Al-Islam Martyred," 11 June 2007, *http://inshallahshaheed.word press.com/tag/lubnan*.

102. "Fatah Al-Islam Planned to Assassinate Siniora, Jumblatt," *Daily Star Lebanon*, 14 June 2007, *http://www.dailystar.com.lb*.

103. Michael Moss and Souad Mekhennet, "An Internet Jihad Aims at U.S. Viewers," *New York Times*, 15 October 2007, *http://www.nytimes.com*.

104. Ignored Puzzle Pieces of Knowledge, 7 November 2007, *http://inshallahsha heed.muslimpad.com*.

105. For a full discussion of the ideological roots associated with CDLR and associated platforms, see Pascal Menoret, *The Saudi Enigma* (London: Zed Books, 2005), 124–26.

106. Gary R. Bunt, *Virtually Islamic: Computer-Mediated Communication and Cyber Islamic Environments* (Cardiff: University of Wales Press, 2000), 92–93.

107. "Police Raid UK Home of Saudi Extremist," *Times* (London), May 15 2005.

108. See the discussion in John Lasker, "Terror Forum Sows Seeds of Jihad," *Wired*, July 19 2005, *http://www.wired.com/news/print/0,1294,68214,00.html*.

109. Qal3ah.org, 7 July 2005, *http://qal3ah.org*. See the discussion by Roger Hardy (BBC News) in "Religious Warning to Saudi Monarchy," 12 October 2001, *http://news.bbc.co.uk/1/hi/world/middle_east/1595394.stm*.

110. For example, see AP, "Cleric's Followers Accused in Attacks," 1 June 2003.

111. Amnesty International, "Worldwide Appeal, Saudi Arabia: Freedom of Expression Denied," 1 September 2005, *http://www.web.amnesty.org/appeals/index/sau-011004-wwa-eng*.

112. Society for Internet Research, "Report No. 3: The Associations, Domains, and Web Sites of the Designated Terrorist Sa'ad Rashed Mohammad Al-Fagih," 28 May 2005, *http://www.sofir.org/sarchives/004190.php*.

113. Al-Rasheed, *Contesting the Saudi State*, 241.

114. Terrorism Monitor, "New Security Realities and Al-Qaeda's Changing Tactics: An Interview with Saad al-Faqih," *http://jamestown.org/terrorism/news/article.php?articleid=2369847*.

115. Al-Rasheed, *Contesting the Saudi State*, 242.

116. Islah.tv, "Vboard, Thread 109684," *www.islah.info*.

117. Revealer, "Search for 'Rightword.net,'" 30 September 2005, *htttp://revealer.org*.

118. Rightword, "Kalama al-haqq," *http://www.rightword.net/Anuke/modules.php?name=News&file=article&sid=6003*.

119. Ibid., 10 September 2003, *http://web.archive.org/web/20030910235111/ www.rightword.net/Enuke/modules.php?name=Sections&op=listarticles&secid=7.*

120. 3asfh.net, *http://www.3asfh.net/vb/showthread.php?t=17023.*

121. Ibid.

122. Revealer.org, result of search for "Abu-Qatada.com Ahmad Ali, sedny st london, london 123," *Abu-Qatada.com Ahmad Ali, sedny st london, london 123,* 8 October 2005, *http://revealer.org.*

123. Kataeb Mojahdat, 5 October 2005, *http://mojahdat.jeeran.com.*

124. Almo123, *http://members.lycos.co.uk/almo123/almodmra-bin-laden.rm.*

125. Saaid.net, *http://saaid.net/.*

126. Abualbukhary.org, 10 October 2005, *http://www.abualbukhary.org/video.*

127. Iraq Patrol, 2 October 2005, *http://www.iraqpatrol.com.*

128. Iraq Tunnel, 2 October 2005, *http://iraqtunnel.com.*

129. SamSpade, "Whois: Islam Memo, Mecca Street, alkhobar 11111, Saudi Arabia," 3 October 2005, *http://samspade.org.*

130. Islammemo, 10 June 2003, *http://www.islammemo.cc.*

131. Ansar.net, *http://www.ansar.net.*

132. Alhesbah, *http://www.alhesbah.org/v/.*

133. Clearguidance.com, 1 December 2003, *http://www.clearguidance.com.*

134. UmmKhubayb, "Copy Taken from Clearguidance Archive," 9 September 2002, *http://clearguidance.blogspot.com/2002_08_25_clearguidance_archive.html.* The archive covers the period between August 2002 and February 2004. The site was registered in New York by an entity known as "Halal Flowers."

135. Abu Muhammad al-Maqdisi, "Translation, Contained in 'Al-Hayat Inquiry: The City of Al-Zarqaa in Jordan—Breeding Ground of Jordan's Salafi Jihad Movement,'" 17 January 2005, *http://memri.org/bin/articles.cgi?Page= countries& Area=jordan&ID=SP84805.*

136. Abu Muhammad al-Maqdisi, "This Is Our Aqeedah," 10 October 2005, *http://www.revivingislam.com/aqeedah/thisisouraqeedah.html#Jihad&Khuruj.*

137. See the discussion by Reuben Paz, "Islamic Legitimacy for the London Bombings," 20 July 2005, *http://www.intelligence.org.il/eng/sib/7_05/london_b.htm.*

138. For a profile on al-Maqdisi and his relationship with al-Zarqawi, see Nibras Kazimi, "'A Virulent Ideology in Mutation': Zarqawi Upstages Maqdisi," *Current Trends in Islamist Ideology,* October 2005, 59–73, *http://www.hudson.org/files/publications/Current_Trends_Islamist_Ideology_v2.pdf.*

139. Abubaseer.bizland.com, "Bayan hawla al-Tafjirat allati Hasalat fi Madin at London (A Statement about the Bombings That Took Place in the City of London)," *http://www.abubaseer.bizland.com/hadath/Read/hadath17.doc.* This is discussed in detail in Paz, "Islamic Legitimacy for the London Bombings."

140. Asharq Alawsat, "London-Based Salafi Scholar Issues Fatwa Prohibiting Suicide Operations," *http://www.aawsat.com/english/news.asp?section=1&id=1427.*

141. Ibid.

142. Ibid.

143. The term was transliterated as *Sout al-Khalifa* on the website, rather than *Sawt al-Khalifa*. There is inconsistency with other sites that proclaim themselves as *sawt*, or the "voice" of a particular cause—in this case an interpretation of the concept of the caliphate. Spellings of sites have been retained as they represented themselves online.

144. Altartosi.com, 11 October 2005, *http://www.altartosi.com/audio/index.html.*

145. "Islamists Step Up Campaign to Stop Muslims Voting," *Guardian* (London), 22 April 2005, *http://politics.guardian.co.uk/election/story/0,15803,1466218,00.html.*

146. "Inside the Sect That Loves Terror," *Sunday Times* (London), 7 August 2005.

147. Peter Stanford, "Preaching from the Converted," *Independent*, 16 May 2004, *http://www.independent.co.uk.*

148. The Saved Sect, "Al-Firqat un-Naajiyah (Gloucester)," 30 September 2005, *http://www.thesavedsect.com.* Address resolved through Whois, 30 September 2005, Google search.

149. "From 18/09/05 to 24/09/05 We Had: 35,173 Hits," *http://www.thesavedsect com.*

150. BBC News, "Blair Bid to Ban Group 'Opposed,'" 19 November 2006, *http:// news.bbc.co.uk/1/hi/uk/6162690.stm.*

151. Islamic Forum, "Lyrics of Al-Ghuraaba nasheed," 1 November 2004, *http:// www.gawaher.com/index.php?showtopic=944.html&.*

152. The Saved Sect, "Newsletters," 30 September 2005, *http://www.thesavedsect. com/publications/newsletters/V1I1.pdf.*

153. The Saved Sect, "Jihaad," 30 September 2005, *http://www.thesavedsect.com/arti cles/Jihaad/IslamDominate.htm.*

154. The Saved Sect, "School Girl Gives a Bad Name to Islaam and Muslims," *http:// www.thesavedsect.com/articles/CurrentAffairs/ShabinaBegum.htm.*

155. The Saved Sect, *The Necessity of Making Takfeer on Ibn Baaz*, *http://www.the savedsect.com.*

156. Al-Ghurabaa, "About Us," *http://www.al-ghurabaa.co.uk/aboutus.htm.* Typographical errors corrected.

157. Al-Ghurabaa, "Jihaad," *http://www.al-ghurabaa.co.uk/Deen/jihaad1/TERROR ISM_SALAF.htm.*

158. Ibid.

159. Ibid.

160. Al-Ghurabaa, 7 October 2006, *http://www.al-ghurabaa.co.uk/Deen/jihaad1/ road2haq.htm.*

161. Ibid.

162. Ahl us-Sunnah wal-Jamaa'ah Muntadaa, 10 April 2007, *http://muntadaa.aswj .net.* See the discussion in Zone-H, "Digital Propaganda Calling to Jihad," 5 January 2007, *http://zone-h.org.*

163. Islam Base, 7 November 2007, *http://www.islam-base.co.uk.*

164. "YouTube Asked to Curb Terror Videos," *Telegraph* (London), 7 November 2007, *http://www.telegraph.co.uk.*

165. Paul McGeough, "Taking Jihad to the Web," *The Age*, 14 February 2006, *http://*

www.theage.com.au/news/world/taking-jihad-to-the-web/2006/02/13/113967 9533905.html#.

166. Reuters/Free Republic, "Al Qaeda Leaders Elusive over 4 Years Post–Sept. 11," 14 February 2006, *http://209.157.64.200/focus/f-news/1578464/posts.*

167. United Shades of Swords, "Sana500do V2.swf," 10 February 2004, *www.united shadeofswords.com/sana500do V2.swf.*

168. The video remained available in 2008, via YouTube, Google Video, and file-sharing sites; see Sheikh Terra featuring the Soul Salah Crew, "Dirty Kuffar," *http://video.google.com/videoplay?docid=9083681522527526242.* A remix had been produced: Sheikh Terra featuring the Soul Salah Crew, "'Dirty Kuffar' Remix 2.1, 2007," 3 March 2008, *http://www.youtube.com/watch?v=qKgkF7H kzNI.* Various other versions and takes on the video have also appeared.

169. Committee for the Defence of Legitimate Rights, December 1999, *http://um mah.org.uk/cdlr.*

170. WildApache786, "9/11 Rap Wows British Muslims," 4 September 2005, *http:// forum.mpacuk.org/archive/index.php/t-2134.html.*

171. "Scarface," 12 February 2004, *http://SomaliaOnline.com.* Original spellings and emphases retained.

172. Fun-Da-Mental, "All Is War: The Benefits of G-HAD," 7 August 2007, *http:// www.fun-da-mental.co.uk.*

173. The Register, "Internet Rap Threatens Dutch MP," 4 July 2005, *http://theregis ter.co.uk.*

174. The Qur'an, *083–036 al-Mutaffin.* Translation unspecified.

175. Global Islamic Media Front, "Jihad Camera," 13 September 2005, *http://cru sader.rulez.jp/files/Jihad__Hidden__Camera.ram.*

176. Al-farouq.com.

177. Jihad Media Battalion, 6 October 2005, *http://d.turboupload.com/d/73550/up 0228.zip.html.*

178. Sheikh 'Abdullah Ar-Rashood, 23 June 2005, *http://www.zippyvideos.com/33 243812477785.html.*

179. Asharq Alawsat, "Zarqawi Says Wanted Saudi Terrorist Killed in Iraq," 23 June 2005, *http://www.asharq-e.com/news.asp?section=1&id=553.*

180. Kathy Gannon (AP/The Standard), "A Date with the Emir of Al-Qaeda," 23 June 2006, *http://www.thestandard.com.hk/news__detail.asp?pp__cat=20&art__id= 21310&sid=8534770&con__type=3.*

181. Al-farouq.com.

182. Sout al-khalifa, 14 September 2005, *http://soutgimf.s5.com.*

183. Ibid., 23 September 2005, *http://s62.yousendit.com/d.aspx?id=1GXNGEUJTU 68M2S6KU6ATQWoXG.*

184. Ibid., 28 September 2005, *http://gimf-taseer.notlong.com.*

185. Asharq Alawsat, "Al-Qaeda Releases Second Online Newscast," 6 October 2005, *http://www.aawsat.com/english/news.asp?section=1&id=2036.*

186. Upload 2005, 12 October 2005, *http://www.up2005.r8.org.*

187. For a full discussion of the themes of this broadcast, see Adnkronos International, "3rd Al-Qaeda 'News Bulletin' Welcomes Hamas' Military Wing,"

11 October 2005, *http://www.adnki.com/index_2Level.php?cat=Terrorism&loid=8.0.217520346&par=0.*

188. Adnkronos International, "Al-Qaeda Talk Show Broadcast on the Internet," 25 November 2005, *http://www.adnki.com/index_2Level.php?cat=Terrorism&loid=8.0.233098355&par=.*

189. Adnkronos International, "Al-Qaeda's 'How to Use a Kalashnikov' Video Guide," 8 December 2005, *http://www.adnki.com/index_2Level.php?cat=Terrorism&loid=8.0.237847294&par=0.*

190. Mi2g, "Growing Need for Cyber Terrorism Vigilance Warn Ex-CIA Directors," 14 December 2004, *http://www.mi2g.com/cgi/mi2g/press/141204.php.*

191. "Pentagon Uncovers Propaganda Failures," *Asia Times*, 30 November 2004, *http://atimes.com/atimes/Front_Page/FK30Aa02.html.*

192. Donald H. Rumsfeld, "How to Fight Terrorism in the Media," *Daily Star/INA Daily/International Herald Tribune*, n.d., *http://www.iht.com/getina/files/312 312.html.*

193. SITE Institute, "Statement by 'Ahmad al-Hatheq Bi Allah,' Cited in 'The Global Islamic Media Front Announces the Initiation of Infiltrating Western Internet Forums, and Issues a Call to Able Muslims to Join Information Jihad,'" 12 January 2006, *http://www.siteinstitute.org/bin/articles.cgi?ID=publications138106&Category=publications&Subcategory=0.*

194. For two detailed Israeli perspectives on this issue, see the Hertziliyya-based academic Reuben Paz, "Project for the Research of Islamist Movements, Israel," *http://www.e-prism.org*; and the Haifa-based academic (and former researcher at the U.S. Institute of Peace) Gabriel Weimann, "WWW.terror.net: How Modern Terrorism Uses the Internet," *http://purl.access.gpo.gov/GPO/LPS47607*, and *Terror on the Internet*. Commentaries on these publications have also been produced by a number of campaigning organizations, including SITE Institute, Northeast Intelligence Network, MEMRI.

195. Al-Neda, "Muaskar al-Battar 1- (al-Battar Camp)," 20 August 2004, *http://free myhost.com/neda6/soout/index.htm* (deleted URL); Al-Neda, "Sawt al-Jihad 1- (Voice of Jihad)," 10 October 2004, *http://freemyhost.com/neda6/soout/index. htm* (deleted URL); Al-Khansaa, "Al-Khansaa," 20 August 2004 (deleted URL).

196. For an early history and overview of al-Qaeda manuals, see Gunaratna, *Inside Al Qaeda*, 70–76; and Dan Verton, *Black Ice: The Invisible Threat of Cyber-Terrorism* (Emeryville, Calif.: McGraw-Hill, 2003), 119–20.

197. Al-Battar, "Al-Battar Issue 17," October 2004 (link deleted).

198. Sawt al-Jihad, "Sawt al-Jihad, Issue 23," October 2004 (link deleted).

199. Details of the case can be found at U.S. Department of Justice, "Joint Statement by Daniel Meron, Principal Deputy Assistant Attorney General, Civil Division and Barry Sabin, Chief, Counterterrorism Section, Criminal Division Hearing before the United States Senate Judiciary Committee," 20 April 2005, *http://kyl.senate.gov/legis_center/subdocs/042005sabinmeron.pdf*. Examples of the manuals are located at U.S. Department of Justice, *http://www.usdoj.gov/ag/manualpart1_4.pdf.*

200. Internet Haganah, "New 'Jihad Encyclopedia' Released; Subject? How to Make WMD," 10 October 2005, *http://haganah.org.il/harchives/005161.html.*

201. OBL Crew, 9 May 2005, *http://www.oblcrew.net.*

202. Military.com, "Iraqi Insurgent Sniper Training, Reproduced as a Translated PowerPoint Presentation, Originally from Baghdad Al-Rashid.com," 10 May 2005, *http://www.military.com/ppt/iraqi_insurgent_sniper_training.htm.*

203. Khansaa was an ancient poet who eulogized her four sons who were killed in battle.

204. The application of the term "blogger" was not entirely accurate in this article.

205. For a profile of al-Suri, see Brynjar Lia, *Architect of Global Jihad: The Life of Al-Qaeda Strategist Abu Mus'ab al-Suri* (London: Hurst Books, 2007). Also see Evan Kohlmann, "Abu Mu'sab al-Suri and His Plan for the Destruction of America: 'Dirty Bombs for a Dirty Nation,'" 11 July 2005, *http://www.globalterror alert.com/pdf/0705/abuMu'sabalsuri.pdf;* and Murad al-Shishani, "Abu Mus'ab al-Suri and the Third Generation of Salafi-Jihadists," *Terrorism Monitor,* 11 August 2005, *http://jamestown.org/terrorism/news/article.php?articleid=2369 766.*

206. SITE Institute, "The Unique Ninja Book for the Vigorous Mujahid," 25 September 2004, *http://siteinstitute.org/bin/articles.cgi?ID=publications8104&Cate gory=pub lications&Subcategory=0.*

207. "Terrorist Website Drops Dirty Bomb," *Arab News,* 11 March 2005, *http:// www.arabnews.com.*

208. See the profile of al-Adel in PHXNews.com, "Adel's New Terrorist Manual and Ayman's 'Shaven Beards,'" 18 January 2004, *http://www.phxnews.com/fullstory. php?article=8734.* Also see Bill Roggio, "The Fourth Rail: Saif al-Adel, Zarqawi, Al Qaeda, and Iran," 16 June 2005, *http://billroggio.com/archives/2005/06/ saif_aladel_zar.php.*

209. MSNBC, "9/11 Report Light on ID Theft Issues," 4 August 2004, *http://msnbc. msn.com/id/5594385.*

210. "Al Qaeda Saudi Branch Has New Chief: Reports," *AFP/Khaleej Times Online,* 4 November 2004, *http://www.khaleejtimes.com/DisplayArticle.asp?xfile=data/ middleeast/2004/November/middleeast_ November37.xml&section=middleeast.*

211. Roel Meijer, "Re-reading Al-Qaeda: Writings of Yusuf al-Ayiri," *ISIM Review* 18 (2006), 16–17, *http://www.isim.nl/files/Review_18/Review_18.pdf.*

212. CBS 11, "Jihadist Web Mag Linked to N. Texas Brothers," 7 February 2005, *http://cbs11tv.com/investigations/local_story_040192418.html.*

213. Adnkronos International, "Iraq: 'Rough Guide' for Aspiring Mujahadeen," 7 June 2005, *http://www.adnki.com/index_2Level.php?cat=Trends&loid=8.0. 174809712&par=0.* Also see *Spiegel Online,* 25 July 2005, *http://www.spiegel.de/ international/0,1518,366723,00.html.*

214. "News Magazine in Secular Turkey Honors Al Qaeda," *Washington Times,* 22 August 2005, *http://washingtontimes.com/world/20050821-112113-2372r.htm.*

215. Birgit Brauchle, "Islamic Radicalism Online: The Moluccan Mission of the

Laskar Jihad in Cyberspace," *Australian Journal of Anthropology* 15, no. 3 (2004): 267–285, *http://www.findarticles.com/p/articles/mi_m2472/is_3_15/ai_n9483585/print.*

216. See Merlyna Lim, *Islamic Radicalism and Anti-Americanism in Indonesia: The Role of the Internet*, vol. 18, *Policy Studies Series* (Washington, D.C.: East West Center, 2005).

217. " 'Cyber-Islamist' Arrested in Jordan," *Arab News*, 12 January 2005, *http://www.arabnews.com/?page=4&section=0&article=57418&d=12&m=1&y=2005.*

218. Jordan Information Center, "Teenager Sentenced to Two-and-a-Half Years in Prison," 18 May 2005, *http://www.jordan.jo/en/en-localnews/wmview.php?Art ID=536.*

219. BBC News, "Terror Suspect Admits Plane Plot," 26 February 2005, *http://news.bbc.co.uk/1/hi/england/gloucestershire/4304223.stm.*

220. "Trial Aims to Expose Euro Terror Network," *Scotsman*, 4 January 2005, *http://thescotsman.scotsman.com/international.cfm?id=7802005.*

221. AP/NJ.com, "Suspected Al Qaeda Members Nabbed in Pakistani Internet Café," 27 September 2003, *http://www.nj.com/news/ledger/index.ssf?/base/news-11/1064638342231930.xml.*

222. "Turkey's Latest Terrorism Act Hatched in Internet Café," Knight Ridder Newspapers, 22 November 2003, *http://www.realcities.com/mld/krwashington/732 7988.htm.*

223. "Jihad Text Gave Rules for Killers, Court Told," *Sydney Morning Herald*, 9 June 2005, *http://www.smh.com.au/news/National/Jihad-text-gave-rules-for-killers-court-told/2005/06/09/1118123959838.html.*

224. Nina Bernstein, "Questions, Bitterness, and Exile for Queens Girl in Terror Case," *New York Times*, 17 June 2005, *http://www.nyt.com.*

225. "Ex-Mujahed Talks about Extremist Groups," *Arab Times*, 3 January 2006, *http://www.arabnews.com/?page=9&section=0&article=75687&d=3&m=1&y=2006.*

226. Anti-Defamation League, "National Guardsman Sentenced to Life for Trying to Aid Al Qaeda," 9 September 2004, *http://www.adl.orgs.* Also see Robert Spencer, "The Enemy Is Not Just Al-Qaeda," *http://frontpagemag.com/Articles/ReadArticle.asp?ID=13454*; and "Trailing Attempted Espionage: Who Is Ryan Anderson, a.k.a. Amir Talhah?," *National Review Online*, 13 February 2004, *http://www.nationalreview.com/comment/malkin200402130909.asp.*

227. ABC News, "Tape Released: American Al Qaeda Member Warns of Attacks," 12 September 2005, *http://abcnews.go.com/GMA/Investigation/story?id=1115 448 &page=1*; "Strange World, Web Reveals Much, Government Little," *South Flor idaSun-Sentinel*, 27 May 2004, *http://www.sun-sentinel.com/news/colum nists/sfl-may027may27,0,1029248.column?coll=sfla-news-col.*

228. "Reports: Student 'Obsessed with Jihad,' " *Casper Star Tribune*, 11 November 2004, *http://www.casperstartribune.net/articles/2004/11/11/news/wyoming/6b6c118ce08a6c2f87256f49000c6698.txt.*

229. U.S. Department of Justice, "Mark Robert Walker Sentenced to Two Years

Imprisonment after Pleading Guilty to Aiding Terrorist Organization," 28 April 2005, *http://www.usdoj.gov/usao/txw/press_releases/2005/walker.sen.pdf.*

230. "Expert Says Sites Linked to Overseas Terrorists," *Idaho Statesman*, 26 May 2004, *http://www.idahostatesman.com.*

231. ABC News, "Saudi Deported after Terror Acquittal," 22 July 2004, *http://www.abcnews.go.com.*

232. "Expert Says Sites Linked to Overseas Terrorists."

233. Crime-research.org, "How Al Qaeda Uses the Internet," 5 August 2004, *http://www.crime-research.org/news/05.08.2004/545.*

234. Bunt, *Islam in the Digital Age*, 56–61.

235. "Terror Suspect Had an Ingenious System of Coded E-mails," *Telegraph* (London), 9 August 2004, *http://www.telegraph.co.uk/news/main.jhtml?xml=/news/2004/08/08/nterr108.xml&sSheet=/news/2004/08/08/ixnewstop.html.*

236. James Ridgeway, "Mondo Washington: All in Favor, Say 'Aiiiee!,'" *Village Voice*, 11 August 2004, *http://www.villagevoice.com/issues/0432/mondo1.php.* Also see Juan Cole, "The Outing of Muhammad Naeem Noor Khan," 19 August 2004, *http://www.antiwar.com/cole/?articleid=3382.*

237. "Seven with Alleged Al-Qaida Links Deny Plotting Terror Bomb Campaign," *Guardian* (London), 22 March 2006, *http://www.guardian.co.uk/terrorism/story/0,,1736523,00.html.*

238. BBC News, "Terrorism's Reach via Internet," 17 September 2007, *http://news.bbc.co.uk/1/hi/scotland/tayside_and_central/6999176.stm.*

239. "'Lyrical Terrorist' Samina Malik Guilty," *Telegraph* (London), 8 November 2007, *http://www.telegraph.co.uk/news/main.jhtml?xml=/news/2007/11/08/npoet108.xml.*

240. Azzam Publications, "What Role Can Sisters Play in Jihad?," 10 October 2007, *http://www.islamicawakening.com/viewarticle.php?articleID=623.*

241. Franco Frattini, "European Commissioner Responsible for Justice, Freedom, and Security: The External Dimension of Security, in Particular the Fight against Terrorism" (paper presented at the Security and Defence Agenda Conference: Defining a European Security Strategy, Brussels, 18 October 2007), *http://europa.eu.*

242. *Violent Radicalization and Homegrown Terrorism Prevention Act of 2007*, 110th Congress, H.R. 1955, Rep. Jane Harman (D-Calif.), 24 October 2007, *http://www.govtrack.us/congress/billtext.xpd?bill=h110-1955 .*

Chapter Six

1. See the discussion by Ghaith Abdul-Ahad, "We Don't Need Al-Qaida," *Guardian* (London), 27 October 2005, *http://www.guardian.co.uk/g2/story/0,3604,1601208,00.html.*

2. Information from Occupied Iraq, 28 October 2005, *http://www.uruknet.info.*

3. Daniel Kimmage and Kathleen Ridolfo, *Iraqi Insurgency Media: The War of Images and Ideas* (Washington, D.C.: Radio Free Europe/Radio Liberty, 2007), 4–6, 10.

4. "Daniel Pearl 'Refused to Be Sedated before His Throat Was Cut,'" *Telegraph* (London), 9 May 2004, *http://www.telegraph.co.uk/news/main.jhtml?xml=/ news/2004/05/09/wpearl09.xml&sSheet=/news/2004/05/09/ixworld.html.*

5. ABC News, "Berg Had Been Advised to Leave Iraq," 2 May 2004, *http://abc news.go.com/wire/World/ap20040512__222.html.*

6. AP/Yahoo! News, "Online Co. Shuts down Site with Beheading," 13 May 2004, *http://story.news.yahoo.com.*

7. "Why Watch a Decapitation?," *Daily Star* (Lebanon), 12 May 2004, *http://www. dailystar.com.lb/article.asp?edition_id=10&categ_id=2&article_id=3844.*

8. "U.S. Must Not Compound the Situation," *Bahrain Tribune*, 13 May 2004, *http://www.bahraintribune.com/ArticleDetail.asp?CategoryId=4&ArticleId=31 561.*

9. AFP/Yahoo! News, "Militants' Use of Horror Images Changes Rules of Propaganda Game: Historian," 13 May 2004, *http://story.news.yahoo.com/news?tmpl= story&u=/afp/iraq_images.*

10. Al-Jazeera, "Bloggers Doubt Berg Execution Video," 14 May 2004, *http://en glish.aljazeera.net.*

11. Middle East Online, "Haunting Documentary of Suicide Attacks in Iraq," 7 June 2004, *http://www.middle-east-online.com/english/?id=10542.*

12. Boston.com, "U.S. Forces and Cleric's Militia Fight in Holy Iraqi City," 20 May 2004, *http://www.boston.com/dailynews/140/world/U_S_forces_and_cler ic_s_militi:.shtml.*

13. NJ.com, "Terrorists Manipulate Reality to Exploit Atrocity's Impact," n.d., *http://www.nj.com/news/ledger/index.ssf?/base/news-17/1096436379137050. xml.*

14. "British Software Relays Hostage Drama to the World Stage," *Times Online* (London), 28 April 2004, *http://www.timesonline.co.uk/printFriendly/0,,1-523- 1279483,00.html.*

15. "Zarqawi Uses Web for Funding, Recruits," *Washington Times*, 29 June 2004.

16. "Blast Kills 3 U.S. Marines; Turks Freed—After Saddam," *Sydney Morning Herald*, 29 June 2004, *http://www.smh.com.au/articles/2004/06/29/1088487963 463.html?from=storylhs.*

17. "Muslims around World Debate Hostage's Fate," *USA Today/Marine Corps Times*, 2 July 2004, *http://www.marinecorpstimes.com/story.php?f=1-292925- 3062605.php.*

18. "Islamic Extremist Group Denies It Killed American Marine on Website," Yahoo!, 5 July 2004, *http://story.news.yahoo.com/news?tmpl=story&u=/cpress/ 20040704/ca_pr_on_wo/iraq_marine_killed&cid=2149&ncid=2149.*

19. SITE Institute, "Jihadists Celebrate Beheadings on Message Boards," 24 September 2004, *http://www.siteinstitute.org/bin/articles.cgi?ID=publications7904& Category=publications&Subcategory=0.*

20. "Amsterdam Home of Ken Bigley's Brother Raided," *Independent* (London), 2 October 2004, *http://news.independent.co.uk/europe/story.jsp?story=568043.*

21. "Victims Die Twice in Obscene Poker Game," *Times Online* (London), 28 September 2004, *http://www.timesonline.co.uk/article/0,,2087-1279480,00.html.*

22. Islamic Army in Iraq, 28 September 2004, *http://www.wanthim.i8.com.*

23. Reuters AlertNet, "Iraqi Insurgents Name Spokesman–Web Site," 3 July 2005, *http://www.alertnet.org/thenews/newsdesk/L03519297.htm.*

24. Reuters, "Al Qaeda Says Kills Egypt Envoy in Iraq-Web," 7 July 2005, *http:// today.reuters.co.uk/news/newsArticle.aspx?type=worldNews&storyID=2005-07 -07T135007Z_01_BAU749585_RTRUKOC_0_IRAQ-EQYPT.xml.*

25. AFP/TurkishPress.com, "Qaeda-Linked Group Posts Website Video of Japanese beheaded in Iraq," 2 November 2004, *http://www.turkishpress.com/news. asp?id=32558.*

26. AFP/TurkishPress.com, "Senior Baghdad Official Shot Dead," 1 November 2004, *http://www.turkishpress.com/news.asp?id=32463.*

27. "Video Shows Execution of 11 Iraqi Guardsmen," *Washington Post/SFgate.com,* 29 October 2004, *http://www.sfgate.com/cgi-bin/article.cgi?file=/c/a/ 2004/ 10/29/MNGMK9ILEB1.DTL.*

28. Medicalnewstoday.com, "Terrorists Know What They Are Doing, They Are Not Crazy, Say Researchers," 11 July 2004, *http://www.medicalnewstoday.com/ medicalnews.php?newsid=10580*; citing the work of Andrew Silke, forensic psychologist, University of Leicester.

29. Zone-H, "Digital Propaganda Calling to Jihad," 5 January 2007, *http://zone-h.org.*

30. Reuters, "Arabs Split over 'Legitimacy' of Iraq Beheadings," 24 September 2004, *http://www.reuters.com.*

31. HindustanTimes.com, "Images of Horror Top Seller in Baghdad's 'Thieves Market,'" 23 September 2004, *http://www.hindustantimes.com/2004/Sep/23/181_ 1017880,0005004.htm.*

32. Newsday/Startribune.com, "Iraqi Beheadings Now Fueling Global 'Snuff' Film Market," 22 October 2004, *http://www.startribune.com/stories/484/5035275. html.*

33. SFGate.com, "Rising Call by Clerics for Jihad; Question Is Not Whether but How to Defeat U.S. Aims," 22 September 2004, *http://www.sfgate.com/cgi-bin/article.cgi?file=/c/a/2004/09/22/MNGLM8SQOC1.DTL.*

34. "Video Shows 'Black Watch Bomb,'" ThisisLondon (*Evening Standard*), 8 November 2004, *http://www.thisislondon. co.uk/news/articles/14555068? source= Evening%20Standard*; "London Muslim Puts Film of Black Watch Deaths on Net," *Sunday Times* (London), 14 November 2004, *http://www.timesonline.co. uk/article/0,,2087-1358677,00.html.*

35. "Sense of Dread Hangs over Fallujah as Battle Looms," *Truthout,* 3 November 2004, *http://www.truthout.org.*

36. "Suicide Squads Await U.S. Troops' Assault on Falluja," *Sunday Times* (London), 8 November 2004.

37. Uruknet.info, "Iraqi Resistance Report for Events of Tuesday, 22 February 2005," *http://www.uruknet.info/?p=m9916&l=i&size=1&hd=0.*

38. BBC News, "U.S. Targets Islamist Group in Iraq," 22 March 2003, *http://news. bbc.co.uk/1/hi/world/middle_east/2875269.stm.*

39. Whitehouse.gov, "U.S. Secretary of State Colin Powell Addresses the U.N. Se-

curity Council," 5 February 2003, *http://www.whitehouse.gov/news/releases/ 2003/02/20030205-1.html*. Also see "U.S. Targets Islamist Group in Iraq."

40. AFP/Kurdish Media News, "Founder of Radical Kurdish Group to Remain in Norwegian Custody: Court," 21 January 2004, *http://www.kurdmedia.com/ news.asp?id=4661*.

41. AP/International Herald Tribune, "Norwegian Appeals Court Upholds Expulsion Order of Ansar al-Islam Founder Mullah Krekar," 22 November 2006, *http://www.iht.com/articles/ap/2006/11/22/europe/EU_GEN_Norway_Mullah_Krekar.php*.

42. AP/MSNBC, "Mess-Hall Suicide Bomber was Saudi," 14 January 2005, *http:// www.msnbc.msn.com/id/6782944/*.

43. AP/Arab Times Online, "Al-Qaida in Iraq Criticizes Al-Jazeera for Wrongly Reporting Its Statement," 13 February 2005, *http://www.arabtimesonline.com/ arabtimes/breakingnews/view.asp?msgID=7993*.

44. BBC News, "Google 'Saved' Australian Hostage," 19 October 2005, *http://news. bbc.co.uk/2/hi/asia-pacific/3755154.stm*.

45. Islam Online, "Iraq . . . The Aftermath," 24 September 2004, *http://www.islamon line.net/english/In_Depth/Iraq_Aftermath/2004/09/article_06.shtml*.

46. For example, see Roy Hallums, "Roy Hallums' Website," *http://royhallums. 4t.com/index.html*. Hallums was kidnapped in November 2004 and freed in September 2005 after a troop operation.

47. Newsweek/MSNBC, "The Hunt for Zarqawi's Webmasters," 4 April 2005, *http://www.msnbc.msn.com/id/7305524/site/newsweek/*. Also see the blog Dread Pundit, "Terrorist Sympathizer Operates Openly in the Netherlands," 17 February 2005, *http://dreadpundit.blogspot.com/2005/02/terrorist-sympa thizer-operates-openly.html*.

48. Adnkronos International, "Iraq: Al-Zarqawi Escapes Capture but Computer Is Seized," 26 April 2005, *http://www.adnki.com/index_2Level.php?cat=Terror ism&loid=8.0.157050001&par=*.

49. Adnkronos International, "Iraq: Al-Zarqawi's Group Launches New Website in Kurdish," 26 April 2005, *http://www.adnki.com/index_2Level.php?cat=Terror ism&loid=8.0. 157386006&par=0*.

50. Reuters/Sierratimes.com, "Zarqawi Tape Says Falluja Victory Certain–Web Site," 13 November 2004.

51. An ongoing list of kidnapping victims was maintained at Wikipedia, "Foreign Hostages in Iraq."

52. CNN, "Video Apparently Shows Public Beheadings," 22 January 2005, *http:// www.cnn.com/2005/WORLD/meast/01/21/iraq.main/index.html*.

53. Mohamad Bazzi, "A Jihadist's Journey," Newsday.com, 27 November 2004, *http://www.newsday.com/news/nationworld/world/ny-wosaud254059317nov 29,0,133515.story?coll=ny-worldnews-headlines*.

54. Reuters, "Militants Use Web in Battle against Polls," 24 January 2005, *http:// www.reuters.co.uk/newsArticle.jhtml?type=worldNews&storyID=659091*.

55. Adnkronos International, "Al-Zarqawi Calls Women to Jihad," 6 July 2005,

http://www.adnki.com/index_2Level.php?cat=Terrorism&loid=8.0.184286030 &par=0.

56. Muqtada, 24 October 2005, *http://www.muqtada.com.*

57. "Post from Noor Fatima" (citing Alhaeri.com, whose original link was down at the time of writing), Shiachat.com, 6 September 2004, *http://www.shiachat. com/forum/lofiversion/index.php/t9303.html.*

58. Ali Akbar Dareini (AP), "Iraqi Cleric's Spiritual Mentor Distances Self from Military Confrontation with U.S.," 2 May 2004; reproduced on Free Republic, *http://209.157.64.200/focus/f-news/1128315/posts.*

59. It was suggested that this discussion had emerged from IslamicDigest.net, but there was no direct link to it. See "Ayatullah al-Udhma Kadhem al-Haeri (HA): Edict Urges Iraqi Muslims to Fill Power," Shiachat.com, 1 May 2003, *http:// www.shiachat.com/forum/lofiversion/index.php/t9303.html.*

60. Muhammad Baqir al-Sadr Tribute, *http://www.geocities.com/Athens/Cyprus/ 8613/index.html.*

61. Islamic Ahlulbayt Foundation of New Zealand, *http://www.islam.org.nz*; Kufa Center of Islamic Knowledge, *http://www.kufa.org*; and the Sunni-oriented Islamic Voice, "Links," *http://www.islamicvoice.com/links.*

62. Radio Free Europe, "Iraqi Political Groups," *http://www.rferl.org/specials/iraq elections/partiesF.asp.*

63. Islamic Dawah Party, 24 April 2006, *http://www.islamicdawaparty.org.*

64. Official website of Ibrahim al-Ashaiqir al-Jaafari's office, *http://aljaffary.com.*

65. Iraq Government, *http://www.iraqigovernment.org/.*

66. Al-Khoei Organization, *http://www.alkhoei.org.*

67. For example, see ibid. (registered in the UK). Also see *http://alkhoei.net* and *http://alkhoei.com* (registered in the United Arab Emirate and Iran, respectively, but containing mirrored content).

68. Alshirazi, 26 June 2006, *http://www.alshirazi.com/index.html, http://www.alshi razi.no.*

69. Banner retrieved from Shi'a Chat, *http://www.shiachat.com/forum/index.php? showtopic=40010.*

70. Al-Karbalaeia, 26 June 2006, *http://www.alkarbalaeia.net.*

71. Iraqi Islamic Party, *http://www.iraqiparty.com/ar/.*

72. Kurdistan Islamic Group, "Index," *http://www.komalnews.net.*

73. Kurdistan Bloggers Union, "Kurds Have the Right to Have Their Own State," 21 June 2005, *http://northerniraq.info/news/index.php?p=391&more=1&c=1& tb=1&pb=1#more391.*

74. Komal, cited in Radio Free Europe, "A Survey of Armed Groups in Iraq," *http:// www.rferl.org/reports/iraq-report/2004/06/20-040604.asp.*

75. Faili Kurds Homepage, "Index," 31 October 2005, *http://biphome.spray.se/faili. kurd/.*

76. Kurds Land and Ecology, "History," *http://www.kurdinfo.com/history.htm.*

77. See "Hamas Expected to Boost Online Activities," *Jerusalem Post, http://jpost. com.*

78. Intelligence and Terrorism Information Center at the Center for Special Studies (CSS), Israel, "Marketing Terrorism by Internet: The Hamas Terrorist Movement Continues Using Internet Service Providers in Eastern Europe and South East Asia to Operate Its Leading Sites," October 2005, *http://www.intelligence. org.il/eng/eng_n/pdf/Internet_m05e.pdf.*

79. Ibid.

80. Palestine-Information Center, *http://www.palestine-info.co.uk/am/publish/.*

81. "Ahmed Yassin," Palestine-info.info, January 2006, *http://www.palestine-info.in fo/arabic/spfiles/yaseen2/yaseen.htm.*

82. "Terror," Palestine-info.info, 10 May 2006, *http://www.palestine-info. info/ara bic/terror/index.htm.*

83. "Hamas," Palestine-info.info, 10 May 2006, *http://www.palestine-info. info/ara bic/hamas/index.htm.*

84. Palestine National Authority, 3 March 2006, *http://www.pna.gov.ps/Arabic/in dex.asp.*

85. Pal-Election, 2 March 2006, *http://www.pal-election.com/.*

86. Khaleelstyle, *http://www.khaleelstyle.com/new/new.htm,* 3 March 2006.

87. Al Qassam, *http://www.alqassam.com/arabic/.*

88. Itamar Marcus and Barbara Crook, "A Self-Portrait of Suicide Terrorists," 2 March 2006, *http://www.pmw.org.il.*

89. Ibid.

90. Palestine Media Watch, "Ask for Death!," *http://www.pmw.org.il/AFD.html.*

91. Fateh, "Al-Shahid," *http://www.al-fateh.net/fa-70/shahid.htm.*

92. An Israeli intelligence perspective on Islamic Bloc(k) activities can be found at Center for Special Studies (CSS), Israel, "The Suicide Bombers and Martyr Culture at Al-Najah University in Nablus," October 2004, *http://www.intelli gence.org.il/eng/sib/11_04/najah.htm.*

93. Alkotla.com, 3 March 2006, *http://www.alkola.com.*

94. PalestineGallery.com, 1 December 2006, *http://www.palestinegallery.com.*

95. Whois, "Palestine Gallery," 7 November 2007, *http://www.whois.net.*

96. AlMaghribi, 3 March 2006, *http://almagribi.blogspot.com.*

97. Palestinian Forum, *http://www.palestinianforum.net.*

98. Register.com, "Whois: Palestinianforum.net," 7 November 2007.

99. Center for Special Studies (CSS), Israel, "The Palestinian Islamic Jihad Internet Infrastructure and Its Internet Webhosts," December 2005, *http://www.intelli gence.org.il/eng/ eng_n/pdf/Internet2_e1205.pdf.*

100. Qudsway, 10 March 2006, *http://www.qudsway.com.*

101. Network Solutions, "Qudsway.com," 7 November 2007, *http://www.network so lutions.com.*

102. Rabdullah.net, 3 March 2006, *http://www.rabdullah.net.*

103. Shikaki.net, 3 March 2006, *http://shikaki.net.*

104. Sabiroon.org, 1 December 2006, *http://www.sabiroon.org.*

105. Whois, "Sabiroon.org," 7 November 2007, *http://www.whois.net.*

106. Palestinian Voice, 5 March 2006, *http://palvoice.com/.*

107. Kataeb Aqsa, *http://www.kataebaqsa.org, http://www.kataebaqsa1.com/arabic/ index.php.*

108. Ibid.

109. SamSpade, "Whois: Kataebaqsa.org," 6 March 2006, *http://www.samspade.org/ t/whois?a=66.235.212.144;server=auto.*

110. SamSpade, "Whois: Kataebaqsa1," 6 March 2006, *http://www.samspade.org/t/ whois?a=203.142.5.230;server=auto.*

111. Fateh Falcons, "Video: Tadreb_30bowat_nasefa," 8 March 2006, *http://www. fatehfalcons.org/vedio/Fateh_Falcons_Tadreb_30bowat_nasefa_1.mpg.*

112. Fateh Falcons, "Video: Shohada2," 8 March 2006, *http://www.fatehfalcons. org/modules.php?name=Shohada2.*

113. SamSpade, "Whois: Fatehfalcons.org," 6 March 2006, *http://www.samspade. org/t/lookat?a=http%3A%2F%2Fwww.fatehfalcons.org.*

114. Khayma.com, "Shuhada," *http://www.khayma.com/nablus-online/shuhada2. HTM.*

115. Al-Watan, "Articles," 6 March 2006, *http://www.alwatanvoice.com/articles.php.*

116. Al-Mudabara, 6 March 2006, *http://www.almubadara.org.*

117. Hussam Khader, 10 March 2006, *http://www.hussamkhader.org/english/De fault.htm.*

118. Free Bargouti, 7 March 2006, *http://www.freebarghouti.org.*

Conclusion

1. Manuel Castells, *The Rise of the Network Society*, 2nd ed. (Oxford: Blackwell, 2000); Dale F. Eickelman, "Muslim Ties That Bind," in *Religious Communities on the Internet*, ed. Göran Larsson (Stockholm: Swedish Science Press, 2006), 50.

2. Daniel Martin Varisco, "Islam Takes a Hit," *ISIM Newsletter*, no. 14 (2004), *http://www.isim.nl*; Peter G. Mandaville, *Transnational Muslim Politics: Re-imagining the Umma* (London and New York: Routledge, 2001), 16; Jon W. Anderson, "Muslim Networks, Muslim Selves in Cyberspace: Islam in the Post-Modern Public Sphere," *http://nmit.georgetown.edu/papers/jwanderson2.htm.*

3. Muslim Space, 5 October 2006, *http://www.muslimspace.com*; IslamicTorrents, *http://www.islamictorrents.net*; IslamicTube, *http://islamictube.net.*

4. Abdussalam Mohamed, "Pornography: Shameful, Silent Disease Spreads in Muslim Community," November 2007, *http://www.infocusnews.net/ content/ view/17445/135/.*

5. Gary R. Bunt, "Decision Making and Ijtihad in Islamic Environments: A Com-parative Study of Pakistan, Malaysia, Singapore, and the United Kingdom" (Ph.D. diss., University of Wales, 1996).

6. YouTube searches for "Islam," "Hajj," "Qur'an," "Khutbah," and "Hijab," *http:// www.youtube.com.*

7. Theo van Gogh and Ayaan Hirst Ali, "Submission, Part 1," *http://www.youtube. com/watch?v=SXGZBs65qMs.*

8. Roberto Preatoni, "Prophet Mohammed Protest Spreads on the Digital Ground; Hundreds of Cyber Attacks against Danish and Western Webservers Spreading Rage in the Name of Allah," 7 February 2006, *http://www.zone-h.org/en/news/read/id=205987/*.

9. See Lawrence Pintak's interview with Nabil Kassem, "Nabil Kassem on Arab Media Darfur Silence," *Arab Media and Society*, May 2007, *http://www.arab mediasociety.com/audio/?item=17*.

10. Electronic Jihad, 10 October 2006, *http://www.al-jinan.org/*; Jamestown Foundation, "New Website Incites Electronic Jihad," *Terrorism Focus* 3, no. 38, 3 October 2006, *http://jamestown.org/terrorism/news/article.php?articleid=23701 47*.

11. DEBKAFile, "Al Qaeda Declares Cyber Jihad on the West," 30 October 2007, *http://www.debka.com/headline.php?hid=4723*; ChannelRegister, "Program Automating Online Jihad Found in the Wild," 8 November 2007, *http://www.channelregister.co.uk*; Gary R. Bunt, "Scare Stories?" (blog posting), 8 November 2007, *http://virtuallyislamic.blogspot.com*.

12. MEMRI, "Saudi Arabia Ministry of Islamic Affairs Launches Arabic-English Website to Fight Extremism," 13 October 2006, *http://memri.org/bin/arti cles.cgi?Page=archives&Area=sd&ID=SP132006*.

13. Tariq Alhomayed, "Bin Laden: Enlightenment Remains the Protector," *Asharq Alawsat*, 27 September 2006, *http://aawsat.com/english/news.asp?section=2& id=6526*.

14. Gabriel Weimann, *Terror on the Internet: The New Arena, the New Challenges* (Washington, D.C.: U.S. Institute of Peace, 2006), 49–58.

15. Abbey Mills Mosque, 17 May 2007, *http://www.abbeymillsmosque.com*.

Index

Islamic Civilization and Muslim Networks

Gary R. Bunt, *iMuslims: Rewiring the House of Islam* (2009).

Fatemeh Keshavarz, *Jasmine and Stars: Reading More than "Lolita" in Tehran* (2007).

Scott Kugle, *Sufis and Saints' Bodies: Mysticism, Corporeality, and Sacred Power in Islam* (2007).

Roxani Eleni Margariti, *Aden and the Indian Ocean Trade: 150 Years in the Life of a Medieval Arabian Port* (2006).

Sufia M. Uddin, *Constructing Bangladesh: Religion, Ethnicity, and Language in an Islamic Nation* (2006).

Omid Safi, *The Politics of Knowledge in Premodern Islam: Negotiating Ideology and Religious Inquiry* (2006).

Ebrahim Moosa, *Ghazālī and the Poetics of Imagination* (2005).

miriam cooke and Bruce B. Lawrence, eds., *Muslim Networks from Hajj to Hip Hop* (2005).

Carl W. Ernst, *Following Muhammad: Rethinking Islam in the Contemporary World* (2003).